*f*P

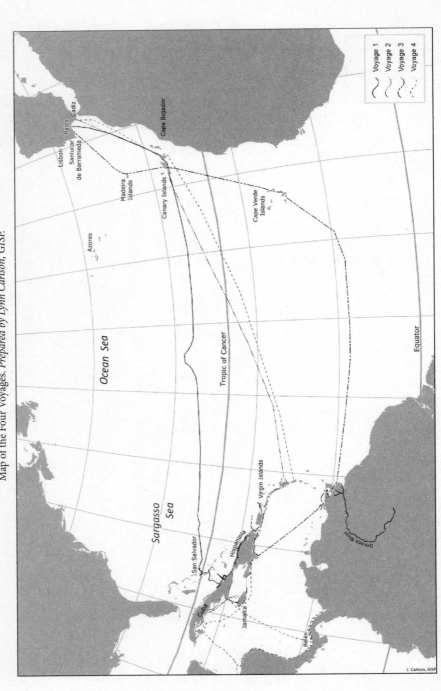

Map of the Four Voyages. Prepared by Lynn Carlson, GISP.

COLUMBUS
AND THE
QUEST
FOR
JERUSALEM

CAROL DELANEY

Free Press

New York   London   Toronto   Sydney   NewDelhi

To Columbus, whose extraordinary journey made mine possible

Free Press
A Division of Simon & Schuster, Inc.
1230 Avenue of the Americas
New York, NY 10020

First Free Press hardcover edition October 2011

FREE PRESS and colophon are trademarks of Simon & Schuster, Inc.

For information about special discounts for bulk purchases,
please contact Simon & Schuster Special Sales
at 1-866-506-1949 or business@simonandschuster.com.

The Simon & Schuster Speakers Bureau can bring authors to your live event.
For more information or to book an event contact the Simon & Schuster Speakers Bureau
at 1-866-248-3049 or visit our website at www.simonspeakers.com.

Designed by Carla Jayne Jones

Manufactured in the United States of America

1   3   5   7   9   10   8   6   4   2

Library of Congress Cataloging-in-Publication Data
Delaney, Carol Lowery
Columbus and the quest for Jerusalem / Carol Delaney. — 1st Free Press hardcover ed.
p. cm.
1. Columbus, Christopher—Religion. 2. America—Discovery and exploration—Spanish. I. Title.
E112.D39 2011
970.01'5092—dc23   2011022360

ISBN 978-1-4391-0232-9
ISBN 978-1-4391-0996-0 (ebook)

∼ Contents ∼

∼ PROLOGUE ∼

This is the story of a boy, born to a family of modest means, who grew up to become the most famous mariner of all time and whose discovery changed the world forever. The story has been told so many times you would think there was nothing more to tell, but the very profusion of books about him suggests that there is something still unresolved.

The story of Columbus does not begin or end with the landfall on an island in the Bahamas on October 12, 1492—the date and event most often associated with him. That day was important to him only because it confirmed what he had been arguing about for years, namely that the Ocean Sea could be crossed. His crew and the three small ships, whose names are almost as famous as his own, had only two days' rest before they were off again, sailing among islands in the Caribbean in search of the Asian mainland and the Grand Khan. Another date to begin the story might be March 15, 1493, for on that day Columbus arrived back in Spain, and that is when Europe learned of his discovery. Had he perished at sea, his name would have perished with him and so, too, any knowledge of his achievement. To me, however, December 26, 1492, is the most important date, for on that day he revealed his motivation and the ultimate goal of the voyage—the vision that would sustain him until the day he died. In his diary, he promised the Spanish sovereigns that in three years' time he would find enough gold and spices to finance a crusade to

conquer the Holy Sepulcher; for thus I urged Your Highnesses to spend all the profits of this my enterprise on the conquest of Jerusalem.

INTRODUCTION
THE PASSIONS OF COLUMBUS

A few years ago, had anyone said I would write a book about Columbus, I would have laughed. To me, Columbus had been a quasimythical figure; I knew nothing about him beyond what every schoolchild of my generation learned, which was not much. I didn't know he had made four voyages, or that he had returned from one of them in chains. Even the Quincentennial of 1992, commemorating his "Discovery" of America, passed me by.

Everything changed during the fall of 1999 when I was teaching a class at Stanford University called "Millennial Fever." The purpose was to observe the apocalyptic frenzy that was gripping America at the turn of the Christian millennium and to explore some of the history of millennial thought. In one of the readings for the course I came across a reference to Columbus and his apocalyptic, millennial beliefs. I learned that Columbus believed his role was to obtain enough of the fabled gold of the East to launch a crusade to conquer Jerusalem in order to prepare for the Second Coming of Christ before the end of the world. I had never heard about these beliefs of Columbus's, nor had anyone else whom I asked. The idea that he envisioned his project as part of the Christian apocalyptic scenario took hold of me and didn't let go.

I spent a summer at the John Carter Brown Library at Brown University in Providence, Rhode Island, exploring its rich collection of material related to the Columbian encounter and seeking the expertise of its knowledgeable staff and fellows. Little did I know that it would change the course of my life. I applied for and received a fellowship for the following year, decided to retire from my teaching position at Stanford, drove across the country again, and settled in Providence to pursue the research for this book. A whole new world opened up for me as I sat riveted to my seat in the library's elegant reading room from the moment it opened until it closed. I read voraciously about Columbus, about fifteenth-century Europe, and about medieval apoc-alypticism.

The more I read by and about Columbus, the more dissatisfied I became with portrayals of him as if he were our contemporary, as if only his clothes or his ships were different from ours, or as if medieval Christianity were merely a belief system he could choose and not the world that enveloped him. Most scholars of Columbus have focused on what he did but there is comparatively little written on why. They have tended to ignore his religious motivation or dismissed it as a way to ingratiate himself with Queen Isabella. Only a handful have taken his apocalyptic, millennial views seriously, and their publications have not reached the general public.[1] Twenty-five years ago Leonard Sweet re-marked that "scholars most interested in millennialism have largely ignored Columbus, and those scholars most interested in Columbus have skipped over his millenialism." To delve into it, he said, would mean taking "a medieval jour-ney into mysticism, dreams, visions, poetry, monasticism, crusading ideology, prophecies, messianic illusions, apocalypticism, and millennialism,"[2] a journey very few academics have wished to take.

I am a cultural anthropologist and, unlike historians, we typically go off to another country to study living people. There is usually a lengthy period of fieldwork in a culture where the language, values, orientations in space and time, notions about human nature, gender, kinship and the meaning of life are often quite different from what many of us take for granted. This prolonged examination of cultural subtleties makes anthropologists keenly aware of the intimate connection between peoples' beliefs, their actions, and the cultural context in which they live. I, for example, lived for several years in a relatively remote village in Turkey and quickly realized that Islam was not separate from the rest of the villagers' lives, but the very context for them. Islam was the mas-ter narrative within which people understood the world and its meanings. A religious narrative, like history, is a story that explains "how things got to be the way they are."[3] The difference is not that the religious story or myth is false and history is true, but rather that they communicate their truths differently. For a believer, the Christian myth is eternal but it also unfolds in time—a belief that encourages a tendency to interpret historical events in terms of the Christian scenario.[4] Just as for the Turkish villagers, for whom Islam was not something they could *choose* to believe but simply "the way things in sheer actuality are,"[5] for people in Columbus's milieu, the master narrative was medieval (Catholic) Christianity.

If "the past is another country," as the common saying goes, then it seemed reasonable that anthropological insights could be applied to a world removed in time, but it was a world I would have to discover. I would have to delve into the history of fifteenth-century Europe and medieval Christianity, and learn more about the geographical and scientific knowledge of the time. But as an anthropologist, I also had to step outside the library and attempt to immerse myself in Columbus's world—the landscapes he would have known, the buildings he would have frequented, the artwork he would have seen, the music he would have heard, and the places where he lived.

I visited Genoa, allegedly the place of Columbus's birth, not only to see some of the precious documents preserved there but to get a sense of the city and its topography. Genoa is still a city cramped between the sea and the mountains: many of the old buildings remain, the harbor is still busy, and the view from the hills above the city gives a sense of the sea's possibilities. In Spain, I visited most of the places of significance to Columbus, including Granada and the Alhambra, whose conquest by Queen Isabella and King Ferdinand he witnessed and where the Capitulations authorizing the first voyage were worked out; I spent several days at La Rábida monastery, where, five hundred years earlier, Columbus met with monks who helped him gain the attention of the Spanish sovereigns; I boarded the replicas of the three small ships docked below the monastery, walked the seven kilometers to Palos in Columbus's footsteps, and entered the church where mass was said before the departure of the first voyage in 1492. While there, I almost missed the small plaque at the crumbling fountain where the crew took on water for that voyage.

Seville was my favorite place. Not only is it the city where Columbus first met the Spanish sovereigns at the Alcázar and the location of the Las Cuevas monastery where Columbus spent a great deal of time, it is also the home of the Biblioteca Colombina—where the remnants of Ferdinand Columbus's library, including some of his father's books and documents, are stored. Although it is open primarily only to researchers, a visitor can sometimes be permitted to catch a glimpse behind glass cases of the old books covered in thick vellum and labeled in fading brown ink. I visited Córdoba, where Columbus lived for several years waiting for the decision about his proposal for the voyage and where he met Beatriz de Harana, who would become the mother of his second son, Ferdinand.

In Madrid, as elsewhere, I visited churches and museums to get a sense of the pictorial repertoire that would have colored his imagination, and was fortunate to meet with Anunciada Colón, a direct descendant of Columbus, and be admitted to the Casa de Alba, which is a private residence for another branch of his descendants and contains valuable documents, including Columbus's drawing of the north coast of Hispaniola.

At the library in Simancas, I actually held five-hundred-year-old letters written by Columbus, fearing that at any moment they would crumble to dust in my hands. Finally, I went to Valladolid to the house, now a small museum, where Columbus is supposed to have died.

A different ethnographic endeavor was to get some feeling of what it was like to go to sea on a sailing ship. I signed up for a stint on a tall ship. I kept the watches—including a very cold midnight-to-three a.m. watch—swabbed the decks, hauled the heavy sails, and attempted to calculate distance by "dead reckoning." Unlike Columbus's crew, I had the luxury of a narrow bunk. However, I have to admit that I got very little sleep due less to the motion of the ship than to the total disruption of one's normal circadian rhythm of wakefulness and sleep and the noise of those on duty. I wanted desperately to sail into the harbor at La Isabela in the Dominican Republic (the site of the first colony) to view the promontory as Columbus did, but that was not possible as the site is under military surveillance. Still, I have spent a fair amount of time in the Caribbean and can understand the wonder Columbus felt at the beauty of the place—the luxuriant foliage, the scent of flowers, and the extraordinary color and clarity of the water.

Today, Columbus is not a flesh and blood person, but a symbol. The dominant picture holds him responsible for everything that went wrong in the New World. Debates about his legacy are politicized and vehement. Every Columbus Day, protests are staged and statues of him are desecrated.[6] No longer is Columbus the man who was proposed for canonization in the nineteenth century; instead, he is an avaricious sinner who fomented genocide. The "Discovery" has come to be seen not as "the greatest event since the creation of the world, save in the incarnation and death of Him who created it," as a sixteenth-century chronicler proclaimed,[7] but as one of the greatest disasters in world history. Judging Columbus from a present-day ethical standard is not only anachronistic, it reduces his intentions to their (unintended) effects; that is, it mistakes the consequences for the motivations. My purpose is not to exonerate Columbus, but to situate him in his cultural context and to shift some of our attention from the man to the religious ideas that motivated him and were widely shared by his contemporaries—ideas that have reemerged in the twentieth and twenty-first centuries.

Years of becoming acquainted with Columbus have convinced me that we must consider his world and how the cultural and religious beliefs of his time colored the way he thought and acted. Columbus lived in a Christian, Catholic world that enveloped his life. For Christians at that time, the concept of *a* religion—one among many others, and each with a name, e.g., Christianity, Judaism, Hinduism, Islam, Buddhism, as we tend to think today—did not exist. Modernity transformed what were different ways and views of life into entities defined by specific beliefs and practices focused on a particular aspect of life, namely, one's spirituality. Indeed, attaching "-ism" to some of them was a late-nineteenth-century invention.[8] For Columbus and his milieu, the Christian way of life and view of the world was the one and only true way; it had been communicated by God through his son, Jesus, described in the *New* Testament, and elaborated in lessons delivered by one's priest. From this perspective, the Jewish way or the Muslim way could only be considered false.

The Christian faith was not just a moral guide to life; it also incorporated a worldview—a view of the world in its widest (cosmological) context. People in Columbus's day took for granted that the world was created by God and held in his embrace, as portrayed in a number of *mappae mundi* (world maps). Where today we tend to think of space and time as expanding, perhaps infinite, that was not the medieval view; space and time were circumscribed. The world, or the earth, was the center of the universe—the pinnacle of Creation; everything else—the moon and planets, the sun and the stars—revolved around it. *Mappae mundi* were not meant to accurately represent the physical world; instead, they were a form of religious education—a topography of faith—pointing out places of religious-historical significance.

T-O map by Zacaría Lilo. *Courtesy of The John Carter Brown Library at Brown University.*

The earth, excluding the ocean, was composed of three "parts"—Europe, Africa, and Asia—believed to be populated by the descendants of the three sons of Noah—Japheth, Ham, and Shem. On the more schematic T-O maps, so called because the O represented the round world and the T the bodies of water that trisected it—the Mediterranean, the Nile, and the Don—Jerusalem was assumed, if not always depicted, to be at the center where the three parts met. While the world was imagined as "the stage on which God's plan for the salvation of mankind was to be enacted,"[9] Jerusalem was center stage both spiritually and physically.

Jerusalem was sacred not only because of events in the past but because of events prophesied to take place in the future. It was the place where Jesus had walked and preached and been crucified, but it was also the place where he would return to usher in the Last Days as portrayed in the book of Revelation or Apocalypse, the last book of the Christian Bible.[10] The big question, always, was "When will He come?" Medieval Christians knew that the "life span" of the world was only seven millennia, one millennium representing each day of Creation, but they did not know when that time was up. Turbulent events experienced over several centuries—wars, famines, pestilences, schisms in the church, earthquakes, and, finally, the fall of Constantinople—were seen as signs that the end time was fast approaching.

Before the end, however, several conditions were necessary to prepare for

Christ's return: all peoples had to be evangelized and hopefully converted so they would be saved from eternal damnation; Jerusalem had to be in Christian hands in order that the Temple could be rebuilt, for that was to be Christ's throne as he sat in judgment. The apocalyptic scenario included a notion of an Antichrist, at that time identified with Muslims, who would try to seduce people from their faith, and a Last World Emperor, who would come forth to defeat the Antichrist, conquer Jerusalem, restore the Holy Sepulchre, and unite the whole world *unum ovile, unus pastor* (one fold, one pastor)—as the Gospel of John (10:16) proclaimed. Then, Christ would come again, the heavenly city would descend, and there would be a brief period of bliss before history, time, and the world would be rolled up.

Medieval Christians considered Jerusalem to be their rightful inheritance, given to them by Christ himself; it was outrageous that it was held by Muslims. Numerous crusades had been launched to wrest the city from them, and Franciscan missions had been sent to Asia to meet with the Grand Khan, who had expressed interest in Christianity. The hope was that he and his people would be converted and be convinced to form an eastern flank to march on Jerusalem as Europeans came from the west.

These ideas had been circulating long before Columbus was born; they were hardly original with him but they would greatly influence his plan to sail west to the "Indies" (cover term for the East). At Cathay Columbus expected to meet the ruling Grand Khan, deliver letters of greeting from Queen Isabella and King Ferdinand, and initiate the process to trade for the gold he had read about in the book of Marco Polo's travels. That gold would finance the new crusade to take Jerusalem. Eventually, he came to see himself as a crucial player in the unfolding apocalyptic drama. His daring and controversial plan—to sail west to reach the East—did not, of course, spring into his mind "full-blown," but developed over the course of his life. In Genoa[11] he found his passion for sailing, heard stories about the crusades in which the Genoese had participated and Marco Polo's travels to the Grand Khan of the thirteen century. He also witnessed the consequences experienced by the Genoese with the fall of Constantinople. While it is not known for certain where and when his passion for crossing the ocean emerged, his early voyages for the Portuguese, during which he learned about currents and winds in the Atlantic, surely contributed to that goal. His faith, as it matured, was of a passionate nature as his contemporaries avowed, and was greatly inspired by the Franciscans, whose vision would help him understand the meaning and purpose of his voyages and discoveries.

Since medieval Christians believed that there was only one true faith, all others were considered false sects; Columbus, like many before him, fervently believed it was the duty of every Christian to try to save the souls of non-Christians so they would not burn eternally in hell. As we know, religious passion can move mountains; it can also lead to wars and suicide bombers. Columbus's passion led him on a great adventure, an encounter such as the world had never seen, but he could hardly have foreseen the consequences of that encounter. Seemingly positive intentions can have negative implications, for the "ends" can be used to justify the "means." Columbus's ends—the otherworldly goal of salvation—provided the justification for his earthly project—the quest for Jerusalem. The crusade to wrest Jerusalem from the Muslims was the first step in the series of events that would make possible the return of Christ before the Last Judgment at the end of the world, and time was running out.

The quest for Jerusalem was Columbus's grand passion; it was the vision that sustained him through all the trials and tribulations he felt, like Job, that he endured—the frustrating years of waiting to secure support for the venture, the sleepless nights and treacherous seas he survived, the mutinous crews and rebellious colonists he put up with, the humiliation of being returned to Spain in chains and, later, being marooned for more than a year on the island of Jamaica with a divided crew and his thirteen-year-old son. He had dedicated his life to the liberation of Jerusalem; on his deathbed, realizing he would never see his project fulfilled, he ratified his will that left money to support the crusade he hoped would be taken up by his successors.

The "Enterprise of the Indies," as Columbus was to call the project that culminated in his arrival in America, was not intended merely to find a new route to the gold and spices of the East, though that was part of it. It certainly wasn't to prove the earth was round, because most people at the time already knew it was round. Nor was Columbus out to discover a "new world," only a new way to reach part of the old one; he died still thinking he had reached the periphery of Asia, never knowing he had discovered a "new world."

This book illuminates the ways the "ends" and the worldview that supported them are bound up with Columbus's vision and venture, and will answer the question why, after all this time, it is important for us to consider them. Today, the apocalyptic vision that inspired Columbus is very much alive among some contemporary Christians and, in slightly different forms, among certain adherents of Judaism and Islam. Columbus's story can be read as a parable for our times.

CHAPTER ONE

OMENS OF THE APOCALYPSE

Christopher Columbus was born two years before an event that would change the world and, in large part, would set the course of his life. The fall of Constantinople to the Ottomans in 1453 was a blow to Christendom from which it has never really recovered. That glorious city—home to the Byzantine Empire for more than a thousand years and to Hagia Sophia (Church of the Holy Wisdom), Christendom's most famous church—lay in ruins, its emperor dead and its people slain or taken prisoner. When news of the sacking reached Europe, Aeneas Sylvius Piccolomini, who would become Pope Pius II a few years later, described the fall of the city as "the loss of one of the two eyes of the church"—the other being Rome.[1]

Constantinople had been a major stopping place for pilgrims en route to Jerusalem, primarily because it was the repository for a number of holy relics. Pilgrims yearned for a glimpse of objects like pieces of the True Cross; the remains of Anne, the mother of the Virgin Mary; and the bones of Saint Luke, brought back from Jerusalem by Helena, the mother of Constantine I, the founder and first emperor of the eponymous city. Helena, who had made pilgrimage to Jerusalem in 326, had also found the location where Jesus had been buried and had ordered a church, the Holy Sepulchre, to be built on the site.

In addition to its religious heritage, Constantinople was also home to European merchants, especially the Genoese who had come to dominate trade with the East through its outposts at ports on the Black Sea. Now, in the mid-fifteenth century, with the fall of Constantinople, the trade route to the East and the pilgrimage route to Jerusalem was virtually closed to the West. Constantinople, like Jerusalem, was in the hands of Muslims. In the struggle between Christianity and Islam, Islam seemed to be winning. Many Christians read this as a sign the end of the world was fast approaching. A pall settled over Europe.

The Ottomans, however, were jubilant; they had finally captured the *"Kizil Elma"* (Red or Golden Apple) of their dreams.[2] Although Muslims had been sweeping across Asia Minor for some time, the Ottomans, known among themselves as *ghazis* or holy warriors, had pushed the farthest. By 1326, they had reached the Sea of Marmara across which they could almost see Constantinople. They lusted after that prize not only because of its opulent buildings, its luxury and learning, and its symbolic importance, but also because of its strategic position.

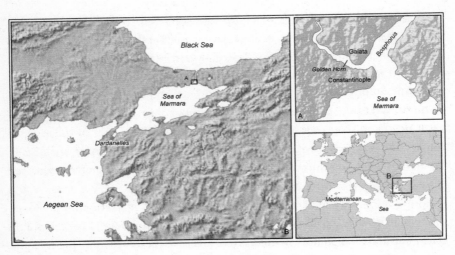

Strategic location of Constantinople. *Map prepared by Lynn Carlson, GISP.*

Constantinople, today's Istanbul, is situated on hills that overlook the place where three waterways meet: the Sea of Marmara, which flows through the Dardanelles out to the Aegean; the Golden Horn, an inlet off the Marmara that divides the city; and the Bosphorus, a strait that leads up from the Sea of Marmara to the Black Sea. Thus, whoever controlled Constantinople controlled travel and trade from ports in the Black Sea to those in the Mediterranean and beyond. Although the Byzantine Empire had contracted considerably over the years to contain barely more than the city itself, Constantinople was thought to be impregnable. It was protected by miles of stone walls that were fifteen feet thick and more than forty feet high, with evenly dispersed towers that were twice as high. There were three sets of walls in all, one inside the other, each separated by a fosse or moat. These fortifications would be put to the test. Ottomans had tried several times to take the city, but had been unsuccessful. They had kept sight of their goal, however, and had made long-term plans; in preparation for the siege of Constantinople, they had conquered a huge swath of territory in Europe: from Gallipoli to Adrianople, from Varna on the Black Sea, to Greece, and then to Kosovo and Bosnia, across the Adriatic from Italy, until Constantinople was effectively surrounded.

The ambitious young sultan known as Mehmet II decided that the "Apple" was finally ripe for the plucking. Late in 1452, he took his army of more than eighty thousand soldiers and marched from his capital in Adrianople toward Constantinople. He quartered his troops at Rumeli Hisarı, a fortress his workmen had quickly constructed on the shores of the Bosphorus, a few miles north of the city walls. Rumeli Hisarı, or "Roman fortress," was built at the narrowest point on the Bosphorus, known as Boğazkesen (throat-cutter), directly across from the Anadolu Hisarı, the Anatolian fortress, built by his great-grandfather Beyazit I. From these two forts, the Ottomans could seize any ships coming from the Black Sea, collecting tariffs or confiscating their goods and capturing their crews. By the beginning of 1453 they were ready to begin the siege.

In the Ottoman camps, the fires burned all night and the men were whipped into fighting mood by the beat of drums, the shrill high notes of the *zurna,* and shouting songs that made it difficult for people inside the city to sleep. They also set up their cannons and began an incessant bombardment of the walls in a strategy of "shock and awe."

> The noise and vibration of the massed guns, the clouds of smoke, the shattering impact of stone on stone dismayed seasoned defenders. To the civilian population it was a glimpse of the coming apocalypse and a retribution for sin . . . [it was] according to one Ottoman chronicler, "like the awful resurrection blast."[3]

Seeing all this activity, the Byzantines inside the city became terrified; Emperor Constantine XI wrote a desperate letter to Pope Nicholas V, promising to unify the Eastern Orthodox and Western Catholic churches if he would quickly send reinforcements. Although both Catholic and Orthodox were nominally Christian, their enmity was of long standing, ever since the two branches of the

Church had split in the eleventh century. "Unity," however, would not mean equality between the two branches, but submission of the Orthodox church to the primacy of Rome. Many Byzantines felt that was too high a price to pay for Rome's support, but they were vastly outnumbered. Although the population of the city was about forty thousand, they could count at most five thousand Greek men available to fight. To be sure, there were also about two thousand foreigners—some Venetians and Florentines, but mostly Genoese who lived in Galata across the Golden Horn from the Greek part of the city—but their loyalty could not be assumed since they were Latin Christians, not Orthodox Christians like the Greeks.

Nevertheless, according to a letter written to the pope by Archbishop Leonard, who had been called from Chios to help negotiate the union, the emperor and his senate had agreed to the union and it was apparently confirmed in mid-December 1452.[4] For a short time hostilities thawed somewhat, if not among priests and theologians, at least among the people imperiled in the city. They celebrated when a Genoese ship arrived in January 1453 filled with food, supplies, and seven hundred soldiers—four hundred from Genoa and three hundred from their colony in Chios, an island in the Aegean. Their arrival provided a much-needed boost to morale to those in the city, especially when they learned that one of the Chian soldiers was Giovanni Giustiniani, who knew how to fortify and repair damaged walls. Knowing that his skill would be essential during the impending siege, Constantine XI, the Byzantine emperor, quickly made him his second-in-command. Some of the Genoese in Galata rushed to join and fight alongside Giustiniani, while others rushed to the ship, hoping to catch passage back to Genoa. But the majority of the Genoese in Constantinople did not want to lose the lucrative trade from their Black Sea colony at Caffa in the Crimea. Luciano Spinola, one of the leading merchants, convinced them to remain neutral in the hope that the Ottomans, like the Byzantines, would appreciate the luxury goods such as caviar and sturgeon that they supplied from that trade.

Spring came; the storks returned from their winter sojourn in Africa, and the scent of roses filled the air and the churches. But these joyful signs could not dispel the unease felt by the people trapped inside the city. To add to their anxiety, at the beginning of April, Easter Week, a couple of small earthquakes rattled their already frayed nerves. For weeks, Mehmet's soldiers had provoked small skirmishes along the length of the walls as a way to tire the Christians before the onslaught. For a time, the Christians had the advantage, despite their numbers. Ottoman cannon fire had damaged but not destroyed the walls, and when the soldiers tried to scale them, the Christians could knock them down with stones. Still, the continual assault and the constant vigilance had exhausted them.

As an alternative strategy to breaching the walls, the Ottomans began to dig tunnels under them. The Byzantines soon discovered some of the tunnels and set fire to them, capturing soldiers and forcing them to give the locations of other tunnels. They were also aware that there were two vulnerable places along the land walls—one at the St. Romanus Gate, located in a depression caused by the Lycus River, and the other at a point where the walls met at right angles, behind the Blachernae Palace. The Ottomans decided to focus on the St. Romanus Gate because the depression rendered the towers lower than hills opposite and also because the riverbed had made it difficult to construct a deep moat. Immediately, they moved their monster cannon into place. It was twenty-seven feet long—probably the largest cannon ever constructed at the time—and could lob a stone cannonball weighing a thousand pounds against the wall or over it. Never had anything like it been seen. It demolished part of the wall, but at night Giustiniani and his helpers were able to repair it and the assault continued.

Near the Golden Horn, the Ottoman fleet was similarly stalled. Aware that their city was most vulnerable through the Golden Horn, the Byzantines had laid a huge chain boom, designed, in fact, by a Genoese, across its entrance to prevent Ottoman ships from entering and attacking both sides of the city. That was a clever strategy but hardly a panacea; they desperately needed more soldiers and supplies from Europe.

The pope in Rome had dawdled in sending aid. He had assumed the city was well fortified and couldn't believe God would let it go to the infidels, and he was waiting for assurance that a "union" between the Greek and Roman churches would be consummated before he sent aid. At the end of March, the pope finally dispatched three Genoese ships, but they got caught in a storm near Chios and did not reach Constantinople until April 20, when they confronted a fleet of Ottoman ships and triremes. Those on land, including Constantine and Mehmet, could only watch as a vicious battle ensued. Against the odds, the Genoese sailors managed to fight off the Ottoman ships and slip through the boom that was opened for them, into the Golden Horn, where they unloaded much-needed supplies.[5] This success of the Genoese greatly embarrassed Mehmet II. In response, he devised an ingenious way to circumvent the boom.

In the dead of night, on April 22, the Ottomans carried out one of the most amazing military maneuvers of the time, perhaps of all time. On greased logs they rolled seventy-two ships overland up from the Bosphorus, over the hill of Galata, and down into the Golden Horn inside the boom, from where they could easily barrage the city. When the Christians awoke and saw this, they must have felt they were doomed. Yet, miraculously, they would continue to hold the Ottomans at bay for another month.

On the twelfth of May, the Ottoman forces came against the palace walls with thousands of soldiers and, according to Nicolò Barbaro, an eyewitness, "these Turkish dogs" let loose with "fierce cries according to their custom, and with sounds of castanets and tambourines . . . they made a strong attack against the walls of the palace, so that the majority of those in the city thought that night that the city was lost."[6] Yet the Christians clung to their belief that God would not allow the city to fall to the "wicked pagans," at least not until a prophecy, attributed to the first Constantine, was fulfilled. He had prophesied that the city would never fall until the "moon rose darkened," and since that had not yet occurred the people inside the city continued hopeful.

Two weeks later, however, their hope ran out. On May 24, there was a lunar eclipse, followed by torrential rain, fog, and a strange light that hovered over Hagia Sophia. Among the terrified citizens a rumor spread that "the time of the Antichrist had arrived," meaning that the end of the world was nigh. In the Bible, the Antichrist is identified as a powerful leader who will come in the last days to tempt people away from their faith.[7] A huge battle will ensue, the Antichrist will be defeated. Christ will come again to judge both the quick and the dead, and the world will end. For the people in Constantinople, it was easy to imagine that Mehmet was the Antichrist and that the end-time was upon them.

At this crucial moment, Mehmet tempted Emperor Constantine with terms of surrender. Constantine refused, and summoning the people to Hagia Sophia, he warned them that the great battle for the fate of the world was imminent. He told them that they should be ready to die for their faith, their country, their family, and their sovereign. Encouraged by his words, Greek and Latin Christians united against their common enemy, the Muslims. After taking communion together, the men went back to their posts, and the women carried water to refresh them and collected stones for them to rain down upon the enemy.

On the night of May 28, after fifty-four days of continual siege, the Ottoman camp was deathly quiet. The Greeks hoped against hope that the Ottomans had given up. But at dawn, when the sun was shining directly into the Christians' eyes, the elite Janissary corps[8] of the Ottoman forces stormed the walls and a ferocious battle ensued. Still, the Christians held on. When the emperor saw that his commander-in-chief was missing, he "went in great distress to see where he had gone" and learned that Giustiniani had been wounded by an arrow and had left his post on the ramparts. When he found him, he pleaded, "I beg you; your flight will encourage others to do the same. Your wound is not mortal; bear the pain and stay at your post like a man, as you promised to do." But Giustiniani fled, and "as he fled, he went through the city crying 'the Turks have got into the city!'"[9] Hearing this, many of the people panicked and abandoned their posts to follow him, hoping to escape on the ships. Many later believed that had he remained, their city might not have been lost. Constantine and his men continued fighting bravely. It is said that the emperor, proclaiming he would rather die fighting for his city than live among the infidels, dismounted his horse and joined the fray. He was last seen, sword in hand, disappearing into the crowd. Not long after his disappearance, the wall was breached. Ottoman soldiers swarmed in and soon their banner flew from the ramparts. The city had fallen to the Muslims. The date was May 29, 1453.

Later in the day, Sultan Mehmet, forever after known as "the Conquerer," rode directly to Hagia Sophia and entered the church. He was awed; never had he seen such a building. It was the largest enclosed space in the world, and the dome was more than 184 feet from the floor (about fifteen stories high) and 102 feet wide. Instead of the customary solid walls, there were windows in the dome that flooded the interior with light. Built in the sixth century, the dome's construction was unsurpassed in Europe for nearly one thousand years; it seemed to float in the air, compelling a close associate of Mehmet's to write that "it vies in rank with the nine spheres of heaven!"[10]

Mehmet's personal cleric mounted the pulpit and recited the Muslim creed: "There is no God but God and Muhammad is his prophet," thereby transforming the church into a mosque. Hagia Sophia would henceforth be called Aya Sofya (a Turkish rendering of the Greek name). Because human images are not permitted in mosques, the golden mosaics and colorful frescoes depicting Jesus and the saints would soon be defaced or covered over.[11]

The damage to the building, and to the city, is said to have saddened Mehmet and caused him to meditate on the transitory nature of all things, but he could not deny his soldiers, who had been fighting for months, the three-day rampage permitted under Muslim law if a city does not surrender. A Christian eyewitness sent a grim report to a cardinal in Florence, who then sent a letter to the mayor of Venice describing Constantinople's terrible fate:

> The public treasure has been consumed, private wealth has been destroyed, the temples have been stripped of gold, silver, jewels, the relics of the saints, and other most precious ornaments. Men have been butchered like cattle, women abducted, virgins ravished, and children snatched from the arms of their parents. If any survived so great a slaughter, they have been enslaved in chains so that they might be ransomed for a price, or subjected to every kind of torture, or reduced to the most humiliating servitude.[12]

The Christian dead totaled about four thousand, many more were wounded, and tens of thousands were taken prisoner. Blood flowed in the streets of Constantinople, encircling the cobblestones like red mortar. Some of the bodies were thrown into the Dardanelles, where they "floated out to sea like melons along a canal."[13] Others were piled up as there had been no time to bury them; the stench was terrible, but even more terrible was the task of identifying the bodies of friends and relatives, because many had been beheaded.

In the city, the Byzantines blamed the Latins, alleging that "Because we made the Union, and paid attention to the Pontiff of Rome, we deserve to suffer the displeasure of God." In turn, the Latins thought the fall of the city was due to the stubbornness and iniquity of the Greeks, whom they compared to a "body which had remained for so many years cut off from its Head,"[14] and who, it was believed, had feigned the union. The chasm between the two wings of the church was dug even deeper. Now, more than two-thirds of the land around the Mediterranean was in Islamic hands and the Muslims had a firm foothold in Europe.

Yet, even upon hearing of the carnage at Constantinople, Christians did not rally to the cause when Pope Nicholas V immediately called for a new crusade; they were not enthusiastic contemplating the realization that they would first have to conquer Constantinople if they were ever to conquer Jerusalem. Nor did they rally when the Ottomans encroached closer to European cities and attacked Belgrade in 1456. Europeans were exhausted from the Hundred

Years' War between England and France and from a number of other interne-cine wars. Despite the apocalyptic mood, they needed a rest. With their forces depleted, there were too few men to commit to a distant war.

The lack of enthusiasm for a new crusade was a sign of the hopelessness of the times. In contrast, three and a half centuries earlier when Muslims had de-stroyed the Holy Sepulchre, armies from all over Europe answered Pope Urban II's call for the First Crusade in 1095.[15] Their fervor was aroused by the belief that Jerusalem belonged to them; its "reconquest" was legitimate. As the right-ful owners, they believed they had to liberate the city and cleanse the sacred places. In the late eleventh century, frequent recitations of Psalm 79:1—"O God, the heathen are come into thine inheritance—thy holy temple have they de-filed, they have laid Jerusalem in ruins," helped to stir the passions of medieval Christians.[16] That fervor, however, had a dark side. Crusaders traveling from all parts of Europe planned to meet in Constantinople, but their religious justifi-cations and lofty ideals did not prevent them from committing terrible crimes against the Jews in response to a rumor that it was the Jews in Jerusalem who had urged the Muslims to destroy the Holy Sepulchre. In cities such as Mainz, Speyer, Worms, Trier, and Cologne, they tortured or simply massacred any Jews who refused to convert. For some Jews, death was preferable to apostasy, and chronicles, liturgies, and poems of the time record that quite a number killed themselves and, in reference to the biblical Abraham, "sacrificed" their children before the crusaders could get to them.[17]

More than twenty thousand crusaders converged on Constantinople be-tween 1096 and 1097. In order to avoid conflict in the city, the Byzantine Em-peror Alexius sent the crusaders to an encampment on the other side of the Sea of Marmara, where their first successful assault was the retaking of Nicaea from the Muslims. Nicaea is the town where the Nicene Creed, the Christian confes-sion of faith, had first been articulated in A.D. 325. Confidently, the crusaders began marching toward Jerusalem, yet their mood quickly deflated when they reached the arid stretches of the Holy Land and found little water or food. They were in no shape to go into battle. Fortunately, as they were marching overland, the Genoese had sent a fleet of twelve galleys, one ship, supplies, and twelve hundred crusaders, and they reached Jaffa, the closest port to Jerusalem, just as the northern Europeans arrived on foot. Thus fortified, the crusaders attacked Jerusalem and conquered it on July 15, 1099. But again the crusaders were ruth-less. Once inside the city, they massacred Muslims and Jews alike. Still, Christians back home praised them for "having purged with swords of piety the place and house of heavenly purity from the filth of the impious." [18]

Following their successful capture of the city, the "Franks," as all Europeans in Jerusalem were called, established the Latin Kingdom of Jerusalem and restored the Holy Sepulchre and other places related to the life of Jesus. They also established a number of other crusader states in the Levant—Edessa, Antioch, Acre, and Tripoli—but there was little peace. The princes of those states fought each other constantly, and the kingdom of Jerusalem often required reinforcements from Europe for support in its ongoing battles with its Muslim neighbors.

Despite European aid, the Latin Kingdom of Jerusalem did not survive a century. One by one, crusader forts fell to Saladin, the Muslim conqueror, and by October in 1187, after a short battle, Jerusalem surrendered to him. Saladin wasn't interested in destroying Christian holy places. Instead, he appointed Franciscans to guard the Holy Sepulchre, permitted the Knights Hospitaller, a monastic order founded before the crusade, to continue their aid to any poor and sick pilgrims still brave enough to make the journey, and allowed the aristocratic, military group known as the Knights Templar to protect them.

After the expending of so much energy on the crusade to take Jerusalem, the loss was devastating to European Christians. Pope Urban III died shortly after hearing the shocking news. It was said that King Henry II "remained speechless for four days," and King William II of Sicily "donned sackcloth and sat in solitude for four days." Cardinals became itinerant preachers, and people flocked to churches that remained open day and night.[19] As scholar Raffaele Pazzelli notes, "Large paintings were made which depicted the Holy Sepulchre trampled upon by horses and Jesus Christ oppressed by Mohammed . . . and minstrels abandoned their love songs to weep over the enormous tragedy." [20] The surrender of Jerusalem created a stain on the hearts of European Christians; they were ashamed, and many blamed the Franks for fighting among themselves and for not fighting harder to defend their city. They also grappled with the theological question: How could God have allowed the city to return to the infidels? The most acceptable explanation, articulated early on in a letter a Genoese merchant had sent to the pope following the surrender, was that God was punishing them for their sins. The new pope, Gregory VIII, sounded the same theme in his encyclical published shortly after he received the news of the loss:

Having heard of the severity of the terrible judgment which the divine hand had used over the land of Jerusalem, both we ourselves and our brothers are so confused with horror and afflicted with such sorrow, that it is not easy for us to discern how we are to act or what we are to do.[21]

He commanded the faithful to repent of their sins and do penance. According to Pope Gregory, God had used the Muslims as a goad to inspire the Christians to change their corrupt ways so that, with cleansed hearts, they would renew the fight for Jerusalem. Their salvation was to be in the future. With the proclamation of this mission, the meaning of Jerusalem changed. No longer was it only the earthly city where Christ had walked and had been crucified, it had become the site of his Second Coming, the site of the Last Days as prophesied in the Gospels, the book of Revelation, and elsewhere in the Bible.

Belief in the impending Apocalypse had stirred friars and priests to redouble their efforts at conversion. In the mid-thirteenth century, a couple of Franciscan friars, John de Plano Carpini and William of Rubruck, journeyed to Central Asia on evangelical missions to convert the Grand Khan in the hope that he would become an ally of the Christians in their fight against the Muslims. Although the khan wanted to learn more about Christianity, he had a more ecumenical approach to religion and could not believe there was only one faith; the friars were unsuccessful in their conversion efforts. The desire to convert the Grand Khan was also part of the motivation for the 1271 journey in which seventeen-year-old Marco Polo accompanied his father Nicolò and his uncle Maffeo to the kingdom of the khan at Cathay in order to fulfill a promise they had made on a previous journey. Because of the khan's interest in Christianity, he had asked them to bring a vial of oil from the lamp of the Holy Sepulchre. He had also sent a letter with them to Pope Gregory X, requesting that he send a hundred priests who could instruct him and his people in the Christian faith. On their return journey to the Mongol kingdom, as recorded in *The Travels of Marco Polo*, they carried the holy oil and some presents and letters from Pope Gregory X to Kublai Khan, the grandson of Genghis Khan. But the few priests who were willing to accompany them soon turned back because of the rigors of the journey. Kublai Khan was sorely disappointed; Marco commented that "if the Pope had sent out persons duly qualified to preach the gospel, the Great Khan would have embraced Christianity, for which, it is certainly known, he had a strong predilection."[22]

During the thirteenth century, eight more crusades had been launched, none of them successful. All left a path of destruction in their wake, but, with the exception of the First Crusade, none was as terrible as the Fourth Crusade. When the crusaders reached Constantinople, they decided to support the young Prince Alexios to depose his uncle Alexios III and install young Alexios as the lawful ruler. But when the prince was unable to pay them as he had promised, the crusaders rebelled and attacked the city with weapons that were meant to be used against Jerusalem. The Latins slew their fellow Orthodox Christians without mercy.

> In April 1204, the greatest city in Christendom was full of smouldering ruins; its palaces and the great houses of its leading families had been pillaged, their hangings and glorious wardrobes torched, their roofs gutted by fire. Entire libraries and archives of documents within, if not already burned, were exposed to rain and would become food for insects and rodents. Many of the revealing small objects of daily life, from tools to kitchenware, icon corners and prayer books, accumulated over hundreds of years, were smashed and broken.[23]

Even Hagia Sophia did not escape destruction; in addition to their looting, the Latin Christians desecrated the church by having a prostitute sing and dance in front of the altar. Much of the booty from the sack of the city now resides in the West, including four monumental gilt horses that had stood atop a column at the ancient Hippodrome where Byzantine emperors had watched chariot races and other major public events. Those horses were taken to Venice, where they stand on pedestals in front at St. Mark's Cathedral. The crusaders never continued on to Jerusalem; instead, for the next fifty-seven years, the Latins occupied the city until the Byzantines, under Michael Palaiologos, took it back in 1261.

The Fourth Crusade wreaked more destruction on Constantinople than the Ottomans would in 1453 and was not forgotten. During the Ottoman siege, it is no wonder that the Byzantines were wary of the Latin Christians, some even going so far as to claim that "they would rather see the turban of a Turk than the hat of a cardinal" in their city. By the beginning of the fourteenth century the major crusades had ended, yet Latin Christians never gave up the idea of a crusade, and their desire for Jerusalem would be revived over and over again.[24]

The crusades did more than stoke religious fervor in Europe, they also helped foster trade in the Eastern Mediterranean. Those involved in transporting crusaders and supplies to the Levant, particularly the Venetians, Genoese, and Pisans, also developed trade routes and trading partners throughout the area, picking up spices, grain, medicines, perfumes, and other goods for the return journey. For their services, these groups were given merchant quarters in Constantinople, Jaffa, Acre, and Jerusalem among other cities. Genoese ships, for example, had sailed to ports on the Black Sea, along the Turkish coast and Aegean islands, to the Levant, Egypt, and as far west as Ceuta in North Africa. By 1298 the Genoese passed through the Pillars of Hercules (the Strait of Gibraltar), after defeating the Moroccans who had controlled them, and thereafter they traded from ports in the Black Sea all the way to their outposts in Lisbon, Seville, Flanders, Bruges, and Southampton.

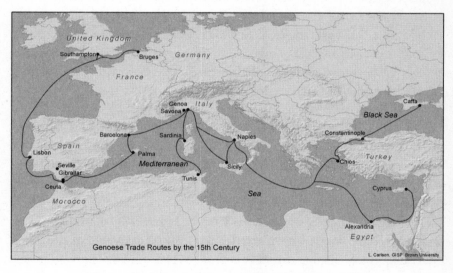

Genoese Trade Routes. *Map prepared by Lynn Carlson, GISP.*

This type of long-distance trade was greatly aided by the invention, around 1270, of the "dry" compass. Instead of a magnetized needle floating in water or attached to a pin, methods that had been used until then, the newer one was set in a wooden box onto which compass points could be marked. Knowledge of the relatively calm and well-traveled waters of the Mediterranean was passed from sailor to sailor and plotted onto *portolani*—charts drawn with fairly accurate outlines of coasts and directions from place to place taken from compass readings—which were compiled in a pilot book known as *Compasso da Navigare* and included distances from port to port, information about landmarks, depths of water, and dangers. With *portolani*, a sailor could both plot his direction and find it, even in cloudy weather, which meant that ships were no longer confined to sailing only in summer. Likewise, changes in ship design also facilitated long-distance trade. Galleys, the oared vessels that had conducted most of the Mediterranean trade and transport, required too many men to row, leaving little room for cargo. They were also too low in the water to easily ward off attackers. Ships for carrying crusaders were designed with higher hulls that made it easier to defend against attacks. Powered by sails, and with only a few side oars at the stern for steering, they required smaller crews. Thus, they could carry more soldiers and, later, pilgrims in addition to supplies and even horses. Other innovations would be introduced in the fifteenth century, including a single rudder attached to the sternpost that was manipulated by a lever, making ships easier to steer.

In Sagres, Portugal, Prince Henry the Navigator (1394–1460) had begun the study of navigation and of ocean currents and winds, and would introduce the caravel, a lighter ship that would become an optimal vessel for exploration. Prince Henry then began to encourage voyages to the Madeiras, the north coast of Africa, and eventually down its western coast.

But just as this trade and innovation were flourishing, and towns in Europe, especially the Italian city-states, were growing in size and prosperity, the Great Famine of 1315 struck. Shortly thereafter, the Great Pestilence (bubonic plague) decimated the European population and wiped out the rest of the region's recent gains.

The origin of the plague that spread like wildfire throughout Europe in the mid-fourteenth century is still being debated. One theory attributes the spread to an early act of what today might be considered biological warfare. Tartar traders traveling along what became known as the Silk Road to the Genoese trading outpost at Caffa on the Black Sea began to die at an alarming rate. When their caravans reached Caffa, there were few men left to wrest the trading post from the Genoese as they had hoped. So instead of fighting, they threw the dead and diseased bodies over the city walls in the belief that whatever had killed their own men would spread and kill the Genoese as well. Though the Tartars failed to take the outpost, they were very successful in unleashing one of the world's greatest disasters. It is thought that in 1347, a Genoese ship left Caffa's port carrying its usual cargo of silks and spices along with its usual accompaniment of rats and their fleas. But the fleas onboard this ship had feasted on the diseased bodies of the Tartars. At every port, the fleas jumped ship, first at Constantinople, then at other ports in the Mediterranean, including Genoa. From each port the bubonic plague spread rapidly inland until all of Europe was affected.

At the time, people didn't know that a tiny flea bite was the cause of their high fevers, headaches, and nausea. The victims were also stricken with painful buboes—swellings the size of an egg or apple—that appeared in the groin, neck, or armpit. When the buboes oozed pus and blackened over, death came quickly, usually within the week. A particularly virulent form of the plague spread through the air; if it lodged in the lungs, a person could die within three days. So many dead meant mass burials. Boccaccio, who survived the plague in Florence, wrote a gruesome description of it in the introduction to his *Decameron*. There were so many bodies, he wrote, that a huge trench was dug, and as the bodies, hundreds at a time, arrived, they were piled up "as merchandise is stowed in the hold of a ship, tier upon tier."[25] Those who survived worried about the souls of their dead relatives and friends. Since many of the clergy, especially the monks who often cared for the sick, also succumbed to the disease, there was often no one left to take victims' confessions and perform the last rites so that their souls might rest in peace.

Though people were unaware of the source of the terrible disease, they had a number of ideas, typically focused on religious motives, to explain it. As with the loss of Jerusalem in 1187, many people believed the plague was God's punishment for their sins, a belief that inspired a number of penitential movements. A venomous theory blamed beggars, lepers or, more often, the Jews, whom people claimed had poisoned wells and were therefore responsible for spreading the dread disease. This rumor led to the torture and burning of hundreds, perhaps even thousands, of Jews.

The Great Pestilence, as it was called at the time—"Black Death" being a much later term—swept across Europe between 1347 and 1348. Because of the paucity of accurate records and lack of information about family size and population, the following can be read only as estimates. Regardless, the figures are stunning; it is thought that the plague killed more than a third of the population, yet that figure is only an average. In some Italian and Spanish cities on the Mediterranean, it is thought that approximately 75 percent of the people died; Florence lost half its population, while Germany and England had the fewest deaths, with an average of about 20 percent. The Great Pestilence took the lives of between 25 and 50 million people.[26]

Although the worst of the plague was over by 1350, it did not disappear.[27] Outbreaks could occur at any time, and did so for more than a century, which intensified the general sense of unease about the imminence of the Apocalypse. It seemed that the signs were there for those who had eyes to see, for Jesus had explicitly warned in the Bible:

> Nation shall rise against nation, and kingdom against kingdom: And great earthquakes shall be in divers places, and famines, and pestilences; and fearful sights and great signs shall there be from heaven. (Luke 21:10–11)

Aware that people were desperately seeking an explanation for the terrible events of the fourteenth century, at the beginning of the fifteenth mendicant friars of the Franciscan and Dominican orders roamed through France, Italy, and Spain, preaching the Apocalypse. Their fiery sermons mesmerized people by warning that the Antichrist could come at any moment, and that he would reign for three years. But Christ would return and defeat him; all people would be evangelized and, to save their souls, would be converted. Forty-five days later, the world would end. The emphasis on conversion had become acute for, by the fifteenth century, the idea that there could be no salvation outside of the church (*extra ecclesiam nulla salus*), stemming from a bull by Pope Boniface VIII in 1302 and reinforced at the Council of Florence in 1442, had become the canonical view. Although some clergy and laypeople doubted that a just God would allow all the good people who had never heard of Christ's saving word to burn eternally in hell, their views did not prevail.[28]

The friars' aim was conversion of Jews and Muslims, but in Spain the pressure to convert became focused especially on Jews. Although Jews had long lived and prospered in Spain, they were ever reminded that their continued residence was at the king's pleasure. *Las Siete Partidas*, the law code compiled by Alfonso X in the thirteenth century, stated that Jews should live in subjection to remind them of their role in Jesus' crucifixion. According to the Spanish friars and priests, because Christ had come to free all people from original sin, the Jews' refusal to be freed was more than obstinate; they were assumed to be under the power of the Devil.[29] After the plague, efforts to convert Jews intensified and as passions were stirred, many were killed. Mass baptisms took place, and it is believed that more than half the Jewish population converted. Baptism was believed to be transformative, so little or no instruction in Christian belief and practice was provided. Many of these *conversos*, as converted Jews were called, rose to high positions in the Spanish government and even in religious orders, but others became suspected of reverting to their old practices in secret.

Muslims, too, were targeted for conversion, but the animus toward them was less than that against Jews, perhaps because they had no alleged role in Jesus' death. Also, they were less involved than the Jews in the life of the big cities, and therefore less visible than the Jews. However, though the Spanish did not aggressively persecute Muslims in their realm, they did aggressively go after the Muslim territories that were at one time held by Europeans. The campaign was called the Reconquista, and by the fifteenth century most of the land the Muslims had conquered in the eighth and ninth centuries had been reconquered by the Spanish. The one exception was Granada, and that would come under attack later in the century.

During the same period, religious ire was directed not only against Jews and Muslims but was also expressed within the Catholic Church itself, due to a critical division of the papacy. This split in the church, known as the Great Schism, was seen as another sign of the impending Apocalypse. From 1305 to 1377, the papacy had moved its seat to Avignon because of unrest in Rome, but accusations of corruption in Avignon and submission to the French king led supporters of the Roman seat to refer to this period as the "Babylonian Captivity of the Church." In 1378, Pope Urban VI returned the papacy to Rome and a new pope was elected; whereupon Catholics in Avignon elected another. Thus, there were two popes. This dilemma threw the Church into disarray and divided Europe into factions. Finally, the schism was resolved during three years of debate (1414–1417) known as the Council of Constance. One of the attendees was Pierre d'Ailly, whose *Imago Mundi* would be avidly read and annotated by Columbus. D'Ailly was a respected theologian, a cardinal, and rector of the University of Paris, who wrote extensively about the schism, suggesting that it might be a sign of the imminence of the Antichrist. That may have moved the council to resolve the crisis; it eliminated the claimants, elected a new pope, and declared that Rome was henceforth to be the true seat of the papacy. Yet the Avignon contingent did not relinquish its position easily, and the popes they elected came to be called antipopes. Just before Constantinople fell to the Muslims, Avignon finally surrendered their claims to the papacy.

The conquest of Constantinople in 1453 represented the capstone to all of these turbulent events that had been rocking Christianity for four centuries.

The city's long history would be encapsulated, like bookends, between the two Constantines—the founder and Constantine XI, its last emperor. With the fall of Constantinople, Muslims now controlled the overland pilgrimage route to Jerusalem, and the city of Jerusalem itself. The loss of the holy city, and then Constantinople, had shattered Christians' once ebullient hopes of unifying the world—*unum ovile et unus pastor*—and turned them introspective; the plague had devastated Europe and was still a threat; and the schism in the church had left deep scars that had not yet healed. Something was clearly wrong with the world; infidel Muslims seemed to be in the ascendant. No wonder the tenor of the time was apocalyptic. This was Columbus's world, and the heritage of these tumultuous events would shape his life and his understanding of the ultimate meaning of his voyages and discoveries.

CHAPTER TWO

LEARNING THE "SECRETS OF THE WORLD"

n the late summer or early autumn of 1451, the man we know as Christopher Columbus was born to Susanna Fontanarossa and Domenico Colombo. While there has been a great deal of speculation about the place of his birth, most of the evidence points to Genoa or its environs.[1] There are no birth records, but the city archives house an incredible number of legal documents that relate to his family. Several mention him by name along with his father and other relatives; one refers to him as "Christopher Columbus, citizen of Genoa," and there are a couple that he wrote himself.

His family can be traced to the area of Fontanabuona, to the mountain village of Moconesi, where his grandfather, Giovanni, was born. In search of economic opportunities Giovanni migrated to the village of Quinto, a short distance down the east coast from Genoa. In 1429, he apprenticed his son Domenico, a boy of eleven, to a cloth weaver in Genoa in the *borgo* (quarter) of Santo Stefano, named after its parish church and monastery. This *borgo* was situated on the right-hand side of the city if one faced it from the harbor and was under the lordship of the prominent Fieschi family.

Domenico must have learned his craft well, for ten years later he was able to lease a house from the monastery, set up shop as a weaver of woolen cloth, and make a contract for an apprentice of his own. These contracts were generally for five years, during which time the apprentice was housed and fed but was not allowed to leave his post unless plague broke out—evidence that the plague was still a fearsome threat.

Plague was not the only threat. The area now known as Italy was at that time composed of a number of independent city-states that were often at war with one another. Genoa and Venice, especially, battled almost continually over dominance of maritime trade in the Mediterranean and the Black Sea and both had outposts in Constantinople as early as the twelfth century. Ships sailing under the flag of one city would attack and confiscate the goods of the other.

In addition to its wars with Venice, the Republic of Genoa was at war with itself. The city-state's fractious history is far too complicated to detail here, but antagonistic parties, defined by allegiances to pope or emperor and to the French or the Spanish, made governance exceedingly difficult. In general, though not always, the merchant class supported the pope, while the landed nobility supported the emperor. These differences, made famous through the Verdi opera *Simon Boccanegra*,[2] were in the fifteenth century most often represented by the (Campo) Fregoso and Adorno families. To bring some order to the city, the Genoese had often resorted to outside rule; each faction needed strong allies to support them against the opposing faction. When Constantinople fell to the Ottomans, Pietro Fregoso was doge (chief magistrate) of Genoa; his faction swore allegiance to the papacy. For outside support, they allied with the French instead of with the Aragonese as had the Adorno faction. In 1458, Pietro Fregoso invited King Charles VII of France to take nominal control of Genoa's government. He sent as deputy his nephew, René of Anjou, King of Naples, titular King of Jerusalem, who seems to have made his headquarters in Savona, a town near Genoa, and to have won the support and hearts of many Genoese. René was known as a good man, an acclaimed painter and great romantic who had written a book on love as well as on tournaments. He was the epitome of the chivalrous knight, and he had fought alongside Joan of Arc in the war with England. But he was a man not so much at odds with the times as temperamentally unequipped to negotiate the tumultuous waters of Genoese politics.

The Fieschi family and, thus, the San Stefano *borgo* was allied with the Fregosos, but at the time Domenico Colombo was setting up shop, Rafaele Adorno was doge. In 1447, however, he was ousted and Domenico's fortune changed. On February 4 of that year,

> The illustrious and excellent Lord Giano Campo Fregoso chose as keeper of the Olivella gate and tower, his beloved Domenico Colombo, serving at the pleasure of the said illustrious lord *doge*, with the customary pay and revenues.[3]

Domenico's support for the Fregoso faction must have recommended him to the doge for the gatekeeper position. This was a distinct honor as the Olivella gate was one of only five entryways into the city.[4] As gatekeeper, Domenico was responsible for keeping track of people who entered the city and thus privy to news and gossip from beyond the walls; he was required to warn the doge of any suspicious activity. Such a job was assigned to only the most trustworthy citizens. According to the editors of the Genoese documents, this position demonstrated

> that Domenico Colombo could not have been a Jew, contrary to a hypothesis recently advanced by some scholars, because the Genoese government would never have entrusted a non-Christian with such a sensitive task as keeping watch over one of the city gates.[5]

This position provided a pretty good living for a man of the *popolo* (ordinary citizen) and was an especially good placement for Domenico, who had migrated only seven years earlier from the village of Quinto. Like all patronage appointments, it depended on the power of his patron to maintain his political control.

During this time Domenico married Susanna Fontanarossa, and in 1451 Cristoforo was born. His mother would normally have gone to Quinto for the birth, where she would have had the assistance of her mother-in-law, but plague had recently broken out in that village and she likely stayed home. St. Christopher's day was celebrated on July 25, so it is possible that Columbus was born on or close to that day.

Columbus was baptized at his parish church, Santo Stefano, named after the first Christian martyr; this church, built in the 1200s but with origins perhaps in the seventh century, is thought to be the oldest church in Genoa. Its bell tower was used as a lookout to see whether approaching ships were friend or foe. The name given to a child at baptism was believed to have an influence on the child's character, so when Susanna selected the name Cristoforo, she may well have been trying to affect his destiny. The name Cristoforo (Christopher) means Christ-bearer and is derived from the story of a pagan man, Reprobus, who once carried a small child across a river. As they crossed, the child became heavier and heavier until he revealed to Reprobus that he was carrying the weight of the entire world. With that, Reprobus realized he was carrying the Christ child. For his service Reprobus became a saint known as Christopher. Indeed, Susanna's choice was prophetic: not only did the patron saint of travelers keep Columbus safe during his extraordinary travels, but Columbus himself, like his namesake, would come to feel that he was destined to be a Christ-bearer, carrying Christianity across the Ocean Sea.

In a short time, Christopher had siblings; three brothers—Bartholomew, Giovanni, and Diego—and a sister, Bianchinetta. In addition to his weaving business, Domenico kept busy with a number of schemes for making (and losing) money; at one point, he was importing cheese from Quinto and other villages and selling it in the city. While hardly rich, the Colombo family was comfortable, and soon Domenico was able to lease a more permanent, but very small house on Vico Dritto from the monastery of Santo Stefano in order to accommodate his growing family. Today, the house at the site, now a small museum, is probably not the original house, but it shows the very cramped quarters in which many people lived. The family would have occupied the upper floors while Domenico maintained his woolen workshop on the ground floor.

Christopher's early life was encompassed by the biblical worldview. Genoa itself was believed to have been "founded by Gianus [Roman Janus], grandson of Noah and the first king of Italy, at the time of Abraham," according to the *Chronicle* written by the Genoese Jacobus de Voragine (ca. 1228–1298). Below a bust of Gianus in the majestic San Lorenzo cathedral an inscription tells of the legend that "celebrates the Trojan prince Gianus who, while searching for a safe and well-protected place, landed in Genoa and seeing it well-defended by the sea and the mountains, enlarged it in name and in power."[6] The god is two-faced, the Genoese say, not because he is deceitful but because he faces in two directions—toward the mountains and toward the sea.

Columbus's daily rhythm was set by the bells of Santo Stefano ringing out at least some of the canonical hours—matins, lauds, prime, terce, sext, none, vespers, and compline. It clearly made an indelible impression on him for, later in life, he would record events by these times. Children may have received some religious instruction from the monks, but more likely through less formal means such as icons, frescoes, and paintings in the churches. Columbus could not have missed the huge fresco of the Apocalypse as he exited the cathedral of San Lorenzo, and would have been taught the lesson it conveyed. Drawn by an anonymous master from the St. Savior in Chora church in Constantinople, in exquisite detail it depicts the heavenly reward for the saved and the hell-fire awaiting sinners and the unconverted. In addition, the yearly calendar was punctuated not only by major holy days such as Epiphany, Palm Sunday, Easter week, Advent, and Christmas, but by frequent processions through the city to commemorate saint's days. Accompanied by horns and drums, these processions, led by city officials, priests, members of confraternities displaying painted images of their patron saints, and prominent citizens carrying gold and silver relics, were not only spectacular events but also served as teaching occasions.

As he grew older, Columbus may have been taken to hear occasional sermons not only from the pulpit of his church but also from popular itinerant preachers who followed in the footsteps of the famous Franciscan St. Bernardino, and perhaps even quoted from his sermons. Bernardino had given his most apocalyptic sermons in Genoa in the years 1417–1418, intensifying people's anxiety created by the schism in the church and in the city's divisive politics, as well as the ever-present threat of plague. The world was coming to an end, Christians had slipped into sin; if they didn't want to be damned for all eternity, they had better quickly repent and transform their lives. People would gather in town squares, day after day, sitting for hours listening transfixed by his fascinating but horrific moral tales about the wages of sin. Bernardino focused especially on sins committed by witches consorting with the Devil, the sin of sodomy, and the sin of fraternizing with the Jews.[7] His sermons were inscribed on wax tablets, dutifully copied, and, after the invention of the printing press (c. 1440), published and widely disseminated, and Columbus surely had heard about them and possibly even read some of them.

Columbus might also have read and found inspiration from the mystical works of his compatriot Caterina Fieschi: *Purgation and Purgatory*, *The Spiritual Dialogues*, and *The Life*, that emphasized the trust and love of God and the spiritual training necessary to ensure eternal life. Caterina was born in Genoa just a few years before Columbus; they may even have become friends, for there is evidence that in later years he wrote to her and her husband.[8] Caterina had wanted to enter a convent, but after the death of her father her brother married her off to Giuliano Adorno, a member of the rival faction. The marriage was unhappy; her husband was a philanderer and had squandered their fortune. Perhaps brought on by these stresses Caterina had a life-changing mystical experience, and became devoted to St. Francis and to working with the poor and the sick, especially at Genoa's famous Pammatone Hospital. Her saintliness even won over her husband, who became a Franciscan tertiary (a lay brother) and helped with her work. She was canonized by Pope Clement XII in 1733.[9]

Painting of Genoa, c. 1481, by Grassi.
By permission of the Museo del Mare, Genoa, Italy.

In addition to Genoa's rich religious context, the city's topography and history would also be reflected in Columbus's interests. Situated on a narrow arc of land wedged between mountains and the sea, Genoa might easily have been a backwater. A steep hill directly behind the city stretches to the rugged Apennines and beyond them the Alps. This made travel and trade overland to other European cities exceedingly difficult. Not surprisingly, the Genoese took to the sea, making the city one of the great mercantile centers of the medieval period. Aeneas Sylvius Piccolomini had described the city in a letter to a friend as early as 1432:

> I wish you were here now with me. Indeed, you would admire an unparalleled city in the whole world. It is located on a hill dominated by very rough mountains to the north, and along the sea to the south . . . Right along the port, on the side bordering the city, rise magnificent palaces, entirely built in marble, reaching to the sky, very elegant with their numerous columns, many adorned with sculptures and figures . . . however, the streets are narrow and only wide enough for 2 or 3 people at a time. [Author's note: Copied from exhibit in the Genoese archives; no citation available.]

As a boy, Columbus may have witnessed the city's voluminous sea traffic when he accompanied his uncle, Antonio, to his post as keeper of the Lanterna, the lighthouse at the end of the quay known as the *mole*. Because of its unforgiving landscape, Genoa had few natural resources and produced few marketable goods except wool and cloth. Its merchants acted mostly as middlemen, transporting goods between ports in the East and those in the West and profiting from that trade. This lucrative business was dominated by a number of prominent families, most notably the Spinolas, di Negros, and Centuriones. They traded soap, woolen cloth, wine, and oil from the West for silks, spices, grain, alum, and slaves obtained from the East. Slavery was common at that time in Europe, and Caffa, on the Black Sea, had been a noted entrepôt for slaves, most of whom were women—Russian, Circassian, Tartar, or Greek—who were then sold in Constantinople, Venice, and Genoa.[10] But with the fall of Constantinople, all of this trade was in jeopardy.

With fewer ships sailing, many sailors were out of work and the city had to accommodate an influx of merchants from the lands conquered by the Ottomans. The *mole*—once so alive with a cacophony of languages, the scents of a thousand spices, the sheen of luxurious silks, the sight of slave women of different features and clothing, and the commotion of ships docking, sailors loading and unloading cargo, and merchants inspecting and registering it—was now more subdued. To generate enough trade to bring Genoa to its former level, some merchants and sailors turned their attention to their outposts in western Europe, hoping to expand their trade, while others were eager to take back the land and the trade lost to the Muslims.

This influx of seafaring men struggling to find work was surely a factor in Genoa's support for the crusade called by Pope Pius II in 1460. Its launch created a great deal of excitement for, as with earlier crusades, Genoa was a major gathering place for crusaders. This was due, in large part, to the Hospitallers, who had established the Commenda of San Giovanni de Pré (St. John the Baptist), a huge building barely a block from the harbor, and still in use, that had offered accommodation to earlier crusaders and had served as a hospital for those who had been wounded in battle. The quest for Jerusalem was the overriding motive for the crusade but, as in the earlier crusades, the Genoese were primed to exploit the trading possibilities.

Columbus would have been nine years old when ships left Genoa's harbor embarking on this new crusade—a sight sure to make an impression on any young boy. He most likely would have heard the stories about earlier crusades in which the Genoese had participated to reclaim the Holy Land, and he may have seen the treasures they had brought back. The most valued treasure, brought back from the First Crusade after the capture of Jerusalem, is an emerald-green bowl, thought to be the Holy Grail in which Jesus washed his hands before the Last Supper. Another revered treasure from the same crusade is a delicate gold-plated silver reliquary containing the ashes of John the Baptist that is still carried in procession through the streets of Genoa every June 24, his saint's day. According to Voragine's *The Golden Legend*, Genoa has only the ashes of his body while those of his head were sent to Constantinople and later to France. However, Genoa holds a gruesome reminder of the Baptist's fate—a plate made of chalcedony believed to have held his head after he was beheaded. This plate was donated in the fifteenth century by Pope Innocent VIII, a member of a prominent Genoese family. Such awe-inspiring relics, housed in the magnificent San Lorenzo cathedral, became the most famous and prized possessions of the Genoese. They were also, of course, constant reminders that Jerusalem, for which the crusaders had fought so hard, remained in Muslim hands, and served as a goad to continue the quest for the holy city.

Like any youth at the time, Columbus could not have avoided hearing stories about the early Venetian traveler Marco Polo. The Genoese were proud of their connection to Marco Polo. He had been their prized prisoner, paraded around the city after the Genoese victory against the Venetians in the battle of Curzola in 1298; adding to his humiliation, he was confined in the Palazzo San Giorgio, which had been built from stones the Genoese had removed from the Venetian embassy in Constantinople. The Palazzo, adorned with colorful frescoes, still stands just across from the *mole*. The Genoese could claim that had they not captured and imprisoned Marco Polo, the stories he told might never have been written. To while away the time, Marco regaled his fellow prisoner, Rusticello, with tales of his twenty-four-year sojourn in the East (seventeen of which were spent in the service of Kublai Khan, the Great Khan of the Mongol Empire, the largest empire in the world). Whether or not Rusticello believed that the tales were true, he was so entranced with them that he wrote them down.

Marco's story began in 1271, when he traveled to Asia with his father and uncle, not only for the purpose of trade but to fulfill a promise they had made to the Grand Khan to bring oil from the Holy Sepulchre as well as priests who could teach about Christianity. From Venice, they traveled to Constantinople, Jerusalem, and Baghdad, and then over the mountainous terrain of Afghanistan, loosely following what later became known as the Silk Road. The arduous journey to reach the court of the Grand Khan took them more than three years. What mesmerized medieval Europeans about Marco's stories were his descriptions of exotic animals they had never seen; of strange customs of peoples he encountered; of the use of charcoal (like our contemporary briquets) to heat their homes and cook their food; and, most surprising, stories about the abundance of gold but the use of paper for money. Of course, they were also interested to learn of the vast extent of the Grand Khan's empire, the opulence of his court, and the advanced civilization of a people who had not had the benefit of Christ's teaching. Because Marco's stories seemed so outlandish to many Europeans, they often felt that his tales were figments of an overheated imagination, and they referred to his book as *Il Milione*, because of the millions of tall tales he told.

The original manuscript of Marco Polo's travels, now lost, was translated into a number of languages—Franco-Italian, Tuscan, Venetian, German, Latin, and a more standard French—and copiously copied. Although more than one hundred manuscript versions exist, none of them are exactly the same, in part because of errors in translation and transcription, deletions of material felt to be immoral, and edifying additions made by some of the copiers. Manuscript copies were owned primarily by monasteries, royalty, and the educated rich, thus most Europeans *heard* rather than read the stories, and that is surely how Columbus first learned about the splendors of the East. Later, when he acquired his own copy of Polo's travels, he made numerous notes in the margins. It is one of the nine books from his library that have survived to this day.[11]

Columbus was especially interested in Polo's descriptions about the location of gold, pearls, precious gems, and spices, and the large island called Cipango (or Cipangu), which is now Japan, and several cities on the Chinese mainland. Marco Polo had written that Cipango had "gold in the greatest abundance, its sources being inexhaustible."[12]

The entire roof is covered with a plating of gold, in the same manner as we cover our houses, or more properly churches, with lead. The ceilings of the halls are of the same precious metal; many of the apartments have small tables of pure gold, of considerable thickness; and the windows also have golden ornaments.[13]

Next to that passage, Columbus had written "copious gold." But he was interested in more than precious commodities. He made notes of things he assumed he would encounter if he ever made it to Asia—the flora and fauna, the names of towns and rivers, and the number of ships in the harbors. Of special interest were the khan's fabulous cities, where he hoped, one day, to meet the reigning khan; the court at Kanbalu (Cambulac) on the ruins of which the Forbidden City in Beijing would later be built; Quinsay (Kin-sai, Hangchow), a sophisticated Chinese city known as the "City of Heaven" that, with its twelve thousand bridges, had reminded Marco of Venice; Zaiton (Zayton), a busy port city with a harbor that could hold a thousand ships and where the "quantity of pepper imported there is so considerable, that what is carried to Alexandria, to supply the demand of the western parts of the world, is trifling in comparison";[14] the summer palace of Shangtu, the Xanadu of Coleridge, where the "stately pleasure domes" held up by gilded canes were actually collapsible and could be moved about like the nomadic *gers* (yurts); and finally, the khan's twelve provinces, especially Cathay and Manji. The latter was said to be the region where the famous Prester John had established a kingdom of Nestorian Christians. Stories popular in Europe in the twelfth through seventeenth centuries told of a Christian patriarch and king who was said to rule over a Christian nation lost amid the pagans and Muslims, in the East. Prester John's legendary realm was thought to be adjacent to the region of Gog and Magog, whose peoples, according to prophecies (Ezek. 38:2, Rev. 20:7–9), were enclosed behind a wall and would be let out at the end of time to help the Antichrist. The Asian location of Prester John's realm figured on a number of maps, including a Genoese map of 1447, Behaim's globe of 1492, and the Mercator map of 1569, but it was never found, even though many travelers before and after Columbus sought it.[15]

Martin Behaim's conception of the Atlantic Ocean. *Courtesy of Felipe Fernández-Armesto.*

Another popular book circulating in the late fourteenth century was the *Travels of John Mandeville*. Though it is not one of the books that survive from Columbus's library, Andrés Bernáldez, a friend of the family, reported seeing Columbus read it, and later Columbus quoted almost verbatim from it in one of his own writings. Today's scholars conclude that Mandeville (a fictitious name) never traveled to the places he described but "borrowed" material from numerous sources, but neither Columbus nor his contemporaries would have known that. The book would have appealed to Columbus and other passionate Christians of the day because its focus was Jerusalem. Pilgrims could use the account as both a map and spiritual guide as they journeyed to Jerusalem. All the important deeds in the life of Jesus were attached to specific physical places, and Mandeville included the stories and legends attached to them so that at each place a pilgrim could relive the Christian drama. "From Bethlehem to Jerusalem is only two miles. On the road to Jerusalem, half a mile from Bethlehem, is a church, where the angels told the shepherds of the birth of Christ. And on that road is the tomb of Rachel, mother of Joseph the Patriarch." To pilgrims taking the overland route that passed through Constantinople, Mandeville noted that there they would be able to see "the sponge and the reed with which the Jews gave drink to Our Lord when He hung on the cross." If, instead, pilgrims had gone by sea, they would arrive at "the port of Jaffa, which is the harbour nearest to Jerusalem. It is only a day and a half's journey from Jerusalem—say thirty-six miles."

As they progressed to Mount Zion, they would come to an even more significant site—"a chapel in which is the huge stone with which the Sepulchre of Christ was covered when He was laid in it . . . Going down thirty-two steps below this chapel is the place where Our Lord washed His disciples' feet—the vessel the water was in is still there." But lo and behold, the very spot where the Resurrection took place was known and accessible and one could walk there. On the Mount of Olives pilgrims could stand where "Our Lord stood when He mounted into Heaven; men can still see the footprint of His left foot in a stone He stood on." How could medieval Christians not want to go to Jerusalem? But Mandeville made sure that pilgrims would not only relive past events, he pointed the way to the future, to the Apocalypse: "From Nazareth to Mount Taber is three miles; it is a high and beautiful hill . . . in that very place on the Day of Judgement will the four angels blow their trumpets and raise all who are dead to life."

Echoing the rallying cry for the crusades, he wrote: "Each good Christian man who is able, and has the means, should set himself to conquer our inheritance, this land, and chase out therefrom those who are misbelievers."[16] In his prologue he admonished his countrymen for their greed and laziness and claimed that if they would make this holy journey, their true heritage—Jerusalem—would be recovered. This appeal to action may be one factor that inspired Columbus's quest.

Although Mandeville's focus was Jerusalem, he "traveled" farther east. Like Marco Polo, Mandeville described the empire, palaces, and court of the Grand Khan as well as some of the customs in India and in the islands near it. But unlike Polo, his interests were biblical rather than commercial. His *Travels* reads more like a kind of "pilgrim's progress," where the journey had both a moral and spiritual purpose. For him, the great lure of the East was not its material riches but the Earthly Paradise which, he said, lay beyond the deserts and the land of Prester John and even beyond the uninhabited wastes. Though "no living man can go to Paradise . . . except through the special grace of God," he, nevertheless, described it in great detail. It "is the highest place on earth; it is so high it touches the sphere of the moon. For it is so high that Noah's flood could not reach it, though it covered the rest of the earth." Should any sailors attempt to approach it, the "great noise of waters" would frighten them away lest they be dashed to pieces because the four rivers that flow down from that height have "so strong a current, with such a rush and such waves that no boat can sail against them." On the third voyage when Columbus believed he had found the Earthly Paradise, not only does he paraphrase these passages from Mandeville, but he, too, is content just to know its location; he would not dare to enter without the "special grace" from God.

The immensely popular stories of both Marco Polo and John Mandeville were known throughout Europe; however fanciful they turned out to be, they colored people's imaginations about the world. Columbus was hardly exempt. Mandeville's lively account confirmed the reasons Jerusalem had to be back in Christian hands while Polo's book told him where to find gold and shaped his thoughts about the geography of the world. Some scholars assume that it was Pierre d'Ailly's work, especially *Imago Mundi*, that furnished Columbus's notions of geography. But according to geographer George Nunn, "the *Imago Mundi* was of little importance in the formulation of Columbus's plans for his first voyage." He noted that in "the *Imago* text, the island of Cipango is not mentioned, Quinsay is not mentioned, neither is Zayton, neither is Mangi [south China]."[17] But these are the very places that would figure so heavily in Columbus's writings of his voyages. Far more likely for Columbus's conception of the world were Marco Polo's book, Ptolemy's geography, and passages from the Bible.

In the late fifteenth century most Europeans were illiterate, but Columbus could read and write, and scholars have long wondered where he learned. He did not attend the University of Pavia, as his son Ferdinand claimed, but instead probably received a rudimentary education at a grammar school on Pavia Street in Genoa for the sons of guild members. There he would have learned basic arithmetic and some Latin, at least enough to be able to read and understand commercial contracts.[18] When the Colombo family moved to Savona, not far from Genoa, on the Riviera di Poniente, Domenico bought a house that belonged to the nobleman Corrado de Cuneo; Corrado's son, Michele, became a close friend of Columbus's, and it is possible that Columbus joined his friend for valuable lessons with his tutor (though no Columbus scholar has considered that possibility).[19] Whether or not Columbus learned to read and write more proficiently with de Cuneo, the two became lifelong friends. De Cuneo would accompany Columbus on his second voyage (1493–1496) and write his own remarkable account of their travels and adventures.

Perhaps they also learned to sail together. The Gulf of Genoa was an excellent place for the young Columbus to learn the mariner's craft,[20] for its sea can become extremely rough, especially when the south wind hits against the mountains and is pushed back toward the sea. This weather pattern creates such huge waves that the Genoese were compelled to build a substantial breakwater to prevent them from inundating the city. While there are hardly any surviving documents about Columbus's early sailing experiences, in his later years, he confessed: "From a very young age I began to follow the sea and have continued to do so to this day. This art of navigation incites those who pursue it to inquire into the *secrets of the world*."[21]

Columbus said that he began his maritime career when he was about fourteen, the age at which boys, in that time, were generally apprenticed to learn a trade. In Savona, Domenico had opened a tavern and began to engage in the import and export of wine in addition to his wool business. His connections with local merchants might have opened a way to his son's apprenticeship; no doubt he hoped that Christopher would be able to help him with his business through his travels to distant lands. Evidently Columbus did act as a merchant for his father's business,[22] but his interest turned more to the business of sailing. There is no evidence that Columbus had any experience on a galley—an oared vessel; more likely he began his apprenticeship on a caravel, a merchant ship rigged with both square and lateen sails. He must have performed well because local merchants signed him on for a number of short voyages in the Ligurian and Tyrrhenian Seas.

The work of an apprentice sailor was surely among the most difficult jobs of the day. According to Pablo E. Pérez-Allaína, young sailors were responsible for the following arduous tasks:

> Climbing to the yards to furl the sails in the middle of a storm or leaping from the gunwale to a ship's boat in the middle of the ocean were tasks specific to the agile and flexible bodies of the apprentices. It was they who served as lookouts on the mast tops or who pulled the oars of the ship's boats and launches, but they were also required to do the back-breaking work of loading and unloading tons of merchandise as well as firewood, water, and ballast.[23]

During approximately six years of such grueling labor, Columbus learned the craft of sailing well—not only how to set and furl the sails, but how to read the weather, the meaning of the shape of the clouds, the strength of the currents, and the direction of the winds. Since voyages in the Ligurian and Mediterranean Seas were rarely out of sight of land, navigation was generally done with no more than a compass and a lead line used to ascertain the depth of the water as a ship neared a port. Beyond sightings taken from the Pole Star (North Star), celestial navigation was unnecessary.

Because the Mediterranean was so well charted, there was little danger from invisible shoals or hidden rocks. Instead, danger most often would appear in the form of an attack by those considered enemies of one's state; for Columbus, it would have meant Pisan or especially Venetian merchants and sailors who could turn pirate depending on the circumstances, attack a Genoese ship, and consider its contents as the spoils of war. They sought mostly foodstuffs such as grain, legumes, cheese, oil, salted fish and meat, and wine, which they would sell in the markets to feed the growing populations in cities.[24] To protect against such attacks, galleys or ships were often sent in convoys.

By 1472, at the age of twenty-one, Columbus was demonstrating the high level of navigational skill that would serve him so well in crossing the Atlantic. One assignment in particular clearly demonstrates that he had learned the art of navigation well enough to use it to manipulate his fellow sailors. In that year, he was commissioned by King René of Anjou (who had continued to oversee the government of Savona) to capture a galleass—a very large three-masted galley that included rowers as well as sails—off the coast of Tunis. En route, Columbus learned that in addition to the galleass, there were two ships and a carrack,

> which frightened my people, and they resolved to go no further but to return to Marseilles to pick up another ship and more men. I, seeing that I could do nothing against their wills without some ruse, agreed to their demand, and, changing the point of the compass, made sail at nightfall; and at sunrise the next day we found ourselves off Cape Carthage, while all aboard were certain we were bound for Marseilles.[25]

Sometime in 1474 or 1475, a branch of the Spinola firm in Savona sent Columbus on a voyage from Savona to the island of Chios (allegedly Homer's home), which had been under Genoese control since the fourteenth century. His assignment was to obtain the aromatic resinous gum called mastic for trading in Europe. This valuable substance was used in varnishes, medicines, perfumes, and breads and puddings and was found only on Chios. At this time, stories about the Muslim conquest of Constantinople were still circulating on Chios, as some of the Genoese living on the island had been part of the effort to aid the people of Constantinople during the siege. Since all the trade on the island was controlled by the Giustiniani family, Columbus would most certainly have heard about Giovanni Giustiniani, who had been put in charge of defense during the siege of Constantinople and had been such a brave fighter. The people on Chios may not have told him the shameful part of the story—

that Giustiniani had deserted when he was wounded and returned to Chios where he died shortly afterwards.

Soon after Columbus returned from the successful voyage to Chios in 1476, the Spinola and di Negro companies sent him out again, this time to England with a convoy of five ships to trade the mastic he had obtained on Chios. This trip would be his first foray beyond the Mediterranean, past the Pillars of Hercules that guarded the Strait of Gibraltar, and would give him his first sight of the seemingly limitless ocean. It would also involve his first recorded taste of its perils. At the southernmost tip of Portugal, the convoy ran into trouble. On August 13, 1476, they were attacked by French privateers, and according to Columbus's account, the two ships

> came to blows, fighting with great fury and approaching each other until the ships grappled and the men crossed from boat to boat, killing and wounding each other without mercy . . . on both sides there was much confusion and fear of the flames, neither side could check the fire; it spread so swiftly that soon there was no remedy for those aboard save to leap in the water and die in this manner rather than suffer the torture of the fire.[26]

Though two of the Genoese ships escaped, three of them sank and many of the crewmen drowned; of the attackers four or five ships went down and hundreds of men died. Although Columbus's ship sank, he reportedly swam to shore near Lagos, a port on the Portuguese coast, hanging on to an oar.

Lagos was an auspicious place for Columbus to land; it was where, almost half a century earlier, Portuguese sailors under the direction of Prince Henry the Navigator had set sail for Africa. These explorations were financed in part by Prince Henry, who managed the funds for the Order of Christ, of which he was a member. He, too, was eager to see Jerusalem in Christian hands and, according to a contemporary, was motivated by his "zeal for God, by the desire for alliance with the Eastern Christians, by an eagerness to know how far the power of the 'infidel' existed, by the wish to convert people to Christianity, and by the desire to fight the Moors."[27] Columbus surely knew about the prince's scientific endeavors, and about his desire for the conquest of Jerusalem. But when he landed at Lagos, he could not possibly have known how the legacy of Prince Henry would become entwined with his personal life.

At that moment all he could think about was the fate of the sailors and the two ships that escaped. From Lagos, Columbus made his way to Lisbon, where he knew there was a substantial community of Genoese. Figuring that the remaining ships had stopped there in order to contact the shipping company about whether to proceed to England, he hoped to make contact with them again.

Indeed, it wasn't long before the Spinolas learned that a few of their ships had survived the privateers' attack, and they ordered the rest of convoy to proceed to England. Columbus joined them again. When he arrived in London, he found the city to be cold and drab, but in seafaring Bristol he felt at home. From there, he accompanied some Bristol sailors for a voyage to the far north:

> In the month of February 1477, I sailed one hundred leagues beyond the island of Tile [Ultimate Thule, as Iceland was known] . . . and to this island which is as big as England, the English come with their wares, especially from Bristol. When I was there, the sea was not frozen and the tides were so great that in some places they rose twenty-six fathoms, and fell as much.[28]

Scholars have long concluded that Columbus was exaggerating about the height of the tide. They did not take into account that Columbus was calculating in terms of a Genoese *braccio* of 22.9 inches, not today's fathom of six feet, which means that the tides rose about forty-nine feet high, not 156. In Bristol, they often reach thirty-six feet and in Avon, forty-seven feet, so it does not seem unlikely they reached forty-nine feet or thereabouts in Iceland. In addition, the actual time of the trip might have been later vis-à-vis current dates since Europeans at the time were using the Julian, not the Gregorian, calendar.

This trip provided an important educational experience for Columbus. First, he learned the feel of the strong east-flowing currents of the Atlantic, and this discovery inspired his idea that, were he to venture across the ocean to the West, those currents would be able to carry him back. On the same trip, he also happened upon a sight that he took as another indication that Asia was closer to Europe than commonly presumed. On the way back from the north, the sailors stopped in Galway, Ireland, and locals brought his attention to two frozen bodies that had washed ashore. Recalling what he'd heard about the physiognomy of Asians, Columbus was so struck by their appearance that he wrote in the margin of a page of his copy of Pope Pius II's *Historia rerum ubique gestarum*:

> Men of Cathay have come from the west. [Of this] we have seen many signs. And especially in Galway in Ireland, a man and a woman, of extraordinary appearance, have come to land on two tree trunks.[29]

Apparently they were dead. Nevertheless, if they had floated from Asia to Ireland, he concluded not only that Marco Polo's estimate of the vast extent of the Asian continent was correct, but also that the ocean in between could not be very wide and, therefore, could be crossed.

When he returned to Lisbon, Columbus began to settle into the Genoese community there. He adopted the custom of the Portuguese elite who spoke Castilian Spanish rather than Portuguese. He also learned to read and write in Castilian, and though his command was never perfect, it is the language of most of his extant writings except for a number of documents in Latin and two brief notes in Italian.[30] Accordingly, he also used the Spanish form of his name, Cristóbal Colón, instead of the Italian, Cristoforo Colombo.

Columbus hardly had time to rest from his northern trip, when he was commissioned for another voyage, again by Paolo di Negro, this time to sail to Madeira to negotiate a load of sugar that was to be shipped to Genoa. Although he was not assigned to accompany the shipment to Genoa, he would be venturing to an island farther out in the ocean; and farther south, than he had ever been. Madeira had been discovered in the fourteenth century but colonized on order of Prince Henry only since 1418. By the time of Columbus's visit, Madeira had become a major exporter of sugar and its profits helped fund Portugal's voyages of discovery.

The visit, undertaken happily and eagerly, had some unexpected consequences for Columbus. As it turned out, di Negro had given Columbus only part of the payment for the sugar, expecting that the Madeira merchants would advance him credit for the rest. When they did not, Columbus was left with no choice but to send a partial load of sugar to Genoa. When it reached Genoa, the Centurione company that had placed the order became suspicious, thinking that perhaps Columbus had pocketed the money, and summoned "Christopher

Columbus, citizen of Genoa" to explain what had happened. Documents in the Genoese archives show that the twenty-seven-year-old Columbus appeared in court on August 25, 1479, explained the situation in full, and testified that he had stolen no money. He swore he had not been bribed to give that testimony, nor did he expect to receive any advantage from it. He received no punishment and was allowed to leave Genoa for Lisbon the day after his court appearance.[31] The reason for his precipitous departure was not recorded, and though it is possible he just wanted to quickly get away from an embarrassing situation, it is more likely that he was eager to get back to Portugal for happier personal matters.

Columbus married Doña Felipa Perestrello e Moniz sometime in 1479, and their son, Diego, was born in 1480.[32] When he was in Lisbon, he had attended mass at the Convent of All Saints, which also served as a boarding school for young women of the Portuguese aristocracy, and it was there, according to his son's memoir, that he met his future wife Felipa. Ferdinand describes their courtship in a brief and unsentimental passage:

> As he behaved very honorably and was a man of handsome presence and one who never turned from the path of honesty, a lady named Doña Felipa Moniz, of noble birth and superior of the Convent of the Saints, where the Admiral used to attend Mass, had such conversation and friendship with him that she became his wife.[33]

His son does not tell us how and where they had "conversation," but he conceded that his knowledge about "matters touching upon his [father's] early days is imperfect, for he died before I made so bold as to ask him about such things; or, to speak more truly, at the time such ideas were farthest from my boyish mind."[34]

The marriage was advantageous for Columbus. Felipa's father, Don Bartholomew Perestrello, was from a noble Italian family that had immigrated to Lisbon. He had served in the colonizing mission of Prince Henry to Porto Santo and Madeira, and for his service he was given the governorship of the island of Porto Santo ("blessed port"), named for having given refuge in a storm to sailors blown off course on a voyage along the coast of Africa. Don Bartholomew died there in 1457. Felipa's mother, Doña Isabel Moniz, belonged to a well-established Portuguese family that had also been honored by Prince Henry. For a brief period, the newlyweds stayed in Lisbon with Doña Isabel, who regaled Columbus with stories about her husband's voyages.

> Seeing that her stories of these voyages gave the Admiral much plea-sure, she gave him the writings and sea-charts left by her husband. These things excited the Admiral still more; and he informed himself of the other voyages and navigations that the Portuguese were then making to Mina and down the coast of Guinea, and greatly enjoyed speaking with the men who sailed in those regions.[35]

Columbus and his wife went to live on Porto Santo, where her brother was the current governor. Porto Santo, once a green and lovely place, had become a barren wasteland after Don Bartholomew brought with him a pregnant rabbit. Imitating the biblical injunction "to increase and multiply," the descendants of that one rabbit denuded the island of anything green and growing. The island was not spiritually barren, however. Not far from the newlyweds' house was a Franciscan monastery where Columbus could take advantage of its library and discuss his plans with the monks, not only to ease his restive soul when he was not sailing, but also to delve more deeply into theology. Columbus wanted to know the "secrets of the world"—to explore its width and breadth, its rivers and mountains and dry land, and to discover for himself its immense variety. But he also wanted to know its meaning and for that, scientific exploration was not enough. Meaning was to be found in religion—for him that meant the Bible.

Columbus was familiar with the Franciscans from his days in Genoa, and their type of spirituality resonated with his own. His contemporaries often noted that he was a passionate man of ardent faith, not of the cool rationalism of the scholastics. Bartolomé de Las Casas, who knew Columbus and his family, wrote favorably of Columbus's spirituality:

> He observed the fasts of the church most faithfully, confessed and made communion often, read the canonical offices like a churchman or mem-ber of a religious order, hated blasphemy and profane swearing, and was most devoted to Our Lady and to the seraphic father St. Francis; seemed very grateful to God for benefits received from the divine hand . . . And

he was especially affected and devoted to the idea that God should deem him worthy of aiding somewhat in recovering the Holy Sepulchre.[36]

Although the recovery of the Holy Sepulchre was something desired by all medieval Christians and was an integral part of the apocalyptic scenario, there were differences of opinion about when or how this would or should occur. In Columbus's day, the official position of the papacy and the established church was that the climax of history had been reached with the Incarnation and that the cataclysm would come in God's good time. Although "apocalyptic was the mother of all Christian theology," [37] Franciscans did not believe in waiting passively for the end. They took a more active stance, believing that St. Francis, the founder of their order, had "been sent by God in the last age of the world to prepare humankind for the final apocalyptic events that would end history." [38]

Their apocalyptic fervor had been sparked by the writings of Joachim di Fiore, a thirteenth-century abbot from Calabria, whose *Expositio in Apocalypsim* expressed a theory of progress toward a more perfect future rather than a return to an idealized past—a theory at odds with the official position of the Church.[39] He believed that the world was moving through three historical, time-limited ages, each of which was subdivided into seven segments. The Age of the Father began with Creation and proceeded through the patriarchs such as Abraham, until the birth of Jesus. The Age of the Son, which was also the age of the Church, persisted up to Joachim's own time, circa 1200, after which he thought the world would enter the third age—the Age of the Spirit—which he envisioned as an age of simple piety and quiet contemplation as all peoples awaited the end. The third age, he believed would begin when the Turks had been defeated, Jerusalem had been liberated, and the Gentiles had been converted. Since none of this had occurred during Joachim's lifetime nor, indeed, by Columbus's time, there was urgency in their work.

Franciscans encouraged Christians to devote themselves to the salvation of their souls and were very active in missions of conversion so that nonbelievers would not be doomed to eternal hellfire. Spurred by their religious zeal, a few Franciscans, e.g., John Carpini (Giovanni de Plano Carpini) and William of Rubruck (Willem van Ruysbroeck), had ventured to the farthest reaches of Asia in the thirteenth century, even before Marco Polo, hoping to meet up with

Prester John and the Grand Khan, whom they imagined would help them in the mission of conversion.

As a faithful Christian, Columbus certainly knew the trajectory of history according to the Christian story, and its forecast of an apocalyptic end. At the monastery on Porto Santo, the urgency of the Franciscans' mission impressed him. If he had not yet read or heard about William of Rubruck's *Journey* to the Grand Khan, the Franciscans at the monastery might have informed him of Rubruck's plan to convert the Grand Khan in order to make him an ally so that he would march toward Jerusalem from the east as Europeans would come from the west to wrest the Holy City from the Muslims. Even more pertinent for Columbus's emerging plan might have been the story of Argun, the son of Kublai Khan, who had a chapel built at his court. Argun had his son baptized and named after the Franciscan pope, Nicholas IV (1288–1292), and he promised "to receive baptism in Jerusalem when it had been won by the allied forces of the Mongols and the West" if the pope would keep his "word and send troops at the appointed time."[40] Although Pope Nicholas began to call for a crusade and even assembled a fleet of ships, nothing came of it.

While many fifteenth-century Christians believed that the end of the world was imminent, the conditions that had to be fulfilled before the end had not yet been accomplished. The Turks had not been defeated, the nonbelievers had not been converted, and Jerusalem was still under Muslim control. There was much to do before Christ could come again, and people felt that time was running out.

Most medieval Christians believed that the "secrets of the world"[41] would be revealed before the end, and it had long been common belief that the world would end after seven millennia had passed. For someone with an inquiring mind, like Columbus, who wanted to know the "secrets of the world," the urgent question was how many years were left before the end. On Porto Santo he had the time and the aid of the monks to figure this out, and like others before and after him, he sought the answer to that question in the Bible.

At the time, Bible reading was highly unusual for laypeople, not only because the text was written in Latin but also because the word of God was supposed to be transmitted primarily through the clergy. Yet Columbus read the Latin Bible with passion, scouring it for clues to God's will.

Columbus began to make calculations for the end of the world by following the well-known practice of using biblical genealogies to reckon the number of years that had already passed, which when subtracted from seven thousand, would yield the number of years left. In 1481 he entered his calculations onto a blank page at the back of his copy of Pope Pius II's *Historia rerum ubique gestarum*, writing "Adam lived 130 years, and then fathered Seth. Seth lived 105 years, and then fathered Enos . . . Thus, from the creation of the world to the flood were 1656 years." From there he went on to calculate the years of the patriarchs, the years of the captivity in Egypt, the years before the completion of the Temple to the Babylonian captivity, and from that period to the building of the second Temple. "And from the destruction of the second Temple, according to the Jews, until the present, this being the year of the birth of our Lord 1481 . . . and from the beginning of the world until this year 1481, there are 5241 years."[42]

If one subtracted 5,241 from 7,000, there were 1,759 years left—plenty of time for fifteenth-century Christians to complete the necessary tasks before the end-time. Twenty years later, however, Columbus revisited and revised his calculations and drastically reduced the number of years left to 155. If his earlier vision had been focused primarily on wresting Jerusalem from the Muslims, he was now beginning to see that as an integral part of the world-historical drama that would culminate in the end of the world. He would put his navigational skills in the service of his faith and play a pivotal role in the unfolding Christian drama.

While it is not known exactly when Columbus's audacious plan to cross the ocean was fully developed, on Porto Santo he had most of the pieces. He knew that another crusade would be necessary if Jerusalem was to be taken from the Muslims. He knew that there was enough gold in the East to finance such a crusade. He also knew that if the Grand Khan and his people could be converted, as seemed likely, he could count on their support.[43]

Because he knew that Marco Polo's travels to the land of the Grand Khan had taken more than three years, Columbus was convinced that the Asian landmass was so vast that the ocean between Europe and Asia was quite narrow. Of course he had no idea of the huge continent that lay between them. Given his view, the ocean could, theoretically at least, be crossed, especially since there were thought to be a number of islands along the way that could be used as stepping-stones.

Furthermore, he had felt the east-flowing winds and currents when he had traveled to the north—the currents and winds that would bring him back to Europe if he should ever be able to cross the ocean. The only piece missing was whether there were west-flowing currents and winds that would take him across it. His intuition told him that he would find them if he went south—farther south than Porto Santo or Madeira. If he was to have a part in the grand Christian drama, he had no time to lose; he was already thirty at a time when life expectancy, especially for a seaman, was low. If his name was to be known throughout the world, as a youthful dream had foretold, he had to move quickly.

CHAPTER THREE

THE PLAN BEGINS TO TAKE SHAPE

Columbus soon had the opportunity to sail south with the Portuguese, farther south than he had ever been. This voyage, in late 1481 or early 1482, was headed to São Jorge da Mina (St. George of the Mine), in what is now Ghana, to the fort the Portuguese had recently built in order to trade their cotton and copper pots for native gold.[1] For centuries, sailors dreaded voyaging south. They thought that if they rounded the huge bulge on the western coast of Africa, called Cape Bojadar, and went "down" the coast of Guinea (Africa), they would not be able to get back "up." None of them believed they would fall off the edge of the world, but the return voyage was very difficult due to the northerly currents and winds along Africa's coast. Eventually they would learn that once they rounded Cape Bojadar, they should first sail farther south to pick up the equatorial current, then head out to sea, go past the Cape Verde Islands, and with the current sail "up" to the Azores before turning east for Lisbon.[2]

In addition to fears of being unable to return from the south, sailors feared the Torrid Zone, thought to be a very hot zone spanning the equator that, according to ancient Greek authorities and Christians after them, no one could pass through without being burned up. Acquainted only with North Africa, Europeans had assumed that the rest of the continent was nothing but sand, seared by the heat of the equatorial sun, and, thus, that the rest of the continent could not be inhabited, not even by the descendants of Noah's son Ham. Such ideas had long precluded further exploration by Europeans down the coast of Africa.

In the early fifteenth century, things began to change. Prince Henry had instituted the study of navigation in Sagres, Portugal, and he is credited, as mentioned, with introducing the caravel. This small light ship could glide over large swells, whereas larger ships, designed primarily for cargo, had to cut through swells or risk being caught between them, which put considerable stress on wooden ships. His introduction of the lateen (a kind of triangular sail) instead of square sails allowed a caravel to sail closer to the wind, making it easier to maneuver along coasts.

With these innovations and the encouragement of Prince Henry, a few intrepid sailors had begun to sail farther south exploring the coast of Africa. In 1433, Gil Eanes had rounded Cape Bojador and returned, though he reported that the desert reached the coast and that there were no rivers where a ship could put in, nor any useful harbors. But in 1445, Dinís Dias reached the Senegal River, where he was astonished to find tropical greenery in the Torrid Zone. Proving the ancients wrong became a great incentive to continue exploration of the West African coast.

At Prince Henry's persuasion, Pope Nicholas V issued a papal bull, *Romanus Pontifex*, in 1455, giving Portugal dominion over all the lands or islands they were discovering by sea along the African coast and the right to enslave any Saracens (Muslims) and pagans they encountered. Henceforth, any exploration down the coast of Africa could only be done under the Portuguese. Alviso Cadamosto, a Venetian in the service of Portugal, was the first European to see the Cape Verde Islands (1456), and sometime in the 1470s Portuguese sailors reached São Jorge da Mina and reported that they had seen natives wearing gold ornaments. To ensure control of the African trade, the Portuguese concluded a treaty with Castile. The Treaty of Alcáçovas, signed by the two parties in 1479, gave the Portuguese control of the coast of Guinea, the Madeiras, and the Cape Verde Islands, while Castile kept the Canary Islands. This treaty also resolved the conflict concerning who would become queen of Castile: Isabella, married to King Ferdinand of Aragón, or Juana, wife of King Alfonso V of Portugal. Rumors had swirled that Juana was not her father's daughter but, instead, the daughter of Beltran de la Cueva; the suspicion that she might not have royal blood led eventually to the crowning of Isabella, whose legitimacy was unquestioned.[3] If Juana had become queen, Spain might not have become Spain. The Treaty of Alcáçovas and its confirmation in 1481 by Pope Sixtus IV's papal bull, *Aeterni Regis*, meant that all exploration and trade down the African coast would be controlled by the Portuguese.

While rumors of these discoveries surely circulated among sailors, they were closely guarded state secrets; Cadamosto's discoveries, for example, were not published until 1507, a year after Columbus's death. There was a very good reason for nations to keep their explorations a secret. The conquest of Constantinople by the Ottomans had cut off western access to ports in the Black Sea and eastern Mediterranean that had long brought luxury items from the East—the spices that enlivened European diets and the fabrics that enhanced their clothing. They did not want to depend on Muslim middlemen charging exorbitant prices; they had to seek an alternative. At the time, the only other way to the East they could imagine was to go around the horn of Africa into the Indian Ocean, and the right to find that route had been given to the Portuguese.

On his voyage to São Jorge da Mina, Columbus became aware of the westerly currents and winds as they passed the Canary Islands and made a mental note of them; *that* would be the place to start a westward crossing. This voyage south was important to Columbus for another reason, too. Mineralogical theories of the time, dating back to Aristotle, maintained that all metal began as one, and then, depending on location and climate, the heat of the sun would cause it to "mature" into different forms—that is, to reach different levels of perfection and purity. The place most conducive to maturing metal into its purest form, namely gold, was none other than the equator, the Torrid Zone. Sure enough, there was gold at São Jorge da Mina; later this region would be called, appropriately, "The Gold Coast." There, Columbus saw that gold "grew" near the equator in Africa, and he gained some practical information about how the precious metal was collected. He witnessed natives panning for gold in the rivers and saw the nuggets they had extracted from the congealed "rivers," the veins of gold in the mines.

Columbus, like Dias, was astonished to see the lush greenery in the Torrid Zone and to discover that the region was inhabited. Refuting the accepted wisdom with his own eyewitness report, he wrote a note in his copy of Pierre d'Ailly's *Imago Mundi*:

Torrid Zone. It is not uninhabitable, since today through it the Portuguese navigate; but it is much populated, and below the equinoctial line there is the castle of La Mina of the most serene King of Portugal, which we saw.[4]

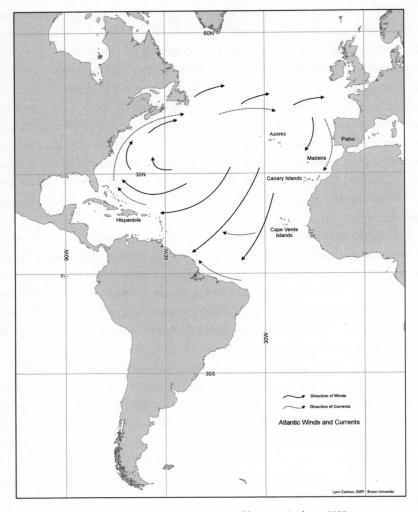

Map of winds and currents. *Prepared by Lynn Carlson, GISP.*

Columbus had amassed considerable information about geography, although he was wrong about São Jorge da Mina: it is not below or even on the equator. But far more important for his grand plan was the newfound knowledge of the winds and the westward-flowing currents. On the return voyage from São Jorge da Mina, when the ship stopped at the Azores, Columbus heard from sailors about logs, seemingly worked by humans, that occasionally appeared on their shores and about islands they had seen while at sea. Columbus probably thought that these were some of the thousands of islands Marco Polo said lay off the Asian coast. With the new information about winds and currents that Columbus absorbed on this trip, combined with his belief about the width of the ocean, he concluded that the ocean could be crossed, and that on the far side of it, in the same climatic zone as São Jorge da Mina, there would be gold.

Columbus did not want to go around Africa; his passion, almost an obsession, was to seek the East by way of the West—*buscar el Levante por el Poniente.* Back in Lisbon, he heard about the 1475 correspondence between King Alfonso V of Portugal and Paolo dal Pozzo Toscanelli, a renowned mathematician in Florence who believed that a voyage west across the Ocean Sea was possible.[5] Somehow Columbus managed to see Toscanelli's letter, for he copied it onto blank pages at the back of his copy of Pius II's *Historia rerum.*

Columbus must have been thrilled to read Toscanelli's claim that the region of the Grand Khan "has an area of approximately one third of the entire globe"[6] and that therefore the ocean was not as wide and impassable as most people thought. Toscanelli described the merchant city of Zaiton, where many ships unloaded pepper and spices, and Quinsay in the province of Mangi near Cathay, where the Grand Khan spent most of the year, and from Cathay he said that Cipango was about 250 leagues away.

> This land is most rich in gold, pearls, and precious stones, and the temples and royal palaces are covered with solid gold. But because the way is not known, all these things are hidden and covered, though one can travel thither with all security.[7]

Toscanelli had encouraged Alfonso to undertake a westward voyage by writing that it would be

> shorter than the one which you are pursuing by way of Guinea . . . Do not marvel at my calling "west" the regions where the spices grow, although they are commonly called "east;" because whoever sails westward will always find those lands in the west, while one who goes overland to the east will always find the same lands in the east.[8]

With his letter, Toscanelli had sent along a chart on which he had plotted the distance west from Lisbon to Asia and included a number of islands—known and imagined—along the way. Perhaps Alfonso had been interested in a voyage west or perhaps he feared that another country would learn of Toscanelli's idea and beat him to the East. Despite this information, Alfonso's good luck with his ventures down the African coast predisposed him to continue that safer, more conservative practice, assuming that his sailors would eventually round the Cape of Good Hope and enter the Indian Ocean.

Columbus was elated to have his own intuitions confirmed by a famous scholar. Although six years had passed since the original correspondence, he wrote immediately to Toscanelli and included a small sphere on which he had drawn his own plans for the voyage. Toscanelli replied, commending Columbus for the courage to attempt a voyage across the Western Ocean, writing

> it will be a voyage to powerful kingdoms and noble cities and rich provinces, abounding in all sorts of things that we greatly need, including all manner of spices and jewels in great abundance. It will also be a voyage to kings and princes who are very eager to have friendly dealings and speech with the Christians of our countries, because many of them are Christians.[9]

Unfortunately, Toscanelli died in 1482. Neither he nor Alfonso lived long enough to see this dream realized. Yet the interest both men expressed in such a voyage lay the groundwork for Columbus to seek support.

Assuming that Alfonso's son, João II, the new king, must have known of his father's earlier interest in a westward voyage, Columbus went confidently to his meeting with João sometime in late 1484. Columbus probably concealed the ultimate purpose of his mission—the liberation of Jerusalem—and played up the riches and spices of the East, knowing that João's interest was more worldly and materialistic. Regardless, Columbus's optimism was quickly deflated. João was cautious. Given the success of his own sailors venturing down the African coast, João was more interested in rounding the Cape of Good Hope to find an eastern route to the spice trade than he was in sponsoring a westward voyage across an uncharted ocean. It didn't help that the plan was proposed by a foreigner; nevertheless, João told Columbus he would think about it.

While he was "thinking," João allegedly "decided to send a caravel secretly to attempt what the Admiral had offered to do,"[10] and thus reap the glory and the wealth for himself. Apparently, João authorized a voyage to find Antilia in

1487, but there are no records about it. In any case, that attempt came to nothing. Whether Columbus ever heard of João's secret venture or whether it was even undertaken is unknown.

King João's negative response was not the only thing that weighed heavily on Columbus's soul around that time. He was in debt, maybe something left over from the sugar deal that had gone sour. Much more devastating was the death of his wife, Felipa, probably sometime in 1484 or 1485, which left Columbus with the care of their four-year-old son. We do not know what he felt about her death—sorrow, guilt, remorse, anger, relief—but it presented another hurdle he would have to surmount. He was thirty-three, the age at which Christ was betrayed and crucified, and for Columbus the coincidence would not have gone unnoticed. His big plans were in jeopardy; he needed to do something, and quickly.

The thought of repeating the process of petitioning sovereigns elsewhere would have been daunting to anyone else, but Columbus had a vision and he would not be discouraged. Figuring that he had to try several strategies in order to save precious time, he asked his brother Bartholomew, who had joined him in Lisbon, if he would be willing to go to England to seek support from King Henry VII.[11] Columbus himself would go to nearby Castile to seek support from Queen Isabella. Then, feeling the weight of the world on his shoulders like his namesake, Christopher carried his son, little Diego, and crossed the water to Castile.

Sometime in the summer of 1485, Columbus arrived at the port of Palos de la Frontera, from which seven years later his famous first voyage would depart. Palos is located up the Rio Tinto on the west coast of Spain in the area known as Andalusia, which was part of Castile. He had sailed into a country embroiled in religious ferment. With the marriage of Isabella of Castile and Ferdinand of Aragón in 1470, the two kingdoms were joined, if not exactly united, and together they made up most of the landmass of what is now Spain. Thus, the way was set for uniting all the land of Spain under the millennial prospect of *unum ovile et unus pastor*, that is, under Catholic Christianity—the one and only true faith.

With renewed vigor the Spanish sovereigns authorized a campaign to convert both Jews and Muslims. Many Jews did convert; for those who refused, the sovereigns revived a rarely enforced 1412 law that stipulated Jews henceforth would have to wear a red patch on their clothing and be confined to separate residential areas. Those who refused to convert would no longer be allowed to practice professions such as "doctors, chemists, drug-sellers, blacksmiths, carpenters, tailors, butchers, cobblers, traders, tax collectors,"[12] while those who did convert were able to rise in professions such as merchants, magistrates, members of religious orders, and royal advisors. Nevertheless, many Christians were suspicious of these *conversos* or *marranos* (a highly derogatory term because it referred to pigs), and believed they were secretly keeping the practices of their faith.

By 1475, the situation had become dire, especially in Seville. In order to ferret out such supposedly backsliding *conversos*, Isabella requested permission from Pope Sixtus IV to appoint inquisitors to investigate allegations of recidivism. Although permission was granted in 1478, Isabella waited a couple of years in order to give *conversos* time to change their ways. For this purpose, she asked Cardinal Mendoza, archbishop of Seville, to "produce a catechism to be sent to every church in the diocese. In a pastoral letter, he requested priests to devote themselves utterly to the instruction of their congregations, in particular that of New Christians,"[13] and sent her confessor, Hernando de Talavera, himself a *converso*, to that city to preach. Practices indicative of relapsed *conversos*, or heretics, were read aloud in church. Such practices included the refusal to eat pork or to work on Saturday, and also practices of omission, such as not keeping Christian holidays. The *Edicts of Grace* allowed thirty days during which a *converso* could come forth and confess or risk being reported.

Several people, including Ferdinand, pushed for stricter measures, and in 1480 a few inquisitors were appointed to Seville. This inquisition was to be solely under the control of the Spanish sovereigns rather than the pope, unlike earlier ones. In 1483 the Spanish Inquisition began in earnest; Isabella appointed Tomás de Torquemada (1420–1498), a Dominican friar, as the Grand Inquisitor. He and his council moved from town to town to try those accused of heresy. An accused individual was presumed guilty and the object of a trial was to elicit a confession. Trials were always held in secret; the accused was not told what the specific accusations were, nor who had made them. Those awaiting trial were held in secret prisons and some of their personal property was confiscated to pay for their maintenance and for the trial. During the trial, the accused would be asked all kinds of questions—about family background, education, and travel and also whether he (or she) knew the words of the prayers. A person who confessed would be reconciled to the church, though not without penance; however, if a defendant's answers to inquisitors' questions were unsatisfactory that person would be tortured. There was a series of increasingly harsh tortures, the first of which was what is now known as "waterboarding." In this procedure,

> The prisoner was tied to a sloped ladder, his head lower than his heels; his mouth was propped open and a cloth was placed over it. On to this water was poured, which the prisoner was forced to swallow. The water jug contained one litre of liquid. During a single session as many as eight jugfuls could be administered to the prisoner.[14]

After the verdict was decreed, the convicted person would remain in prison until a public ceremony, known as an auto-da-fé, was held. These generally took place in the major town square where the populace of the town gathered to watch the procession of the condemned, to hear the charges and the verdict, and see whether the accused admitted his guilt and repented. There were different punishments depending on the severity of the heresy. Some were given "life" sentences (which rarely lasted more than three or four years), others were garrotted before being burnt at the stake, presumably a more benign death than awaited those who had not confessed and were unrepentant. Those were burned alive.[15] However, since the Church does not kill, the Inquisitors were compelled to hand the condemned over to the secular authorities for execution. No matter the numbers, these horrific events could not help but terrify the people and enforce conformity of practice, at least publicly.

At the same time that the Inquisition was being conducted, two other events occupied the Spanish sovereigns. In May of 1480, Mehmet II, the conqueror of Constantinople, died just as he was preparing to invade Italy. His successor, Bayezid II, went forward with the plan and by August had taken Otranto in the kingdom of Naples. From there, he intended to attack Sicily, which was nominally, at least, under the sovereignty of Isabella and Ferdinand. The Ottomans, or Turks as they were more often referred to in Europe, were striking much too close. Isabella immediately mounted a fleet of seventy ships to sail to Naples, to help retake the city and prevent the Turks from invading Sicily. However, many sailors had succumbed to the plague, and when those remaining reached

Naples they learned that the local rulers had already retaken the city. Nevertheless, this brush with the Turks renewed Isabella's intention to rid her kingdom of Muslims who refused to convert.

Isabella was committed to the Reconquista—the effort to regain all the territories in the Iberian peninsula that Muslims had taken in the eighth century, presumably from her ancestors. The purpose of the Reconquista at home was to unify the nation religiously, but it was also imagined as the first stage of the millennial mission that should lead inevitably to the reconquest of Constantinople and Jerusalem. Over the course of centuries, the Spaniards had regained much of their former territory and many of the Muslim enclaves that existed had become vassals of the Crown. But some held out.

In addition to establishing the Inquisition in 1480, Isabella announced her decision to go to war against the last bastion of the Moors in her realm: the kingdom of Granada, which incorporated the provinces of Málaga and Almería—and included more than fourteen cities and many villages. Isabella obtained a Bull of Crusade from the pope in 1482, elevating her war theologically. Her subjects understood that this war was not simply some local skirmish for power but was part of a much larger religious battle intended to bring Castile, and eventually the world, under the one true faith. Such a heady concept helped rally the people to her cause despite the heavy tax burden they sustained to support it.

Just before Columbus arrived in Castile, plague had broken out in Seville and carried off a third of its population. Because Jews had often been blamed for causing or spreading the plague, many chose that time to leave. With so few people left in the city, it could hardly function. The plague knew no religious or class boundaries; it had even hit the royal family. A century earlier it had killed King Alfonso XI, a distant relative of both Isabella and Ferdinand, and now Isabella must have been haunted by the awareness that she owed her succession, in part, to the death of her younger brother, who is thought to have died of the plague in 1468.[16]

Isabella was fully occupied; it seemed hardly the moment for Columbus to attempt an audience. His personal situation was precarious—he had very little money and a young son to care for. He may have thought to leave Diego with his sister-in-law, Violante Moniz, who lived with her husband, Miguel Moliart (also spelled Molyart) in the village of Moguer, while he pursued his plan. Although Moguer is not so distant from Palos, it would have been much too far for a little boy to walk on their first day in the new land, and Columbus might not have alerted his wife's relatives about his plans.

While sailing into Palos, Columbus would have glimpsed the tower of a monastery perched high on a bluff overlooking the confluence of the Rio Tinto and the Rio Odiel and thought of stopping there. Perhaps he had already been told about it. Regardless, Columbus and Diego walked the seven kilometers from the port of Palos up the bluff to the monastery where, tired and thirsty, Columbus "asked the porter to give him bread and a drink of water for that little boy who was his son." [17]

Arrival of Christopher Columbus and his son Diego at La Rábida
by Antonio Cabral-Bejarano. *Courtesy of La Rábida Monastery.*

They were taken in as guests. Columbus stayed on for many months while he considered his options; Diego remained for several years and was schooled by the monks.

Founded in 1261, La Rábida was and still is a Franciscan monastery. While the name suggests it might have been established by rabid monks, inflamed with their apocalyptic beliefs, the name was actually taken from an Arabic word that means "watchtower," which seems very appropriate, for the tower is the first thing visitors see if they approach the monastery from the long flower-lined dirt road that leads to it.

Today, the monks at La Rábida are very proud of their connection to Columbus and open the monastery to visitors on certain days. While it has undergone a number of renovations and additions since the fifteenth century, several rooms where Columbus spent time have been kept relatively unchanged. The refectory where he ate with the monks is bare but elegant; there are built-in benches along three sides, and the narrow tables, hewn of rough dark wood, are set with pottery ware and pitchers for wine or water. The only decorations are a simple iron candle holder suspended from the ceiling, colorful tiles along the rim of the benches, and a crucifix. When the monks entered the refectory, conversations would have become muted as they gazed at the inspirational inscriptions in Latin painted on the walls near the ceiling, and waited for one of the other monks to deliver a lesson from the pulpit at the far end.

Like the refectory, the conference room is also very simple. Its walls are thick and whitewashed, and the ceiling has rough-hewn beams of dark wood, polished with the patina of age. This room is especially prized by the monks, for they claim it is "where America was born," meaning that this is where Columbus's plan was most fully articulated and taken seriously. So alive is the memory of Columbus at the monastery that, sitting at the table in the middle of the wide room that looks out over the river below, it is easy to imagine the whispers of the conversations he had with Antonio de Marchena, head of the Franciscans in the Seville area, who was visiting La Rábida at the time.[18] Marchena was well educated; he had studied not only theology but also astrology and astronomy, at that time considered to be parts of the same science, and had an open mind when it came to geographical debates. Later, Columbus would write:

> In all this time every mariner, pilot, philosopher and every other man of learning deemed my enterprise to be false; never did I get help from anyone except Father Antonio de Marchena, barring that from God . . . Everyone regarded it as folly except Father Antonio de Marchena.[19]

Marchena was intrigued with Columbus and thought his plan was worthy of being heard. He made arrangements for Columbus to meet his friend, Enrique de Guzman, the duke of Medina Sidonia, one of the wealthiest men in Castile, who might be able to support the voyage. The duke was very interested, but at that point he was not on good terms with the sovereigns, whose permission for such an enterprise was advisable, if not necessary. De Guzman sent Columbus to Luis de la Cerda, the duke of Medina Celi, a wealthy man who could claim descent from King Alfonso X, and who owned a fleet of ships moored at Puerto Santa Maria, near Cádiz. He was prepared to outfit the fleet himself, but as he later reminisced in a letter to the archbishop of Toledo, he, too, thought he ought to inform the queen.

> Most Reverend Lord: I do not know if your Lordship is aware that for a long time I had in my house Cristobal Colombo, who came from Portugal and desired to go to the King of France in order that by his favour and aid he might undertake to go and search for the Indies: and I would have liked to try it and to send an expedition from the Port [of Santa Maria], as I was well prepared with three or four caravels, which was all he asked of me. But as I saw that this undertaking was worthy of the Queen, our Lady, I wrote to Her Highness about it from Rota and she replied telling me to send him to her.[20]

That was how Columbus, a commoner and a foreigner in Spain for less a year, gained the attention of Queen Isabella. Despite her preoccupation with the Inquisition and the war against Granada, Isabella summoned Columbus to court sometime in late 1485 or early in 1486. This was a more complicated gesture than it might seem; the court did not have a fixed residence but moved from place to place, residing sometimes in a palace and at other times in a monastery. At the time Columbus was summoned, the court was in Córdoba, about 250 kilometers from Puerto Santa Maria, where Columbus was staying with the count. Columbus couldn't just rush off to meet the queen; a court visit required money for the journey and, more important, money for the proper attire.

In such an aristocratic age, in which each person had a position within the social hierarchy, one's rank was displayed by one's comportment and manners, and even more conspicuously by one's clothes. Men's clothes were as elaborate as women's. Court life was spectacular in the sense that wealth, position, and power were visibly displayed; luxury symbolized power. The opulence of one's attire exhibited not only one's personal wealth or the wealth of the nation, but also functioned to reassure the aristocracy that all was well with their world. The clothing of the rich was made of costly materials such as cloth of gold, brocade, velvet, silk, and satin, much of it embellished with intricate embroidery, that did not clean easily even with the labor of a retinue of servants. In the royal household, clothes might be worn only once or twice, and then given to members of the household, including servants. Isabella admonished her young son, Prince Juan, for not giving away his clothes, saying that "princes should not be old-clothes men." After that, every year on June 30, his birthday, he had to distribute his used garments to his servants and others whom he wished to favor. The state treasurer recorded that the year the prince was fifteen, Isabella spent 805,790 *maravedis* on his clothes, sixty-seven times more than the annual salary of a sea captain.[21] Her own attire must have run in the millions.

For his audience with the queen, Columbus would have had to calibrate the appropriate attire for the occasion, and his choices would have reflected his understanding of his place in the elaborate social hierarchy. Fortunately, he had the advice of his patron, the count, who probably also assumed the expense. Each item had myriad variations of cloth and color: embroidered hose or plain, slashed sleeves or paned, flat hat or brimmed (if the latter, brim up or down), and for shoes—square toe, pointed toe, buskin, or boot; each choice subtly conveyed a social message. No doubt Columbus's outfit was modest but elegant; it likely consisted of hose and garters, a doublet made of velvet or fine wool, a linen jerkin and shirt, probably a velvet cap with the brims folded up and attached with points, a woolen cape, and soft leather shoes rather than boots. Although sailors were permitted to wear red caps, Columbus would not have dared to wear red to his meeting with Isabella, for that color was usually reserved for royalty, cardinals, and some of the high nobility.[22]

By the time Columbus finally arrived in Córdoba, in January 1486, the court had moved on to Madrid. After all his preparation, the delay must have been a huge disappointment to him. But despite his eagerness to present his plan to the sovereigns, Columbus decided against pursuing the court and chose to wait in Córdoba until they returned in the spring. It would not have been a bad place to wait. Like Istanbul, it is a veritable palimpsest of history. An old Roman bridge spans the Guadalquivir River; on the far side is a tower that used to guard the entrance to the city and, on the city side, a short walk up from the river takes one to the renowned Mezquita.

That great mosque, first built around 785 by Arabs and added to throughout the centuries, is a massive complex of buildings surrounded by a wall. Despite the Muslim ambience, the Mezquita was transformed into a cathedral in 1236 and was being used for Christian worship when Columbus arrived. On entering, he may have been startled by its design, so different from the churches he knew. The entrance, through the Patio de los Naranjos, a courtyard planted with orange trees, gives no hint of what is inside. The Mezquita has neither the huge, cavernous spaces of the great mosques in Istanbul, nor the soaring heights of European cathedrals. Instead, Columbus, like a visitor today, would have been confronted with a forest of columns, over eight hundred and fifty of them, connected at the top by arches, so that rather than being in a large space, one has a sense of being underground as, perhaps, in the cistern in Istanbul or deep in a mine where the earth is held up by pilings. The effect is overwhelming, disorienting, even disquieting.

Córdoba had long been a lively and intellectually stimulating city. Several important thinkers were born in that city, including Averroës (also known as Ibn Rushd), whom Columbus would quote in his argument for the voyage, and Moses Maimonides. In the twelfth century these two men—one Muslim, one Jewish—helped incorporate Aristotelian philosophy into their respective theologies. In the vibrant atmosphere of Córdoba, Columbus sought out contemporary thinkers with whom to discuss politics, geography, and theology, finding them in and around the Mezquita and the picturesque *Juderia* (Jewish quarter), with its tiny streets, secret gardens, and synagogue. In Córdoba, he may also have become acquainted with the work of the Roman playwright and philosopher Seneca, who was born in the city, and he may have bought his copy of *Medea* during this time; it is one of the nine books that survive from his library. Verses from that play became a kind of spiritual talisman for Columbus:

> *The time will come*
> *In a number of years, when Oceanus*
> *Will unfasten the bounds, and a huge*
> *Land will stretch out, and Typhis the pilot*
> *Will discover new worlds, so*
> *The remotest land will no longer be Thule.*

Because he had already been to Tile/Thule, Columbus may have begun to imagine himself as the one who would "unfasten the bounds" and, like Jason's pilot, discover new worlds. Later he would reword the verses and insert himself into the prophecy.

Columbus at the Spanish Court by Václav Brožík. *Courtesy of the Library of Congress.*

Columbus went to his first audience with Queen Isabella sometime in May 1486, when the court returned to Córdoba. The Alcázar de los Reyes Cristianos (Palace of the Christian Kings) is just a short walk from the Mezquita. There, behind high walls, Spanish royalty could walk in peace through beautiful gardens. At the end of a pool in one of the gardens, visitors today will see a huge statue of Columbus with Isabella and Ferdinand that commemorates their first meeting.

Today advertisements selling anything with the name Columbus portray him as a round-faced, pudgy man with black curly hair, clearly someone's very bad, stereotypical idea of an Italian. This portrait does not fit many Italians today and it does not at all capture the image of Columbus as described by those who knew him. Although no known portraits of Columbus were painted during his lifetime, contemporaries were fairly consistent in their descriptions.[23] Columbus was an attractive and articulate man of aristocratic bearing and courtly manners. Angelo Trevisan, a contemporary, said he was "a tall man and well built, ruddy, of great creative talent, and with a long face."[24] Bartolomé de Las Casas, who later became famous as a defender of the Indians and wrote an invaluable history of the Indies, knew Columbus and concurred with how Ferdinand, Columbus's second son, described his father:

> The Admiral was a well-built man of more than average stature, the face long, the cheeks somewhat high, his body neither fat nor lean. He had an aquiline nose and light-colored eyes; his complexion too was light and tending to bright red. In youth his hair was blonde, but when he reached the age of thirty, it all turned white. In eating and drinking, and in the

adornment of his person, he was very moderate and modest. He was affable in conversation with strangers and very pleasant to members of his household, though with a certain gravity. He was so strict in matters of religion that for fasting and saying prayers he might have been taken for a member of a religious order . . . And so fine was his hand that he might have earned his bread by that skill alone.[25]

Columbus was clearly a charismatic figure, and women, including the queen, seemed to be attracted to him. Isabella was a devout Catholic and determined to make her realm entirely Christian. She, like Columbus, was partial to the Franciscans. His desire to help in the liberation of Jerusalem would have received a sympathetic hearing if he mentioned it to her at that time. In the royal household she must have heard about her grandfather's pilgrimage to Jerusalem with his brother, her great-uncle, Prince Henry the Navigator, and about their desire for it to be under Christian control. At that meeting with Isabella, Columbus might have suggested how important it was to bring the saving grace of Christianity to the Grand Khan, because, as he later wrote in his diary, so many times the Grand Khan

and his predecessors had sent to Rome to ask for men learned in our Holy Faith in order that they might instruct him in it and how the Holy Father had never provided them; and thus so many peoples were lost, falling into idolatry and accepting false and harmful *sectas*.[26]

Converting the Grand Khan to Christianity would make it easier to convince him of the necessity of forming an eastern flank to converge on Jerusalem at the same time that the Spanish crusaders would come from the west. Conversion of the Grand Khan was hardly a new idea. It had been voiced early in the thirteenth century by the Franciscan missionaries who had traveled there and also by Marco Polo and John Mandeville. What Columbus added was the means to make the conquest of Jerusalem possible, namely gold.

Isabella was clearly favorably impressed by Columbus and agreed to think over his proposal. Since she was not interested in an overland expedition to the riches of Asia, and the papal bull as well as the Treaty of Alcáçovas prohibited her from exploring the sea route around Africa, she realized that the only way she might beat the Portuguese to the gold and spices of the East was across the Western Ocean. No doubt Columbus mentioned the theory of the learned mathematician Toscanelli. Soon after their meeting, she convened a commission, headed by Friar Hernando de Talavera, to study Columbus's proposal.

Columbus went to Salamanca sometime in 1486 to present his proposal to the commission in person. The commission's primary concern was the issue of the width of the Western Ocean. Columbus marshaled his arguments about this topic and, thus, the possibility of crossing the ocean to reach the East, with support from ancient pagan and Arab geographers, philosophers, biblical texts, and the assessment of the vast extent of Asia put forth by both Marco Polo and Toscanelli. The width of the ocean also involved an estimate of the circumference of the globe. Instead of using Eratosthenes' (ca. 276–196 B.C.) almost correct calculations of the circumference of the globe, Columbus used those of Alfragan, a ninth-century Arab mathematician, but he misunderstood the length of Alfragan's nautical "miles," effectively making the world at least 25 percent smaller than had Eratosthenes.[27] Columbus skated close to heresy when he cited the pagan philosopher Aristotle, who

> says this world is small, there is very little water, and one could easily go from Spain to the Indies. Averroes, as reported by Cardinal Pedro de Aliaco [Pierre d'Ailly], agrees, adding further authority to this theory and to that of Seneca who agrees with them also, saying that Aristotle was able to know many *of these* secrets of the world.[28]

In contrast to Aristotle, the commission relied on the wisdom of St. Augustine, who believed that the globe consisted mostly of water and that the dry land constituted but a small fraction. No doubt the commission was not pleased when Columbus countered their arguments by citing the noncanonical, apocryphal text of 2 Esdras 6:42:

> On the third day thou didst command the waters to be gathered together in the seventh part of the earth; six parts thou didst dry up and keep so that some of them might be planted and cultivated and be of service before thee.

In other words, Esdras was saying that six-sevenths of the world was dry and only one-seventh was watery, which implied that the ocean could not be very wide and therefore could be crossed.

While Columbus waited for the commission's decision, he was supported by a retainer of 12,000 *maravedis*, the normal annual salary of a ship's captain, for one year. After a time the stipends ceased, and he and his brother Bartholomew, who had not yet gone to England, made their living by selling books and maps. Some maps might have been drawn by Columbus himself, for he was considered a skilled draftsman.

Meanwhile, Columbus had made the acquaintance of Diego de Harana, whom he met at a shop owned by Luciano and Leonardo Esbarroya, both Genoese, that doubled as a meeting place of the local intellectuals. One day Diego invited Columbus back to his house, and there he met Beatriz Enríquez de Harana (sometimes spelled Arana). She was the daughter of Ana Nuñez de Harana and Pedro de Torquemada, a remote relation of the grand inquisitor. Both of her parents had died when she was quite young, and she went to live with her mother's first cousin Rodrigo Enríquez de Harana and his son Diego. Although the daughter of a peasant and the niece of a wine presser, she was educated and could read and write. These were extremely rare accomplishments among women of the day but qualities that appealed to Columbus. Always a courtly gentleman where women were concerned, his relationship with her might have been somewhat avuncular at the beginning given their difference in age. Beatriz was only twenty-three, while Columbus was thirty-five or thirty-six and on the verge of leaving for his great adventure. The introduction to book four of *Las Siete Partidas*, an influential thirteenth-century Spanish code of laws, noted in relation to marriage that "those who wish to be joined in the name of God should consider some practical matters: spouses should be of equal condition and age."[29] But as his wait for the commission's report lengthened into months, and the months into years, he spent more and more time with her.

At some point their relationship became intimate, for on August 15, 1488, she gave birth to Ferdinand, Columbus's second son. There is no record that Columbus and Beatriz were ever officially married. A difference in rank could have been the reason, as some scholars have suggested, but at the time Columbus actually had no rank, only ambitions of attaining it. After his return from the first voyage in 1493, when he was "showered with the highest honours and raised to the topmost dignity in Spain, becoming overnight one of the most illustrious figures at the Spanish court," he became "subject to restrictions, in matters of marriage and extra-marital associations, imposed on the nobility by extant laws."[30]

Nevertheless, relations between the sexes in that period were more flexible than they were to become, and having a child out of wedlock did not carry the stigma it has since acquired. Medieval canon law, in concurring with Roman law on many matters related to sex, held that if "marital affection existed between the parties, they were married . . . Ceremonies were a matter of decorum, but were not essential . . . consent alone created a marriage."[31] So perhaps Columbus and Beatriz considered themselves married.

Regardless of their legal status, Columbus was accepted into Beatriz's family and maintained good relations with them even when he was away. Her cousin Diego would accompany him on the first voyage and her elder brother would go on the third. So, for a time, Columbus was cushioned in the bosom of their family, delighted and distracted by the charms of Beatriz and the baby, and perhaps these familial pleasures mitigated his anxiety over the outcome of the report.

The year his son Ferdinand was born, Columbus received an invitation from King João asking him to return to Portugal to discuss again the plan for the westward voyage; since he was still waiting for the results of the commission's deliberations, Columbus accepted the invitation. He arrived in Lisbon sometime in December. Later, he wrote in the margins of his copy of Pierre d'Ailly's *Imago Mundi* of a major event he witnessed while he was at the Portuguese court:

> Note that in this year '88 in the month of December arrived in Lisbon *Bartholomaeus' Didacus* captain of three caravels which the most serene king of Portugal had sent to try out the land in Guinea. He reported. . . . that he had reached a promontory which he called *Cabo de Boa Esperança . . .* I was present in all of this.[32]

Bartolomeu Dias had sailed not only farther south than anyone else before him had done, he had rounded what he named the Cape of Good Hope and sailed north into the Indian Ocean. His fleet went only as far as the Great Fish River and carried out no explorations on land, for his men refused to continue, and Dias was forced to turn homeward. Nevertheless, theoretically, a sea route to the riches of the East had been found; King João was no longer interested in the westward voyage that Columbus had proposed, and Columbus went back to Spain to wait some more.

Isabella was still involved in her war against the Moors, although one city after another had fallen. The first to fall was Alhama, for which a melancholy lament *Ay mi alhama!* (Alas, my Alhama)[33] was quickly composed. Soon Ronda and Málaga fell. Columbus joined Isabella at Jaén in 1489, and after that city fell, they moved on to Baza, where Columbus was said to have fought courageously.

Columbus was present when two Franciscans from the Holy Sepulchre in Jerusalem arrived to inform Isabella and Ferdinand that the sultan of Egypt would persecute Christians in his realm and destroy the holy church if they did not stop their siege against Muslims. Isabella did not take the sultan's threat too seriously because she was aware that he had recently "requested the help of an Aragonese fleet against the Turks."[34] Instead, she sent them back with a conciliatory message, saying that she was merely trying to reclaim the land of her ancestors which Muslims were ruling unjustly. Not only that, she declared that they had always negotiated fairly with those they defeated and permitted them certain rights and privileges. She promised to send money to Jerusalem to help with the upkeep of the church and gave the visitors a veil she had made to cover the Holy Sepulchre. But she would not be deterred from her war; she had been successful so far, believed she was following God's will, and though the prize, Granada and its glorious Alhambra (not to be confused with the city of Alhama), still eluded her, she believed she would be victorious. Since she understood the Reconquista as part of the larger project, the reconquest of Jerusalem, Columbus may have chosen this occasion, if he had not done so earlier, to speak to her about the ultimate goal of his enterprise in order to spark her resolve.

The Talavera commission did not submit its report about Columbus's proposal until late in 1490, and, as Las Casas reported, it "judged his promises and offers were impossible and vain and worthy of rejection."[35] Talavera, arguing from ancient authorities such as St. Augustine, named at least six reasons it was unfeasible: (1) first and foremost, Talavera did not believe that so many centuries after Creation anyone would find unknown lands of any value, (2) only three of the five zones were habitable because the frozen lands at the poles could not be inhabited, (3) there are no Antipodes because the globe is covered mostly by water, but (4) if he should reach the Antipodes (the opposite side of the earth), he would never be able to get back, (5) for the Western Ocean was too vast to be crossed, and finally, (6) a voyage to Asia would take at least three years.[36] Talavera's report, when studied critically, seems shortsighted and riddled with contradictions: if the ocean was so vast and unnavigable, how could they calculate a three-year voyage to Asia? At the Antipodes, everything was thought to be upside down, but then the committee claimed the Antipodes didn't exist. Not only that, but the report misrepresented his mission: Columbus was not seeking unknown lands but a new route to Asia—"the unknown space in question was the route, not the destination."[37]

Columbus did his best to keep his anger under control, but he was furious. Still, as Las Casas commented, Columbus

> began to sustain a terrible, continued, painful and prolonged battle; a material one of weapons would not have been so sharp and horrendous as that which he had to endure from informing so many people of no understanding, although they presumed to know all about it, and replying patiently to many people who did not know him or had any respect for his person, [and] receiving insulting speeches which afflicted his soul.[38]

The committee's objections were not as strange as they seem, for their skepticism has roots deep in Christian theological/cosmological terrain. Augustine had believed that all peoples were created by God and descended from Adam and Eve. After the Flood, the three sons of Noah—Japheth, Shem, and Ham—were dispersed to the three continents and repopulated them. Finally, Augustine believed that most of the earth was covered by water on which the landmass of the earth floated like a relatively small lonely island. If the other side—the Antipodes—was water, it could not possibly be inhabited.

Despite the committee's negative judgment, the queen told Columbus to wait until her war against Granada was concluded. By this time Columbus had been waiting for more than six years and thinking about his project for more than a decade. Such perseverance is an indication both of Columbus's patience and his passion. But both were wearing thin; from the time he arrived in Castile to the time he embarked for the "Indies," he never put out to sea. For a sailor with such experience and grand plans, that must have been agony. Other men would have given up. But Columbus had a vision, and he was convinced he could make it a reality. By then he was a man of forty and already feeling the effects of age—primarily through a painful form of arthritis. Knowing his time for accomplishing his goal was limited, he was under a great deal of stress. He had had enough with waiting. He decided to go to try his luck with Charles VIII, the king of France.

Disappointed but determined, Columbus went back to La Rábida to retrieve his son Diego, by this time a boy of about eleven, whom he hoped to place with his sister-in-law in nearby Moguer while he prepared to go to France. At

La Rábida he confessed his disappointment to the new head, Friar Juan Pérez, formerly Isabella's confessor. Pérez counseled patience and sent a letter to the queen asking her to reconsider her decision. She summoned Columbus again and sent him 20,000 *maravedis* to outfit himself in clothes proper to a royal audience—almost twice the amount of the annual stipend she had given him. Thus properly attired, Columbus set off for Santa Fe (Holy Faith), just outside Granada, where the queen was preparing for the final siege against this last bastion of the Moors.

When Columbus arrived at Santa Fe, Isabella told him to remain with the camp until the war was over, at which time she would reconsider his project. The encampment at Santa Fe was more like a medieval fair than a battlefield. Isabella had erected a city in the shape of a cross, replete with roads, moats, and towers. The queen and her entourage, which included her children, numerous servants, and ladies-in-waiting, were housed in sumptuous tents, festooned with silk and brocade. For the spiritual well-being of all assembled, Isabella had brought a makeshift chapel, musicians, and a choir consisting of fifteen to twenty-five boys, and soon Juan de Anchieta would compose a mass to commemorate the fall of Granada.[39] In this chivalrous age, the presence of the queen and her ladies-in-waiting emboldened the knights to show their bravery in battle. Yet, their confrontations resembled tournaments more than pitched battles between armies. Only two men fought, one from each side, which meant, obviously, less loss of life than in battles between opposing armies.

Isabella, however, almost lost her life. It was mid-July; a fire started with a candle she had left next to her bed. As her tent went up in flames she escaped in her nightgown, but the fire spread so quickly that soon most of the camp was ablaze, lighting up the night sky. Now she feared that the Muslims would take advantage of the disorder in her camp and swoop down on them. Her army quickly prepared to stop any attack.[40] The Muslims did not attack, the Spanish soldiers rebuilt the city, and the battle continued.

Boabdil, the Muslim ruler of Granada, had agreed to surrender the city as soon as the other Muslim-controlled cities had been conquered, but now he procrastinated. Some of the people inside the walls of the Alhambra wanted to fight to the death, but others were weary of war and recognized that without reinforcements and with dwindling supplies of food, they could not hold out for very long. Finally, on January 2, 1492, Boabdil formally surrendered. Columbus was there. On January 6, Epiphany, King Ferdinand entered the Alhambra, carrying a huge silver cross given to him by Pope Sixtus IV as his standard. For his bravery Columbus was allowed to be part of the procession. He wrote:

> I saw the Royal Standards of Your Highnesses placed by force of arms on the towers of the Alhambra, which is the fortress of the said city; and I saw the Moorish King come out to the gates of the city and kiss the Royal Hands of Your Highnesses.[41]

Over the ramparts of the Alhambra flew the banner of Castile with the "motto of the messianic kingdom . . . *Unum ovile et unus pastor*—One flock and one shepherd." [42] The Spanish victory over the Moors demonstrated to Isabella and Ferdinand that their desire to unite their territory under one faith was ordained by God. When news of their victory reached Pope Innocent VIII he bestowed on Ferdinand and Isabella the title "the Catholic monarchs."

Still, there was one remaining obstacle before the nation could be united under one faith—the Jews who refused to convert. On March 30, 1492, the Catholic monarchs gave the unconverted Jews an ultimatum: they must convert or they would be expelled from the Spanish kingdoms. They were given only four months to decide whether to abandon their faith or their property.[43]

With the conquest of Granada, and the order for the expulsion of the Jews, Columbus must have thought his project for the greater glory of Christendom would finally be approved. Isabella did convene another commission to study the more technical aspects of Columbus's proposal and asked members to send their conclusions to the Royal Council, a group composed mostly of theologians and grandees, people who had little knowledge or experience with navigation. But the new council also rejected it; again the sway of Augustine's worldview was too powerful and prevented the council members from appreciating what Columbus had proposed. Reluctantly, the queen assented to their decision. Columbus's high hopes were dashed; he was enraged but could do nothing against a royal decision. Cool and determined, he gathered up his charts and his books and set off for Córdoba to visit briefly with Beatriz and their young son Ferdinand before going on to France to present his proposal to King Charles.

He was on the road when a courier sent by Isabella caught up with him near the village of Pinos-Puente, only about four miles from Santa Fe, with her request that he return to her at once. The courier couldn't tell him the reason for her urgency, but Columbus could not defy a royal order. He could not have known that his decision to stop waiting and to take his ideas elsewhere had started a chain of events that worked powerfully in his favor. During the short time Columbus had been on the road, his friend, Luis de Santangel, who was also the queen's confidant and keeper of the privy-purse, rushed to her as soon as he heard that the commission had again rejected Columbus's proposal. He told her that she was losing a great opportunity—he felt that Columbus's project was a small investment for what might yield a high return.

Trusting her heart and intuition, Isabella went against the advice of the commission and her husband, who had never been very enthusiastic about Columbus. Perhaps Ferdinand resented Columbus because the Genoese had imprisoned his grandfather, Alfonso of Aragón, or because Columbus had sailed for René of Anjou, who had been at war with the king of Aragón. The queen followed her own counsel and lost no time pondering her decision; immediately she dispatched the courier to intercept Columbus.

CHAPTER FOUR

VISION BECOMES REALITY

I sabella and her entourage were still camped at Santa Fe, where they were making the necessary arrangements to establish her rule over Granada. It was there that the agreement between Columbus and the sovereigns was hammered out. The sting of three rejections, beginning with the one from King João of Portugal, rankled Columbus and probably encouraged him to raise the bar about the conditions he would accept, for they were exorbitant by the standards of the day. He told the queen that he wanted to be called "Don," a noble title, and given a coat of arms to go with it; he also wanted the titles of Admiral of the Ocean Sea and Viceroy and Governor of the islands and mainlands he might discover. The coat of arms and all the titles were to be hereditary so that his sons and their sons could inherit them in perpetuity. Besides these honorary benefits, he wanted a tenth of "whatever merchandise, whether it be pearls, precious stones, gold, silver, spices, and other things," was found.[1] In addition, he asked that if he paid an eighth toward the expense of any ship, he would be able to keep an eighth of the profits in addition to the tenth that would be automatic.

Columbus was confident that he would be successful in his endeavor, gaining a fortune and nobility in the process, while the sovereigns—somewhat dubious about his grandiose claims and with relatively little to lose—capitulated to all of his demands.

The Capitulations of Santa Fe, as the documents spelling out the terms of the agreement between Columbus, Queen Isabella, and King Ferdinand are known, were signed on April 17, 1492. An addendum, dated on April 30, stipulated in more detail Columbus's powers to hear and decide both civil and criminal cases on board ship or in the lands he might discover. On that date Columbus was also given a kind of passport as well as three letters of greeting from the sovereigns to any rulers, such as the Grand Khan, whom he might meet. The name of the addressee was purposely left blank so that Columbus could fill it in with the appropriate name of the ruler.

> *To the Most Serene Prince _____ Our very dear friend,*
>   *Ferdinand and Isabella, King and Queen of Castile, Aragon, Leon, Sicily, etc., greetings and increase of good fortune. . . . We have learned with joy of Your esteem and high regard for Us and Our Nation and of Your great eagerness to be informed about things with Us. Wherefore, we have resolved to send you Our Noble Captain, Christopherus Colón, bearer of these, from whom You may learn of Our good health and Our prosperity. . . .*
>
> *I the King   I the Queen*

Ships in the port of Cádiz were being readied for the deportation of Jews, so the sovereigns chose Palos on the Rio Tinto as the site for Columbus's departure. Apparently, the people in that town had incurred some kind of debt for which they had to provide two ships for whatever use the sovereigns demanded. The time had come to make good on that debt. The sovereigns sent a letter to the mayor of the town, and on May 23, 1492, he read it aloud to the townspeople:

> *Don Fernando and Doña Isabel, by the grace of God, King and Queen of Castile, León, Aragón [etc., etc.]. To you, Diego Rodríguez Prieto, and to all the other persons, your associates and other citizens of the Town of Palos, and to each one of you, Greetings and Grace. You well know that, because of certain acts performed and committed by you to Our detriment, you were condemned by Our Council and obliged to provide Us for twelve months with two caravels equipped at your own cost and expense, whenever and wherever you should be required by Us, under fixed penalties, as is provided in detail in the aforementioned decree, which has been pronounced against you.[2]*

Hardly happy greetings. The people of Palos were commanded not only to provide two ships but, unrealistically, to do so in ten days. They were greatly pressed by this demand, but they could not go against a royal order. Perhaps the resentment triggered by this onerous task has lingered on through the years, because today the town of Palos celebrates its native son Martín Alonso Pinzón, captain of the *Pinta*, as the "discoverer." In Palos, there are many reminders of Pinzón but no statue or any hint that Columbus had any connection to this place except a fresco adorning the nave of the church of San Jorge, perched above the harbor.

Summer days in Palos are luminous and long. In the summer of 1492, the ten days given to obtaining and supplying the ships stretched into ten weeks. The court had moved on to Barcelona. While waiting for the fleet to be readied, Columbus may have gone there briefly to go over the plans, for it is believed that he was present when the sovereigns received a letter from Genoese ambassadors which claimed: "we did read that Joachim the Abbot of Southern Italy has foretold that he is to come from Spain who is to recover again the fortunes of Zion." [3] Some people had already begun to think that Ferdinand was the prophesied Last World Emperor—the one who would defeat the Antichrist and recover Jerusalem so that Christ could come again. The letter must have stirred Ferdinand's imperial desire. Now that the Moors had been conquered and the Capitulations had been signed, Columbus might have felt more confident to raise the issue of Jerusalem with the sovereigns if he had not yet done so. Had he already broached the topic with them, the arrival of the letter would have been the opportune moment to remind them again of their commitment to the cause of Jerusalem's liberation.

Back in Palos, preparations for the voyage were well under way. Two local ships, the *Niña* and the *Pinta*, both caravels, had been commandeered. Because so many ships were needed for the deportation of the Jews from Spain, Columbus's choice for the flagship was limited; he had to take what he could get. He chartered the *Santa María*, a *nao* which, though larger and equipped with a captain's cabin, Columbus never liked. He wrote that it was "very sluggish and not suited for the work of exploration" (*Diario*, p. 291),* preferring the fast little *Niña*, which he commissioned for his second and third voyages. Samuel Eliot Morison, a historian and himself a mariner, claimed that the *Niña* "logged 25,000 miles under the Admiral's command" and called her one "of the greatest little ships in the world's history." [4]

---

* See Readers Note on p. 266 on version of *Diario* used.

On these small wooden ships, there was very little protection from the sea; there was no insulation, no inner wall—no disguising the proximity of the water slapping against the bare wooden planks. The sailors of the preindustrial era had a saying that only four fingers separated them from death,[5] because in a standard ship of that era, the planks were no wider than that, and the planks on Columbus's ships were not even that wide. No wonder the merest leak or evidence of shipworms (really a form of clam) would create a panic.

No extant drawings or plans exist of the *Niña*, the *Pinta*, or the *Santa María*, but scholars have used those of other ships of the time to make approximations. Columbus's ships were very small. Most of the space on ship was taken up with the storage of supplies—primarily food, water, wine, wood for cooking, cooking equipment, arms and armor, and trinkets for trading. The *Niña* was probably no more than seventy feet long, the *Pinta* maybe as much as seventy-five feet, and the *Santa María* was not much bigger than the others. These lengths are very approximate, and modern scholars have estimated their size from their tonnage, which was reported. Tonnage then did not mean what it does today— namely, the tons of water a ship displaces. Instead, tonnage in Columbus's day was a measure of the number of wine tuns a ship could hold, and a wine tun was a particular kind of wooden cask. Columbus used a Seville tun, which held approximately 1.405 cubic meters of wine, or 40 cubic feet, and the *Santa María* is thought to have had the capacity for 100 tuns of wine.[6] Modern shipbuilders have constructed models, including one in Barcelona and three replicas in a small harbor on the Rio Tinto just below La Rábida. These made the transatlantic crossing in 1991 in anticipation of the Quincentennial of Columbus's discovery.

Even more daunting than finding suitable ships was the difficult task that remained: recruiting men to go on a voyage that had never been tried and from which there might be no return, and with a foreigner in charge. Not only did Columbus have to find the requisite number of crew to handle the three ships, he had to make sure that all the necessary jobs were filled. Each crew member had specific duties, and there was a distinct hierarchy of position and pay. At the top of the hierarchy were the captain, pilot, and master. Columbus, as captain general, had the ultimate authority for the fleet and the highest pay; captains of the other two ships would have authority on board their ships. The pilot's role was perhaps the most important, for a good pilot should be capable of predicting a storm simply by observing the color of the seas, the disposition of the clouds, or the direction of a flight of sea birds . . . and with a single glance at the wake of his ship or the way in which the prow broke the waves, an expert pilot should be able to calculate the speed of the ship.[7]

Generally it was the pilot who plotted the route and kept the charts and knew, from previous voyages, the dangers to avoid in order to direct a ship to its destination, but, of course, on this voyage no one could claim that experience. The master of a ship had responsibility for economic issues—for instance, ordering the cargo and distributing the pay. He would also often transmit orders from the captain to the boatswain, who, as overseer in charge of the rigging, anchors, and cables, would shout the orders to the rest of the crew.

As an outsider and foreigner Columbus would not have been able to convince sailors to sign up without the help of the Pinzón brothers of Palos and the Niño brothers from the nearby town of Moguer. These men, known to the locals who had sailed with them, were able to convince most of the ninety men who became crew to join up. Martín Alonso Pinzón would captain the *Pinta*, and his brother, Vincente Yáñez Pinzón, would be captain of the *Niña*. Juan Niño, who owned the *Niña*, would be its master under Vincente, and Juan's brother, Peralonso Niño, was the pilot on the *Santa María*. Several friends of Columbus also signed on, including Diego de Harana, the cousin of his mistress Beatriz.

Due to the indefatigable efforts of Alice Bache Gould, an American who made discovering their names her life's work, the names of eighty-seven of the ninety crew members are known.[8] All but five of the eighty-seven men were Spaniards, though not all of them were from the Palos area. Columbus had only one of his countrymen aboard along with three other foreigners—a Calabrian, a Venetian, and a Portuguese. Only a couple of the men were criminals, convicted of minor crimes, and they would be pardoned upon their return from a successful voyage. Columbus also had the services of an interpreter, Luis de Torres, a *converso* who knew Hebrew and a little Arabic. Because Arabic was commonly supposed to be the mother of all languages, it was assumed that de Torres would be able to communicate with the Grand Khan.[9]

Officers whose jobs were of more immediate importance were those of a steward, to watch over the food and distribute the daily rations; a surgeon to deal with injuries; a carpenter to repair anything made of wood, especially the pulleys and the masts; a cooper to attend to the casks of wine and water; and a caulker to fix leaks. Below them were those called able seamen—they had to have had considerable experience, attested to by captains for whom they had sailed, and be over the age of twenty. Some of them had extra talents: one was also a tailor, another a painter. No one on this voyage was listed as a gunner or trumpeter, jobs that were filled on later voyages. Normally, below the rank of able seamen were the apprentices—young sailors not yet twenty—who because of their agility could quickly climb up the mast to look out for dangerous reefs or clamber about on the yards to fix a loose rope, but no apprentices were listed as crew on this voyage, perhaps because Columbus wanted only very experienced sailors. Nevertheless, he did have twenty-three ship's boys, or gromets, who were often only eight or ten years old—nine on the *Santa María* and seven each on the other two ships. These boys, at the bottom of the social hierarchy, were felt to be indispensable as they served the other sailors and were responsible for turning the "hour" glass, for singing the ditties at the change of the watch, and performing any number of odd jobs as needed. No one was assigned the job of cook, since cooking was not a manly role. Crew members cooked their own food or paid someone, most likely the gromets, to do it.[10]

Given that religion was one of the reasons for the voyage—for Columbus, a primary reason—scholars have wondered why Isabella did not send along a priest as the Grand Khan had specifically requested. At the time, it was highly unusual for a priest to accompany any voyage, let alone an exploratory voyage whose ostensible purpose was to see if the ocean could be crossed and then, if possible, to set up a trading post. Moreover, Columbus was more than capable of conducting prayers on ship and informing the Grand Khan of the basics of the Christian faith.

Although Columbus had no idea how long the voyage would take, Isabella told him to plan enough provisions for a voyage that might last a year. Water, of course, was the most essential item, and many barrels of water were stored, doubling as ballast. The only other beverage was wine. But it was not just "wine," as most scholars write; given the huge amounts needed, it had to be something local, and that would have been sherry. If properly coopered, sherry would keep better than other wine over long voyages, and as a fortified wine it would provide more calories and warmth to the sailors (not to mention increasing morale). The area from which Columbus departed is known today as the "sherry triangle" and includes Sanlúcar de Barrameda, Jerez de la Frontera, and Puerto de Santa María: all authentic sherry is produced in this area and was being produced in the fifteenth century. Within that small region, each of the towns specializes in a different kind of sherry, due to the different types of grapes and soil as well as its microclimate and degree of sunlight. It seems safe to conclude that the "wine" Columbus loaded was sherry and not just any sherry, but a specific sherry from one of the three major producers. For the first voyage it was probably the manzanilla sherry from nearby Sanlúcar.

Tea and coffee, chocolate and tobacco were unknown to Europeans at the time; in fact, the last two would be introduced *from* the New World. Without such stimulants, one wonders how the men stayed awake during the long night watches, especially after drinking their daily ration—a liter and a half—of sherry wine.[11]

Theoretically, provisions for the voyage were quite varied and probably not very different from the food the men were accustomed to eating at home. Because Columbus was Italian, our immediate culinary associations are pasta and tomato sauce, but tomatoes would also be a gift from the New World. However, when Europeans first saw tomatoes they thought they were poisonous due to the flower's resemblance to the "deadly nightshade" plant. Columbus probably took a quantity of the Genoese invention—pesto—a highly aromatic sauce made from basil, garlic, pine nuts, and cheese, for it keeps well and was known to have been taken by the Crusaders on their long journeys. On board, the sailors' diet likely consisted of legumes, rice, hardtack (twice-baked biscuits), salted meat and fish, onions, garlic, olive oil, and some spices (cinnamon, black pepper, chilies, cloves). If they became sick, they might receive some raisins and almonds, which were thought to be beneficial. Not all of the food was dried, cured, or preserved in oil; they also carried live chickens, eggs, squash, apples, pears, cabbages, cauliflower, green peppers, pomegranates, peaches, and figs.

The fresh food did not last long in the heat and without refrigeration, so sailors tried to supplement their diet with birds and fish they caught at sea. Much more discouraging was that the wine often soured, the water became brackish, the hardtack got moldy, and the fish and meat wormy. Sometimes the men ate in the dark to avoid seeing the mold and the insects. If they did not get sick from such unappetizing morsels, the stench from the slops dumped into the hold to feed the few animals they kept must surely have turned the stomachs of many. Yet, to Columbus's credit, none of the men developed scurvy, which would soon become a scourge on long voyages.

Since sailors preferred their food cooked, they often prepared their meals on a fire laid on top of a bed of sand enclosed in some kind of a box to block the wind. But cooking in cramped quarters on wooden ships could be dangerous, as a strong wind could easily scatter the embers over people and provisions. Nevertheless, Columbus did not mention any outbreak of fire on board. Since there was hardly any place on the cramped ship where a sailor could retreat or be alone, a fire would have been noticed before it got out of control and quickly extinguished.

There were few sleeping quarters. Only Columbus had a cabin and a bed of his own; the officers might have had a mattress or a grass mat, and a few of them might also have had a tiny cell under the quarterdeck. The rest of the crew slept exposed on the upper deck anywhere they could find a place. With so many men confined in such close proximity for weeks—not unlike a prison—conditions were ripe for the temptations of homosexual activity, which was understood not as a matter of sexual orientation but as a particular kind of act, namely sodomy. Especially vulnerable were those with little authority, namely the younger boys, who often performed personal favors for their masters. While it is possible such behavior occurred on board, sodomy was both a sin and a crime that had lethal consequences—if caught, men were killed by hanging, by being thrown overboard and left to drown, or by beatings.[12]

Each of the men was permitted to bring a chest to hold his belongings. These might consist of a linen shirt, a woolen vest of green or black, wool underpants, wool stockings, wool tunic, shoes, and maybe a long overcoat. Although the color red was reserved primarily for royalty and members of the nobility, Spanish sailors were permitted to wear red caps and bonnets. Columbus had a pair of red shoes. Other items in the men's chests were linen handkerchiefs, perhaps a towel, a few pieces of cloth, scissors, a sword, and for those who could read, a prayer book.[13] Columbus had additional items such as cloths, plates, and cutlery for his table; linens for his bed; and books, charts, and paper, pens, and ink for writing.

Ever optimistic, the visionary Columbus was confident about the journey; for the crew, however, it was an entirely different matter. Though most of the men were experienced sailors, none had been as far out into the ocean as they were about to go. They knew the earth was round, but no one had confirmed it because no one had ever gone around it. Thus, suspicion lingered; perhaps they *would* fall off the edge of the earth or would not be able to get back up from the other side. Maybe it was different in the "antipodes," maybe everything *was* upside down. They simply had no idea what lay in wait; after all, at the edges of the known world, maps warned "there be dragons."

Mostly, however, they worried about two things: first, that the ocean was too wide and that they might not reach land before running out of food, and second, about what they might encounter if they should reach land. Sailors were worried about encountering the "Plinian" races, named for the Roman naturalist Pliny (d. 79), who exhaustively catalogued them in his *Historia naturalis*. These monstrous races—Amazons (without breasts); Blemmyae (headless creatures); Cynocephali (dog-headed); Monoculi (one-eyed); hairy men; men with a foot so large they could use it as an umbrella; and, finally, the Anthropophagi (man-eaters, cannibals)[14]—were familiar to everyone. They were mentioned in many popular stories, briefly in Marco Polo, more so in John Mandeville, and were vividly depicted in medieval paintings and on maps, where they were located in the unexplored areas of the world. Today they seem preposterous, but our imaginative renderings of extraterrestrial "aliens" point to the same unease about how and where to situate such beings in relation to humans. In the medieval world, the issue of the "Plinian" races was an urgent one, especially for those venturing into the unknown.

H. Schedel, *Nuremberg Chronicle*, 1493.

Courtesy John Carter Brown Library at Brown Univeristy.

For medieval Europeans the possible existence of such monstrous peoples challenged the story told in Genesis where all humans are said to have descended from Adam whom God himself had created perfect. Either these monsters were not human, in which case they would be assimilated to animals hitherto unknown, or they must have degenerated from the human state due to sins they had committed, and thus were worrisome.[15]

Because of the challenge to the biblical view, theologians had to find an acceptable explanation. Christian commentaries on Genesis, influenced by St. Ambrose and St. Augustine, suggested that the monstrous races were descendants of Cain, who was cursed by God. God told the children of Seth (the good lineage) not to mix with those of Cain's (bad) lineage, but they ignored the warning and had "mixed race" children from whom all the monstrous races allegedly had sprung. Although the descendants of Cain did not survive the flood, Ham, one of the sons of Noah, was thought to have inherited the curse because "he uncovered the nakedness" of his father when he saw his drunken father unclothed.[16] When Noah awoke, he cursed Ham and his son Canaan, saying "a servant of servants shall he be unto his brethren" (Gen. 9:25). Since Ham was the son dispersed to Africa after the flood, he was considered the "father" of Africans. The Spanish believed that the Moors, who came from North Africa, were from the line of Ham. Medieval Christians used both Aristotle's notion of natural slavery and the curse of Ham as a rationale for the disparagement and enslavement of African people.[17]

Although Columbus owned a copy of Pliny's *Historia naturalis*, he was not so gullible; he dismissed the stories of monsters because he was sure he would meet civilized Asians in the court of the Grand Khan. The crew, however, was far more credulous.

In addition to legends about monstrous races, there were legends about islands in the western ocean. The most famous of these were Antilia, sometimes identified with the Island of the Seven Cities, Brasil, and St. Brendan's island. Antilia was said to have been founded by seven bishops, each of whom had established a fabulous city on that island after they had escaped from Spain when it was taken over by the Moors. It appeared north of the Canaries and the Madeiras on a Venetian map of 1424 and west of the Azores on the chart that Toscanelli had sent to Columbus in 1474. Brasil or Hy-Brasil, also known as the Isle of the Blest, was thought to be off the coast of Ireland and though it appeared on a map as early as 1325 and was sought until the eighteenth century, it was never found. St. Brendan's island, also originally off the coast of Ireland and sometimes conflated with Brasil, had supposedly been found by St. Brendan and fourteen monks who stayed there for a few weeks in the sixth century. As more of the Ocean Sea was explored, these islands "moved" farther west, always to the beyond. According to John Gillis, who has made a study of the place of islands in the European imagination, "[T]he notion of roving islands was not at all strange."[18] Because space, especially the unexplored ocean, was fluid, there was really no way of fixing an island to a particular place on the globe.

Sailors continued to seek these fabled islands by venturing farther west into the ocean; indeed, until late in the sixteenth century the Portuguese continued to provide grants to sailors who would try to discover them,[19] and until the 1870s they continued to be placed on maps, but none were ever found. As we know, Antilia gave up her name to an archipelago in the Caribbean and Brasil to a country in South America; the Seven Cities moved inland to Mexico, where Cortés searched for them; and St. Brendan's island moved to the coast of Newfoundland.

But just as he was skeptical about monsters, Columbus was skeptical of the existence of these mythical islands. He fully expected to encounter some of the 7,440 islands Marco Polo said lay off the Chinese coast. When he was in Portugal, armed with Toscanelli's chart, Columbus may have suggested to King João that he could use Antilia as a stepping-stone on the way to Asia, and plotted his route from Lisbon to the Azores, which belonged to Portugal. But, sailing for the Spanish sovereigns, he could not go that way.

In late July 1492, as Columbus was preparing for his momentous voyage, another equally momentous journey was also under way. The Jews who had refused to convert to Christianity were departing from the nearby port of Cádiz and heading east to North Africa, and to Constantinople, where the Ottomans embraced them, a glaring reminder to the Christians of their failed efforts at conversion.[20] The coincidence of the simultaneous journeys—one evangelical, one fleeing for his faith—could not have been lost on Columbus; he knew about the Jews' departure, and he may even have passed by Cádiz as they were embarking or used them as a cover to avoid the Portuguese, who, he feared, were planning to intercept him. Yet, in the only versions we have of Columbus's diary, that is, the abridgements made by his son Ferdinand and by Bartolomé de Las Casas, there is no mention of these events; whether Columbus purposely omitted any reference to them or whether these editors had reason to excise them is unknown.

The evening before Columbus's departure, Juan Pérez, the influential friar at La Rábida and his friend and confessor, said mass at the Church of San Jorge. Below the church, the ships sat in the harbor, awaiting their crews.

Imagine that night, so many years ago, when ninety men in three small ships prepared for the biggest adventure of their lives. They cannot have gotten much sleep. As they lay awake watching the transit of the moon across the summer sky, they must have wondered if the leader of their voyage—a foreigner full of dreams of crossing the ocean that had never been crossed—was crazy. It is unlikely Columbus got much sleep either, but his musings were different. After all the years of waiting, his dream was about to be realized; perhaps, as Fellini once said, "the visionary is the only true realist." His persistence had finally won royal support, the ships were outfitted and provisioned, the sailors were on board. But how long would they be gone? Would they ever see their loved ones again? No way of knowing and no way of sending news back. Columbus was not exempt from these qualms: he was leaving his two sons—Ferdinand, only four, was with Beatriz in Córdoba; Diego, a boy of eleven or twelve, was also in Córdoba, but at school.

Finally, everything was ready; a shiver must have passed through the crew as the lines were lifted. Slipping out of the harbor before dawn on the morning of August 3, 1492, the ships were hardly noticed, and the only sounds were the crew's muted voices in prayer as they glided out with the tide over the bar of Saltes.

Departure of the *Santa María*, the *Pinta*, and the *Niña*
from Palos in 1492 by Antonio Cabral Bejarano.
Courtesy of La Rábida Monastery.

Soon they picked up the wind and headed for the Canary Islands. This leg of the trip was relatively calm, but if there were any first-time gromets aboard, they would quickly experience what a rolling ship could do to their balance and stomachs. Columbus had chosen the Canaries as the optimal place to begin the crossing, not only because he assumed they were at the same latitude as Cipango, but more important, because of the winds and westward currents that he had noticed on his voyage to São Jorge da Mina.

Almost immediately he began to keep a diary of the voyage, which, following Las Casas, is generally referred to as the *Diario*. The *Diario* begins with a letter to the sovereigns that serves as a preface or prologue.[21] In a tone that is somewhat dry and controlled, given the momentous occasion, he informs them that

> On the third day of August of the said year, on a Friday, half an hour before sunrise; I took the route to Your Highnesses' Canary Islands, which are in the said Ocean Sea, in order from there to take my course and sail so far that I would reach the Indies and give Your Highnesses' message to those princes and thus carry out that which you had commanded me to do. And for this purpose I thought of writing on this whole voyage, very diligently, all that I would do and see and experience . . . writing down each night whatever I experience during the day and each day what I sail during the night . . . and above all it is important that I forget sleep and pay much attention to navigation in order thus to carry out these purposes, which will be a great labor (*Diario*, p. 19).

The *Diario* was very unusual for its time. Not only were ships' logs uncommon, since many sailors could not write, but even after record keeping was mandated in 1524, the logs generally recorded only wind, direction, and speed. Columbus included his observations about people and places, and despite the dry tone as in the quotation above, he also confided his feelings about the enterprise and his encounters. In the same letter he recapitulated his understanding of what the voyage was all about, for he reminded the sovereigns of the report he had given them about a prince who

> is called "Grand Khan," which means in our Spanish language "King of Kings" . . . to see how their conversion to our Holy Faith might be undertaken. And you commanded that I should not go to the East by

land, by which way it is customary to go, but by the route to the West, by which route we do not know for certain that anyone previously has passed (*Diario*, p. 17).

The six-day sail to the Canaries provided an opportunity to test the crew, fix any problems, and obtain additional provisions. On the way to the Canaries, they passed through what later became known as the Horse Latitudes, because this was the route over which the Spanish began to transport horses to the New World. Some have speculated, however, that the area was named because sailors often had to throw the horses overboard to save on water and food when the ships were becalmed due to the dry, hot air and lack of wind.

Despite their relatively calm sail, on Monday, August 6, the rudder of the *Pinta* came loose. In his diary entry for that day, Columbus wrote that he "believed or suspected [it] to be by design of one Gómez Rascón and Cristóbal Quintero, whose caravel it was, because he disliked going on that voyage" (*Diario*, p. 23). Yet since Quintero sailed on the *Pinta* with Martín Pinzón, as did a relative, Juan Quintero, it seems highly unlikely that he would have risked their lives by tinkering with the rudder. (Quintero sailed again with Columbus on the third voyage and Juan Quintero went on the fourth.) While at sea, Pinzón fixed the rudder with ropes, but Columbus became concerned about the ship's ability to make it to the Canaries, let alone across the ocean. His "anguish lessened knowing that Martín Pinzón was a valiant person and very ingenious" (*Diario*, p. 23), but Columbus's trust in Pinzón would be tested as the voyage progressed.

When the *Pinta*'s rudder came loose again, Columbus decided to leave Pinzón in Grand Canary to see if he could get a better ship. Columbus had envisioned the Canaries as a resting and refueling stop; now it would also have to serve as a place of repair. The *Santa María* and the *Niña* went on to Gomera, another of the Canary islands. While there, they heard from some Spaniards about land they had seen to the west, "toward the setting sun," and Columbus recalled that when he had sailed for Portugal in 1484, a man from the Azores had said the same thing. If he thought they referred to Antilia or another of the mythical islands, he doesn't say. He simply records that they took on firewood and meat and made ready to leave Gomera, for he was frustrated when ten days had elapsed and the *Pinta*, or its replacement, had not caught up with him. Reluctantly, he turned back to Grand Canary to find out what was keeping them.

When he reached that island, he learned that Pinzón had been unable to obtain a different ship, but he had repaired the *Pinta*'s rudder as best he could. His caravel, like the other ships, was using a single rudder attached to the sternpost—a fifteenth-century innovation—which, if it was working properly, made steering a ship much easier than the earlier side rudders. Its repair was absolutely necessary if they were to proceed. Columbus decided to change the *Niña*'s rigging from lateen to square in order to make better time. While the lateen sail is better for sailing close to shore, the large square sail can catch more wind and thus help make better speed.

While the ships were technically sound, such repairs and changes before heading across the ocean were not good omens. To make matters worse, the crew's apprehension became outright terror when a volcano erupted on nearby Tenerife, the largest of the Canary Islands, spewing flames and ash into the air. They had never before seen such a thing; it could only be another evil omen. Columbus tried to calm the men by telling them about a volcano he had witnessed on Mt. Etna in Sicily. Yet the devilish red sky kept the men awake all night as they mulled over whether to continue on this voyage into the unknown. Desertion was common on voyages at the time, but remarkably, none of the men chose that option.

Leaving Grand Canary on September 1—having already spent almost a month there before the real part of the voyage had even begun—the fleet headed back to Gomera, which was ruled by a young and very beautiful widow, Doña Beatriz de Peraza. It was rumored that Columbus fell in love with her; whether true or not, the dalliance was of short duration, for on the morning of September 6, Columbus and the crew hoisted the sails, said goodbye to the only world they knew, and set out for the unknown. The great voyage had finally begun.

While the volcano and other omens had frightened the crew, Columbus was thrilled to be under way. For him, the world was not a fearful place; it had, after all, been created by God and was held in his embrace. Columbus's world was a much cozier place than our world is today. His world was geocentric and the center of the universe. Copernicus was alive at the time, but his heliocentric view that the earth revolved around the sun, had not yet been published. Galileo had not even been born. If it is difficult to imagine what it was like to live in such a world, the following passage from Andrés Bernáldez, a priest and a good friend of Columbus's, should help:

In the Name of God Almighty. There was a man of Genoa, a dealer in printed books, trading in the land of Andalusia, whom they call Christoval Colon, a man of very high intellect without much book-learning, very skillful in the art of Cosmography and the divisions of the world; who received, by what he read in Ptolemy, and in other books, and by his own discernment, how and in what wise is formed the world into which we are born and in which we move. This he places within the sphere of the heavens, so that it touches them on no side, nor has aught of firmness to rest upon, but is only earth and water globed by heat within the hollow vault of the sky.[22]

The last sentence gives a visceral sense of how people perceived the earth and the heavens. The sun, the stars, and the planets were set in separate spheres that revolved around the earth. Despite the much more circumscribed space, such a view did not greatly impede navigation by the stars.

Columbus had time to think about the meaning of the journey and his role in it. He was beginning to think of himself as the Christ-bearer like his namesake, St. Christopher, carrying the Christian faith across the waters. A map of the lands Columbus discovered, drawn by Juan de las Cosa (ca. 1500), includes an image of St. Christopher bearing Christ across the water. Some scholars think the drawing might actually be a portrait of Columbus. But he also had earthly concerns that inspired him to compose a letter to the sovereigns that reiterated the terms agreed to by them:

you granted me great favors and ennobled me so that from then on I might call myself "Don" and would be Grand Admiral of the Ocean Sea and Viceroy and perpetual Governor of all the islands and lands that I might discover and gain and [that] from now on might be discovered and gained in the Ocean Sea; and likewise my eldest son would succeed me and his son him, from generation to generation forever (*Diario*, p. 19).

Rather than a sign of his greed, as many scholars have suggested, it seems more likely that the letter was in lieu of a private will, which, in the custom of the time, he could not make without permission from the sovereigns. Laws of inheritance were strict and relatively automatic, preventing most people from dispersing their estates however and to whomever they wished.[23] Not until 1497 did Isabella and Ferdinand grant Columbus permission to draw up a formal will, known as a *majorat*, and it was not signed until February 22, 1498.

But such thoughts of legacy would have been for rare, contemplative moments; aboard ship, his life was filled with activity. Having moved out into the open sea, Columbus and the crew were constantly on the lookout for islands, regardless of whether they were the mythical islands of popular imagination, or the islands discussed by Marco Polo, or indicated on Toscanelli's chart, or those Columbus had heard about from sailors in the Azores. Finding even a small island could prove to be a dubious blessing: in the vast ocean, a bit of land would help to calm their nerves and replenish their water and food supplies, but what if they encountered the strange creatures alleged to inhabit them? Fortunately, there was so much to do on ship that the men did not have much time to ruminate on the enormity of the ocean and the possible dangers ahead, and what "free" time they had was spent sleeping.

During clear sailing, the day was taken up with routine chores—setting the sails, swabbing the decks, checking for leaks, repairing the lines, washing clothes, and while in coastal waters, a bit of fishing. The crew did these chores according to a strict rotation of "watches." The men were divided into two named groups, and there had to be one "watch" on duty at all times. Watches lasted for four hours each and rotated around the "clock," but there seems to be some debate about the sequencing of watches on Columbus's voyages. While modern sailors assume the rotation of watches is at four, eight, and twelve o'clock, there is evidence in Columbus's diary that they changed at three, seven, and eleven, the time being determined by how many turns of the *ampoletta* (half-hour glass) had occurred. Pérez-Mallaína claims that there were three night watches: the first beginning at 7:00 p.m., followed by one from 11:00 p.m. to 3:00 a.m. (the "sleepy" watch), and then 3:00 a.m. to 7:00 a.m. (the "dawn watch").[24] There would also have been a time to shift the order of the watches so that each group would not have the same schedule day after day. The rotation of the watches ensured that a sailor's day was never the same, nor was the time during which he could sleep. Each "watch" had particular tasks; for example, in the morning, one of the first tasks may have been to light the fire for breakfast, another task to swab the decks. Hoisting or lowering the sails was an enormous job that, because of the weight involved, required many men to pull and secure the ropes. In emergencies, all men were called on deck, but if the sea was calm and the sailing was going smoothly, they may have been able to relax. The work got done but there was no sense of trying to "beat the clock" because there were no portable clocks until after 1500.

Although Peter Henlein, a locksmith in Nuremberg, invented a portable clock around that time, it was not seaworthy and did not have a minute hand. Time on board was kept by the *ampoletta* that a gromet or one of the crew turned when the sand ran out, every half hour. Because this instrument, imported from Venice, was expensive and very fragile, turning the glass and keeping the time was an important job. No doubt Columbus carried a couple of extras on board in case of breakage. Nevertheless, inattention caused minutes, even hours, to be "lost" over the course of the voyage, though theoretically they could be "found" again at high noon. But even such corrections were not always accurate.[25] Modern-day navigation uses technology to calculate the most minute changes in the winds and direction, and it is hard to imagine travel without the most basic equipment such as a timepiece.

Cross-cutting the work watches was the steady round of canonical hours: the day was divided into eight "hours" traditionally beginning with matins, which were prayers read during the night. Lauds were said at sunrise, prime at the first hour of the day, terce at the third, sext at midday, nones at the ninth hour in midafternoon, vespers as evening approached, and compline read before bed. Morison claims that as "as a pious Christian, faithful in his religious duties, Columbus kept a book of hours in his cabin, and whenever possible said his prayers in private at the appointed hours, as he had learned to do when staying at La Rábida." Apparently the crew only joined in the evening prayers after sunset and before the night watch began.[26] Because of their voices, the gromets were the ones to call the men to prayer and to lead the singing, but all joined in to recite the Pater Noster, Ave Maria, and the Nicene Creed and then sing the "Salve Regina."[27] Columbus often recorded events according to the canonical hour in which they occurred.

While most members of the crew had varying sets of responsibilities depending on their watch, Columbus and the pilot could devote themselves to navigation. Columbus was "a dead-reckoning navigator pure and simple," according to Samuel Eliot Morison, who, in 1939 with a Harvard team, tried to trace the route of Columbus's first voyage using the technology available to him. Morison went on to write one of the most engaging works about Columbus. Dead reckoning, he says, consists in "laying down your compass courses and estimated distances on a chart." [28] But as there were no charts, like the *porto-lani*, for an uncharted, never-crossed ocean, Columbus would have to make one. Morison commented that "No such dead-reckoning navigators exist today; no man alive, limited to the instruments and means at Columbus's disposal, could obtain anything near the accuracy of his results." [29] He believed Columbus "must have had a born navigator's innate sense of direction, a practiced seaman's knowledge of what to expect from a cloud formation, the look of the water, and the behavior of the wind." [30] Columbus's talents or gifts were demonstrated over and over during his voyages and frequently remarked on by those who sailed with him.

Morison's awe is well placed when the resources Columbus had at his disposal are considered. Although Columbus had estimated the distance across the ocean from biblical, ancient Greek, and Arabic sources, he really had no idea of its width; no one did because no one knew of the American continents in the way. Columbus's estimate of the extent of the ocean was based on his erroneous calculations of the circumference of the globe rendering it much smaller than what we now know and even what some ancients, such as Eratosthenes, had calculated. Columbus's intention was to sail due west, as he believed that Cipango (Japan) and Mangi, a province of China, were on the same latitude as the Canaries. So after leaving the Canaries he calculated his daily distance and added it to a blank chart as they went along. Easier said than done; the method was fraught with problems at every stage. Distance equals speed times time, and in the fifteenth century, there was no *technical* way to measure speed. Time also had to be estimated because even the finest half-hour glass was much too rough a gauge. Instead, knowing the length of his ship, Columbus could calculate the time—counted off in seconds—it took for sea bubbles, bits of weed, or a piece of wood to traverse the distance from bow to stern to get an approximate sense of the speed. [31] A good mariner with a lot of experience, like Columbus, could estimate speed quite accurately. The distance they had traveled in a day was recorded in terms of leagues; Columbus is said to have "estimated speed in Roman miles per hour, and distance in leagues of 4 Roman miles each, his league being equivalent to 3.18 nautical miles." [32] In an average day, he estimated that a caravel could go about fifty leagues—sometimes more but at other times much less.

There was also the problem of ascertaining the depth of the ocean, which became more important as they neared land. Most ships carried lead lines of forty fathoms, but Columbus had several lines that measured 100 fathoms. Yet, it is difficult to know with certainty the actual length of what Columbus considered a fathom; he used the Castilian term *braças*, which some scholars say is 2.5 feet, others claim it is 5.5.[33] And Columbus may actually have meant the length of a Genoese fathom, which is 22.9 inches, a measurement he had used on earlier voyages. Regardless, whenever they took soundings—that is, letting the line down to ascertain the depth of the water—the line came up considerably short of the actual depth of the sea. No wonder the sailor shouted out, "No bottom, sir."

There were also problems trying to figure out where they were on the globe. Celestial navigation for finding one's position at sea, according to Morison, was in its infancy during Columbus's time, and he did not really use it much except for his sightings of Polaris (the North Star or Pole Star) and the sun. Columbus had a very simple quadrant that he could use for trying to ascertain latitude. His quadrant was "a simple quarter-circle of hardwood, with sights along one edge through which the heavenly body could be lined up, a plummet attached to the apex by a silk cord." As the cord cuts the arc of the quadrant, it indicates the altitude.[34] Altitude is the angle between the star and the horizon, the distance from the North Pole estimated from the width of the angle. Longitude was much more difficult; the only way Columbus could have tried to calculate his longitude was during an eclipse of the moon, but there was no eclipse on the first voyage.[35] Had there been one, he would have taken his copy of Regiomontanus's *Ephemerides*, which predicted the time of an eclipse in Nuremberg and compared that with the local time. Then on the basis of the difference, he could figure out how far west he was from the German city.

Nevertheless, in the middle of the ocean with nothing to see on the horizon, the night sky was a familiar and comforting sight; sailors knew all the stars and constellations and took their bearings from the Pole Star—the still point in the turning sky. However, on September 13, eight days out from the Canaries, Columbus noticed something strange on the ship's compass. He wrote in his diary: "On this day at the beginning of night the compasses northwested and in the morning they northeasted somewhat" (*Diario*, p. 31). Pilots on the other ships had noticed it too. The same thing happened a few days later. What they had noticed, but without understanding the significance of, is what we now know as magnetic variation—the difference between true north as shown by the North Star and magnetic north, which can vary considerably depending on where one is.[36] In the Mediterranean, where he had learned his navigational skills, there is very little variation, but the Atlantic is an area of tremendous variation. The discrepancy in their one sure direction unnerved the crew.

Events of the next few days played more havoc with their emotions. Their trepidation increased on the night of September 15 when "they saw a marvelous branch of fire [a meteor] fall from the sky" (*Diario*, p. 33) very close to the ships. But they calmed down when a flock of birds passed overhead because, as Columbus wrote, "these birds never depart from land more than 25 leagues" (*Diario*, p. 31). The men were on constant lookout for land not only because of their fears but also because the sovereigns had promised that the first man who correctly sighted land would receive an annuity of 10,000 *maravedis*. Their hopes soared when they "began to see many bunches of very green vegetation which a short time before (so it appeared) had torn loose from land" (*Diario*, p. 33). But instead of approaching land, they were becoming entangled in what is now known as the Sargasso Sea—a true sea in the middle of the ocean—between the Azores and the West Indies. Clockwise-moving currents surround this sea, and the sargassum weed that flourishes in it was so thick that the ships had difficulty getting through, making the crew even more anxious. Their spirits rose again on September 20, when "Two boobies came to the ship and later another, which was a sign of being near land," and the next day "they saw a whale, which is a sign that they were near land, because they always go close." However, they finally broke free of the weeds and sailed into the open ocean again, but there was no land in sight and the smooth water did nothing to calm the men; they wondered how they would ever get back home. Aware that the men were jumpy, Columbus wrote that because the ocean was "calm and smooth the men complained, saying that since in that region there were no rough seas, it would never blow for a return to Spain" (*Diario*, p. 41).

To this point in the crossing, Columbus's course had been mostly due west from the Canaries, but he began to steer north to try to catch some wind. A short while later, miraculously, there was a high sea, which Columbus took as a heavenly sign "which had not appeared except in the time of the Jews when they left Egypt [and complained] against Moses, who took them out of captivity" (*Diario*, p. 41). He was referring to the biblical story about how God had caused a trough in the middle of the Red Sea so that "the children of Israel walked upon dry land in the midst of the sea; and the waters were a wall unto them on their right hand, and on their left," and so they were able to escape from pharaoh to the Promised Land (Exodus 14:21–31). The wind felt by Columbus and his men, as well as the north-bound currents and the high sea, helped to quell the men's fears about ever being able to return home.

A couple of days later Columbus resumed his travel west. On September 25, Martín Alonso Pinzón called out that he had sighted land. Everyone was over-joyed. Columbus knelt down "to give thanks to Our Lord, and Martín Alonso and his men said *Gloria in excelsis deo*" as did those on the *Niña*. But there was no land, it was a mirage. Again their hopes were dashed. "In order to prevent men from crying, 'land, land!' at every moment and causing unjustified feelings of joy, the Admiral had ordered that one who claimed to have seen land and did not make good his claim in the space of three days would lose the reward"—that is, the annuity the sovereigns had promised. But to whoever correctly sighted land, Columbus said that he would add a silk jacket to the reward.[37]

On October 7, Columbus decided that the fleet should turn to the south-west, for "great multitudes of birds were passing from north to southwest, which made it seem likely that they were flying off to sleep on land." He also "knew that most of the islands that the Portuguese hold they discovered through birds" (*Diario*, p. 55). After several weeks of sailing with all these signs of land but without sight of any, the crew became restive, and they began to murmur among themselves about their commander. Their fear made them side with the Pinzóns, and that whiff of power may have been the beginning of Martín Alonso Pinzón's attempt to distance himself from Columbus, a move that would prove disruptive to the mood of the voyage and eventually cause his demise. On October 10, Columbus records that "the men could no longer stand it; they complained of the long voyage." It was not just the rotten food and sour wine but the close, cramped quarters with the same men day after day, with no place to hide or be alone. But a full-scale mutiny was useless, as they well knew. To assuage their anxiety, Columbus is said to have told them that if they did not sight land within three days, he would turn around.[38]

The next day more signs of land appeared—a green branch floating past the ship (but they had seen so many green weeds), "a green fish of the kind that is found near reefs" (but they had been wrong about the fish before), and a stick they thought had been carved (it could have been gnawed by a fish). That night, "at the tenth hour, while he was on the sterncastle, [Columbus] saw a light, although it was so faint that he did not wish to affirm that it was land. But he called Pedro Gutiérrez . . . for him to look: and thus he did and saw it." Yet, given his own injunction, he feared to call it out. After midnight, Rodrigo de Triana, on board the *Pinta*, which had gone ahead, called out *"Tierra, tierra,"*[39] The tension was palpable; this, too, might turn out to be a mirage. At night, there was no way of knowing. Columbus did not take any chances; if there was land, he could not continue sailing straight ahead for fear of hitting hidden shoals or reefs. As they waited for morning to come, he ordered the captains to tack back and forth—a maneuver of turning one way then another—as a means of keeping in place. In this way, they spent an agonizing few hours until dawn.

CHAPTER FIVE

DAYS OF WONDER

Their vigil was rewarded. Early morning, October 12, a veil of mist opened and Columbus's crew "saw an island about fifteen leagues in length, very level, full of green trees and abounding in springs, with a large lagoon in the middle."[1] The men rubbed their bleary eyes, suspicious that Columbus had conjured the island so soon after pledging to turn back if they did not find land within three days. But the land was real; this time it was not a mirage. Columbus's vision had been realized; just as he had predicted, he had crossed the ocean that no one thought possible and did so in thirty-three days, a feat that few sailors in small boats have surpassed. Instinctively he had chosen the route that, since then, sailors traversing the Atlantic continue to follow.

The crew were delirious with relief. After so many days cooped up in the tiny ships, they couldn't wait to go ashore. As the anchors were dropped, the men stood on the decks and gazed at the green island—a soothing sight after so long at sea with only gray-blue water and sky—and "saw naked people." Columbus summoned the Pinzón brothers (the captains of the other two ships), donned his armor, and went ashore in the launch, carrying the royal banner and two flags emblazoned with a green cross and the initials of Ferdinand and Isabella.

With unsteady steps after so many days at sea, they waded onto the beach, knelt to kiss the ground, and gave thanks to God for having brought them safely across the great water. Soon "a multitude of people . . . hastened to the shore, astounded and marveling at the sight of the ships."[2] A momentous encounter between two peoples neither known to nor imagined by the other was about to take place. Emotions were running high, each group wondering whether their meeting would be friendly or hostile. Although the natives were not clothed, the sailors must have been relieved to see that they were not the freakish monsters described by Pliny.

Soon, "in the presence of the many natives assembled there," Columbus named the island San Salvador, for their salvation. He called for the *escrivano* (scribe), and, as protocol dictated, he had him record as witness that "he took possession of it in the name of the Catholic Sovereigns with appropriate ceremony and words."[3] Taking possession of lands hitherto unknown or undiscovered was primarily a signal to other European nations to "keep off," a sign that whoever "took possession" first had the preeminent right to discover, explore, and establish trading posts; it did not automatically imply conquest or ownership.[4]

In the hope that he and his men would be received hospitably, Columbus's first impulse toward the native people was one of benevolence and friendship, motivated, not surprisingly, by a concern for their conversion to Christianity:

> I, in order that they would be friendly to us—because I recognized that they were a people who would be better freed [from error] and converted to our Holy Faith by love than by force—to some of them I gave red caps, and glass beads which they put on their chests, and many other things of small value, in which they took so much pleasure and became so much our friends that it was a marvel (*Diario*, p. 65).

The natives, too, were friendly and "came swimming to the ships' launches where we were and brought us parrots and cotton thread in balls and javelins and many other things, and they traded them to us" (*Diario*, p. 65). Columbus's description of the people, reflecting an almost anthropological attention to detail, comes across as open-minded and objective, writing what he saw with his own eyes:[5]

> All of them go around as naked as their mothers bore them. . . . They are very well formed, with handsome bodies and good faces. Their hair [is] coarse—almost like the tail of a horse—and short. They wear their hair down over their eyebrows except for a little in the back which they wear long and never cut (*Diario*, p. 67).

The natives must have been just as astonished to see such heavily dressed and bearded men as the latter were to see people "naked as their mothers bore them." The beards of the Europeans would have held a special curiosity since the natives had very little or no facial hair. Continuing his description, Columbus wrote that while they "are of the color of the Canarians, neither black nor white," they painted themselves with black or red or white paints. The very next day, October 13, he noted again that they are a "very handsome people with hair not curly but straight" (*Diario*, pp. 67, 69).[6] The skin color and straight hair of the natives confirmed for Columbus the truth of geographical theories of the day, which held that people living in similar climates or along the same latitudes would share similar racial features. "Nor should anything else be expected since this island is on an east-west line with the island of Hierro in the Canaries" (*Diario*, p. 69). He felt it was natural that the natives would be the same color as the people on the Canary Islands.

When the native people approached Columbus and his men, they raised their arms in greeting and by this gesture, Columbus surmised they were saying something like:

> "Come see the men who came from the heavens. Bring them something to eat and drink." Many men came, and many women, each one with something, giving thanks to God, throwing themselves on the ground; and they raised their hands to heaven, and afterward they called to us in loud voices to come ashore (*Diario*, p. 75).

The natives would have been hard-pressed not to be curious about these strange interlopers, but their gesture was, most likely, their normal form of greeting and indicated their customary sign of hospitality. These first encounters had gone well; there was a flurry of visiting back and forth. The natives seemed delighted to introduce these strangers to some of their ways. Columbus marveled not just at the innocent pleasures of the natives, but also at their technology. Many of the people

> came to the ship in their dugouts that are made from the trunk of one tree, like a long boat, and all of one piece, and worked marvelously in the fashion of the land, and so big that in some of them 40 and 45 men came. And others smaller, down to some in which came one man alone. They row with a paddle like that of a baker and go marvelously (*Diario*, p. 69).

Columbus was impressed with these vessels and the ease and speed with which the natives got around in them, for he goes on to say that "if it capsizes on them they then throw themselves in the water, and they right and empty it with calabashes that they carry" (*Diario*, pp. 69–71). No doubt he was feeling the weight and difficulty of maneuvering his own heavy, bulky ship, and longed for a light, fast little boat to explore the coastline. At first Columbus used a Portuguese word (*almadías*) to denote these vessels, but in a few days he was already using the native word *canoa*, which later entered English as *canoe*.

Despite his relief at having crossed the ocean and found land, Columbus was wondering exactly where they were. As we now know, they had come ashore in the Bahamas, on an island the natives called Guanahani. Scholars identify it as Watling Island, but most people know it by the name Columbus gave it, San Salvador.[7] Yet, having enticed the crew with stories from Marco Polo about the gold, jewels, and silks of the richly attired, sophisticated people in the realm of the Grand Khan of Cathay that they would meet on the other side of the ocean, Columbus must have been baffled by what he saw. His expectations were challenged, but if he was disappointed or perplexed by what he saw, he does not reveal it in his diary. To head off the disappointment of the men, Columbus told them that they must have landed on one of the many islands that Marco Polo had said lay off the Chinese coast. Surely, they would soon find the mainland or the large island of Cipango (Japan).

Columbus thought he had the answer to their location when some of the natives showed him marks of injury on their bodies and tried to explain with gestures how and where they had received them. Columbus interpreted their signs as indicating that "people from other islands nearby came . . . and tried to take them, and how they defended themselves; and I believed and believe that they come here from *tierra firme* to take them captive" (*Diario*, p. 67). He was already imagining that the mainland was near and that there were different, perhaps warring groups in the vicinity. Because the natives "do not carry arms nor are they acquainted with them" and "they say very quickly everything that is said to them," Columbus believed they would become "good and intelligent servants . . . and Christians" (*Diario*, pp. 67 and 69).[8]

Although he had just accomplished an extraordinary feat, Columbus could not relax. It was all too apparent that this tiny island was not the Asian mainland. He was getting restless; after spending only two days on San Salvador, Columbus wrote that "in order not to lose time I want to go to see if I can find the island of

Cipango." If he could find Cipango, then he would know that the mainland was not too far away. So on October 14, they weighed anchor and headed southwest in search of the island Marco Polo had said was laden with gold.

The quest for gold, and especially for the source of it, was relentless. No wonder people reading Columbus's diary conclude that greed was the primary motive behind his quest. But it would be wrong to equate the material goal with his personal motive. For Columbus, the search for the precious metal was less a commercial venture than a "spiritual quest," a medium not so much of exchange as a "medium of redemption."[9] In a letter to the Spanish sovereigns, Columbus later wrote:

> Gold is a metal most excellent above all others and of gold treasures are formed, and he who has it makes and accomplishes whatever he wishes in the world and finally uses it to send souls into Paradise.[10]

It is important to remember that as an agent for Ferdinand and Isabella, Columbus was driven to find gold in order to repay them, with profit, so they might continue to finance his future voyages. More important, he knew that if he didn't find gold, his grand plan to wrest Jerusalem from the Muslims would quickly come to an end.

When the fleet set sail from San Salvador, Columbus took several native men to serve as guides.[11] But since they didn't really know what he wanted or where he wanted to go, they simply gestured "onward, onward." As they sailed among other small islands, Columbus, like a new Adam, bestowed names in "a proper order." San Salvador had been named "in honor of God, who had first pointed it out to him and saved him from many dangers; the second island, Santa María de la Concepción, out of devotion to Our Lady and because she is the principal patroness of Christians";[12] and the next Fernandina, after the Spanish king, and Isabella, after the Queen. These last three islands are now identified as Rum Cay, Long Island, and Crooked Island in the Bahamas.

On their way to Fernandina, Columbus wrote: "These islands are very green and fertile and with sweet-smelling breezes" (*Diario*, p. 83). The abundance of tropical greenery and brilliantly colored flowers was exhilarating and soothing at the same time. For Columbus it was literally a "sight for sore eyes," because his eyes constantly pained him.[13] His first impressions give a hint of the therapeutic value of the beauty of the place:

> I also walked among those trees, which were more beautiful to see than any other thing that has ever been seen . . . I do not know where to go first; nor do my eyes grow tired of seeing such beautiful verdure and so different from ours . . . and the smell of the flowers or trees that came from the land was so good and soft that it was the sweetest thing in the world (*Diario*, pp. 93 and 101).

As they passed among these small islands, they came upon a man alone in his dugout. Columbus realized he had come from San Salvador because he had with him some of the glass beads the crew had just distributed there. He learned that this man was on his way to Fernandina.

> He came up to the ship and I had him enter, which was what he asked, and I had his dugout put in the ship and all that he brought watched over, and I ordered him given bread and honey and something to drink, and so I will transport him to Fernandina (*Diario*, p. 85).

Columbus confided that, by this kind gesture, he hoped the man would give a good report of them so that the foreigners would be well received in the future. After taking this man home, they sailed on.

At every island they passed, or harbor they explored, Columbus continued to marvel at the beauty. Curiously, he does not mention the extraordinary clarity and color of the water. One would think that after so many days crossing the ocean he would have been taken by the color of the tropical water—from the palest aqua to turquoise, teal, and deepest blue. But most of all he marveled at the flowers, the trees, and the animals. Near the island of Fernandina he commented:

> the fish are so different from ours that it is a marvel. There are some shaped like dories, of the finest colors in the world: blues, yellows, reds, and of all colors; and others colored in a thousand ways. And the colors are so fine that there is no man who would not marvel and take great delight in seeing them (*Diario*, p. 89).

A few days later, on another island, he can barely contain himself, and uses some form of the word *marvel* three times in one paragraph:

Here there are some big lakes and over and around them the groves are marvelous . . . And the singing of the small birds [is so marvelous] that it seems that a man would never want to leave this place . . . And [there are] flocks of parrots that obscure the sun; and the birds of so many kinds and sizes, and so different from ours that it is a marvel. And also there are trees of a thousand kinds and all [with] their own kinds of fruit and all smell so that it is a marvel (*Diario*, p. 105).

In addition to the beauty of the place, Columbus was impressed by the generosity, intelligence, and ingenuity of the people as displayed by their canoes and their houses. Like an anthropologist, Columbus used the strategy of making a foreign custom comprehensible by creating an analogy with something familiar. He compared native houses positively with Moorish campaign tents he had seen during the siege at Granada, saying the huts were "very high and with good smoke holes" (*Diario*, p. 93). But some things were incomparable. Men whom he had sent for water "told me how they had been in their houses and inside they were well swept and clean and their beds and furnishings were made of things like cotton nets" (*Diario*, p. 93). Soon he was using the native word *hamaca*, which eventually became the English word *hammock*. More than what we now think of as a piece of leisure equipment, this native invention "solved the shipboard sleeping problem for seamen of all nations,"[14] for the use of hammocks became customary on ships from that time until the present, surely one of the great gifts from the natives to the Europeans.

From the native men he had on board, Columbus and some crew members were beginning to learn a few words and the rudiments of their language, at least enough to tell the native people "not to be afraid" when they encountered them. In his optimistic way, Columbus thought that they were getting along marvelously. He realized that the natives were not speaking gibberish as, later, so many Europeans attributed to "primitive" peoples, and that it was important to learn their language. But six weeks into their explorations, he had to admit that his understanding of the language was woefully inadequate. He confessed:

I do not know the language, and the people of these lands do not understand me nor do I, nor anyone else that I have with me, them. And many times I understand one thing said by these Indians that I bring for another, its contrary; nor do I trust them much, because many times they have tried to flee. But now, pleasing Our Lord, I will see the most that I can and little by little I will progress in understanding and acquaintance, and I will have this tongue taught to persons of my household because I see that up to this point it is a single language (*Diario*, p. 183).

In order to better understand the native culture and to be able to communicate, Columbus planned to take six Indians back with him when he left for Spain so that they could learn Spanish; at the same time, this educational experience was to be reciprocal for he wanted members of his household to learn their language.[15]

Although Columbus realized that it would be impossible to understand a culture without knowing the language, somehow he imagined that he would be able to understand something of the natives' religious beliefs. In his diary, he wrote: "I do not detect in them any religion [*secta y creo*] and I believe that they would become good Christians very quickly because they are of very good understanding" (*Diario*, p. 89). When he used the word *secta*, Columbus did not mean "religion" as it has often been translated. (See discussion in introduction, page xi.) In Columbus's view, there was only one true faith, the Christian faith; *secta* indicated those like Jews and Muslims, who had false beliefs and practices. So when he wrote that the natives had no *secta y creo*, it was a positive evaluation of the natives, not a negative one as most scholars have claimed. Because they did not have a *secta*, they would not have to be weaned, like the Jews and Muslims, from their false beliefs and practices. Instead, because they were "of very good understanding," Columbus believed they could very easily be brought into the fold of the true faith.

There is no evidence of hostilities during these early encounters with the native people, only curiosity on both sides. After sailing among the islands in the Bahamas, the fleet set sail, on October 24, for the large island which has retained the name the natives called it—Cuba. If, as Columbus believed, this must be the Cipango described by Marco Polo and depicted on some of the maps he had seen, then the mainland was within reach. Before they had even reached Cuba, Columbus optimistically wrote: "I have already decided to go to the mainland and to the city of Quinsay and to give Your Highnesses' letters to the Grand Khan" (*Diario*, p. 109).

After several days' delay due to rain and lack of wind, Columbus finally reached Cuba on October 28, and renamed it Juana after the Spanish infante

Don Juan. He sent some men ashore, giving instructions as usual, that if the natives fled at their approach, the men must not touch or take anything from their houses. From the very beginning, Columbus notes how generously the natives shared whatever they had, and he did not want his crew to take advantage of them. He demanded that there be an *exchange*, for example, beads and bells for needed food supplies. It was unequal to be sure, but trade nonetheless. He continually recounts having to restrain his crew from looting villages when the residents fled at their approach. Throughout the diary he repeats: "I did not allow anything to be taken, not even the value of a pin" (*Diario*, p. 107).

When they went inside one of the houses on Cuba, the men found "many statues in the shape of women and many masklike heads very well made." Wondering about their possible religious significance, Columbus continued, "I do not know whether this is because they consider them beautiful or whether they worship them." They also reported that "[T]here were dogs that never barked; there were small tame wild birds around their houses; there was wonderful equipment of nets and hooks and contrivances for fishing . . . and the singing of the grasshoppers all night delighted everyone" (*Diario*, pp. 121–122).

Trying to find out more about the people they were encountering, Columbus thought that some of the natives on board told him about a people who lived in a faraway place called Bohío where, he understood, "there were one-eyed men, and others, with snouts of dogs, who ate men, and that as soon as one was taken they cut his throat and drank his blood and cut off his genitals" (*Diario*, p. 133). In his marginal notes Columbus said these were "*Caribes*" and decided they were probably a warlike group and enemies of the people with whom he had made contact.[16] Rather than man-eaters, these *Caribes* were probably marauders who came with their ships and weapons and captured some of the men from this island. When they didn't return home, their friends and relatives assumed they had been eaten (*Diario*, p. 167). More likely, they had been killed or enslaved, for people in the Caribbean had been enslaving each other before Columbus arrived.

Columbus also thought he understood from one of the natives "that large ships from the Grand Khan came there and that from there to *tierra firme* was a journey of ten days" (*Diario*, p. 119). But there were conflicting reports. Martín Alonso Pinzón told him that he had come to understand "that Cuba was a city and that that land was a very big landmass that went far to the north, and that the king of that land was at war with the Grand Khan" (*Diario*, p. 125). From this report, Columbus concluded that the Grand Khan was not far away, and on November 1 he believed he was "off Zayto and Quinsay a hundred leagues more or less."

The next day, November 2, Columbus decided to send Rodrigo de Xerez and Luis de Torres, the interpreter, with instructions to

> inquire about the king of that land . . . in order to learn of his circum-
> stances and to obtain his friendship, and to favor him in whatever
> he might need from them, etc . . . And with these men he sent two
> Indians . . . gave them strings of beads to buy food if they needed to and
> six days limit in which to return (*Diario*, p. 129).

As he waited for their return, Columbus tried to ascertain his location; first he "took the altitude [of the Pole Star] with a quadrant and found he was 42 degrees from the equinoctial line" and with his calculations "found he had gone 1,142 leagues from the island of Hierro" (*Diario*, p. 131) in the Canaries. With this information, he changed his mind about Cuba, and decided it was not the island of Cipango, but the mainland itself. This was not necessarily good news—although he thought he was not too far from the realm of the Grand Khan, he was becoming increasingly nervous that he had found so little of the gold on which he had staked the voyage. When some of the natives told him about an island to the southeast where "there was a vast amount [of gold] and that the people wore it on [the] neck and in ears and on arms and legs, also pearls" (*Diario*, p. 133), he decided they would go there next unless the men he sent inland brought news of gold and the big city.

At the same time that his head was filled with those grandiose hopes, Columbus turned his attention to earthier concerns. During the wait for the men to return, he made some notes about native foodstuffs: "These lands are very fertile; the Indians have them full of *mames*, which are like carrots and have the taste of chestnuts" (*Diario*, p. 133). He was probably describing cassava. Later he even described their method of growing it. It is

> some little twigs that they plant, and at the foot of the twigs some roots
> like carrots grow, which serve as bread; and they scrape and knead and
> make bread of them. And later they plant the same twig elsewhere and it

again produces four or five of those roots which are very tasty, have the same flavor as chestnuts (*Diario*, p. 233).

Columbus liked their bread (cassava bread) better than his own hardtack and decided to load up on it for the return voyage to Spain.

When the men returned from their explorations inland, they reported that they had found only one settlement with fifty houses and perhaps a thousand inhabitants, who treated them well, but they saw no gold and had no information about a large city, or the Grand Khan. Columbus was undaunted; he believed he would eventually find the Grand Khan and together they would set up a brisk trade. His men had brought a sample of what appeared to be mastic, the valuable product he had seen in Chios, and thought there was enough in that region "to take out a thousand *quintals* each year" (*Diario*, p. 135). He also thought he recognized aloe and had seen plenty of cotton. Of the latter he wrote, optimistically: "I think that it would sell very well here without taking it to Spain, but to the big cities belonging to the Grand Khan, which doubtless will be discovered, and to many other cities belonging to other lords" (*Diario*, p. 145). The men who had gone inland also related an interesting sight that had caught their eye.

[T]wo Christians found along the way many people going back and forth between their villages, men and women with a firebrand of weeds in their hands to take in the fragrant smoke to which they are accustomed (*Diario*, p. 139).

Columbus's account is the first report of Europeans' encounter with the stimulating weed known as tobacco—a weed that would sweep across the world and ultimately prove more profitable than gold. Although he had been given a gift of some dried leaves when he first landed on San Salvador, he didn't know their use and tossed them out. The man he had picked up on his way to Fernandina told Columbus that the leaves were highly valued for their fragrance and healthful qualities. But Rodrigo de Xerez and Luis de Torres explained its use: they said that the natives inhaled the smoke through fork-shaped tubes inserted into each nostril and that sometimes they "became benumbed and almost drunk, and so it is said that they do not feel fatigue." [17]

Rodrigo, apparently, became the first European smoker and introduced the practice to his countrymen when he returned to Spain. However, when they saw smoke coming out of his nose and mouth they thought he had been taken over by the devil and they brought him before the Inquisition. He spent a number of years in jail and when he was released he saw that his fellow Spaniards had taken up the habit. Tobacco plants became the fashion in Europe and were appreciated for their aesthetic and medicinal qualities; the leaves were said to heal sores and skin ulcers and even cure headaches when held against the forehead. The practice of smoking quickly spread throughout Europe and by the mid-sixteenth century Europeans were growing tobacco.

Columbus's overall impression of Cuba was so favorable that eventually, he wrote, "the whole of Christendom will do business in these lands," and that their "Highnesses ought not to consent that any foreigner set foot or trade here except Catholic Christians" (*Diario*, p. 185). One of the original ideas for the voyage was to set up a trading post, presumably with the Grand Khan, to exchange European goods for gold and spices that would both reimburse the sovereigns and other investors in the voyage and finance the crusade to Jerusalem. Since Columbus had found neither the Grand Khan nor any gold, he might have been trying to alleviate their doubts about whether there was enough potential profit to continue with the enterprise.

On November 12, they left Cuba to explore other nearby islands where, according to the natives on board, the people "collected gold at night on the beach with lanterns, and afterward, with a hammer . . . they would make bars of it" (*Diario*, p. 143). Since these islands were closer than the realm of the Grand Khan, Columbus decided to explore them first. The fleet spent several weeks wandering about in search of the gold. While Columbus needed to find gold, both for the sovereigns and for his big plan, he was also delighted with all the discoveries they were making—about the many verdant islands and the resources they yielded and about the numerous friendly natives and their culture. Others in his expedition, however, were becoming impatient and anxious to discover the gold that had been promised. On November 21, Martín Alonso Pinzón "because of greed and without the permission and will of the Admiral, departed with the caravel *Pinta*, . . . in order to go to the island of Baneque where the Indians say there is much gold" (*Diario*, p. 165). That night, Columbus put a lantern out so that Pinzón could find his way back to him for "the night was very clear and the light wind good for coming to him if he were so to wish" (*Diario*, p. 167). Apparently, Pinzón did not so wish. Columbus would not see him again for more than six weeks.

The weather had turned foul and the winds so contrary that he could not continue west; Columbus had to abandon his search for the Grand Khan, at least for the time being. Instead, he and Martín Pinzón's brother, Vincente Yáñez, headed east, still along the north coast of Cuba, where Columbus noted that there were so many islands that he believed they were the "innumerable ones that in the maps of the world are put at the eastern end." Columbus believed he was at the point that, depending from which direction one came, was both the beginning and the ending of the Orient. He called the place Cabo Alpha and Omega, an allusion, perhaps, to the passage in the book of Revelation (Rev. 1:8) where Jesus said: "I am Alpha and Omega, the beginning and the ending."

From that easternmost cape of Cuba, Columbus decided to cross the Windward Passage to the western cape of what the natives called Hayti (now Haiti). But bad weather prevented them from making much progress. While the ships crept along the eastern coast of Cuba, the natives again told Columbus about a cape or an island called Bohío where "there were people on it who had one eye in their foreheads, and others whom they called cannibals [canibales], of whom they showed great fear" (Diario, p. 167). Columbus thought it was merely another version of carib, caniba, or canima, but he also understood that the natives on board were afraid because these canibales were well armed and were said to eat people. They became mute with fear when Columbus sailed in that direction.[18] Columbus wrote in his diary that the locals apparently "believed the same about the Christians and about the Admiral when some Indians[19] first saw some of them" (Diario, p. 167).

The crew was more gullible than Columbus and tended to believe tales about strange animals, monsters, and cannibals rumored to inhabit the unexplored parts of the world. Perhaps they thought they were soon to meet up with the Cynocephali, the dog-headed people described by Pliny. Sometime later, when "two men showed the Spaniards that some pieces of flesh were missing from their bodies, and they gave the Spaniards to understand that the cannibals had eaten them by mouthfuls," Columbus "did not believe it" (Diario, p. 237). Columbus had extrapolated from what the locals told him that they believed the people of Bohío had faces like dogs; maybe it was really the dogs who had bitten the men and torn their flesh. Yet no one seems to have thought of that.

There were many incidents that could have incited terror had Columbus not had such a pragmatic view of the natives' customs. When some of his men "found in a house a man's head inside a basket covered with another small basket and hung on a post of the house," Columbus did not think "cannibalism." Instead, he thought that the heads "must be those of important persons of the family . . . probably relatives, descendants of one man only" (*Diario*, p. 189), that is, a practice that included some kind of veneration and notions of kinship.[20]

Columbus's skepticism can be taken as a sign of his equanimity, calmness, and trust when confronting persons and cultures so different from his own. Anthropologist Margaret Hodgen notes that the

> more significant of his [Columbus's] contributions to the history of ethnological ideas were his realistic, down-to-earth judgments of the Caribs and their culture. These, if the anthropology of Herodotus be excepted, were almost unique departures in ethnological attitude and method of inquiry . . . [He] approached ethnological phenomena with an amount of tolerance and critical detachment unusual in his day—and possibly also in ours.[21]

Despite the fearful stories and the bad weather, Columbus continued to extol the beauty of the places he saw. Going into a secluded harbor, he wrote, again, that it was so beautiful "that one might not wish to leave that place," and told his men that "the things they were seeing, a thousand tongues would not suffice to tell it or his hand to write it; for it seemed to him enchanted" (*Diario*, p. 183).

On the night of December 5, Columbus and his men made a dash southeast for Haiti (Hayti) and searched for a safe harbor. "At the hour of vespers, they entered the said harbor and he named it Puerto de San Nicolás in honor of Saint Nicolas, whose day it was" (*Diario*, p. 203).

They had reached the island of Haiti, which Columbus renamed Hispaniola, and though it is considerably south of the latitude of Castile, the December weather was wintry. They encountered torrential rain and strong winds and made very little progress. But wherever they went many Indians came out to see them. At one stop, Columbus asked his men to try to grab some of them "in order to treat them courteously and make them lose their fear." It seems an odd way to make the natives less afraid. They caught only a young woman who "was wearing a little piece of gold in her nose, which was a sign that there was gold on that island" (*Diario*, p. 221). She came aboard, was well treated, given gifts, and returned ceremoniously to her village, where she told her group not to fear the strange men. The next day, many Indians, including the woman and her husband, came to the ships. In gratitude to Columbus for the courtesy he had shown, and the gifts he had given, they brought food and parrots. Columbus was particularly fond of parrots because they had a special place in the Christianity of the time—in Eden, all animals except parrots had lost the faculty of speech due to original sin. Because of parrots' ability to speak and their longevity, they were considered closer to humans.[22] Columbus hoped to take several back to Spain and was delighted with the gift.

Every native group invited the men to feast and wanted them to stay, but Columbus pushed on. On December 16, when some of the natives came aboard, Columbus

> ordered that they should be treated courteously because they are the best and most gentle people in the world, and especially, because I have much hope in Our Lord that Your Highnesses will make all of them Christians and that they will all be your subjects, for I consider them yours already (*Diario*, p. 231).

Columbus envisioned the Spanish sovereigns as both the lords and protectors of these people who felt threatened by those of the Grand Khan. But, because of their guilelessness and malleability, he also suggested that they could be put to work.

They had seen a few small pieces of gold and they were excited and hopeful; perhaps soon they would find their source. On occasion, Columbus sent some of his men inland to explore an area, but he was becoming more and more annoyed with his crew because of their greed and disorderly conduct, and compared them unfavorably with the dignity and generosity of the natives. Meanwhile, news of their arrival traveled fast along the coast. Columbus received an invitation from Guacanagarí, the cacique (chief) of another area farther along. Moved by Guacanagarí's sense of decorum, Columbus accepted.

On December 24, Columbus raised the anchor and moved out of the harbor where they had been staying. The sailing was exceedingly difficult, and they had to navigate waters filled with reefs and shoals. Columbus recorded directions in his diary about how to maneuver through them, as if he was writing to some future sailor or possibly for his own future reference. As it was late when they arrived near Guacanagarí's village, Columbus decided the ships should anchor outside the harbor and wait for daybreak to enter. By eleven o'clock that night, he was so exhausted "because there had been two days and a night when he had not slept" (*Diario*, p. 277) that he went to bed.

On that starry Christmas Eve, 1492, the sailor keeping watch aboard the *Santa María*, seeing that the night was clear and the sea was "as smooth as water in a bowl," left the tiller in the hands of a ship's boy, which Columbus had always forbidden, and went off to get some sleep. Before dawn, "the currents of water carried the ship upon one of those banks . . . and the ship went upon it so gently that it was hardly felt" (*Diario*, p. 277). Except by Columbus.

In an instant, he knew his flagship had run aground. He jumped up and roused the crew, for they would have to work fast to dislodge the ship or it would become too deeply embedded in the sand to ever free it. He immediately ordered the men to throw the anchor astern so that they might be able to pull the ship out of the sand. But the crew panicked. They hadn't seen their sister ship the *Pinta* for more than a month, not since Martín Alonso Pinzón, its captain, had set off in the direction of Baneque in the hope of finding gold. If the *Santa María* was wrecked, the crew's only hope for passage back to Spain was the small *Niña*, which was anchored nearby. In desperation, they jumped into the launch and rowed over to the *Niña*, where they begged to be taken aboard. But the captain refused, sending the men back to Columbus.

With the tide ebbing, the *Santa María* was becoming more and more lodged in the sand and was already listing to one side. Columbus and the crew frantically tried to lighten the ship's load and even cut down its mast, but to no avail. Soon the pressure of contact with the sea floor forced the planks of the ship's hull to separate and water rushed in. The *Santa María* would never sail again.

When Guacanagarí heard about the grounding of the *Santa María*, according to Columbus's description in his diary:

> he cried and sent all his people from the town with many large canoes to unload everything from the ship. And thus it was done and in a very brief time everything from the decks was unloaded . . . without a crumb of bread or any other thing at all being taken . . . [He also ordered] it put all together near some houses that he wished to provide, which were being emptied, where everything might be put and kept. He placed armed men around everything and ordered that they keep watch all night (*Diario*, pp. 281–283).

Additionally, Guacanagarí offered two very large houses for Columbus's crew, and said that he would provide them with more if necessary.

That night, in gratitude for his hospitality, Columbus invited Guacanagarí to join him for dinner on the *Niña*, but the chief revealed that he had already ordered a feast. Wearing a shirt and gloves that Columbus had given him, Guacanagarí led Columbus ashore where more than a thousand naked people greeted him. Of Guacanagarí, Columbus wrote: "In his table manners, his urbanity, and his attractive cleanliness, he quite showed himself to be of noble lineage" (*Diario*, p. 285). The chief presented him with a few pieces of gold and told him that there was much more in a place called Cybao, which Columbus assumed was their term for Cipango. Columbus was extremely grateful to Guacanagarí for his help and generosity, but he also seemed genuinely fond of him. "All through the Log," Robert H. Fuson, another translator of the diary, commented:

> Columbus expresses nothing but love and admiration for the Indians. His affection for the young chief in Haiti [Guacanagarí], and vice versa, is one of the most touching stories of love, trust, and understanding between men of different races and cultures to come out of this period in history.[23]

Columbus had equally effusive praise for all the islanders, writing glowingly, "I believe that in the world there are no better people or a better land. They love their neighbors as themselves, and they have the sweetest speech in the world and [they are] gentle and always laughing" (*Diario*, p. 281). Already, they seemed to be natural Christians, so no wonder Columbus thought they would be easily converted.

While once his men had desperately feared they would not be able to return to Spain, they now began to haggle over who would be fortunate enough to stay on the island while Columbus and the rest of the crew would attempt to return to Spain on the tiny *Niña*. Ultimately, thirty-nine or forty-two men were left on the island, depending on whether the three overseers mentioned by Columbus—Diego de Harana, the cousin of Beatriz, Columbus's mistress; Pedro Gutiérrez, the man who confirmed Columbus's sighting of the light just before landfall; and Rodrigo Escobedo, the *escrivano*—were among the thirty-nine or in addition to them (*Diario*, pp. 301–302).[24] Luis de Torres, the interpreter, would also remain.

His flagship grounded on the far side of the world and a perilous winter voyage looming, Columbus might well have been distressed. Instead, he wrote in his diary that "the anguish and sorrow that he had received and felt because of the loss of the ship were tempered" by the kindness of Guacanagarí (*Diario*, p. 287). He retreated to the *Santa María*'s listing deck, where, calm like the Caribbean night, he wrote one of the longest of all his diary entries from the voyage. As a man of profound faith, he wrote that the grounding was "not a disaster, but great luck . . . If I had not gone aground I would have passed at a distance without anchoring in this place . . . [and] would not have been able to learn about the country . . . nor on this voyage would I have left people here" (*Diario*, pp. 287 and 291). Believing that the shipwreck, on Christmas Day, was a sign from God that his mission was ordained, Columbus christened the nascent settlement Navidad in recognition of its birth from the body of the *Santa María*.[25]

Map of La Española, allegedly drawn by Columbus himself.
Courtesy of Biblioteca del Palacio de Liria, Madrid.

Not only was Columbus confident that Guacanagarí would treat his men well, he was also confident that the enterprise would eventually fulfill his dreams. He had crossed the ocean, which few thought possible; he had seen gold but had not yet found the source; he felt he knew the whereabouts of the Grand Khan even though, for the moment, he could not continue the search. Confident about the site's prospects and the journey ahead, he wrote in his diary, addressing the sovereigns, that when he returned to Navidad to rescue his men, he would find a barrel of gold that those who were left behind would have acquired by exchange; and that they would have found the gold mine and the spicery, and those things in such quantity that the sovereigns, before three years [are over], will *undertake and prepare to go conquer the Holy Sepulchre; for thus I urged Your Highnesses to spend all the profits of this my enterprise on the conquest of Jerusalem* (*Diario*, p. 291, my emphasis).

And he reminded the sovereigns that they had agreed and had said "that even without this profit they had that desire" (*Diario*, p. 291). For the moment, however, Columbus had to begin preparations for departure; there was to be no more exploring, for with only the tiny *Niña* at his disposal, he had to return to Spain as quickly as possible to get reinforcements for the tiny settlement and to rescue those who wanted to go home. He gathered all his men together and told them that after he left for Spain, those remaining should strip the *Santa María* of its planks and nails and use them to construct a fort.

Columbus named Diego de Harana as captain in his stead and gave explicit instructions about how the men should conduct themselves. Columbus ordered them to do no harm to the Indians and to respect chief Guacanagarí, to whom they owed so much. He also decreed that the men were "not to scatter themselves or enter inland" but to stay together; and especially to

avoid doing injury or using violence to the women, by which they would cause scandal and set a bad example . . . rather they should strive and watch by their soft and honest speech, to gain their good-will, keeping their friendship and love, so that he should find them as friendly and favourable and more so when he returned.[26]

The next few days, while Columbus was preparing to leave, the chief presented him with several large worked pieces of gold, including a mask. For a farewell party, Guacanagarí built a dais for Columbus, invited five minor chiefs to attend, and in the presence of all, took off his crown and placed it on Columbus's head. In exchange, Columbus "took from his own neck a collar of fine agates and handsome beads of beautiful colors" and gave it to Guacanagarí. In addition, he gave him the red cape he had been wearing, "some colored, high-laced shoes" and "a large silver ring," all of which gave the chief much pleasure (*Diario*, pp. 293, 295). During the feast "an Indian came, saying that two days before he had left the caravel *Pinta* in a harbor to the east" (*Diario*, p. 297). So, it seemed that Pinzón would rejoin Columbus for the voyage back to Spain.

It was time to leave Hispaniola. The *Santa María* was no more: its remains would be recycled in the buildings of the tiny settlement at Navidad. For the men who would remain, Columbus left trinkets to be used to barter for food and gold. He

> also left them biscuit for a year, and wine, and much artillery, and the ship's launch . . . [and] seeds to sow and his officials, the *escrivano* and the bailiff, and among them a ship's carpenter and a caulker and a good lombardier who knew about machinery, and a barrel maker and a physician and a tailor (*Diario*, p. 303).

Two days prior to departure, Columbus had his men feign a skirmish and fire a lombard (a kind of cannon) "telling the cacique not to fear the Caribs even if they were to come" (*Diario*, p. 301). Of course, this display of arms also functioned to make Guacanagarí wary of attacking Columbus's men.

On January 4, 1493, with everything riding on (and in) the *Niña*, Columbus said a sad goodbye to his new friend Guacanagarí and raised the *Niña*'s anchor to begin the voyage home. He took six Indians aboard on the return voyage to Spain, and he says that even more wanted to go.[27] He took them primarily so that they might learn the language and customs, and be instructed in the faith of the Spaniards, so that they might serve as cultural translators upon return. Columbus also needed them as evidence that he really had found a route across the ocean.[28]

Before leaving, Columbus gave a letter to Rodrigo Escobedo charging him to administer justice and to watch over a chest filled with some gifts Guacanagarí had given him. The letter was signed with a mysterious sigil that Columbus must have designed during the voyage. The letter to Escobedo is the first example of it, but henceforth this was the way Columbus signed all his letters and other documents. Later, when he was permitted to make a *majorat*, he instructed his heir, Diego, and those after him to sign in this fashion. The sigil resembles a ship in full sail, and consists of three rows of letters in the shape of a triangle:

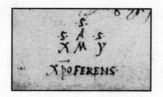

Columbus's signature.

The meaning of the last line is clear. Xpo-ferens is a combination of Greek and Latin words meaning "Christ-bearer." Columbus must have believed he had made good on his identification with his namesake, St. Christopher. Though during the voyage Columbus must have given much thought to the letters and their arrangement, to this day they remain undeciphered, despite the efforts of many people through the ages. One interpretation is that the initials stand for: SERVUS at the top; then SUM ALTISIMI SALVATORIS on the second line and XRISTE MARIA YESU on the third, all of which translates as: "I am the servant of the Most High Savior, O Christ, Mary, Joseph." Another interpretation is: SERVIDOR; SUS ALTEZAS SACRAS; CHRISTO MARIA YSABEL, that is: "The humble servant of their most Sacred Majesties, Christ, Mary, and Isabella." [29]

Since there are three lines and seven letters, one might also imagine he was referring not only to the Trinity, as a few scholars have proposed, but also to the three ages prophesied by Joachim, and the seven millennia of the world's duration. In addition, the S at the apex may be SANCTUS (Holy), the second line representing the age of the patriarchs with the initial S for SPIRITUS referring to the Spirit that visited Sarah, the A for Abraham and S for Sarah. The third line representing the age of the church beginning with Christ, Mary, and Joseph or possibly John the Baptist, and, finally, the Christ-bearer who would initiate the third age before the end. [30]

Columbus began to sail east along the north coast of Hispaniola, trying all the while to keep free of the many reefs and shoals. In the distance he saw an island that he thought must be Cipango, but he could not, now, go discover it; he needed to get to Spain as quickly as possible in order to send a relief ship back to his men stranded at Navidad. On January 6, while he was still just off the coast of Hispaniola, Martín Alonzo Pinzón showed up, having been gone for more than six weeks. Pinzón pretended he had gone off course, yet according to one of the natives on board the *Pinta*, he had purposely gone to the island of Baneque, where he had heard there was much gold. Apparently they found none and so returned to Hispaniola empty-handed. Columbus confessed "that he did not know whence had come the arrogant behavior and dishonesty with which Martín Alonso treated him on the voyage," but he concealed his feelings "so as to give a good ending to his voyage" (*Diario*, p. 313). When Columbus learned that Pinzón had taken "four Indian men and two young girls by force," he became angry because he viewed these people as subjects of the sovereigns and, thus, they "should be honored and favored." Columbus "ordered that they be given clothes and returned to their land, and they went away to their houses" (*Diario*, p. 323).[31]

On January 13, while still sailing east along the coast, Columbus came across a group of natives whose language and customs were quite different from those with whom he was familiar. He said "their speech matched their appearance, which was fiercer than that of any other Indians they had seen . . . [and] they wore their hair long and gathered behind the head into nets of parrot's feathers."[32]

The differences in language, bodily ornamentation, and hair styles indicated to Columbus that he was entering what twentieth-century anthropologists would call a different cultural area. One scholar believes that

[t]he most advanced concept [Columbus] offered was that of a cultural region, unified by language and customs. As he approached the eastern part of what is now the Dominican Republic, he became increasingly aware of the Caribs, of whom he had heard reports. And as the language began to shift, he attributed this to distance from the cultural hearth.[33]

Columbus assumed they had met the fierce, supposedly man-eating Caribs that the natives on board had been telling him about. The Caribs came out armed with bows and arrows that Columbus said were "made of yew and are as large as English and French bows," and he wanted to take a few samples back with him to Castile. He sent some men in the launch to barter for them using their usual truck of glass beads and hawks bells. They were able to obtain two bows and some arrows, but unlike the Indians with whom they were famil-iar, these were reluctant to continue to trade; instead, they began making signs to attack the Spaniards. Seeing what was happening, the Spaniards who were ashore attacked the Caribs with their swords and crossbows in the first skirmish of the entire voyage, wounding a couple of the Indians. Columbus called the place Golfo de las Flechas (Gulf of Arrows), now Samana, Dominican Republic. He "hoped that when the [other] islanders learned what seven Spaniards had done against fifty-five ferocious Indians, they would feel more respect for the men left behind in the town of Navidad and would not dare annoy them." [34]

During their brief stop at the Gulf of Arrows, Columbus heard stories about Matinino, an island supposedly populated only with women—women who, it was said, at a specific season entertained men, then cast them off again, keeping any girl children who resulted from their unions and sending the boys back with the men. It was one more confirmation that he had reached the East, for he had read in Marco Polo of the islands Masculina and Feminea, one inhabited by men, the other only by women. But he could not spare the time for more exploring.

By January 16, Columbus set sail for Spain. The voyage home would be much longer than the outbound one into the unknown. By February 14, Martín Pinzón and the *Pinta* were again nowhere in sight. Having experienced some of Pinzón's treachery, Columbus may have thought that he had gone ahead to claim the glory of the discovery for himself or, perhaps, due to the storm and bad shape of the *Pinta*, it had sunk. Despite several days spent searching for him, Columbus did not see Pinzón or the ship again.

His own ship was fraught with problems. The boat had been leaking even before they arrived at the Golfo de las Flechas, for which Columbus blamed the caulkers back in Palos for scrimping on the work. But he did not want to stay to make repairs among the hostile natives. So he prayed to God, "who brought him [to the Indies], to return him" (*Diario*, p. 337). From his earlier trips to northern Europe, Columbus had felt the pull of the east-flowing currents and the winds that would take them back to Spain; he may even have felt the northern current on his outward journey just before landfall, that made it necessary for him to turn south. He knew he had to go north even though it was getting quite cold. Although he intuitively chose the "right" route heading toward home, the weather was stormy, and the seas treacherous.

> The storm was raging so badly they could hardly keep the ship upright, because of a lack of ballast, so much of her provisions having been consumed. To make up for this lack they filled all the empty water casks with seawater which helped some because it made the ship more stable and thus lessened the danger of capsizing. [35]

The task of trying to fill the casks with seawater during a storm must have been extremely dangerous, with the distinct possibility of falling overboard. The crew also had to lower the mainsail for fear it would be ripped to shreds and taken by one of the huge waves; thus, they were sailing with bare poles and would be at the mercy of the waves since without sails it is much more difficult to keep to a course.

In his diary, Columbus confided that he was less concerned about his own life than about those of "the people I had brought with me . . . [and] my grief was redoubled when I remembered my two sons at school in Córdoba, left friendless in a strange country, before I had done or at least made known to Your Highnesses some service that might dispose you to remember them." [36]

At the time of that entry, they had not yet reached the Azores. Columbus was desperate, his thoughts in a whirl; if the *Niña* didn't make it, no one would ever know they had actually crossed the Ocean Sea and found land and people on the other side. No one would know of their days of wonder. No one would see the evidence—the Indians on board, the gold, the samples of flora and fauna, and his descriptions so carefully written in the *Diario*. Nor would they learn about the fate of the *Santa María* and about the men left behind. Columbus and the men prayed fervently, and if they were saved, they vowed to make pilgrimages when, and if, they got home. At the height of the storm when their survival seemed unlikely, Columbus wrote the proverbial "note in a bottle" (actually a letter sealed in a wine cask), in which he described all they had seen and done, and threw it overboard. Neither that letter nor a copy has ever been found.

When the tiny *Niña* limped into a harbor at the Azores on February 18, 1493, the residents were astonished. They could not believe the tiny ship had survived such a storm. Columbus had promised the crew that they could make a pilgrimage to a shrine of the Virgin in gratitude for their safe deliverance, but because they were in Portuguese territory, he was wary and decided to let only half of the men go at one time, telling the others they could go when the first group returned. But the first group was captured and held for ransom by the Portuguese, who thought Columbus had illegally entered "their" waters—that is, the coast of Africa. One of their leaders came out to the ship and demanded to know where they had been and whether they had "a commission from the King of Castile." Columbus was affronted but once again "concealed his resentment." [37] After he showed them the Spanish documents authorizing the voyage, his men were released. Eager to be gone from this place, he did not let the remaining men make the pilgrimage. They were still about one thousand miles from the Spanish coast.

En route they encountered another storm or, perhaps, the continuation of the one they had just come through. "On March 3rd there arose so terrible a tempest that after midnight it split their sails . . . [so that] driving on under bare poles in a terrible sea with high wind and dreadful thunder and lightning"[38] made it seem that this time they would certainly go down. Columbus feared that the first letter he had thrown overboard might never reach its destination. As the ship was "drawing closer to Castile, I placed a similar cask at the head of the stern, so that if the ship sank, it might float on the waves at the mercy of the storm."[39] A copy of a letter dated March 4, 1493, surfaced in 1985. It was not pulled from the sea, but was found in a private collection; it is thought to be a copy of the one attached to the stern.[40] Most likely it contained much of the same information as the one thrown overboard. Addressed to the sovereigns, Columbus recounted his discoveries and described the people he met, and the flora and fauna he saw. Furthermore, he made two personal requests. First, considering the fate of his sons if he did not return, he asked that a "cardinalate" be provided for his son Diego, "for there is little difference in his age and that of the son of the Medicis of Florence, to whom a cardinal's hat was granted." Second, in a more optimistic mood hoping that he, or someone else, would return to the Indies, he asked that Pedro de Villacorta, one of his crew members, be made "paymaster of the Indies, for I vouch that he will do it well."[41]

Finally, he concluded:

> that through the divine grace of Him Who is the fount of every victory and every good thing and Who grants favors and victory to all who follow His Way, within seven years I shall give Your Highnesses enough money to pay for 5,000 knights and 50,000 foot soldiers for the conquest of Jerusalem— the ultimate goal behind your decision to undertake this enterprise.[42]

Between the diary entry on Christmas Day, 1492, and this letter of March 4, 1493, Columbus must have realized he would need more than three years in which to obtain enough gold from the newly discovered lands to launch the crusade for the conquest of Jerusalem. The more reasonable estimate of seven years was balanced by the specific, and no doubt inflated, claim regarding the number of men he would provide for that project. He urged their Highnesses not to delay in the project of Jerusalem as they had in launching his voyage.

Miraculously, the *Niña*, the crew, and the Indians made it to the European coast, but instead of Castile, they found themselves off Portugal. Columbus managed to pull into Lisbon's waters, and wrote to King João asking permission to anchor. Immediately, the master of a Portuguese ship came over to demand that Columbus give a report to the king's administrators. The master turned out to be none other than Bartolomeu Dias, the very man whose rounding the Cape of Good Hope in 1488 cost Columbus King João's support for his own project. Columbus refused to comply with Dias's request and said:

> that he was Admiral of the sovereigns of Castile and that he would not give such an account to such persons nor would he leave the ships . . . [and that he would send] neither the master nor anybody else if it were not by force, because he considered giving up someone else to be the same thing as going himself, and that it was the custom of the Admirals of the sovereigns of Castile to die before they gave up themselves or their people (*Diario*, p. 393).

Conflict was avoided when Columbus showed Dias the documents from the Spanish sovereigns that authorized his voyage west.

> When the Portuguese heard that Columbus had come from the Indies so many people came from the city of Lisbon to see him and to see the Indians that it was astounding; and they all marveled, giving thanks to Our Lord and saying that it was because of the great faith that the sovereigns of Castile had and their desire to serve God that his High Majesty gave them all this (*Diario*, p. 395).

A few days later, Columbus received a letter from the king inviting him to come and tell him about his travels. Columbus was wary, but he could not so easily refuse a royal invitation. In the letter, João greeted him cordially but intimated that he believed Columbus had entered the waters around Guinea (Africa), which were under Portuguese control, and thus had violated the Treaty of Alcáçovas. Pleasantries must have been exchanged, but João soon declared that the gold and other goods Columbus had in his possession rightfully belonged to Portugal, but he added that he would negotiate directly with the Spanish sovereigns. Columbus refused João's offer to send him overland to Spain, fearing, with good reason, that he would be captured and killed by João's agents. Instead, he took the opportunity to send a letter overland to the Spanish sovereigns to inform them of his safe arrival and asked them to send their response to him in Seville. He, as captain, would remain with his crew and sail back to the place from which they had set out.

CHAPTER SIX

TRIUMPH AND DISASTER

At midday on the Ides of March, 1493, seven months and eleven days after his departure from Palos, Columbus and the tiny *Niña* entered the harbor as quietly as they had left. People on the quay could not believe their eyes. Quickly they gathered round to see if it was really Columbus and to learn who was with him. News spread rapidly around town that one of the ships and some of the men had returned from the Indies. People ran to the harbor, incredulous. Columbus and many of the townspeople made a procession to the church to give thanks for their safe return. Those who had relatives on board joyfully embraced, while others received the more sobering news that their husbands or sons, fathers or uncles had remained at Navidad and that the fate of the *Pinta* was, as yet, unknown.[1]

Later, Columbus would learn that Pinzón had landed near Vigo in Galicia, a province in northern Spain, sometime in February. He had written to Queen Isabella and King Ferdinand with the intention of going directly to Barcelona to inform them of the voyage and discoveries and, thus, gain the glory and the honor for himself, but the sovereigns responded that he must not come alone but only in the company of Columbus. This "snub caused Pinzón such chagrin and annoyance that he went home to Palos a sick man, and a few days after his arrival died of grief."[2] Sometime on March 15, Columbus made a final entry in his diary. He thanked God for the miracles He had performed for him, but he couldn't resist a barb at those who

> were all against me, alleging my enterprise to be ridiculous. I hope in Our Lord that it will be the greatest honor to Christianity that, unexpectedly, has ever come about (*Diario*, p. 403).[3]

That first night back in Spain Columbus either walked or was carried by an exultant mob up to the monastery of La Rábida, accompanied by the six Indians he had brought. There he spent several days recuperating from the difficult journey and described to the astonished Friar Juan Pérez the marvels he had seen and the trials overcome. But after such an accomplishment, Columbus could not be sequestered for long, as the news of his miraculous deed "spread over Castile like fire." And truth be told, he was eager to hear from the sovereigns. Soon he set off for Seville to await their summons. All along the road people from the surrounding countryside flocked see him and the exotic, nearly naked men carrying "beautiful green parrots, *guayças* or masks made of precious stones and fishbone, . . . samples of very fine gold, and many other things never before seen in Spain."[4]

On Palm Sunday—the day that commemorates Jesus' triumphal entrance into Jerusalem[5]—Columbus entered Seville, probably sitting upon a donkey just as Jesus had, and heralded by horns and drums. That entrance, on March 31, 1493, was Columbus's most triumphant moment. His entrance at the beginning of the festivities of Holy Week could not have been more auspicious and confirmed his belief that his voyage was an integral part of the greater religious story.[6] His contemporaries came to see the discovery as "the greatest event since the creation of the world, save the incarnation and death of Him who created it."[7]

While Holy Week culminates on Easter Sunday—the holiday that marks Jesus' resurrection; the larger Christian story is the hope of his return to Earth, the Second Coming. To many people, Columbus's return from the other side of the world must have seemed an earthly parallel. Columbus himself felt he was on the verge of fulfilling two of the conditions necessary for Christ's return: he had met many people ripe for conversion and he had found the means—the gold and spices—that would finance the crusade to liberate Jerusalem.

The news of Columbus's discovery and triumphant return must have been balm to the sovereigns, who were still reeling from an assassination attempt on Ferdinand's life in December, only a few months earlier. It happened in Barcelona during one of Ferdinand's regular audiences to hear petitions from his subjects. Instead of kneeling in supplication, one of them stabbed him in the neck. The wound was deep but not fatal because, according to Peter Martyr (humanist, priest, and tutor to the children at court), the knife was deflected by a gold chain Ferdinand wore around his neck. The attempt was made by a poor and crazed man acting alone rather than as a targeted political gesture, but it was deeply disturbing all the same; the man was gruesomely tortured and dismembered, and his parts were ultimately burnt.[8]

As Columbus awaited the letter from the sovereigns that would summon him to court, he stayed with Friar Gaspar Gorricio, an Italian family friend who was a resident monk at the Monastery of Nuestra Señora Santa María de las Cuevas. The Indians were put up nearby at the Gate of the Imagines, where Columbus often visited them to make sure they were being well treated; after all, they were his evidence that he had found the "Indies." Friar Gorricio would likely have accompanied him in order to bless them and begin their introduction to the practices of the Christian faith.

The letter from the sovereigns, dated March 30, 1493, reached Columbus around April 7, and it addressed him as "Don Cristóbal Colón, Admiral of the Ocean Sea, Viceroy and Governor of the Islands discovered in the Indies"— that is, with all the titles they had promised him. Their response indicated they had received his letters, and they invited him to come, as soon as possible, to Barcelona, where they were holding court. It would be a journey of about five hundred miles. Columbus had to arrange for transportation and assemble clothing appropriate to his new rank, which despite the title in the letter still had to be conferred publicly, and prepare the Indians for the journey. Once all of these details were accomplished, Columbus set off with one of his officers, several servants, and the six Indians. The mode of travel is not recorded, but such an entourage would likely have used a cart as well as mules and/or horses. For the Indians, who had never seen such animals, it must have been an amazing and perhaps frightening experience, especially if they were expected to ride one.

Isabella and Ferdinand were awaiting Columbus's arrival with great anticipation.[9] For the event, they had prepared an elegant but solemn reception as befitted his new station. They set out their royal throne in public view and commanded the attendance of many of the nobility. When Columbus entered into their presence looking ever more the Roman senator with his graying hair and aristocratic bearing, they requested that a chair be brought so that he could sit beside them—a favor rarely bestowed even on the highest-ranked nobles. Then Columbus, quietly and modestly, related the highlights of his voyage and discoveries. To their delight, he brought forth the six Indians, who presented the sovereigns with a number of pieces of gold. Las Casas exclaimed: "Who can describe the tears which sprang from the Royal eyes and from the eyes of many Grandees . . . ? What joy, what pleasure, what ecstasy bathed the hearts of all!" [10] Everyone assembled thanked God and sang the "Te Deum Laudamus."

The Indians were baptized a few days later, with the king and queen, the infante Don Juan, and Columbus standing as godparents.[11] One of the Indians, a relative of the cacique Guacanagarí, was named Don Fernando, after the king, another Don Juan, after the infante, and the one who was close to Columbus was named Don Diego Colón—the name of both his brother and his son. Don Juan chose to remain at court; the others chose to return home on Columbus's next voyage. Apparently only two of them survived the journey; one was Columbus's "godson," Don Diego, who became his able interpreter and accompanied him on many of his travels.

Now that Columbus had accomplished what he had set out to do, he was officially made a nobleman, who would be addressed as Don and was allowed a coat of arms that included, in the upper quadrants, a castle representing Isabella's Castile and a lion representing Ferdinand's Aragón, and, in the lower quadrants, several islands and a number of anchors, symbolizing his rank as Admiral—a title he always preferred to Governor or Viceroy. The arms and the titles would be hereditary. In addition, both of his brothers would have the title of Don. Diego had been summoned from Genoa to be present for the ennoblement, but Bartholomew was still in England, trying to convince King Henry VII to sponsor the voyage, oblivious to the news that his brother had already returned from it.

Elsewhere, however, news of the discovery had traveled very quickly. Even before Columbus had reached Spain, the duke of Medina Celi, who had been willing to outfit the voyage, heard that Columbus had arrived in Lisbon, and he quickly wrote the news to the grand cardinal of Spain. Peter Martyr was present when Columbus arrived in Barcelona. On May 14, he wrote to a friend in Milan about other matters and added, almost as a postscript, a sentence saying that a few days ago "a certain Christopher Columbus, a Ligurian, who with barely three ships . . . returned from the Western antipodes," and closed by saying, but "we must pass over these foreign matters." [12] His seeming indifference was short-lived, for soon he would write the first history of Columbus's discoveries.

Columbus. *Epistola de insulis nuper inventis.* Latin letter announcing Columbus's discovery.
Courtesy of The John Carter Brown Library at Brown University.

Columbus's letter announcing the discovery and describing what he had found was an immediate media success. Printed in Castilian, Italian, German, and Latin, it was widely circulated. Generally known as the letter to Santangel, it was actually addressed only to "Senor." Another slightly different version, known as the letter to Sanchez, is also addressed to "Senor." It is likely that they are the same letter, published in slightly different forms due to editorial license, difficulties of translation, and deciphering the handwriting.

The letter, though fairly short, recaps almost verbatim from Columbus's diary some of what he considered the most interesting and important information. He describes the beauty of the islands, and the "very keen intelligence" of the natives who "know neither sect nor idolatry." He also comments positively about their comeliness, saying: "I have found no human monstrosities, as many expected . . . nor had report of any, except on an island . . . inhabited by a people who eat human flesh," by which he meant the Caribs. He describes the people with whom he was familiar as generous to a fault, giving all they have with "as much love as if they were giving their hearts." Because of this, he assures the sovereigns that the men left at Navidad are "without danger for their persons, if they know how to behave themselves."

As evidence that he had been to the Indies, he wrote that he had brought a few *Indios*—the first time in print of the name given to the native people[13]— and promised the riches that he will be able to provide in the future—gold, spices, cotton, mastic, aloe wood, rhubarb, cinnamon, and "slaves, as many as they shall order, who will be from the idolaters," that is from the man-eating Caribs.

Scholars have long wondered why the letter was not addressed, as was appropriate, to the king and queen, for surely Columbus was unlikely to have offended the sovereigns with such a serious breach of etiquette. The answer is simple. In a note wrapped around the letter addressed to "the Keeper of the Priory Purse [i.e., Santangel], about the islands discovered in the India," there was "*another* for their Highnesses" (emphasis mine). That is, he did write a letter to the sovereigns and included it along with the one addressed to Santangel. Although the original letter to the sovereigns has been lost, the recent discovery of the *Libro Copiador* may resolve the issue. It contains copies of a number of letters presumed to be written by Columbus, including one, addressed to the sovereigns, that he wrote at sea on March 4, 1493. That letter contained information considered confidential—about the route he had taken, the location of the islands, and their professed goal, the conquest of Jerusalem. In it, Columbus also included personal matters; he requested the cardinalate for his son Diego and voiced several complaints—about the clunky *nao* (the *Santa María*), about the humiliations he had suffered from those who thought the voyage impossible, and about his frustration over the long wait—complaints that were meant only for the sovereigns' eyes.[14]

Since that letter included items that were confidential, the sovereigns must have suggested changes and/or simply let the one sent to Santangel be the one promulgated.[15] By June 15, 1493, Giuliano Dati, an Italian bishop, composed a rhymed version in Italian that was sung in the streets of Florence. Following is a translation of one stanza:

> *Back to my theme, O listener, turn with me*
> *And hear of islands all unknown to thee.*
> *Islands whereof the grand discovery*
> *Chanced in this year of fourteen ninety-three,*
> *One Christopher Colombo, whose resort*
> *Was ever in the King Ferdinand's Court,*

Bent himself still to rouse and stimulate
The King to swell the borders of his State.[16]

After all the excitement and fanfare over the discovery had calmed somewhat, Queen Isabella began responding to some of Columbus's requests. While
hardly the cardinalate Columbus had requested for his son, the sovereigns must
have taken his concern for his son into account; still, they took their time. Diego
did not go to court until early in 1494. There, he would soon become a member
of the queen's inner circle. She also provided a house for Columbus in Seville—a
house that had been confiscated from Jews who had been expelled. For the first
time, Columbus would have a home of his own. This house became his base for
many years, and there

> he cultivated a large social network that included family members, busi-
> ness associates from among the Florentine merchant community in the
> city, and local Franciscan and Dominican friars. Columbus seemed to
> enjoy having family and friends, especially family around him . . . he
> arranged to bring his sister-in-law Violante Moniz and her husband
> Miguel Moliart from Huelva to join him. . . . In Seville, Violante main-
> tained a home for Columbus and his son Diego, in between the admiral's
> voyages and when Diego was free from his duties as a page at the royal
> court.[17]

Despite having a house of his own, Columbus had little time to rest and enjoy
the rewards of his success. Instead, he had to get ready to sail again.

Riding the waves of his triumphal return to Castile, Columbus had no trouble convincing Isabella to launch a second voyage; as promised, he had found a
new route to the East, had found gold and spices, and many people to be converted to the one true faith. Now that Isabella knew the route was successful,
she lost no time in trying to establish her dominance over the area and to begin
to reap the benefits of Columbus's bravery.

Isabella was eager to beat her rival, King João of Portugal, to the newly discovered riches, examples of which she had seen with her own eyes. King João
wanted to make sure he was not left out if there were riches to be had, and Isabella was aware that João was preparing to send a fleet of his own to find out the
truth of Columbus's account.

Isabella was shrewd. She had quickly alerted the pope, Alexander VI, of Columbus's discovery and of all the potential souls to be converted to Christianity. The pope responded knowingly: as God's emissary in the world, he felt he had the right to bestow on Christians lands that were in the hands of non-Christians. In the Papal Bull of May 3, 1493, known as *Inter caetera*, Pope Alexander VI acknowledged that since he had given regions in Africa, Guinea, and "the Mine of Gold" to the Portuguese, he could now bestow the lands newly discovered by Columbus to the Spanish king and queen in perpetuity. The very next day, realizing that was not specific enough, he issued another bull. Today we hear of "lines drawn in the sand," but the pope drew an imaginary line in the ocean—from the North to the South Pole—dividing that ocean between Spain and Portugal. To the Spanish monarchs he gave all lands 100 leagues west and south of the Azores and the Cape Verde Islands (which were Portuguese possessions). San Salvador, Cuba, Hispaniola, and the other islands Columbus had discovered were more than 2,400 U.S. nautical miles to the west, or about 820 U.S. nautical leagues.

Still, the bull was not clear enough. A few months later, the pope issued another, *Dudum siquidem*, which acknowledged that by sailing west, one could reach the East and the lands of "India," and to the Spanish sovereigns he granted that they could "freely take corporal possession of the said islands and countries and to hold them forever." These were the very lands the Portuguese had been trying to reach for decades, by sailing to the "Indies" by way of Africa, and they had already entered the Indian Ocean. *Dudum siquidem* appeared to nullify Pope Nicholas V's bull of 1455 that had given the rights to those lands to the Portuguese. The Portuguese were outraged; in order to avoid a major conflict with Spain, they came to an agreement that modified the pope's decision. The Treaty of Tordesillas (1494), as it is known, extended the line of demarcation from 100 to 370 leagues west of the Cape Verde Islands. It meant that anything discovered east of that line, whether by the Portuguese, the Spanish, or any other nation, would belong to Portugal and anything west of that line would belong to Spain. So when Brazil was discovered, it turned out to be within the Portuguese limits—which explains why Portuguese remains the predominant language of Brazil.

With the bulls decreed and the pope's support, the queen could turn her attention to the second voyage. Isabella requested that Columbus write up a memo describing his vision for the settlement. Columbus's memo contained a very detailed outline for the structure of the settlement, its government, the registration of any gold found through exchange or extraction, the people who should be permitted to be involved in the enterprise, and the kinds of occupations to be undertaken by the settlers. It was to be a *factoría*—a trading post—based, in large part, on what he had seen in Guinea.[18] A *factoría* is not a colony but rather a settlement established for the purpose of trade—presumably beneficial to both parties. Colonization of the newfound lands was not being considered at this time, for it was clear that the lands belonged to local chiefs and possibly even to the Grand Khan or some other overlord. Although the trade was to be undertaken in the interests of the sovereigns and their equivalents in Hispaniola and elsewhere, a *factoría* was also a kind of medieval fiefdom held by individual families. This one would be hereditary in the Columbus family; Columbus and his heirs would be entitled to ten percent of any profits.

When gold was collected, Columbus wanted the transactions to be conducted openly. He requested that nothing be concealed and that when gold was placed in a locked chest, "the record of all the gold placed in the said chest should be made public, so that each may have what belongs to him . . . [and] that this business be managed honorably and in the interest of Your Highnesses."[19] Then, for the first time on an official document, Columbus signed the memo with his peculiar sigil and Xpo-ferens (the Christ-bearer).

The sovereign commended Columbus for his service and gave him explicit instructions for the administration of the settlement. The first issue they addressed concerned the conversion of the Indians, whom he had found "to be very ripe to be converted to our Holy Catholic Faith, since they have neither dogma nor doctrine,"[20] and for this purpose the sovereigns assigned several *religiosos* and Friar Buil, a Benedictine and the pope's delegate to the Indies whose primary job was to instruct and convert the natives. These men would be assisted by the native interpreters who would return with Columbus from Spain, where they had acquired some greater knowledge of the language and of the Catholic faith during their six months' stay. In order that all interactions with the natives be conducted with dignity befitting a royal enterprise, the sovereigns commanded the settlers

> to treat the said Indians very well and lovingly and abstain from doing
> them any injury, arranging that both peoples hold much conversation and
> intimacy, each serving the others to the best of their ability (and if any

person) should maltreat the said Indians in any manner whatsoever, the said Admiral, as Viceroy and Governor of their Highnesses, shall punish them severely by virtue of the authority vested in him by their Majesties for this purpose.[21]

After taking leave of the sovereigns in Barcelona, Columbus began his overland journey to Cádiz, where the ships were being readied. Not only would the second voyage depart from the major port of Cádiz, but the sovereigns had designated it as the only port to receive the cargo from the "Indies," as a way to keep better track of it. On his way to Cádiz, Columbus stopped first in Guadalupe in Estramadura to worship at the shrine of the Virgin. Columbus was especially devoted to her but so, too, were many sailors; they felt, and many still do today, that she protects them from drowning. In Guadalupe, Columbus promised the monks that he would name an island after their sacred city.

If Columbus had not stopped in Córdoba to see Beatriz and his sons before he went to court, he certainly stopped there after his visit to Guadalupe. They already knew that he had returned safely from the first voyage, for he had sent letters to them and to the town officials as soon as he had arrived in Spain. After so many months without news and without any assurance he would ever return, their reunion could not have been anything but joyous, but also tinged with sadness. We do not know if Columbus ever intended to marry Beatriz, but now that his nobility was conferred, it was probably impossible; in those times, there were laws prohibiting intermarriage between commoners and nobles. It is also likely that they did not have much time alone together with so many people wanting to see and hear and touch the person who had performed such a miraculous deed of reaching the East by sailing west across the Ocean Sea.

All too soon Columbus had to make his way to Cádiz to check on the preparations. His sons clamored to accompany him. There, they watched as an extraordinary sight unfolded.

Seventeen ships were bobbing up and down in the harbor, straining at their ropes as if to say, "let's get going." Men were frantically securing wine casks (this time filled either with amontillado sherry from Jerez or the variety made at nearby Puerto de Santa Maria) and other provisions in the holds, and leading the animals—horses, livestock, pigs, and chickens—up the gangplanks. Other sailors were stowing their personal chests wherever they could find a place— which would also probably serve as their sleeping place. Compared to the modest fleet of the first voyage, Columbus must have been overwhelmed by the size and logistics of this one, but also very proud of his achievement.

Thousands of men had flooded Columbus with petitions to join as crew and as worker-settlers, lured by his descriptions of balmy weather, of easily obtainable gold, and, undoubtedly, of naked women. Columbus had to turn away at least as many as he signed on. Significantly, the crew included quite a few of the sailors who had been with him on the first voyage, evidence of the respect he had garnered despite their grumbling on that voyage. Although the list of the men who embarked on this voyage has been lost, some of it has been reconstructed from various letters and other documents. The men came from all parts of Spain, from Italy and Portugal, and included "Spanish knights and Castilian labourers, proud *hidalgos*, exacting priests, irresponsible magistrates, and wild soldiers"[22]—a cross-section of the social world.

In a memo the sovereigns sent to Juan de Fonseca, the man in charge of provisioning the ships, they told him that from among the settlers, Columbus could take "ten squires and another twenty men as his personal retainers, and that these should be paid like the others and included in the number of people who are going." Besides the crew members, it is difficult to know who were the other paid employees of the Crown, certainly not the notaries, for in the same memo the sovereigns instructed that there should be a notary on each of the ships but that "neither they nor their accountants should receive a salary."[23] The man who was assigned as doctor for the fleet, Diego Alvares Chanca, did receive a salary. Some of the men were volunteers, including at least two hundred of the common laborers. Expectations that these men from different classes would work together for the common good of the settlement seem to be the ideals of a dreamer but, of course, that is just what Columbus was.

A number of men with personal ties to Columbus accompanied him on this voyage. Among them were Pedro de Las Casas, the father of Bartolomé; Antonio de Torres, to whose sister, a lady-in-waiting to the queen, Columbus would later write a letter pouring out both his misery and his exultation; Juan de la Cosa (possibly a different Juan de la Cosa from the one who had been master of the *Santa María* on the first voyage), whose map is considered the first of the islands Columbus had discovered, excepting the sketch Columbus had made of the north coast of Hispaniola; and Pedro de Terreros, who had been on the first voyage. Columbus's brother Diego also accompanied him on this voyage and was considered "a virtuous person, very discreet, peaceable and simple, and of good disposition, neither artful nor mischievous, who went very modestly clothed in a sort of clerical garb."[24]

A few gentlemen came along as volunteers for the adventure: Michele de Cuneo, Columbus's boyhood friend from Savona; Ponce de León, future discoverer of Florida and the "Fountain of Youth"; and Guillermo Coma, an Italian gentleman, whose letter along with those of de Cuneo and Dr. Chanca, when printed, were among the earliest firsthand descriptions of the "new world." Columbus had also requested "that the Holy Father provide prelates and devout, wise friars as unaffected as possible by lust for temporal goods." For this voyage Columbus obtained the services of five ecclesiastics; in addition to Friar Buil there were three Franciscans and Ramón Pane, "who knew the language and was charged by me to set down all their rites and antiquities." Although Pane's pamphlet is the first study of Caribbean religion and folklore, Columbus later thought that his account was totally inadequate and simply wrong on several accounts, writing that "it contains so many fictions that the only sure thing to be learned from it is that the Indians have a certain natural reverence for the after-life and believe in the immortality of the soul."[25]

No European nation had ever undertaken a voyage on such a scale; amazingly, the people of Cádiz managed to get the ships and provisions ready in record time, barely six months.[26] Crowds of people gathered at the harbor to see them off. Despite the excitement, ambivalence played with the emotions of those leaving and those being left. The voyage had been successful once before, but that was no guarantee. Would those departing make it across the ocean? If so, what awaited them on the other side? Would any of them ever see their families again? When would those remaining receive any news? Columbus and his sons were not exempt from those pangs of fear; Columbus instructed Diego, now thirteen, to watch over his little brother Ferdinand, who was only five. Perched on a cliff overlooking the harbor, the two boys waved goodbye as their father and their uncle Diego departed, along with twelve hundred men, on a sunny September 25, 1493.

The fleet made a brief stop at the island of Gomera in the Canaries to take on water and supplies, perhaps affording another, brief opportunity for Columbus to see the other Beatriz. On October 7, according to his son Ferdinand, Columbus

set his course for the Indies, having first given to each captain sealed instructions which he must not open unless separated from the fleet by stress of weather. The reason for this secrecy was that in the instructions he showed how to reach the town of Navidad in Española, and he did not want anyone to know that route save in case of great need.[27]

The ships left Gomera on October 13, barely missing the hurricane season, and made a record crossing in just twenty-one days. During the voyage Columbus was sure to be thinking about the thirty-nine (or forty-two) men he had left behind at Navidad, curious to learn about their adventures and accomplishments in his absence. One can imagine his excitement and various expectations while on the high seas, including him wondering if the men had collected a barrel of gold, as he hoped, and had followed his instructions to avoid conflict, to respect Guacanagarí, who had done so much for them, and perhaps most important, not to go marauding around the island.

Columbus found his way back "as if we had been following a known and accustomed route," marveled Dr. Chanca. As noted previously, this voyage established the route that would be used for the next four hundred years and is still the most common route for those who *sail* across the Atlantic. Regarding Columbus's sailing ability, Michele de Cuneo wrote that

since Genoa was Genoa, no other man has been born so magnanimous and so keen in practical navigation as the above mentioned Lord Admiral: for, when navigating, only by looking at a cloud or by night at a star, he knew what was going to happen and whether there would be foul weather.

Furthermore, in a storm he often took the helm himself and when it passed, "hoisted sail while the others were sleeping"[28]—which seems almost impossible as the sails were very heavy and usually required a number of men to hoist them.

Whether to confuse the other captains about the route, or whether Columbus wanted to explore the area a bit more, the fleet went about discovering other islands before heading straight to Navidad. They discovered more than twenty islands, including one that Columbus named Guadalupe as he had promised to the friars at Guadalupe in Spain. They arrived at that island on November 4 and spent some time loading water and making bread. Whenever they found fresh water, Columbus ordered the men to bathe and wash their clothes; after so many days working in the sun, the men and the few items of clothing they had brought with them must have been ripe.

On Guadalupe, according to both Dr. Chanca and Michele de Cuneo, they encountered the Caribs, whom they distinguished from other Indians. De Cuneo commented that the Caribs practiced the "accursed vice," the "extreme offense," of sodomy and believed that they had probably introduced it to the other Indians. Both men asserted that the Caribs were "cannibals." Dr. Chanca, who must have known something of human anatomy, wrote that the men who went ashore found many body parts in the huts and one of them brought back "four or five bones of the arms and legs of men."[29]

Less remarked upon by historians is their observation that some of the boys had been castrated. These "Caribs," according to the captured members from the native group that Columbus knew, had eaten the men, made the women concubines, and castrated the boys—"each has had his penis cut off." The crew assumed that the Carib practice of castration was done to "fatten up" the boys as a prelude to eating them. While the issue of cannibalism in the Indies has been hotly disputed, the castration of the enslaved boys is rarely mentioned. Yet the practice seems likely, given that these eyewitnesses, one of whom was a doctor, reported seeing genital organs that had been "cut to the belly" and still sore.[30] It seems highly unlikely they mistook castrated boys for girls as some scholars have suggested. Despite the revulsion the Europeans felt about these practices, Dr. Chanca wrote that this group of Caribs seemed "more civilized than those who were in the other islands which we have visited." He was not referring to their practices or manners but rather to their houses which he said were much better made than those seen elsewhere, and to other "signs of industry" that included "cotton sheets, so well made as to lose nothing by comparison with those of our own country."[31]

Columbus captured some of the Caribs and planned to send them to Spain, but he did not burn their villages; instead, he ordered that the Carib canoes be destroyed so that they could not continue to raid his friends. From among the girls, mutilated boys, and adults that the Caribs had enslaved, Columbus rescued as many as he could, took them aboard the already crowded ships, and returned them to their homes. In addition, Columbus wrote that the men found an orphaned year-old baby whom he "entrusted to a woman who came from Castile" and said that once the child learns the language he would send him to Spain. Columbus did not specify whether the woman was Spanish or an Indian, though it is possible she was Columbus's domestic servant, Maria Fernández.[32]

Columbus navigated his way back to Hispaniola as if he had been there many times. Of this voyage Morison said that Columbus

> had conducted across the Atlantic seventeen vessels, many of them very small, made a perfect landfall, and continued through a chain of uncharted islands, with no accident serious enough to be recorded. He had discovered twenty large islands and over two-score small ones, upon which the eyes of no European had rested before. Over the biggest fleet that had yet crossed deep water, bearing twelve hundred seamen, colonists and men-at-arms, he had kept discipline during a voyage that lasted fourteen weeks.[33] [Author's note: Morison is wrong about the duration or perhaps it is a misprint. Columbus left Spain on September 25 and made landfall at Dominica on November 3. The trip across the ocean from the Canaries to the first island in the Caribbean was twenty-one days.]

Some of the islands discovered were Puerto Rico and the Virgin Islands, which Columbus named The Eleven Thousand Virgins. The name comes from the legend of St. Ursula, who was on her way to meet her future husband with 10,999 virginal handmaidens when a storm blew them off course. Perhaps she had not really wanted to marry for, upon landing, she decided to make a pilgrimage to Cologne during a siege by the Huns. There, legend goes, she was beheaded in or about 383. For Columbus, the virginal appearance of the islands, not Ursula's fateful end, must have been the operative idea behind the name.

When the fleet anchored at St. Croix on November 14, Morison wished "that some chronicler of this voyage had told us the technique of laying-to a fleet of seventeen vessels for the night" so that they didn't foul each others' lines or, worse, crash into each other.[34] Some of the men went ashore and encountered more hostile Caribs. There was a skirmish in which one of their men was killed. Apparently these Caribs had captured people from the group Columbus knew and taken them as slaves. During the skirmish, Michele de Cuneo captured a beautiful Carib girl with whom he wished to take his pleasure. She put up quite a fight but was unable to fend him off. Describing the rape, de Cuneo wrote that they eventually came to an agreement and commented "that she seemed to have been brought up in a school of harlots."[35] In a move that was in contrast with much of Columbus's behavior, Columbus let him keep her aboard.

The ships were now filled to more than capacity, for they contained not only the Spanish settlers but a number of Caribs as well, some of whom would later be sent to Spain as slaves since it was legitimate policy to enslave warlike, resistant peoples. On the other hand, Columbus returned to their homes the gentle people that the Caribs had enslaved. Loaded with these additional people and the supplies, there was no opportunity for more discoveries. They had to make their way through all these islands, taking care to avoid the coral reefs which, fortunately, they could easily see due to the clarity of the water, and then headed straight for Navidad.

On November 28, eight weeks after their departure from Spain, the fleet approached Navidad. As they sailed into the harbor, Columbus and the crew were greeted by a gruesome sight—several bodies were floating in the water. From the condition of the bodies, it was clear that their deaths were fairly recent, and they appeared to be Europeans. Immediately on landing, Columbus learned that every last one of the men he had left at Navidad was dead. A macabre detail did not go unnoticed by the terrified voyagers: the eyes of the dead had been removed. Michele de Cuneo wrote to a friend that whenever the Indians beheaded someone they scooped out the eyes and ate them.

The incoming Spaniards, including Friar Buil, wanted revenge. Buil told Columbus that he should put cacique Guacanagarí and his people to death. Columbus, though devastated by the massacre, did not jump to the conclusion that it was Guacanagarí's people who were responsible. Columbus displayed enormous patience and forbearance despite his shock and the particular grief he must have felt since one of the dead was his friend, Beatriz's cousin Diego de Harana. He surmised, correctly as it turned out, that the Spaniards had defied his explicit instructions and done everything he had told them not to do.

Reserving judgment until he could find out the truth, he first turned to Diego, his Indian godson, to find out what had happened. Columbus's worst fears were confirmed. He learned that the men had begun to fight among themselves, had formed into groups and gone on raiding parties to the neighboring area belonging to cacique Caonabó. They stole goods, raped the women, kidnapped them, and took them back to Navidad as concubines. Not surprisingly, Caonabó retaliated by attacking the garrison, killing all the men, and burning their village. Columbus decided to pay a visit to Guacanagarí and learn his side of the story. Dressed in full regalia, he and one hundred men, accompanied by pipes and drums, marched to Guacanagarí's village, about ten miles inland. Guacanagarí confirmed Diego's report. He felt responsible to Columbus and was chagrined that he had not been able to keep his promise to protect the European men. He said that when he tried to help them, he was struck by a large stone and injured. Dr. Chanca could see no evidence of a wound, but Columbus decided not to press the issue and invited Guacanagarí on board for dinner. There, for the very first time, the Indian chief saw a horse.

Over dinner, Columbus learned that the men had been hoarding gold that they had either found or stolen, and had not reported it for the Crown. They had also been taking women and even girls as concubines. Although the three men he had put in charge—Rodrigo Escobedo, Pedro Gutiérrez, and Diego de Harana—had tried to restrain the debauchery of the men, they were unable to and, unfortunately, perished with them. Columbus wrote that he

> felt great pain . . . and though I know it happened through their own fault, there is much to be sad about in such an event, and for me it is a punishment greater than any experienced by their relatives, because I wanted them to win great honor at little danger, which would have been the case had they governed themselves according to my instructions as they pledged to do.[36]

He had a difficult task ahead. He would have to inform the families about the deaths of their relatives, and at the same time find a way to delicately explain the circumstances. It was perhaps easier to tell families about the death of loved ones who had paid with their lives while trying to put a stop to the evil behavior of others; there was some nobility in that kind of death. Although that task was personally painful as well, for he would have to tell Beatriz about the death of her cousin. But it was a more odious duty to tell families of the death of relatives who had committed despicable deeds.

While the friendship between Guacanagarí and Columbus survived, the relationship between Columbus and the newcomer-settlers began to deteriorate. Morison believed that

> despite numerous provocations Guacanagarí remained so steadfastly loyal to the Admiral that we may be certain that Navidad would have been unmolested as long as the Spaniards behaved themselves.[37]

But instead of blaming the men who had gone on the rampage, the newcomers blamed Columbus for what had happened to them. The Europeans who had sailed with Columbus and were likely still overwhelmed by the journey resented his trust and seeming support of the Indians; they wanted revenge, not allies.

With such sad memories hovering in the air like ghosts, Navidad was not the place to found a settlement. After a few days commiserating with Guacanagarí and burying the dead, Columbus pushed on, searching for a more suitable site. The weather was so bad and the currents so strong that it took them more time (twenty-five days) to sail the 160 kilometers from Navidad to the new site than it did to cross the Atlantic. The new site, also on the north coast of Hispaniola and close to the current border with Haiti, was named La Isabela, after the queen, and was established with full ceremony on Epiphany, 1494.

Columbus liked the site because the promontory on which the settlement would be built formed a natural fortification. He wrote that "it does not have a closed port, but there is a big bay that could hold all the ships of Christendom." [38] In his analysis of the area, he claimed it was never touched by the violence of storms. He also liked the availability of stone and water from a nearby river. Curiously, many modern scholars have been of the opinion that the site of La Isabela was a bad choice precisely because of its location and lack of resources. However, archaeological excavations conducted by Kathleen Deagan and José María Cruxent in the 1980s have overturned that opinion; they believe the site was an excellent choice and note that "there was no censure voiced by those chroniclers who were actually present." [39]

Several of the men who *were* present extolled the site in letters they later wrote to friends back in Europe. Guillermo Coma's florid letter to his professor friend Nicolò Syllacio described the site of La Isabela as surpassing "all others by virtue of its strategic position and benign climate . . . [it] is next to an excellent port, that abounds in fish of succulent flavor, and which, as the doctors have shown, cause the sick to recover their health." [40] Dr. Chanca, another eyewitness, concurs. In his long letter he wrote:

> The land is very rich for all purposes. Nearby there is one main river, and another of reasonable size, not far off, with very remarkable water . . . they have begun to canalize a branch of the river, and the foremen say that they will bring this through the center of the town and that they

will place on it mills and waterwheels and whatever can be worked with water.[41]

Columbus's plans for the settlement were grandiose; the problem was how to translate them into reality. The settlement would have to be built from scratch; this would involve the arduous labor of cutting down dense foliage in order to clear an area for the buildings and gardens, and they would have to fashion some of the wood so it could be used in construction. They would also have to collect stones for the buildings and very quickly get a water supply for drinking. It was a daunting task that lay ahead.

Columbus was a sailor and a navigator; he was not cut out for the job of administrator, even less as contractor, and he had had no training for this role. But now, he was confronted with the task of organizing his motley group of settlers into cadres for work. Although he had warned them before they left Spain that there was a lot of work to be done, some had clearly been blinded by the descriptions of the wealth and ease of life on Hispaniola and were only now being rudely awakened to the reality. Columbus the visionary naively assumed everyone would do his share. The common laborers, with expectations of improving their lot, adapted more easily to their tasks and did most of the heavy work: clearing and planting the fields, hauling the stones, and constructing the buildings. But the *hidalgos* were a problem from the beginning. They were unaccustomed to manual labor and refused to work; instead they expected to be given Indians as servants to work for them. They thought of themselves as vassals of the king and queen, despite the directive from the sovereigns that had delegated their authority to Columbus. They resented Columbus as a foreigner whose authority they had only reluctantly accepted to begin with. Not only did the *hidalgos* refuse to work, they refused to let "their" horses be used for the labor of hauling timber and stone. Columbus countered that since the *hidalgos* did not own the horses (they had been paid for by the sovereigns), and since he was governor, he could commandeer them when necessary; still they refused. Their truculence sorely tried Columbus's patience and put a tremendous burden on the other settlers.

Columbus wrote a letter to the sovereigns saying he did not want to deal with such "petty disputes" every day. He asked them if he could buy the horses from the *hidalgos* to put an end to that conflict. Of course, the letter could not be sent until some of the ships returned to Spain, and he would not receive their response for more than six months. When he did, the sovereigns told him not to buy the horses; instead, they commanded the *hidalgos* to relinquish the horses when needed and render whatever service Columbus deemed necessary.[42] The *hidalgos* bristled under these commands and did not comply; their refusal, therefore, was not just against Columbus but against the explicit instructions from Isabella and Ferdinand. The tensions between the *hidalgos* and Columbus continued to grow more and more acrimonious.

Despite these problems, the settlement was an impressive undertaking even as it was being built. One of the first things to be built, at Isabella's command, was a customs house where goods acquired would be stored and registered before being shipped to Spain. This storehouse was large even by Spanish standards. Years later, Las Casas recalled his amazement about its dimensions—48 meters long by 13 meters wide, and a roof of 800 square meters covered by tiles weighing a total of 52.5 tons.

From the promontory, the laborers next built walls around the settlement, making it a kind of wedge shape. Inside the walls, the settlement was described as having a wide avenue and a plaza for ceremonies, ball playing, and dancing. Columbus liked music and had asked the queen to send musicians on this voyage, for he felt they would help to make the settlers feel at home and, perhaps, to ease relations with the Indians.[43] Inside the walls, Columbus

> hastened to proceed to the building of a fort to guard their provisions and ammunition, of a church, a hospital, and a sturdy house for himself; he distributed land plots, traced a common square and streets; the important people grouped together in a section of the planned township and everyone was told to start building his own house. Public buildings were to be made of stone; individuals used wood and straw for theirs.[44]

De Cuneo wrote that they quickly built two hundred little houses, like hunting cabins, with thatched roofs. Although these would shelter many of the settlers, even two hundred structures could hardly house everyone, but he does not say how or where the others were housed.[45] The furnishings on the settlement were simple regardless of what kind of housing one had—a trunk and bedroll the settlers had brought with them, and possibly a table and chairs that were made there.[46] One imagines they soon adopted the native hammocks. Perhaps they bartered with the Indians to obtain some wall hangings made of braided reeds in different colors to offset the drabness of their huts. Columbus's house was larger, made of stone, and nicknamed *Palacio* just in case the sovereigns decided to visit.

Outside, along the promontory, was a shipyard for building and repairing ships and a smelting forge. Columbus also built a mill on the river and a "satellite" village called Marta which, although mentioned in Dr. Chanca's letter, most historians had dismissed until recent excavations uncovered it. Here, due to the abundance of mud and clay, Columbus established a kiln for making tiles and pottery.[47]

In addition to the geographical advantages of the settlement, the land was exceedingly fertile. Columbus said that "seeds germinate in three days and we ate the produce after fifteen days except for melon and squash," which were ready in thirty-six days.[48] As a premonition of things to come, he wished that more of the sugar cane they had brought had survived the voyage, for it grew very well. Eventually, he wrote, it could provide a million *quintals* (hundredweights) of sugar a year so that in the future it would not be necessary to send anything but clothing to the settlement. The men "have sown many vegetables, and it is certain that they grow more in eight days than they do in twenty in Spain," wrote Dr. Chanca.[49] Such statements were reiterated by some of the others who were there. In addition to what the men had sown, the natives also brought food. As Dr. Chanca continued:

There come here constantly many Indians . . . [A]ll come laden with *ages* [yams] which are like turnips, very excellent for food; of these we make here many kinds of food-stuffs in various ways. It is so sustaining to eat that it comforts us all greatly.

Guillermo Coma wrote that these yams were especially delicious when soaked in almond milk, which conveys an impression that those who tried the local food were eating well.

The reports of these gentlemen volunteers might be more reliable than those of the settlers since they were along for the adventure and did not have a vested interest in amassing gold. Food was obviously abundant, but many of the settlers, especially the *hidalgos*, would not eat the food the Indians brought, and most did not "think of supplementing the inadequate rations with the fish, manatees, turtles, fruits, cassava, and other crops of the region."[50] One man who tried an oyster for the first time was hailed a hero. The rest were disappointed because they found no pearls in them. A few of the settlers tried local food, including even dog, which one claimed tasted like goat, but most would eat only imported Spanish food. In addition, the Spaniards clung to traditional cooking practices and refused to learn native ones, even demanding their own types of cooking vessels. The archaeologists found a significant amount of glazed majolica that had clearly been imported from Spain. Columbus tried to accommodate their needs by constructing a kiln, and requesting skilled potters to make the kinds of pottery they were accustomed to. The complaints of the *hidalgos* that they were starving had little to do with the availability of food or the fertility of the land and more to do with their refusal to eat the local produce and to engage in the necessary agricultural labor.

As a sailor and explorer, Columbus was chafing under all this administrative minutiae; he was not suited for the thankless task of managing a settlement, nor did he like it. The barrel of gold he had expected the men at Navidad to have collected in his absence did not exist, so he was now under even more pressure to produce it for the sovereigns and to be able to fund the crusade. Columbus was also concerned about his location; although he continued to think he was in Asia, he was unable to decide exactly where he was. In the 1493 letter that announced the discovery, he had said that Juana (Cuba) "might be the mainland province of Cathay"; but at other times he was sure he was in Cipango (Japan), and now at La Isabela, hearing the native word *Cibao*, he thought he might not be far from the land of the biblical Sheba. To resolve the issue, according to a letter sent by Guillermo Coma to a friend, Columbus soon sent an expedition off to the interior, where he hoped they might "visit the Sabaeans" and their King Saba "from whom frankincense is obtained."[51]

Columbus had heard from the natives that there was gold in Cibao so he sent another expedition with Alonso de Hojeda, "a big strapping lad and very trustworthy,"[52] to see if they could find the gold mines; perhaps they might also be able to learn the whereabouts of the king of that area. The expedition was to be a reconnaissance mission only; the men were instructed not to start digging and only to bring back a few samples because Columbus didn't want the natives to "be provoked at seeing strangers taking things from their lands."[53]

Hojeda returned on January 20 with some sizable nuggets of gold. From Hojeda's report about gold in Cibao, Columbus decided they should erect a small outpost on the site in order to facilitate its extraction. But just as things were beginning to look up, there were more problems in the settlement that forced Columbus to postpone that project; there were simply not enough healthy men able to work. Many of the men at La Isabela had fallen ill but it is unknown whether the cause was the water, the heat and humidity, their refusal to eat local food, or, according to a recent suggestion, swine flu.[54]

Columbus's vision for the *factoría* was not working out as he had hoped and planned. His expectation that everyone would work for the common good and for the higher purpose to which the project was dedicated was a dream that was quickly evaporating. The insolence and disobedience of the *hidalgos* not just to his commands but, more shocking, to the directives from the sovereigns, created a very tense situation. Their refusal to work put even more strain on the laborers.

The conflicts that had arisen in the settlement were taxing his patience and must have taken him by surprise—the very people who had celebrated his discovery and been so eager to join him now turned against him. These tensions would soon put both the settlement and his grand plan at risk. Columbus was getting sidetracked from his mission to find the Grand Khan, to convert the natives, and to find the gold that would finance the crusade. He could not wait for more gold to be collected before sending some of the ships back to Spain; he desperately needed food and other supplies for the settlement. So on February 2, 1494, not even a month after the establishment of La Isabela, twelve of the seventeen ships departed in the hope that they would be able to return with the supplies by May.

The ships were under the command of Antonio de Torres, no relation to the interpreter Luis de Torres who had been killed at Navidad. Though Antonio de Torres and the other captains had made the crossing from Europe to Hispaniola with Columbus, now they would be the first to navigate back to Europe without him. Columbus's directions must have been excellent, for the ships returned safely to Cádiz on April 10, 1494. De Torres carried Columbus's letters and an official memo to the sovereigns. A couple of the letters, the memo, and the sovereigns' reply still exist.

The memo reported what had been accomplished to date, asked advice about certain matters, and requested more supplies—especially wine. Much of the wine had soured and leaked out due to badly constructed barrels by the coopers in Seville. Columbus requested 12,000 *arrobas* (48,000 gallons) of wine and pleaded that it be sent as soon as possible.

> The greatest need which we now have, or which we expect to have for the present is wine . . . nothing disappears as fast here as the wine, for it is a strengthening provision . . . food is found everywhere, a ration of wine fills and satisfies people.[55]

He asked the sovereigns to punish the men responsible for the badly made wine barrels and also those whom he suspected had substituted weak horses for good ones at the last minute.

In response to his memo and other letters, the sovereigns sent the list of supplies requested by Columbus to Juan de Fonseca. While the list specified items "for the people" and those "for the Admiral and his household," it is not known how these items were distributed or for exactly how many people Columbus was responsible. The "people" may have meant the common laborers, while Columbus's household may have included the officers, the gentlemen volunteers, and some of the *hidalgos*. His requests for his household included 80 shirts and 120 pairs of shoes, 12 mattresses, sheets, and blankets. Based on this, one might deduce that at least twelve men were sleeping in his house. Some of the food may have been prepared in his kitchen and distributed to the people, other foodstuffs may have been kept at his house to be given to the sick by the doctor.

Regardless of who was actually included in his household, the list does indicate a significant disparity in lifestyle between the nobles and the commoners. Apparently, Columbus had requested rose-colored sugar, water scented with orange blossoms, other water scented with roses, raisins from Almuñécar, good honey, and fine oil. The mattresses, he said, were to be of fine Brittany linen, and he also wanted some cloth tapestries depicting trees.[56] With so many "marvelous" trees around him, one wonders why he would want even more. In addition, he requested tablecloths, towels, pewter cutlery, salt cellars, brass candlesticks and candles, large pots, small pots, graters, a grill to roast fish, and a colander.

Columbus also requested miners from Almadén who were skilled in the extraction and processing of precious metals.[57] With their expertise, he wrote, they would be able to accomplish in seven years what he had earlier promised— a reference, no doubt, to the letter of March 4, 1493, in which he had promised to have obtained enough gold during that time to provide soldiers and cavalry for the liberation of Jerusalem. However, Columbus implied that the accountant they had sent to the settlement to keep track of the gold collected, Bernal de Pisa, was turning out to be a troublemaker. Columbus alluded to this only briefly in his memo but more fully in his letter. At the time, he didn't know the full extent of de Pisa's animosity, but "[S]hortly after de Torres sailed, a paper of his full of false charges against the Admiral and outlining a plan to seize some of the caravels and return to Spain was discovered in an anchor buoy."[58] De Torres must have corroborated de Pisa's mutiny for, in their response, the sovereigns gave permission to Columbus to send de Pisa back on whatever ship would next return to Spain.

With the ships, Columbus sent back cinnamon, pepper, cotton, parrots, and sandalwood, and some of the gold samples they had collected, in order to show that the enterprise would be profitable.[59] In addition to the profitable materials gathered from nature, Columbus also sent human cargo—twenty-six Indians, from the man-eating Caribs. In doing this, he was following papal policy at the time, which permitted enslavement of those captured in a "just war," those who resisted Christianization, or those who went against the law of nature. The Caribs appeared to fit all three definitions; not only had they resisted and fought against the Christians, they contravened the law of nature by their acts of sodomy and cannibalism. As a fan of Pope Pius II, Columbus must have known of his 1462 address to the rulers in the Canaries where he stated that natives who became Christian could not be enslaved, but once enslaved conversion did not automatically free them. "Salvation, escape from the ills and evils of this world, and eternal life were what Christians sought, not social and political reform in this world."[60] Christians accepted slavery as long as it complied with the conditions just cited, but conversion was the goal; not only would it civilize them in this world but, more important, it would free them from eternal damnation. In any case, Columbus, as a man of his time, was surely not one to go against accepted policy and a practice that had been justified by the pope. Throughout, it seems he first wanted the natives to become Christian but for Columbus that meant they had to be instructed, not just baptized. He wrote, "owing to the fact that there is here no interpreter, by means of whom it is possible to give these people understanding of our holy Faith . . . although every possible effort has been made, there are now sent with these ships some of the cannibals, men and women and boys and girls."[61] Although they were to become slaves, he asked that they be treated better than other slaves and given instruction in both the language and religion. He felt he was doing a good deed, for sending them to Spain "would not be anything but well, for they may one day be led to

abandon that inhuman custom which they have of eating men." If they learned
the language they would become good interpreters, and if they learned about the
Christian faith they would "much more readily receive baptism and secure the
welfare of their souls."[62]

In addition to saving their souls, Columbus thought that by capturing the
Caribs "great credit will be gained by us" for they will serve as an example to
"all the people of this great island . . . [who] when they see the good treatment
which is meted out to well-doers and the punishment which is inflicted upon
those who do evil, will quickly come to obedience so that it will be possible to
command them as vassals."[63] Columbus is clearly making a distinction between
the Caribs and the other natives, for vassals cannot be enslaved. He did, however, intend to put them to work because he wrote: "I believe that if they started
to receive something in payment they would work, being exceedingly eager,
and so set themselves to do anything if it should profit them."[64] This is an extraordinarily important statement; it shows that Columbus's primary intention
was that the natives should be employees of the Crown, not slaves, though he
admitted that he didn't know the language well enough to ask them what might
be an appropriate payment.

When the sovereigns received Columbus's memo, they responded that, in
the future, they would prefer that he try to convert the natives while they were
still in the islands. Yet, given the failure of Friar Buil to convert any natives,[65]
no doubt because he never learned the language and could not communicate
with them, let alone instruct them in the intricate theology of the Christian
faith, Columbus seemed to think it was better to send the cannibals/Caribs to
Spain, where "their inhumanity they will immediately lose when they are out
of their own land." However, when he elaborated a plan to send more Caribs
back as slaves as a way to defray the costs of supplying the settlement, the sovereigns demurred.

The sovereigns must have been pleased with the items returning from their
new settlement, but not with the 330 disaffected Europeans. Now, they would
begin to hear complaints about Columbus from the disgruntled and disillusioned *hidalgos* who had returned from La Isabela, and from letters, including
one from Friar Buil, sent by those who had remained in Hispaniola. Unfortunately, they never heard the opinions from those lower on the socioeconomic
ladder, whose lives may well have been better in Hispaniola than they had been
in Spain: their voices went unheard because most of them were illiterate, thus

the historical record is considerably skewed. The *hidalgos* complained that they were starving and criticized Columbus's governance. In contrast, de Cuneo wrote that he was not surprised when so many of them left, for the elites' resistance to adapting to the local culture was a sure sign that they didn't want to be there. Some of them had gambled away their money "thinking they could get rich without work or effort." Writing to the sovereigns, Columbus said that he had told those who wanted to come with him that they

> would have to work for everything. They were so greedy they thought I was lying. There is a chance they could have succeeded had they made sacrifices and worked, but their laziness and bad habits would not let them demonstrate even a minimum of virtue.[66]

Although Antonio de Torres was able to corroborate Columbus's version of the Spaniards' behavior, the sovereigns were concerned.

Columbus's memo did not focus on the pettiness that the other nobles engaged in. Instead, it focused on more practical matters and the better interest of the men who were still his responsibility. It was a straightforward report requesting the items already noted and beasts of burden to relieve some of the labor from the men's shoulders. To replace the men returning to Spain, Columbus requested that the sovereigns "appoint in their service men who get along with one another and who value more the reason for which they were sent than their own personal interests."[67] He commended some of the men still living at the settlement by name and asked that their pay be increased; he also asked that some not yet on the payroll should be added to it in order to show that "good service pays . . . [and] those who work so diligently should not be underestimated."[68] Columbus was concerned with issues of pay, both for his men and for their wives and children back in Spain. He requested that some money be sent not only to the families of the artisans, but even to the wife and children of the nobleman Pedro Margarit, who "has done good service." (He would have reason to regret that statement.) The issue of payment for his men was to become a constant refrain for the rest of his life.

CHAPTER SEVEN

UNRULY PASSIONS: THE COLONIES

I n April 1494, two months after de Torres left for Spain, Columbus took seventy men, including artisans, carpenters, and miners, to Cibao in order to erect a small settlement and begin extracting the gold the men had seen on their recent reconnaissance expedition. When they arrived at the site, Columbus named it Santo Tomás for the "doubting Thomases" who had not believed they would find gold. During the few days Columbus was there, the men collected "two thousand castellanos' worth of gold . . . including nuggets that weighed twenty-four castellanos."[1] All felt they must be in the vicinity of the mine and would soon be rich. In good spirits, Columbus left fifty of the men and some horses at Santo Tomás under the direction of Pedro Margarit, and returned to La Isabela. In his usual optimistic way, Columbus thought he had come across the land of Sheba, which the natives had mispronounced Cibao. That led him to believe they might actually be in the vicinity of the legendary mines of Ophir—the mines that had provided the gold for the temple of Solomon in biblical times. How marvelous it would be if gold from the very same mine could be used to reclaim and gild the Holy Sepulchre in Jerusalem. Actually, it was more than marvelous; for Columbus would have taken it as one more sign that the apocalyptic times were upon them.

When he arrived back in La Isabela, Columbus's high spirits were quickly deflated. More than three hundred men remained ill and several had died. While they claimed it was because they were starving, most continued to refuse to eat local food, despite provisions being very low, but they may also have come down with swine flu.[2] While Columbus was away, a fire had broken out and destroyed nearly two-thirds of the houses, and the men were in no condition to work on rebuilding. Unruly passions were erupting; the tiny settlement was in a critical state.

To add to Columbus's distress, a messenger arrived from Santo Tomás with news that Caonabó, the cacique believed to have killed the men at Navidad, was planning to attack the fort at Santo Tomás. To counter Caonabó's attack, Columbus sent four hundred men with Alonso de Hojeda, whom he appointed as *alcalde* (mayor, something akin to a chief justice), back to Santo Tomás to replace Margarit and defend the fort. In January, Hojeda had been on the reconnaissance mission to Santo Tomás, had made contact with the Indians, and knew the area pretty well.

In order to distract Margarit from the change in power, Columbus sent instructions that he should take his men on an exploratory mission around the rest of the island. The purpose of the trip would be to induce the Spaniards to become used to eating native food and to pacify the Indians by making sure that they "receive no injury, suffer no harm, and that nothing is taken from them against their will; instead make them feel honored and protected so as to keep them from becoming perturbed."[3] Columbus also commanded that Margarit should pay the Indians with glass beads or hawk's bells—items much prized by them—whenever they brought food or gold, and that detailed records of these transactions be kept; Columbus wanted the Indians to go away happy and believed that a show of force would only strike fear in their hearts.

What Columbus didn't know was that Margarit, and the men under his command, had gone on rampages, marauding the native villages and raping the women, and that it was their actions which had aroused Caonabó's anger. Michele de Cuneo, who had accompanied Hojeda on this expedition, had witnessed Margarit's men secreting away as much gold as they officially reported having collected, which was "against the rules and our own agreement." Columbus would not learn of their duplicity until de Cuneo returned to the settlement. Later, after he had returned to Savona in 1495, de Cuneo wrote a long and colorful letter to his friend Hieronymo Annari detailing what he had seen and experienced in Hispaniola; in it he blamed the greed and rapaciousness of the men on the Spanish character:

As you know, the devil makes you do wrong and then lets your wrong be discovered; moreover, as long as Spain is Spain, traitors will never be wanting. One gave the other away, so that almost all were exposed, and whoever was found guilty was well whipped; some had their ears slit and some the nose, very pitiful to see.[4]

In addition to asking him to explore more of the island, Columbus gave Margarit a mission of another kind. He wanted him to capture Caonabó so he could be punished for having killed the men at Navidad. Columbus suggested a clever stratagem that would not make Caonabó suspicious. Since Caonabó, like all the natives, was naked, there was nothing to grab on to; catching him would not be easy. Columbus told Margarit to present him with a gift of clothes, which Caonabó would interpret as a sign of friendship. His defenses would be down, so that when he put on the clothes, he would not suspect Margarit's intentions of grabbing him by them.[5]

With Margarit dispatched and Hojeda instated, Columbus had specific instructions for how he wanted things to change at Santo Tomás. He ordered that any bartering for gold should be done in the presence of Hojeda "because, as I said, I found our people so unbelievably greedy that it makes one wonder, and at times they molest the Indians because I do not punish them enough."[6] Columbus likely felt that the Indians were retaliating against the settlements in response to the Spaniards' violence, and he clearly wanted his men to hold themselves to a higher standard. But Columbus misjudged Hojeda's character. He would later learn that Hojeda used brutal tactics against the Indians to demonstrate the dire consequences of their attacks. For example, when Hojeda heard that a few Indians had robbed several Spaniards of some of their clothes, he cut off the ears of one of the natives and sent the chief and several others in chains to La Isabela. Years later, Las Casas wrote that this "was the first injustice, with vain and erroneous pretension of doing justice . . . and the beginning of the shedding of blood, which has since flowed so copiously in this island."[7] Yet the first injustice committed by the Spaniards against the natives began at Navidad when the men who had been left behind after the grounding of the *Santa María* raided Caonabó's villages, raping, killing, and enslaving his people. Columbus was angry over what Hojeda and his men had done, and he should have punished them, but he realized that would only infuriate them further and make insurrection more likely. So to demonstrate his authority, he made a show of preparing to execute the captives. When the Spaniards were distracted, he released them.

After he thought he had restored some order at Santo Tomás and normalized the situation at La Isabela, Columbus left his brother Diego in charge along with Friar Buil and several other notables, while he went on a voyage to explore Cuba in the hope of making contact with the Grand Khan. His plan implied that he still believed Cuba to be part of the Asian mainland. He took three of the remaining ships, sixty men, including his friend Michele de Cuneo and his interpreter-godson Diego, and several men who had been on the first voyage. They left on April 24, 1494, and would be gone five months. On that day, Columbus wrote:

> I sailed west in the name of Our Lord Jesus Christ with three square-rigged caravels in fine weather. In a few days I reached the excellent port of *San Niculás*—before *Cabo de Alpha et Omega* on *Juana*, which is not an island but the mainland, the end of the Indies to the east.[8]

Believing that Cuba (Juana) was the Asian mainland, Columbus had named the place Cape Alpha and Omega, assuming it was either the beginning of the East or the end of the West. He then declared that the whole inhabited world, the landmass between Spain and Asia, lay between Cape Alpha and Omega and Cape Finisterre in Spain. When they arrived at Cape Alpha and Omega, they erected some posts to commemorate its significance. While there, the crew voted to explore the south coast since Columbus had already been along the north coast on the first voyage. A few days later they entered what would become Guantánamo Bay. Columbus wrote: "I figure I was in the region of Magón, adjacent to the noble region of Cathay . . . [and] I intend to go to see this region and the city of Quinsay" to ascertain whether it "is as noble and rich as described and whether it is still friendly to Christians as claimed."[9] For Columbus, Magón sounded close enough to Mangi, which to him meant southeast China, and since it was thought to be near Cathay, he imagined he was not that far from the Grand Khan.

Continuing westward, they reached Cape Cruz, where Columbus was astonished when they met a man who knew all about him and about his converted native interpreter Diego. Since the first voyage had only stopped on the northern coast of Cuba and they were now on the south, this was clear evidence that the natives had a very efficient way of spreading news. While he was at Cape Cruz, Columbus heard that there was gold in Jamaica, so he took a brief detour from his westward passage and crossed over to Jamaica, landing at Santa

Gloria. Columbus thought Jamaica was the most beautiful of all the islands he had seen, saying that he considered its fertile land more valuable than gold. Even the food was better than on any of the other islands, but they found no gold.[10] On May 13, after a week of sailing west as far as Montego Bay, they headed back to Cuba and continued west along the south coast.

They had entered a very shallow gulf littered with tiny islets and shoals and the sailing was very difficult. For reasons known only to Columbus, he named this area Jardín de la Reina (the Queen's Garden). It extended for more than a hundred and fifty miles. Because of the milk-white color of the water, often they could not see the bottom. On several occasions, the ships lodged in the soft mud and had to be dragged out of it, causing damage to them and extra work for the sailors.

For several weeks Columbus barely had a full night's sleep due to these treacherous waters. Still, he was alert enough to record that they saw many turtles, butterflies that swarmed the ship, and most startling, a flock of "pink birds like cranes" (flamingos). Columbus and the crew were also intrigued when some natives demonstrated their ingenious method of catching fish. To the end of their lines, they attached a species of fish that had a mouth with a strong sucking apparatus. When they let out the line, this fish swam fast and attacked its prey by latching onto it. Then, all the fisherman had to do was reel in both. No hooks, no nets: they let the fish do the work for them.

All along this coast, the natives came out bearing gifts to the men they believed came from heaven. Diego, the interpreter, tried to dissuade them from this view but was rarely successful. However, at one stop an old man who had heard of Columbus approached him with a desire to engage in a theological discussion; perhaps he had heard that Columbus was interested in religious beliefs, or he may have cleverly used this dialogue as a way to protect his people. Columbus, for his part, must have jumped at the chance to have a discussion with a learned native about their beliefs. They talked about the soul and what happens to it after death. The old man explained that his people believed that any injury to the body also affected the soul and begged Columbus not to injure any of the people. Columbus assured him that he only hurt bad people because that was what his sovereigns had commanded. Unlike others who had believed Columbus was some kind of god, this man told Columbus to his face that he "was mortal like everyone else."[11] Columbus was not offended and wrote that the old man "expressed his thinking with excellent judgment and courage."

When Diego, the interpreter, told the old man about the wonders he had seen in Castile and about the Spanish sovereigns, the man decided he wanted to go with them, but his wife and children wailed and wouldn't let go of him.

The ships proceeded farther west along the south coast of Cuba. When Columbus sent his men inland to seek water, they came back a bit spooked because they claimed they had seen light-skinned men in long white tunics. From the stories of Marco Polo and Mandeville, Columbus wondered whether his men had encountered the people of Prester John, the group of Nestorian Christians who were thought to live in Central Asia. This sighting would have confirmed Columbus's belief that he was in the vicinity of Cathay, and perhaps he thought Prester John's people could lead him to the Grand Khan. But although the men spent several days searching for the men in white tunics, they never caught sight of them again.

The land curved to the southwest, and Columbus believed he was moving farther away from Cathay and the region of the Grand Khan. They had been sailing for seventy days and had gone over 335 leagues (more than a thousand miles) without seeing the end of the land. Although the Indians, de Cuneo, and an abbott/astronomer on board had told Columbus that Cuba was an island, Columbus was convinced that Cuba was part of the Chinese mainland. Surely, on their next explorations, they would find Cathay. He went so far as to ask Fernand Pérez de Luna, a notary from La Isabela, to go to each of the ships and ask the men to sign a document saying they had never seen such a long island. If they had questions, Columbus said he would talk to them in order to "remove any doubt and would show them . . . that it is the continental land."[12] Bartolomeu Dias had done the same kind of thing in 1488 believing that, having rounded the Cape of Good Hope, he did not need to sail farther to prove he had found the Indian Ocean.[13] A more likely motivation in this case was de Cuneo's suggestion that Columbus may have had the men sign the document because he feared the Spanish sovereigns would abandon the whole project if he did not soon find Cathay and the riches long promised.

Columbus reconsidered his position; thinking they were now far south of Cathay, he reasoned that they must be "very close to the Golden Chersonese [Malay peninsula]"[14] and he began to think about the possibility of circumnavigating the world. Columbus was not the first to contemplate such a voyage; he may have read in Mandeville's *Travels* "that a man could go round the world, above and below, and return to his own country, provided he had his health, good company and a ship." [15] From the Chersonese, Columbus imagined that he "could have tried to return to Spain from the east by way of the Ganges, Arabian Gulf, and Ethiopia," [16] then on to Jerusalem and, by way of the Mediterranean, return to Cádiz. He was imagining the Chersonese as a peninsula, unaware of the huge South American continent around which he would have to navigate. [17] Had he even tried, he soon would have discovered that continent and no doubt it would have been a disappointment since he would have come to the realization that he was nowhere near either the Chersonese or Cathay.

In truth, undertaking such a voyage was a pipe dream, for they were running out of food. Their daily rations, including those of Columbus, consisted of "a pound of rotten biscuits and a pint of wine," [18] so they had to turn back toward Hispaniola. In order to avoid the treacherous waters they had just come through, they decided to return to La Isabela by heading south around Jamaica. There, a fleet of canoes, very elaborately decorated, came out to meet them. The most regal one carried the cacique

> with his wife and two daughters, one of whom was 18, very beautiful, completely naked, as is their custom, and very modest; the other much younger. There were also two young boys, the cacique's five brothers, and 18 servants . . . in his canoe was a standard bearer, who stood alone in the prow wearing a tunic of colored feathers like a coat of arms and a great plume on his head. [19]

Other canoes carried subjects of the cacique including several musicians. When the cacique greeted Columbus, he said: "Friend, I have decided to leave my homeland and come with you to Castile and see the King and Queen . . . of the world." Columbus wrote: "He said all this so reasonably I was wonder struck." [20] Columbus didn't think it was a good idea to take the cacique with him, in part because they were not returning to Spain at this time. He did not want to disappoint such an important local personage, but he knew he had to find a way to discourage him. Seeing that a storm was brewing and hoping that the rough weather would dissuade the cacique, Columbus welcomed the entire retinue aboard and took them for a ride out to sea. It was windy and they encountered some big waves, and as expected, the cacique and his family decided to return home and await Columbus's next visit. They left in dignified procession.

Everyone with Columbus was eager to get back to La Isabela. After leaving the south coast of Jamaica, they headed toward Hispaniola. De Cuneo was the first to sight land on this "homeward" journey, so Columbus named the place, Cabo de San Miguel, after his friend. De Cuneo also sighted a small island, hitherto undiscovered, and wrote that "the Lord Admiral called it *La Bella Saonese*" in recognition of their home town in Italy. Columbus gave it to de Cuneo as a present and made a brief stop so that Cuneo could take "possession of it according to the appropriate modes and forms . . . and [he] planted the cross and also the gallows, and in the name of God baptized it." [21] Today that tiny, uninhabited, and waterless island is known as Navassa. Because of its lucrative guano deposits, the "United States Congress quickly placed the island under American jurisdiction based on the Guano Islands Act of 1856." [22]

When they reached Hispaniola, they landed on the south coast and were quite a distance from La Isabela to the north. Columbus sent some men overland to alert those at the settlement that they had returned safely. In the meantime, he would approach La Isabela by sailing east around the island. At a stop on August 23, an Indian surprised Columbus by calling out to him by name; clearly word of the Europeans and their "chief" had spread across the island. They were still traveling three weeks later when, on September 14, they witnessed an eclipse of the moon. With his dog-eared copy of Regiomontanus's *Ephemerides*, which gave the time of the eclipse in Nuremberg, Europe, Columbus calculated the time difference between Hispaniola and Cádiz was five hours and 23 minutes. [23]

Finally on September 29, Columbus limped into port at La Isabela with leaking ships and a crew that was tired, dirty, and sick. And the sickest of all was Columbus: "I was struck with an illness that robbed me of my faculties and intellect, as if it were the plague or lethargy." [24] He thought his many years at sea were taking their toll, but especially on this voyage his illness was due to the difficult sailing and his reluctance to leave the helm to anyone else. In addition to a high fever, he wrote that "over the last 30 days I slept no more than five hours, in the last eight only an hour and a half, becoming half blind, completely so at certain times of the day"—a terrifying experience. He might have suffered from what, today, is called a nervous breakdown or, in the view of Dr. Renato Lungarotti, it might have been typhoid fever brought on either by the water or from oysters that Columbus, unlike the other sailors, had been eating. [25]

Ferdinand, reading his father's journal of this voyage, understood better than anyone how very sick his father must have been because from the twenty-fourth of September he

> ceased to record in his journal the day's sailing, nor does he tell how he returned to Isabela. He relates only that because of his great exertions, weakness, and scanty diet he fell gravely ill . . . he had a high fever and a drowsiness, so that he lost his sight, memory, and all his other senses . . . [and] sometimes went eight days with less than three hours' sleep. This would seem impossible did he not himself tell it in his writings.[26]

Whatever it was that caused his collapse, Columbus was plagued most of his adult life with a painful form of arthritis and eye problems, about which some doctors today assessing the symptoms believe may have been Reiter's syndrome—a severe form of rheumatoid arthritis that affects the joints, eyes, and urinary tract.[27] He remained ill for more than five months. The only thing that cheered Columbus was the arrival of his brother Bartholomew, whom he had not seen in six years, and the news he brought that Diego and Ferdinand were at court, where they had been appointed as pages to the infante.

While Bartholomew had been away in his unsuccessful attempt to persuade the kings of England and France to finance the first voyage, Columbus had already sailed under the Spanish sovereigns. Bartholomew was eager to see his brothers and the much talked-about lands. The sovereigns had sent him with three ships filled with needed supplies for the settlement. He had arrived sometime during the summer of 1494 while Columbus was still away on this voyage of exploration, and dove quickly into the political fray.

Bartholomew joined Diego and the council to try to bring some discipline to the unruly settlers, especially to Margarit and his men whose tour had, not surprisingly, included plunder and rape. When Margarit returned to La Isabela, he found Bartholomew in charge. In the opinion of Las Casas, Bartholomew "lacked the 'sweetness and benignity' of the Admiral, and erred on the side of rigor as Christopher did on the side of gentleness."[28] In order to avoid Bartholomew's wrath, Margarit managed to commandeer the ships that had brought Bartholomew to Hispaniola and, along with Friar Buil, took off for Spain, leaving in his wake natives seething with resentment, and the settlement in turmoil. Thus Margarit managed to escape a confrontation with Columbus, who had done so much for him and his family. Once back in Castile, Margarit spread rumors undermining Columbus's management of the settlement, not admitting his own part in creating the tense relations between the natives and the Europeans. Columbus was unaware of these events during his absence. On his return to the settlement, Columbus appointed Bartholomew as *adelantado*, a position that made him second-in-command, and the person who would take Columbus's place when he was away exploring.

Before the end of 1494 another four caravels arrived from Spain, commanded, once again, by Antonio de Torres. The ships carried more supplies and a letter from the sovereigns requesting that, if at all possible, Columbus return to Spain to discuss the situation at the settlement. But because so many of the men were sick, Columbus thought he could not leave La Isabela at that time. Instead, when de Torres left for Spain a few months later, Columbus sent a memo to the sovereigns describing his recent explorations and requesting supplies and people who had specific skills. Since the memo would be public, he also sent a private letter asking the sovereigns to send a few good friars. He had been displeased with Friar Buil, who had not learned the language and seemed to think that baptism alone, without any prior instruction, was enough to make the natives Christian. In contrast, Columbus wanted the natives to receive religious instruction before being baptized so they would understand the faith. "I say again, repeating it one more time, that the only thing I am lacking to make them all [the natives] Christian is the ability to tell them how; i.e., to preach to them in their language, because in truth they have no sect or idolatry." [29]

In addition to good friars, Columbus again requested that they send more miners from Almadén because, although the rivers contained gold, the major source would be the mines. Las Casas wrote that Columbus's request for miners was proof "that the Admiral never intended to make the Indians work in the mines." [30] In his letter, Columbus tried to assuage any doubts the sovereigns might have about the presence of gold by telling them that the men had found the source of it, and in two places reiterated the promise he had made after the first voyage, that in seven years' time he would have collected enough gold to accomplish their plan, namely the crusade for the conquest of Jerusalem. [31]

What Columbus did not quite let on in his letter back to the sovereigns was that the settlement was in dire straits. There was famine in the land and the Indians, too, were ill; they could no longer produce enough food to feed themselves, let alone the Spaniards. Some of the settlers left La Isabela in search of food and continued their violence and rapacity. Peter Martyr, in his history of this period, wrote that a

> number of the principal caciques of the frontier regions assembled to beg Columbus to forbid the Spaniards to wander about the island, because, under the pretext of hunting for gold or other local products, they left nothing uninjured or undefiled.[32]

Martyr went on say that in order to prevent these rampages and gain protection, the natives between the ages of fourteen and seventy years had agreed to pay tribute to Columbus. In Columbus's world, tribute was nothing new; all vassals of the queen, except the nobility, paid tribute, and the natives were considered her vassals. The tribute that Columbus collected, ultimately, belonged to the Crown. The system in the Indies required that, every three months, the natives bring to La Isabela a certain amount of gold or other products, depending on where they lived. But like the Spaniards, the Indians were weak and dying and could not afford the tribute requested even when he cut it by half.

When de Torres left for Spain on February 24, 1495, he took with him Columbus's memo and letter, his brother Diego, his good friend Michele de Cuneo, some more of the disillusioned Spanish settlers, and according to de Cuneo 550 natives who were being sent to Castile as slaves. Some of them were probably the Caribs they had captured at Guadalupe, but others may have been hostile natives rounded up in Hispaniola perhaps by Margarit and/or Bartholomew. If the natives' resistance was the reason for their capture, then their enslavement was justified by the beliefs of the time; no one, including the pope, the sovereigns, or Las Casas, who only decades later came to the defense of the Indians, had doubts or qualms about the practice of slavery under certain conditions. Furthermore, it was assumed that once in Spain, the slaves would become good Christians and that at least their souls would be saved. But, at wit's end in the unruly colony, Columbus may have conveniently told himself that these natives had attacked the Christians at several forts that had been established in the countryside or resisted them when they went on their marauding excursions, or refused to be baptized. No doubt the natives did resist the atrocities committed by Margarit and his men.

In reality, the distinction between "good" natives and those who attacked the Spaniards and resisted Christianization was probably often blurred in practice, and Isabella must have been concerned about whether the natives in this shipment had been captured justly. She had already expressed her desire that the natives, whom she considered her vassals, be converted in the islands. Vassals cannot be enslaved, so their conversion was one way of halting the shipment of dubiously captured slaves. Regarding future shipments of slaves, she wrote that "their Highnesses have not made up Their Own minds, so nothing can be said to the Admiral about this now."

Upon arrival at Cádiz, de Torres sent Columbus's letter to the sovereigns. When they received it, they instructed Fonseca, as the man in charge of outfitting the ships, to comply with Columbus's requests. At the same time, King Ferdinand decided to investigate the allegations made by the settlers that they were starving, and about what they considered Columbus's mismanagement. No doubt there was some truth in the allegations, but far more likely their complaints were due to the restraints Columbus had placed on their behavior, whether forbidding them to take native women as concubines or native men as slaves. The king chose Juan Aguado to investigate. Aguado had been on the second voyage and may have captained one of the ships; he also captained one of the twelve ships Columbus had sent back to Castile early in 1494.

The sovereigns gave Aguado detailed instructions about the rations each man in the settlement was to receive because they had complained these had been unequally divided when Bartholomew was in charge. Columbus was told to find a couple of trustworthy men to oversee the distribution. "[E]ach man was to receive one-half arroba of wine every two weeks [approximately a gallon a week] at full strength, for they say it is often watered down, and for good measure, one pint per day, and this is to continue until We send more provisions, at which time the ration may increase." [33] In addition, they should receive four pounds of bacon and cheese every two weeks, some oil and vinegar, beans until the chickpeas arrived, and on fish days each month—the days Catholics were required to abstain from meat—they were to receive three pounds of dried fish. The sovereigns also conceded to the men's request that if they brought their own seeds, chickens, or other plants and animals from Spain, they should be permitted to retain the produce for their own use.

Aguado left Seville in August of 1495 and arrived at La Isabela in October, when Columbus was away in another part of the island. Without license to do so, Aguado immediately began to usurp the authority of Bartholomew. With the demeanor of a priest hearing confessions, he began to hear the complaints of the colonists who were all too ready to blame the Columbus brothers for their problems. When Columbus returned from the other side of the island, he realized that he could no longer put off his departure for Castile. But despite his readiness, he could not leave immediately. Most of the ships had been destroyed in the summer of 1495 during a hurricane—a word that derives from the native *hurakán* via the Spanish *huracán*. In order to leave at least one ship at Hispaniola, they had to construct another.

While waiting for the new ship to be built, Columbus had concluded that, despite his efforts to make La Isabela successful, the settlement had not thrived, and he decided that a new location might be a change for the better. He told his brother to begin construction of a new settlement at the site found sometime earlier by Miguel Díaz, on the south side of the island. Díaz, who had served under Bartholomew, had gone into the hinterlands after an argument with another Spaniard. He took refuge in an Indian settlement ruled by a female cacique with whom he fell in love. Their relationship was not a mere affair; they married, and eventually she became a Christian known as Princess Catalina. Although happy in his marriage, Díaz began to pine for the fellowship of his own people. His wife, the cacique, was wise; she took him up to the top of a hill where

> she pointed to the beauties of her home, the safe harbour, the tireless river, the responsive fields, and the mines of gold. "Here," she cried; "here bring thy people and here found a new city." [34]

And so they did. Miguel Díaz became the *alcalde* (mayor) of the new city that Bartholomew named Santo Domingo after his and Christopher's father. For a time, it was simply referred to as New Isabela, while the old Isabela was abandoned and left to ruin. Forever after, people thought it was haunted, and only pirates, smugglers, and looters dared to visit it. Today, the archaeological site can be visited by land, but because it is so close to the border between Haiti and the Dominican Republic, it is under military surveillance and, thus, is difficult to approach by sea and to view it as Columbus first did.

When he was finally ready to embark for his trip back to Spain, Columbus was able to sail his favorite ship back, the newly repaired *Niña*. Juan Aguado captained the *India*, so called for being the first ship built in the Indies. Separated only by ship, Columbus and his foe left Hispaniola in March 1496.

Between the two ships they carried 225 Christians and 30 natives. When they arrived in Cádiz on June 11, 1496, those on the quay were curious not only to see the Indians and the new ship but also Columbus, who disembarked wearing the coarse brown habit with knotted cord indicative of a Franciscan friar of the Observatine order—an outfit that he continued to wear for the rest of his life and that, at the end, became his burial shroud. If he wrote about when and why he had made this change of clothing, it doesn't survive, but many believe he had become a tertiary, a lay brother in the order. Columbus the monk! Hardly the image we have of him. Perhaps the words and example of his Franciscan friends had come back to him in the midst of all the greed and turmoil in the settlement and he had adopted it as penance; perhaps he also recalled the meaning of his name—the Christ-bearer—and rededicated himself to his mission.

In Cádiz, Peralonso Niño, who had served as pilot of the *Santa María*, was preparing to sail to La Isabela with relief ships. Before setting out for the court, Columbus may have had the opportunity to apprise Niño of the situation at La Isabela, and reciprocally Niño could give Columbus a sense of the court's thinking about the settlement. When Columbus learned that the court was in Valladolid, quite a distance away, he decided to stop in Seville and stay with his friend, the priest Andrés Bernáldez. Although Columbus was able to move easily between the opulent life at court and the simple life of the monastery, he preferred the latter and especially the conversations with men of religion. Andrés Bernáldez enjoyed the stories Columbus told him about the marvels and the beauty of the Indies; he relished them so much, in fact, that he included them in his *Historia*. Columbus, for his part, entrusted Bernáldez with many of his papers, including the journal of the second voyage that Bernáldez drew upon for his *Historia*. Bernáldez's account is so valuable because through it, "it is possible to gather the impression made by the discovery upon an ordinary man, of simple mind and simple tastes and habits," who shared with Columbus the sense of wonder.[35]

After recuperating from the journey at the modest home of Bernáldez, Columbus set off for Valladolid, eager to see his sons and to make his case before the queen. On the way, he stopped again at Guadalupe to tell the monks about the island he had named for them. According to records at the church, some of the Indians who were with Columbus were baptized there; thus they could not be enslaved. When he finally arrived at court, which had moved on to Burgos, Columbus presented the sovereigns with more gold ornaments, told

his view of what was happening at La Isabela, and pleaded with them to sponsor another voyage so he could return to Hispaniola. It would be a long wait.

Meanwhile, the fleet that had sailed with Peralonso Niño arrived in Hispaniola during the summer of 1496, bringing the much needed supplies and permission from the sovereigns to enslave any Indians who attacked the Christians.
Whether or not they fit that description, Bartholomew loaded three hundred
Indians on board the returning ships. Bound for Cádiz, they left on September
29, 1496, but many of them died due to overcrowding, seasickness, and disease.

Columbus continued to petition the sovereigns to support another voyage,
but they were fully occupied on very different matters. They were waging a war
against France, and Ferdinand was contemplating the conquest of Naples. Three
marriages were also in preparation; the infante Don Juan would marry Margarita of Austria; the sovereigns' eldest daughter, Doña Isabel, would marry Don
Manuél of Portugal, and a younger daughter, Doña Juana, would marry Philip,
the archduke of Hapsburg. Columbus and his sons, who were pages to the infante, attended the wedding on April 3, 1497.

Time was slipping away, Columbus was becoming more and more anxious
about the settlement; by the time of the weddings, he had already been back
in Spain for nearly a year. He was itching to return, but he couldn't leave without royal authorization. There was good reason for urgency in this matter; the
sovereigns were concerned not only that the Portuguese were sending ships to
investigate the Spanish claims, but that the English were also intending to make
voyages of their own. During his wait, Columbus had received a letter from
John Day of England informing him of the 1497 voyage of a fellow Genoese by
the name of Jacobo Caboto, in England known as John Cabot, and his discovery
of Newfoundland. Soon, Caboto would undertake another voyage.[36]

On April 23, 1497, Ferdinand and Isabella issued an order to Columbus to
prepare for a third voyage. On the same day, they finally granted Columbus
permission to draw up his *majorat*:

> As Don Christopher Columbus, our Admiral, Viceroy, and Governor
> of the Ocean-Sea . . . we give you our power and authority, to make and
> establish out of your possessions, vassals, hereditaments, and perpet-
> ual offices, one or two majorats to the end that there may be perpetual
> memory of you and your house and lineage, and that those who come
> after you may be honoured.[37]

A huge weight was lifted from his mind. Having come close to death several times and knowing of the dangers that could easily befall him, Columbus was continually concerned about what would happen to his sons if he died.

Due to the custom of primogeniture, Columbus left all of his property, privileges, and titles to his eldest son Diego. If Diego should meet an early death, his estate would go to his son Ferdinand, then brother Bartholomew and his eldest son, and after them to brother Diego and his eldest son. At the same time, however, he instructed his son Diego to disperse a certain percentage of the revenue each year—a million *maravedis*—to his son Ferdinand and his brother Bartholomew. Regarding his other brother, Diego, Columbus left a lump sum in order to "maintain him honestly . . . because he wishes to be of the church, and they will give him what is right." In addition, Columbus wrote:

> I direct the said Don Diego, my son, or whoever inherits the said Majorat, to keep and always maintain in the city of Genoa, a person of our lineage who has a house and a wife there, and I direct that he shall have an income so that he may be able to live honestly, as a person so near to our lineage: and that he may be the root and base of it in the said city, as a citizen thereof, so that he may have aid and protection from the said city in matters of his own necessity, since from it I came, and in it I was born.[38]

Furthermore, Diego should "always strive and labour for the honour and good and increase of the city of Genoa."

Columbus also bequeathed a fund at the Bank of St. George in Genoa to relieve the citizens of taxes. For Hispaniola, he left money to be used to build a hospital, as good as any in Spain or Italy, attached to a church, and dedicated to Santa María de la Concepción, where masses would be said for his soul and those of his ancestors and successors. But it was not just for his soul and those of his family members that he was concerned; he was also concerned for the souls of the natives. Part of the fund was to be used to maintain four men of religion—not theologians, he said, but teachers and preachers who would instruct the natives in Our Holy Faith and work to convert them, because he did not want them to be condemned to Hell when Christ returned to judge both the living and the dead.[39]

Regarding the Church, Columbus left instructions that if a schism should again occur in the church, his beneficiary—that is, whoever of his beneficiaries was alive at the time—should endeavor "with all his power and revenue and estate" to work to deliver "the church from the said schism" and prevent it "from being dispossessed of its honour and property."

His passion for the conquest of Jerusalem never left him. For the purpose of financing a crusade to retake Jerusalem, he established a trust in the bank of St. George in Genoa and hoped that this bequest would inspire future sovereigns, whoever they would be, to undertake it. However, if they were not so inspired, he instructed his son Diego (or whoever would inherit) that when the money had multiplied and was sufficient for the purpose, he should gather together a great force and go even without royal support.

When Columbus's will was completed and signed on February 22, 1498,[40] he could rest easier knowing that when he was away his sons would be provided for in the event of his death. Soon thereafter, plans for the voyage began to take shape. It would be still another year from the time that the order was issued before the ships and crew were ready.

Before Columbus left on the third voyage, he wrote a letter to his son Diego:[41]

Very dear son:—

I have written you by another courier that I will send you two marks of virgin gold nuggets and thus I do now, by . . . , the bearer of this letter, fastened in a cloth and sealed, in order that you may give them to the Queen, our Lady, at such time as you see to be best, with the consent of Jeronimo and of the Treasurer Villacorta, to whom I am also writing at length by another courier: and in my opinion the best time will be just after dinner. This is a treasure of such value that I have hitherto suffered a thousand necessities rather than sell it or melt it in order to serve the Queen, Our Lady, with it, as her Highness had granted it to me. Further, I saw that it was charged upon my conscience not to destroy it but to return it to her that she may see the miracles of our Lord and that it may make her see to whom her Highness will apologize. Kiss her Royal hands for me and give it to her with this letter which goes with it. And as I tell why I write to you and to all greatly at length in other letters, I do not enlarge more than to supplicate our Lord to have you in His holy keeping, and thy brother, whom, may you have greatly in your charge. Done in Seville April 29 [1498]

> Your father, who loves you as himself.
> .S.
> .S. A .S.
> X M Y[42]

El Almirante.

This letter provides a charming insight—the father telling his son the best time to present his gift to the queen. It implies, too, that Diego might actually be dining with the queen, or at least in attendance, and thus very close to her. In addition, he instructs Diego to watch after his little brother.

The sovereigns authorized six ships for Columbus, one of which should be old so that it could be dismantled on arrival and its nails and wood recycled as building material. The six ships were to form a single fleet as far as the Canaries, where they would split up. Three of them would go directly to Hispaniola with the supplies, and the three under Columbus would go on another voyage of discovery before reaching the settlement. The sovereigns specified the total number and kinds of people to accompany him. In sharp contrast to the twelve hundred men who went on the second voyage, they told him that this time he could take only three hundred and thirty people and, although they said that he could specify their occupations and rank, they recommended that there be: "40 squires, 100 foot soldiers, 30 sailors, 30 cabin boys, 20 gold washers, 50 farm workers and gardeners, 20 skilled tradesmen of different types and 30 women."[43] Whether these women were wives of some of the colonists, domestic servants to make unnecessary the use of Indians as servants, or prostitutes meant to deflect the rape of native women, is not clear. The sovereigns wanted farmers to go "so that the persons who are and will be on the island may be sustained better and at less cost," and for this purpose, they also sent seeds, cows, and mares, as well as "a suitable number of hoes, spades, pickaxes, sledgehammers, and crowbars."

They also sent the miners that Columbus had requested but told him that in addition to miners there should be men and equipment for minting the gold into "Granadan *excelentes* . . . because by doing this, deceit and fraud related to the said gold in the Indies can be avoided." All of the skilled workmen would be on the royal payroll, and the sovereigns specified the amount each should be paid. For the health and happiness of the settlers, the sovereigns sent: "a surgeon, and apothecary, and an herbalist" and, per Columbus's request, "some musicians and instruments for the entertainment of the people there." The sovereigns also granted pardon to any criminal who wanted to go, although they gave no pardons for murder, treason, arson, counterfeiting, or sodomy; they wanted to make clear that they were not creating a penal colony. The length of a man's service in Hispaniola would be commensurate with his crime. These men were free once on board ship, and Columbus said he had far less trouble with them than with the men who had pleaded to go on the first two voyages.[44] In their letter to Columbus the sovereigns also suggested, regarding the tribute required of the Indians, that they

> should wear a brass or lead coin around their necks, and that this coin be marked differently each time they pay the tribute, so that anyone not paying the tribute may thus be known; and that when persons not wearing the said coin on their necks are found on the island, they should be arrested and given some light punishment.[45]

The sovereigns authorized the construction of a new settlement, perhaps unaware that work on it had already begun. They also authorized Columbus to make grants of land to the settlers (a system known as *repartimiento*), meaning that each settler would have ownership of a parcel of land where, previously, the land had belonged to the Indians. Claiming possession of land was a clear indication that the sovereigns' thinking had shifted from creating a *factoría*, or trading post, to a colony—the beginning of Spanish imperial designs on the New World, and for Columbus, the beginning of the end of the privileges specified in the original agreement known as the Capitulations. In that document, the trading post was supposed to be a fief and, in this case, would be hereditary in the Columbus family, which meant that Columbus and his descendants would oversee the trade, collect their "tenth," and decide who would be permitted to engage in it.

To outfit and pay the expenses of this voyage, the sovereigns had allocated 2,824,326 *maravedis*, but they didn't have that much money on hand due to their wars and marriages. Part of the amount was transferred "through the Seville branch of the Genoese house of Centurione that had employed Columbus in his youth." By February 17, 1498, Columbus had received only 350,094 *mara-vedis*; in addition, the proceeds from the sale of the slaves brought by Peralonso Niño in 1496 were turned over to Columbus, but neither of these sources of money was enough to pay the men's wages, nor to pay for a cargo of wheat that he had ordered from Genoa. For a long time Columbus bore the brunt of the settlers' hostility.[46]

Finally, on May 30, 1498, after Columbus had been in Spain for two years, and a year after the order for the third voyage was given, he was ready to set sail. The fleet left from Sanlúcar de Barrameda, a town situated at the mouth of the Guadalquivir river that flows to the coast from Seville. That town was and still is famous for its Manzanilla sherry, which, no doubt, Columbus loaded for the voyage and for the people on Hispaniola.

Columbus's third voyage was almost dead in the water before getting very far. Just off the coast of Portugal, some French ships appeared intending to attack and take Columbus as a prize in their war with Spain. He managed to elude them and gave effusive thanks to the Holy Trinity to whom he had dedicated this voyage: "May That which is Three in One guide me by Its charity and mercy."[47] He made a brief stop at Porto Santo, where he had lived with his wife years before and where his son Diego had been born, and then sailed on to the Canaries, where the ships would separate. The three ships with Columbus would head farther south to the Cape Verde Islands, where they would begin the ocean crossing.

The three ships that would go straight to Hispaniola were commanded by a group of people close to Columbus. One was Giovanni Colombo, a son of Columbus's uncle Antonio, for whose voyage detailed court records in Genoa describe who would pay for his travel to Seville so he could meet his famous cousin (further evidence of Columbus's Genoese origins). Others included Antonio Alonso de Carvajal (who had been captain of a ship on the second voyage) and Pedro de Harana. The fact that Pedro, the brother of Columbus's mistress Beatriz, went on this voyage indicates both that Columbus was still in contact with Beatriz and her family and that neither she nor her brother held Columbus responsible for the death of their cousin who was killed at Navidad.[48] Columbus gave these captains directions to Hispaniola and strict instructions that when they needed supplies, they must *trade* with the Indians, not just take what they wanted; the use of force, he said, was unnecessary and only served to create hostility. Columbus sent a letter to his brother Bartholomew, telling him to pay a group of these men to go work in the mines. Others were to help build a new settlement and plant wheat and other foodstuffs.

Despite Columbus's directions and the fact that one of the captains had already been to Hispaniola, the ships went off course. They finally arrived sometime in July 1498, shortly before Columbus himself would arrive. But instead of landing at the settlement of Santo Domingo where Columbus's brother was in charge, they landed at the far side of the island in the region of Xaragua, where they confronted a rebellious group of settlers led by Francisco Roldán. Because no supply ships had come to Hispaniola for a long time and the people were unaware that any were on the way, some of them had wondered if they had been abandoned. Taking Columbus's long absence as evidence that he was never coming back, Francisco Roldán became emboldened. Columbus had trusted Roldán and had appointed him as *alcalde* of La Isabela to oversee

> the laborers and craftsmen and making them do their work; but since he was an intelligent and able man, the Admiral, recognizing that he was capable of holding more responsible positions and to do him honor, appointed him first town magistrate of Isabela and later on chief magistrate of the island: and in return for this, Roldán decided to rebel against him.[49]

Although he was a commoner, he had ambitions and had come to resent the Columbus brothers' leadership. He decided to change the balance of power. Perhaps Roldán also resented the appointment of Miguel Díaz as *alcalde* of the new city which left him presiding over the abandoned settlement. When Bartholomew was on a trip to the hinterland to investigate a few of the outposts, Roldán capitalized on the complaints of some of the colonists who claimed that they were being worked too hard, that Bartholomew showed favoritism in distributing the rations and by telling them that they could not "take" native women. They disliked Bartholomew's imposition of the monastic rules of poverty, chastity, and obedience. Roldán rallied them to his side by promising them food, women, freedom to live wherever they wanted, and permission to collect gold for themselves.

Roldán's rebels had stormed the storehouse stashed with weapons and stolen them.[50] Then they slaughtered all the cattle and left them to rot—a very odd move since the men complained they were starving. The few men who were loyal to Columbus and his brother were in danger of their lives; they could do little to stop the looting. The rebels proceeded to steal all the horses and rode through the country crying "Viva el Rey," a sign of their fealty only to King Ferdinand and not to Columbus. They had settled in Xaragua, where they began to form alliances with the Indians by promising to lift the tribute Columbus had imposed on them. However, Roldán's promises were short-lived; instead he diverted the tribute to his own use, and when he and his men began plundering native villages and raping the native women, the Indians realized their mistake in allying with him. But it was too late; they were no match for the weapons of the Spanish.

Nevertheless, the natives were to get their revenge by transmitting the "French sickness" to the Spaniards.[51] Today it is believed that the natives had a form of yaws, a highly contagious disease caused by a spirochete similar to that of syphilis, which is thought to have developed into syphilis when contracted by the Europeans. When these men returned to Spain, the disease began to spread throughout Europe.

When Bartholomew returned to Santo Domingo from the outposts, he attempted to quell the rebellion by meeting with Roldán to hear his complaints and try to negotiate a settlement. But by this time, Roldán had talked with the men who had arrived with the ships and had seduced them with his promises. For example, he told the men who had come to work in the mines that they could make the Indians work for them.

Columbus had sent a letter with those ships that included the news that the sovereigns officially appointed Bartholomew as *adelantado*. When Bartholomew received the letter, his first official order was to strip Roldán of his office. He threatened Roldán with criminal proceedings if he continued with his rebellion, stating that it was not just against Columbus and himself, but against the sovereigns. Yet Roldán now had the majority of the settlers and the new arrivals with him and all the weapons. He was in no mood to negotiate. This was the situation Columbus would have to deal with when he returned from his explorations.

CHAPTER EIGHT

PARADISE FOUND AND LOST

Columbus was oblivious to the rebellion happening in Hispaniola. He was glad to be exploring again, but he was preoccupied. He knew that if he did not soon find major sources of gold, spices, and other valuables, the "Enterprise of the Indies" would come to an end and so, too, would his dream of financing the crusade to Jerusalem. The sovereigns were becoming anxious about the expense of voyages that had resulted in so little return. Las Casas captured the importance of this voyage to Columbus when he wrote:

> Truly this man had a good and Christian purpose . . . was thoroughly content with his station in life, and wished to live modestly therein and to rest from the great hardships which he had undergone so meritoriously . . . But he saw that his signal services were held of slight value, and that suddenly the reputation that these Indies at first had enjoyed was sinking and declining, by reason of those who had the ear of the Sovereigns, so that day by day he feared greater disfavors, and that the Sovereigns might abandon the enterprise altogether, and that he might thus see his labor and travail go for naught, and he in the end die in poverty.[1]

For Columbus, the enterprise was not just about finding gold; he felt that his discovery of islands in the sea, all the people to be converted to the Holy Christian faith, and of a new route to the east were as important as finding riches. But the issue of gold was ever present and the source of it had to be found, soon. The sovereigns asked Jaime Ferrer, a lapidary with extensive knowledge about the probable location of gold and gems, to write to Columbus and suggest that he go farther south on this voyage since gold ought to be found nearer the equator. Most of Ferrer's letter was taken up with stories of the achievements of great men of antiquity with whom he favorably compared Columbus, adding that Columbus was "an Apostle and Ambassador of God, sent by His Divine judgment to make known His Holy Name in unknown regions." Slowly, Ferrer came to the topic at hand; prefacing the gem of wisdom he was meant to communicate, he wrote that "temporal things . . . are not evil or repugnant to the spiritual things" if they "will be for the service of God and of all Christianity, especially of this, our Spain." Those words were well calculated to ease Columbus's conscience for, though his ultimate goal was the liberation of Jerusalem, he was not so naive as to think that could be accomplished without gold.

Ferrer went on to give his opinion "that within the equinoctial regions there are great and precious things, such as fine stones and gold and spices and drugs," which are "from a very hot region where the inhabitants are black or tawny." Ferrer concluded that if Columbus found such people he would also find the valuables.[2] This information about the location of gold was hardly news to Columbus, who already knew of Aristotle's theory that gold "grew" closer to the equator and had seen confirmation of it at São Jorge da Mina. He also knew that people living in similar latitudes would have similar characteristics, and thus he assumed that other people living near the equator, like the blacks in Africa he had seen, would also be black.

Columbus followed the sovereigns' plan to sail farther south than he had on his first two voyages and only then turn to the west. He had left from the port of Sanlúcar de Barrameda on May 30, 1498, with six ships and headed for the Canaries, as usual. After separating from the other three ships there, he sailed south toward the Cape Verde Islands, located off the west coast of Africa not far from the places Columbus had visited when he sailed for the Portuguese years earlier. While not quite at the equator, these islands were close enough; at that latitude in Africa, Columbus had already seen gold and people who were black. He reasoned that if he sailed due west on the same latitude, he would find black people and gold on the other side of the ocean. In the process, Columbus would also be able to discover whether there was any land before he reached the line of demarcation, 370 leagues west of the Cape Verde Islands, that was set by the Treaty of Tordesillas. Columbus prayed that he would not find any undiscovered land east of the line because if he did and there was gold, it would belong to Portugal.

When he reached the Cape Verde Islands, Columbus was surprised to see that they were not as verdant and fertile as the coast of Africa he had seen. The Cape Verde Islands, he remarked, "have a false name, since they are so barren that I saw no green thing in them and all the people were infirm, so that I did not dare to remain in them."[3] However, he did exchange some of his fresh Castilian victuals for the local salted goat meat. While anchored at one of the smaller islands, Columbus learned that "lepers came thither to be cured of the leprosy because of the great abundance on that island of turtles . . . [B]y eating their flesh and washing repeatedly in their blood they are cured of leprosy."[4] Columbus went on to describe the life cycle of the turtles and the inhabitants' methods of catching them.

On July 4, 1498, Columbus left the Cape Verde Islands and set his course due west. Two weeks later he had still not found any land. Instead of land, the ships hit what has come to be known as the Doldrums, an area in the mid-Atlantic known for its lack of wind, and they became absolutely becalmed.

> So suddenly and unexpectedly did the wind cease and the excessive and unusual heat come on that there was no one who would dare to go below to look after the casks of wine and water, which burst, snapping the hoops of the pipes; the wheat burned like fire; the bacon and salt meat roasted and putrefied. This heat and fire lasted eight days.[5]

Columbus must have been beside himself with wanting desperately to get on with his explorations, but his long training in patience came in handy. Fortunately, several of the days were overcast; if the sun had been shining, Columbus said, "it would have been impossible for even one of them to escape with his life." No doubt their suffering in the sweltering heat was exacerbated because, as was seamen's custom, the men never removed their heavy, dark, woolen clothes.

Finally the wind picked up and they were able to set sail again; but because some of their food had spoiled, and they were running out of fresh water, Columbus had to change course to the north in the hope of finding one of the islands that he had discovered on his other voyages. Had he continued due west he would very quickly have come to the north coast of South America. Instead, on the last day of July, a man keeping watch in the crow's nest sighted an island that Columbus did not know. When the island's three hills came into view, Columbus named the island Trinidad as a sign that the Holy Trinity was watching over this voyage. Then, as usual, he had the whole crew assemble on deck to give thanks with prayer and song. In his journal, he wrote, as if to the sovereigns, that

> It pleased Our Lord by His Divine Majesty that on the first sight there were three rocks, I mean mountains, all in a group, all at once and in a single view. May His Almighty power guide me by His charity in such wise that He be well served and Your Highnesses have much pleasure, for it is certain that the finding of this land in this region was a great miracle, as great as the discovery on the First Voyage.[6]

The men reached the island at the hour of compline, but the harbor was too shallow to enter; they sailed on until they found a safe place to anchor where they would also find fresh water and be able to bathe.

Columbus had never seen natives like the ones they now encountered; here, they wore their

> hair long and smooth, and cut in the manner of Castile. They had their heads wrapped in scarves of cotton, worked elaborately and in colours, which, I believed, were *almaizares* [a kind of head covering worn by Moors in Spain]. They wore another of these scarves round the body and covered themselves with them in place of drawers.[7]

Because the natives spoke a language that none on board had ever heard, Columbus asked the ship's musicians to play the *tanborín* [8]—a kind of drum—and encouraged the ship's boys to dance as a gesture of hospitality and friendship. But the frightened natives misinterpreted the gesture as an announcement of war, and took up their bows and arrows. When Columbus saw this, he ordered the music stopped. The pilot of one of the other ships attempted to make contact by proffering gifts, but the natives left in their canoes and were not seen again.

On August 4, as Columbus sailed along the south coast of Trinidad, he could see the coast of South America; at the time, however, he assumed it was just another island, and he named it the isle of Gracia. Between Gracia and Trinidad lay a narrow strait that led into a large gulf, but

> there came a current from the south as strong as a mighty flood, with such great noise and din that it terrified all hands, so that they despaired

of escaping, and the ocean water which confronted it from the opposite direction, caused the sea to rise, making a great and lofty tidal wave which tossed the ship on top of the bore, a thing which none had ever heard or seen.[9]

The ships may have been lifted up on a water spout or *bore*, a nautical term for a dangerous wave caused by the collision of different tidal currents, or raised on a wave caused by some kind of volcanic activity. The huge wave could easily have capsized the ship, but somehow Columbus managed to keep it upright. He named the strait Boca de la Sierpe (Mouth of the Serpent). Later, when Columbus described this event to the sovereigns, he said, "Even today I feel that fear within me, lest the ship be swamped when she came beneath it."[10]

Having survived the treacherous strait, the men sailed into the gulf and searched for a harbor on Gracia. On land, Columbus was pleased by the grapes that grew plentiful there, and something he described as an orange with an inside like a fig (it was a guava). He also saw many *gatos Paulos* (monkeys).[11] The Europeans saw a multitude of oysters hanging on branches with their tiny mouths open to receive the dew, which the explorers believed created pearls. Soon natives appeared bearing bread and several kinds of wine, one which Columbus said was made from maize, and all of which he enjoyed.

Columbus was entranced with this place which the natives called Paria, part of Venezuela today. From there, he took four natives on board with the hope they would act as guides along the coast of Paria.[12] The people they met were eager to trade their "gold" ornaments for European brass because of its copper content. Natives very much liked the smell of copper. Columbus suspected these ornaments were not pure gold and later, when he was able to send some to Spain to be analyzed, he learned that they were made of an alloy of gold, silver, and copper, called *guanin* by the natives, and obviously far less valuable than either gold or silver.

He was perplexed, though, for the people at Paria were whiter than those with whom he was acquainted, and the weather was so cool that he had to wear a lined coat in the morning. After their days sweltering in the heat, the men now shivered from the cold. Yet, anthropological and geographical theories of the time purported that it would be hot near the equator, and the people would be black because they would be scorched by the sun. Columbus believed he was at the same latitude as Sierra Leone, not far from the equator. He would likely have been concerned about this turn of events; since the color of the people and the climate were at variance with the prevailing theory, this did not bode well for finding gold.

Columbus wished he had more time for exploring the area, especially when he saw women wearing strings of pearls round their necks and learned that the pearl "fisheries" were not too distant. But, at this point he was waking up to the reality that the colonists at Hispaniola were expecting the supplies he had on board and most of the food was already rotten.

At the canonical hour of terce, Columbus exited the Gulf of Paria, through a dangerous channel, and encountered another terrifying bore. Grateful to be released from what he called the Boca del Dragón (Dragon's Mouth), Columbus collapsed due to fatigue and burning eyes. He asked God to release him from such pain, which he so often endured for the sake of the voyage,

> for He knows well that I do not bear these sufferings to enrich myself or to find treasures for myself, for, certainly, I know that everything in this age is vain, except what is done for the honor and service of God, which is not the amassing of wealth and riches and many other things which we use in this world, to which we are more favorable than to the things which can win salvation for us.[13]

While lying in bed with his eyes closed, Columbus had time to reflect on what he had seen and experienced. Recalling the strong flow of water from the river, and knowing that "neither the Ganges nor the Euphrates nor the Nile carried so much fresh water,"[14] he came to the conclusion that he had discovered not another island, as he had first thought, but *tierra infinita*—a continent. Only from a "continent," he said, can water exit with such force and be carried so far out into the sea. In his letter to the sovereigns, he wrote:

> I have come to believe that this is a mighty continent which was hitherto unknown. I am greatly supported in this view by reason of this great river, and by this sea which is fresh, and I am also supported by the statement of Esdras in Book 4, Chapter 6, which says that six parts of the world consist of dry land, and one part water. This work was approved by St. Ambrose in his *Exameron* and by St. Augustine [in his commentary] on the passage *Morietur filius meus Christus*, as cited by Francisco de Mayrones.[15]

He had, in fact, come upon the Orinoco River on what we know as the South American continent. If he imagined he had found a "fourth part" of the world, he was not ready to say so as it would have challenged the conventional and canonical view; instead he probably thought he had found a part of Asia "unknown" to ancient authorities whom he cites, or to Marco Polo, or simply not yet explored by Europeans.

Columbus also thought about the compass variations and changes in the location of stars that he had been noticing since the middle of August.[16] From these, he started theorizing about the shape of the earth, and in the same letter to Ferdinand and Isabella, Columbus came to this startling conclusion:

> I find that it is not round as they [authorities] describe it, but that it is the shape of a pear which is everywhere very round except where the stalk is, for there it is very prominent, or that it is like a very round ball, and on one part of it is placed something like a woman's nipple, and that this part, where this protuberance is found, is the highest and nearest to the sky, and it is beneath the equinoctial line and in this Ocean sea at the end of East. I call that "the end of the East," where end all the land and islands.[17]

Columbus's conclusion about the shape of the earth led, in quick succession, to several other astonishing ideas. On maps of the day, East was usually placed "up" at the top, often with the Terrestrial Paradise (the Garden of Eden) somewhat raised (like a protuberance) and also often surrounded by water or flames. Because the protuberance was at "the end of the East," Columbus deduced that it must be the place where the first light appeared because the "sun, when Our Lord made it, was at the first point of the east."[18] His mind was racing; they had been sailing near the place where Creation began, the place where God had said: "Let there be light." Columbus knew his Bible well enough to know what followed: As they sailed along, he couldn't help but imagine they must be nearing the Terrestrial Paradise. This was hardly a crazy idea; many people today believe that the Garden of Eden was a real place, and every so often archaeologists propose a possible site.[19]

In the Garden, Columbus knew that God had "placed the tree of life, and from it issues a fountain from which flow four of the chief rivers of this world, the Ganges in India, the Tigris and Euphrates . . . and the Nile,"[20] one of which

Columbus believed he had just seen. His recent experience may also have evoked a recollection from the fourteenth-century account in John Mandeville's *Travels*; perhaps he had his copy on board, for Mandeville's description of the Terrestrial Paradise had clearly influenced Columbus's thoughts about what he had just seen, heard, and experienced:

> The Earthly Paradise, so men say, is the highest land on earth; it is so high that it touches the sphere of the moon. For it is so high that Noah's flood could not reach it, though it covered all the rest of the earth . . . In the middle of Paradise is a spring from which come four rivers . . . [which] flow with so strong a current, with such a rush and such waves that no boat can sail against them. There is also such a great noise of waters that one man cannot hear another . . . and so no man, as I said, can get there except through the special grace of God.[21]

The spring in Paradise was the source not only of the four rivers, but was believed to travel through the center of the earth and rise up again in a well in Jerusalem, at the exact opposite side of the world. Columbus and Mandeville may also have been aware of the old myth that Dante recounted in his *Purgatorio* which claimed that the location of Eden was not only at the "end of the East," but also at "the extreme height of the world." But unlike either Dante or Mandeville, Columbus had just heard the roar of the water and believed he had actually come to the region where the Terrestrial Paradise was located, even if he could not yet see it. Because it was so high and had escaped the Flood, some people thought that Paradise was protected by an unsurpassable sea; others thought that it was "surrounded on all sides by a flaming sword."[22] Based on what he had just experienced, Columbus decided that it was surrounded neither by water nor by a flaming sword, but was both at "the end of the east" and "at the extreme height of the world." No wonder the rivers flowed with such force; they were flowing *down* from the Garden. Thus, it is not surprising that Columbus began to think he would have to sail *up*, against the flow of the rivers, if he was ever to reach the Terrestrial Paradise.

While trying to decide what to do, Columbus must have mulled over the various stories about the Garden of Eden that came flooding into his mind. He knew the story of Seth, the son of Adam who had been admitted to Paradise. And he knew that an angel had given Seth three seeds from the Tree of Knowledge of

Good and Evil which, when planted, would "grow the wood for Christ's Cross." [23] Because that story formed a bridge between the Old Testament and the New, it was essential for "the wider Christian scheme of salvation history." [24] Since Columbus felt he had an important part in that scheme, he must have wondered if he, like Seth, might be admitted to the Garden. Yet, without a sign from God, Columbus did not dare to approach, thus, paraphrasing Mandeville, he explained to the sovereigns "to it, save by the will of God, no man can come." He had come close enough; he knew its location. Columbus did not try to enter the Terrestrial Paradise, but he could not stop thinking about what his discovery might mean.

The widely held belief that the Terrestrial Paradise would be found only near the end-time was part of the medieval Christian interpretation of the story of Enoch and Elijah. These two figures from Genesis were associated with the "two witnesses" in Revelation (11:3), thought to be waiting in the Garden until the end-time, when they were prophesied to fight the Antichrist. [25] Having found the Terrestrial Paradise must have confirmed Columbus's belief that the end was nigh, and that his enterprise was the beginning of the fulfillment of prophecy. The extraordinary discovery of the Terrestrial Paradise was the first step in the apocalyptic drama; he hoped this event would spur the Spanish sovereigns to take the next steps.

The discovery of the Terrestrial Paradise was, for Columbus, an event that signaled the truth of biblical prophecy. Yet, he worried that the sovereigns had forgotten the purpose of the enterprise and its religious goals. He wrote to them saying, "all will pass away, save the word of God, and all that He has said will be fulfilled. And He spake so clearly of these lands by the mouth of Isaiah, in many places of his Book, affirming that from Spain His holy name should be proclaimed to them." [26] Columbus often felt that the real achievements of his voyages—the new route to the East, the islands discovered, and the people ripe for conversion—were overshadowed by the demand for gold and other precious commodities. The miraculous discovery of the location of the Terrestrial Paradise should have completely dwarfed these mundane issues that were becoming so tedious for Columbus. His complaints reflected his feeling that he was not being appreciated for his true gifts and the value of his discoveries. So he wrote, as if to remind them:

Your Highnesses will leave no greater memorial [for you] have won these vast lands, which are an Other World, in which Christendom will have so much enjoyment and our faith in time so great an increase . . . so that in the end of your days you may have the glory of Paradise.[27]

Not only were the sovereigns forgetting the religious motivations, Columbus thought they were being too influenced by the negative reports of the returning colonists, which might lead them to abandon the project altogether. In the same letter in which he exulted about finding the location of the Terrestrial Paradise, he complained that so many people had disparaged the enterprise "because I had not immediately sent caravels laden with gold, no thought being taken of the brevity of the time and the other many obstacles which I mentioned."[28] Not too discreetly he also compared the commitment of the Portuguese to their voyages with the lack of it by the Spanish sovereigns. He wrote that

in Castile, in the household of Your Highnesses, there are persons who each of them annually earn greater sums than it is necessary to expend on this enterprise.

In his journal he added that

the kings of Portugal spent . . . both money and men for four or five years before receiving any profit.[29]

In "the very same week of August, 1498, when he was working up a fantastic cosmographical hypothesis, he . . . [was] successfully concluding one of the finest bits of dead-reckoning in his maritime career." He was setting out from a direction he had never taken toward Santo Domingo, the new town in Hispaniola which he had never seen, and he came within a few miles of it. He had set the course northwest by north, but how he arrived at that is anyone's guess. Morison, the great sailor and writer about Columbus, concluded that Columbus had "that mysterious knowledge, partly intuitive, partly based on accumulated observation and experience, which has enabled so many unlettered mariners in [the] days of sail to 'smell their way' safely around the seven seas."[30]

Columbus landed at Beata Island, just barely off the coast of Hispaniola and about one hundred miles west of Santo Domingo. The near-miss Columbus attributed, correctly, to the strong currents, but he was nonetheless deeply disappointed that he hadn't hit the bull's-eye. Later, when Las Casas read Columbus's diary of this voyage, he noted that it often took many months for ships to get from the place where Columbus had landed to Santo Domingo, but Columbus had made it in eight days. By any standard, it was an extremely successful voyage.

On arrival, Columbus was probably anxious to see his brothers and to learn the news of the colony. When he'd landed on the last day of August, he had sent a party to Santo Domingo to announce his arrival. Diego, who had probably returned to Hispaniola sometime in 1495 or 1496, was still at La Isabela; Bartholomew was near Santo Domingo, and when he heard that Columbus had landed, he set out to meet him. They had not seen each other in two and a half years. They hardly had a moment to savor their reunion before Bartholomew conveyed the terrible news of Roldán's rebellion and the chaos in the colony.

Although Columbus was angry with Roldán, especially after the trust he had placed in him, he did not want war; instead he hoped to find a way to resolve the issues peacefully. On September 12, 1498, Columbus promised "food and free passage home to all who desired it."[31] Columbus invited Roldán to a peace conference where, as he wrote to the sovereigns, he "promised to give them their salaries and letters for Your Highnesses saying they had served well, and agreed to many other dishonest things," namely things he had reluctantly agreed to in order to get the rebels off the island so they would stop stirring up trouble for, he said, "every day they raid and annoy me."[32] At the same time, he asked Miguel Ballester, a loyal servant whom he had made the *alcalde* at the outpost at Concepción de la Vega, to tell Roldán that he, Columbus,

> greatly deplored his sufferings and all that had happened and that he wished to bury the past in oblivion, granting a general pardon to all; Roldán should come to confer with him without fear of reprisal, that they might consider how the interests of the Catholic Sovereigns could best be served.[33]

Ballester wrote back on September 24, reporting to Columbus that Roldán and Adrian de Mujica, another rebel leader, were so brazen and insolent that they would not agree to anything unless certain conditions were met.

Roldán refused to meet with Columbus; instead, on October 16, he enumerated his demands in writing. Roldán demanded that Columbus provide two fully equipped ships, the men's wages until the time of sailing, letters to the sovereigns about their good service, and a slave to each of them "as compensation for the sufferings they have endured on this island." Roldán swore that within fifty days after receiving Columbus's assent and signature to the document, "we shall embark and sail for Castile."[34] The next day Ballester wrote a note to Columbus beseeching him

> to conclude an agreement with them, whatever it involves, above all so they may go back to Castile as they ask, otherwise I am certain that the affairs of Your Lordship would not be carried on properly as you would wish.[35]

On October 18, before he had received this note, Columbus sent five ships back to Spain with letters to the sovereigns. In one letter Columbus recounted finding the new continent, his musings about the shape of the earth, and the location of the Terrestrial Paradise; another letter was "a detailed account of all that had happened, saying that he had delayed the departure of those ships since his arrival in the belief that Roldán and his men would leave in them as they had announced they would do."[36] But the rebels didn't leave. Instead, on October 26, Roldán finally agreed to meet with Columbus in Santo Domingo. Columbus sent him a "safe-conduct," but when they could not come to any agreement, Roldan stomped off determined to get his way. Under such provocation, other leaders might have executed the rebels, but Columbus did not give up his efforts to resolve the conflict peacefully.

On the 11th of November, Columbus published a general amnesty which would be good for thirty days. Eager to bring peace to the island, Columbus signed Roldán's document on November 16, 1498, with hope that now, the rebels would depart. By January of the new year, 1499, two ships (the *Niña* and the *Santa Cruz*) were being readied for them, and in February they set out from Santo Domingo for Xaragua, Roldán's compound on the other side of the island. On the way, a huge storm arose that forced the ships to put in to a harbor before they reached the rebels. They were not able to sail again until March. When the ships finally arrived at Xaragua, Roldán and his men refused to embark. They claimed that Columbus, "out of spite had delayed sending the caravels," that they were not seaworthy, and that "they had consumed their provisions in waiting." These were clearly excuses; it seemed the rebels had changed their minds or maybe they had never intended to leave. On April 25, 1499, the empty ships returned to Santo Domingo. In May, Columbus wrote again to inform the sovereigns about what had transpired since his last letter and to try to clear his name.

Exalted Princes: When I came here, I brought for the conquest of these lands, many men who had begged me to take them along, saying that they would give as good service in this as anybody else; but the opposite was the case, as has been seen; because they were so blinded by greed that they came believing that the gold said to be found here could be gathered with a shovel, and that the spices were already tied up in bundles all along the coast, all ready to be loaded aboard the ships. It did not occur to them that even if there were gold and other metals, it would be found in mines, and the spices on the trees; and that it would be necessary to excavate the gold and to pick and cure the spices. I had told them all of this in Seville . . . and of all the hardships normally endured by those who settle distant lands, but they responded that this is what they were going for, and in order to gain honor from it.[37]

Columbus countered all the complaints of the settlers and, again, pleaded with the sovereigns to send someone, *at his own expense*, to investigate the situation—

someone who should inform himself of the wicked deeds committed by the rebels, in order that they might be punished with fitting severity by another than himself—who might be charged with partiality because the outbreaks had been directed against his brother.[38]

Sometime late that spring, Columbus received word from Roldán that he agreed to meet again; in order to save Roldán the trouble of traveling the long distance overland, Columbus decided to sail and meet him. He arrived toward the end of August and heard the rebels' additional demands: (a) to let fifteen of them return to Spain on the next ship, along with a slave each, which they had demanded as compensation, (b) to give land and houses to those who chose to remain, (c) to "publically proclaim that all that had happened was caused by false testimony of a few evil men," (d) to appoint Roldán as *alcalde* for life, and (e) to allow them to use force against Columbus if he did not keep the agreement.[39] The latter two demands, especially, were an outrage to Columbus's leadership. Nevertheless, he signed the document because he wanted to end the strife that had caused him so much pain, had created such tension among the settlers, and had soured relations with the Indians.

Isabella had already instructed Columbus to make grants of land (*repartimiento*) to the settlers; now he had to make them to the rebels who decided to remain. Soon they demanded that he formalize a system they had already enacted, that the Indians who lived on that land be assigned to them as laborers. While not exactly slavery, it was about as close as one could get. Initiated by Roldán, this plan was soon to become institutionalized as the *encomienda* system of "quasi-serfdom . . . [that] allowed the European recipients of land grants to treat the native peoples on the land as their property."[40] Columbus capitulated but it was not his idea. Still, he knew the system was nothing new, for a parallel already existed in Castile: in lands taken from Muslims, *hidalgos* were given grants of land and peoples; in return they were obligated to serve the Crown when necessary but were exempted from taxes [tribute] and local jurisdiction, making them almost autonomous.[41] Not only did Roldán's plan further erode the sovereigns' original plan for establishing a trading post on Hispaniola, it also worked against Columbus's interests whereby he and his family would receive a certain percentage of the profits from it.

Columbus was becoming more and more concerned not only about the rebellion but also about his position. He wrote to the sovereigns requesting them to confirm his command of the enterprise; he also requested that he be given the same benefit as the Admiral of Castile, who was awarded a third of all the earnings he brought in. He ended the letter by saying he believed that as God was pleased "when the temple in Jerusalem . . . was built of wood and gold from Ophir," so now He would be pleased that "the same gold will restore the Holy church and build it up even more sumptuously than before," and sealed the letter "written in Hispaniola, formerly Ophir" thereby identifying the island he had discovered with the biblical Ophir from which Solomon's gold had come.[42] He had to wait months before he could send the letter with departing ships, and whether this letter ever reached the sovereigns is unknown.

Adding outrage to outrage, soon after Columbus had concluded the agreement with Roldán, Alonso de Hojeda arrived in September with news that he had been to Paria and had collected pearls, brazilwood, and slaves. Columbus was outraged that Hojeda had gone to Paria without his permission since the agreement made with the sovereigns stipulated that he had the sole right to choose who would be permitted to go exploring and where. Either Hojeda had no right to go there, or the sovereigns had reneged on their agreement with Columbus and permitted it. In either case, it was not a happy situation for Columbus, even more so because Hojeda was the same man he had so warmly embraced a few years earlier, as "a big strapping lad and very trustworthy," and had appointed as *alcalde* at Santo Tomás. Now, this same "lad" sought ways to discredit Columbus's discoveries and undermine his power. Later, Hojeda would even claim that because he had been to Paria, he had been the first to discover the mainland of South America.[43] Soon after landing on Hispaniola, Hojeda began to spread rumors that the queen was very ill, and that if she died, Columbus would lack her staunch support. Worse still, Hojeda began to stir up more trouble by claiming that Roldán, by signing the agreement, was now working for Columbus, and persuaded some of the former rebels to join him so they could take over governing the island. Not only did he want to get rid of Columbus, he also planned to capture and kill Roldán. In the dead of night, Hojeda attacked, killed, or wounded those who opposed him. Roldán was not there, but when he heard of what Hojeda had done, he went in pursuit. He found Hojeda on his boat, and using a ruse of agreeing to talk with him, Roldán attacked and killed some of Hojeda's men, after which he was able to extract a promise from Hojeda that he and the rest of his men would leave the island immediately.

Hojeda's departure did little to bring peace to the island. Adrian de Mujica, who had up until then worked with Roldán, now turned against him. He and several other rebel leaders continued their mayhem and planned to kill Roldán. Roldán learned of their plot and managed to capture a few of them including Mujica. When Roldán wrote to Columbus to ask what he should do with the captives, Columbus "replied that they had disturbed the peace without cause and it would be the ruin of the country if they went unpunished; Roldán should punish them as their crimes and the law required."[44] As *alcalde*, Roldán could administer justice and order punishment; he ordered that Mujica be hanged, and the others banished or handed over to Columbus as prisoners.

Meanwhile, when the fifteen disgruntled settlers returned to Spain along with their slaves, Isabella was furious and was quoted as saying, "What right does My Admiral have to give away My Vassals to anyone?"[45] She was not yet aware of the circumstances under which Columbus had been forced to capitulate to Roldán's demand that each Spaniard returning to Spain be granted a slave. Isabella ordered that the slaves be returned to Hispaniola on the next ship. When she received the letters from Columbus, she decided to comply with his request that she send someone to investigate the situation on the island.

Why she chose Knight Commander Francisco de Bobadilla is unknown, but it was a bad choice, as she would soon find out. "Bobadilla already had a reputation for being harsh and had been sued for malfeasance by citizens of the towns" he commanded.[46] More harsh and more biased against Columbus than Roldán, Bobadilla made matters in Hispaniola even worse.

As Bobadilla approached Santo Domingo in August 1500, he saw a terrible sight—two Spaniards hanging from a newly constructed gallows. These were men who had been punished for their rebellion and the hideous deeds they had committed against the Indians. Columbus intended their deaths to serve as an example not only to the rest of the colonists, but also to show the Indians that the rule of law also applied to his own men. Before he even heard Columbus's side of the story, Bobadilla was enraged at what he saw and sympathized with his disaffected compatriots.

At the time of Bobadilla's arrival, Columbus was inland, checking on one of the outposts. Taking advantage of his absence, Bobadilla marched to the fortress, which was being guarded by only Miguel Díaz and a few men, who were unable to prevent Bobadilla from entering. When Columbus heard that Bobadilla had arrived, he returned swiftly to Santo Domingo in order to greet and welcome him, under the assumption that the sovereigns had answered his request for someone to investigate the rebellion and the charges against him. But when he arrived in Santo Domingo, Columbus was shocked at Bobadilla's behavior. Abandoning any sense of courtesy, Bobadilla immediately put Columbus in chains and imprisoned him in the fortress. Bobadilla never explained the reasons for Columbus's arrest, never took any testimony from him, and never went to visit him.

Columbus was devastated; in an instant everything he had worked so hard for was gone, and all his dreams for the enterprise were dashed. When Bobadilla's men came to take him from his prison, Columbus wrote that he was under great fear that they were going to behead him. Instead, they marched him to one of the ships waiting to return to Spain. His brothers Bartholomew and Diego were already on board, enchained and imprisoned. As Columbus shuffled to the ship, he suffered the same humiliation his brothers had received: Bobadilla "permitted the malcontents and rabble to shout innumerable insults at them in the public squares, to blow horns in the harbor when they were being taken aboard, and to post scandalous handbills about them on the street corners."[47] Commenting on the fate of Columbus, Las Casas wrote:

It seemed absurd and completely out of proportion, and at the same time miserable and wretched, that a person who held such high dignities as those of Viceroy and perpetual Governor of all of this New World, and who bore the grand title of Admiral of the Ocean Sea, having been chosen by God for the singular privilege of finding and presenting to the world, and particularly to the rulers of Castille, these lands that had been concealed for many centuries, and who, through his difficult and dangerous labors, had put the Monarchs perpetually in his debt, could be treated with such inhumanity, cruelty, and dishonor; certainly this was unworthy of reasonable men and more than grotesque.[48]

Columbus and his brothers left Santo Domingo for Castile at the beginning of October; Bartholomew was on one ship while Columbus and Diego were put on the *Gorda*, named after its owner and captain, Andrés Martín de la Gorda.

With Columbus dispatched, Bobadilla released the rebel prisoners and ingratiated himself with the colonists who remained. He was supposed to investigate the crimes that Roldán and his men had committed, but instead he told them to "[T]ake as many advantages as you can since you don't know how long this will last."[49] By "advantage" he meant for the men to take as much of the gold, women, and labor of the Indians as they could. Las Casas said the obvious: "The Spaniards loved and adored him in exchange for such favors," and because they were allowed to get away with murder, literally, they were not about to denounce Bobadilla.

Las Casas, himself a Spaniard, had terrible things to say about his compatriots. Not only did they oppress the natives and take women as concubines, they also killed many on a whim. Recounting one of the most horrendous deeds of that time, Las Casas wrote: "Two of these so-called Christians met two Indian boys one day, each carrying a parrot; they took the parrots and for fun beheaded the boys . . . Another shot arrows into an Indian in public, announcing the reason for punishment as his failure to deliver a letter with the speed he required."[50]

Instead of investigating and recording the actions of the rebels, Bobadilla began to take "testimony" from the rebels against Columbus. This "testimony," published in 2006 as *La caída de Cristóbal Colón: El juicio de Bobadilla*, has recently been found.[51] One accusation against Columbus was that he did not want the natives to be baptized because he wanted to make them slaves. Yet there is plenty of evidence that Columbus objected to the ritual of baptism only if the natives had not first been given instruction about the faith, and he repeatedly asked the sovereigns to send friars who could do that. Secondly, while it is true that Columbus began to punish some of the Spaniards and ordered the execution of a few of them, it is highly unlikely that he executed his own brother-in-law Miguel Moliart, as the rebels claimed. Testimony gathered from such malcontents, without Columbus's presence and ability to challenge it, is hardly credible. Far more likely is that the rebels themselves committed many of the deeds of which they accused Columbus, and that Bobadilla's "testimony" was an elaborate cover-up to exonerate them.

Bobadilla declared himself governor and took up residence in Columbus's house. He confiscated or sold all of Columbus's belongings, including his share of gold that had been collected, "along with all the books and the public and secret documents he had in his chests, which pained the Admiral more than anything else."[52] Later, regarding Bobadilla's theft of his property, Columbus wrote:

All that he found there, he appropriated for himself; well and good, perhaps he had need of it . . . Concerning my papers I complain most, that they have been taken from me by him, and that I have never been able to recover one, and those which would have been useful for my defense, he had most carefully concealed.[53]

Though devastated and humiliated, Columbus kept his own counsel and his dignity on the voyage to Spain. The captain, Andrés Martín de la Gorda, who greatly esteemed Columbus, offered to remove his chains, but Columbus obstinately refused. He said he would wait until, and if, the sovereigns released him. In the biography of his father, Ferdinand wrote that Columbus "was resolved to keep those chains as a memorial of how well he had been rewarded for his many services. And this he did, for I always saw them in his bedroom, and he wanted them buried with his bones."[54]

Immobilized on the journey back to Spain, Columbus had time to reflect. Although he was officially a prisoner, the captain treated him with respect and gave him pen and paper so he could write. Columbus wrote a letter to Doña Juana de Torres, sister of Antonio de Torres, his friend, supporter, and sometime captain of ships on the transatlantic route. Doña Juana was the governess to the infante, and after his death she became confidante to the queen. Since

Columbus's sons served as pages to the queen, Doña Juana must have become close to them. Columbus may have written to her so that she could alert them to his condition before they learned it from someone else.

The letter begins, "Highly Virtuous Lady: If it be something new for me to complain of the world, its custom of maltreating me is of very old standing . . . With cruelty, it has cast me down to the depth." [55] He reminded her of how he had so devotedly served the queen and how God had given Isabela the "spirit of understanding and great courage" so that she supported the Enterprise in the face of all those who argued against it. He felt wronged and continued his lament:

> If I had violently seized the Indies or the land [now] made holy because in it here is today the fame of the altar of St. Peter, and had given them to the Moors, they could not have shown greater enmity towards me in Spain. Who would believe such a thing? [56]

The persecution Columbus felt may have brought to mind the words of Jesus at the height of His passion: "Father, forgive them, for they know not what they do" (Luke 23:34). Had he thought of them, these words would have brought some comfort to him, for Columbus's faith was a refuge. Through comparisons with biblical figures, like Job, Daniel, and David, Columbus was able to comprehend his own trials and transcend them. The Bible provided solace and the context within which Columbus understood the world, his discovery, and his own role in the larger Christian drama. This became clear in his letter to Doña Juana:

> Of the new heaven and earth which Our Lord made, as St. John writes in the Apocalypse, after he had spoken it by the mouth of Isaiah. He made me the messenger thereof and showed me where to go. [57]

By this time Columbus had clearly come to see himself as a messenger, and his message urged people to think about how his discoveries—all the lands he had found, all the people to be converted, and the location of the Terrestrial Paradise—related to prophecy about the end-time. His characterization as messenger skated close to heresy because of the analogy to Muhammad, who was, and is, known as the Messenger. Muhammad's message was to recall people to repent and return to the one true faith given in the beginning to Abraham; for

Christians like Columbus, the only true faith was the Christian faith. In contrast to Muhammad's message, Columbus's focused on the future and called people to pay heed to the signs of the coming Apocalypse. His message would soon become more urgent. But as his ship neared the coast of Spain, having made an extremely fast crossing, Columbus could only think about how the sovereigns would receive him when he returned, without gold in his hands and with chains on his feet.

CHAPTER NINE

PRIVILEGES AND PROPHECIES:
COLUMBUS'S STAKE IN THE FUTURE

W hen the white-haired, arthritic, fifty-year-old Admiral of the Ocean Sea disembarked at Cádiz,[1] he was a pathetic sight. With his chains clanking, Columbus made an unsteady descent down the gangplank and shuffled along the quay on the arm of his jailer. People stared; some of them were truly horrified to see the great explorer brought so low, while his detractors took great pleasure in jeering as he passed. Captain Andrés Martín had told Columbus that he would gladly remove his chains, but Columbus vowed to retain them until he was released by the sovereigns. Martín made sure that Columbus's letters to the sovereigns were sent to them before a report from Bobadilla.[2] Martín was compassionate, perhaps because he knew, as the bystanders did not yet know, that the man they were looking at had just discovered an unknown continent and the location of the Garden of Eden.

The record is unclear about where Columbus spent the next few weeks. Because Bobadilla had confiscated all of his belongings, Columbus had arrived in Cádiz without any money. Most likely he and his brothers made their way to Columbus's house in Seville, where his sister-in-law, Violante Moniz, was probably still residing.[3] Columbus also spent some time at the Carthusian monastery of Nuestra Señora Santa María de las Cuevas, with his friend, Friar Gaspar Gorricio.

When the sovereigns learned that Columbus had returned in chains, "they ordered him set free and wrote expressing their good will toward him and their displeasure at Bobadilla's harsh treatment of him."[4] With that letter of December 12, 1500, they sent him two thousand ducats of gold (about 750,000 *maravedis*, a considerable amount of money) and told him to proceed with his brothers to Granada, where the court was residing. Fortunately, Granada was not far from Seville, and they arrived at court on December 17. There, the sovereigns told Columbus that "his imprisonment had not been by their wishes or command, that they were much displeased by it, and would see to it that ... the rebels would be tried and punished as their offenses deserved."[5] They promised to send someone to relieve Bobadilla of his post and to ensure that Bobadilla return all of the property he had confiscated from Columbus. The sovereigns also promised to restore all that belonged to him "according to the Capitulations," which, to Columbus, meant all of his titles and privileges.

Columbus was relieved by the reception the sovereigns gave him and was able to regain some of his dignity. In that happy frame of mind, he spent Christmas with his brothers and with his sons, whom he had not seen in more than two years. Diego was now a man of twenty, and Ferdinand a young man of twelve. As heir to his father's estate Diego had a stake in his father's business matters. He was more worldly than Ferdinand and had developed aristocratic tastes at court, and Columbus leaned on him for information about relations among the court personnel—who was in or out of favor, whom to trust, and of whom to be wary. Columbus's writings suggest that his relationship with Diego was more reserved and more formal than that with Ferdinand. As a little boy of twelve, Ferdinand was not expected to know much about business; instead, he endeared himself to Columbus with his wit and his curiosity. Emotionally, Columbus seemed closer to Ferdinand.

A shadow fell over their reunion, however, as Columbus heard of his sons' recent humiliation by some of the men who had returned from the colony. Ferdinand recounted:

> fifty of these shameless wretches bought a quantity of grapes and sat down to eat them in the court of the Alhambra, loudly proclaiming that their Highnesses and the Admiral had reduced them to that pitiful state by withholding their pay ... And if my brother and I, who were pages to the Queen, happened by, they followed us crying, "There go the sons of the Admiral of the Mosquitoes, of him who discovered lands of vanity and illusion, the grave and ruin of Castilian gentlemen."[6]

These barbs, aimed at his sons, struck Columbus's heart. He was deeply grieved by what they had suffered and concerned about his own position.

Despite the sovereigns' assurances that they would reconfirm what they had promised Columbus, they had given permission to Hojeda to make a voyage of discovery. Columbus had an intimation that they were whittling away at some of his entitlements. His suspicions were soon confirmed. In a letter of September 16, 1501, the sovereigns wrote to Nicolás de Ovando, a friar and a commander of a military order, appointing him governor of the islands and mainland that Columbus had discovered, thus stripping Columbus of his title of governor. They told Ovando to prepare to go to Hispaniola to replace Bobadilla and to oversee the restitution of Columbus's property. Columbus valued the title of Admiral of the Ocean Sea above all, and that title was not taken away, but after all he had done for the Crown, Columbus must have been furious about his replacement. He began to solicit opinions from legal experts regarding his rights and privileges as recorded in the Capitulations and other documents, and with them initiated a series of litigations.

In order to secure his future and that of his sons, his first task was to clear his name and collect the papers that Bobadilla had confiscated. Most important were the documents from the king and queen regarding rights and privileges they had bestowed on him. Columbus was concerned primarily about his hereditary titles and his percentages of the profits from the Indies. Although he had made a will, it would be of no use if there was nothing left of his estate. Keenly feeling his infirmities in an era when life expectancy rarely exceeded sixty years, Columbus wanted to make sure that his sons and descendants would be provided for when he died, for he knew that promises made were not always kept.

He had taken some of the documents with him on his voyages but had realized how easily they could be lost or damaged. Back in Spain, he wanted to make a complete set and deposit several copies with friends for safekeeping. His first priority was the Capitulations of Santa Fe signed by the king and queen in April 1492, authorizing the first voyage. That document also set out the titles and privileges that Columbus would receive once he had fulfilled his part of the agreement, namely crossing the ocean, finding land on the other side, and returning. Other documents that Columbus collected were letters from the sovereigns that spelled out his authority for government in the islands; papal bulls regarding the line of demarcation that had given Ferdinand and Isabella sovereignty over the islands he had discovered; authorizations for provisioning the second and third voyages; the sovereigns' letter giving him permission to make a will; letters detailing the persons permitted to sail, their roles and their pay; and orders about taxes and imports. Columbus also included a letter from the sovereigns of September 27, 1501, restoring his property that Bobadilla had taken; a copy of their letter to Ovando; two legal opinions about his rights and privileges as set out in the Capitulations; and the royal instructions of March 14, 1502, authorizing an impending fourth voyage. When he finally gathered together all the documents, Columbus called the collection his *Book of Privileges*; it was his most valuable wordly possession.

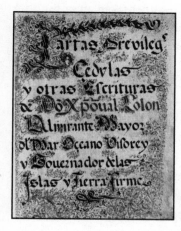

Cover of *The Book of Privileges*.

By permission of the Museo del Mare, Genoa, Italy.

Columbus had several copies made, which was in and of itself a complicated task: copying, of course, had to be done painstakingly by hand, and each copy had to be notarized. One copy was sent to Genoa to Nicolò Oderigo, the former Genoese ambassador to Castile and Aragón, along with a poignant letter that begins: "The loneliness in which you have left us cannot be expressed."[7] Columbus sent a second copy of the *Book of Privileges* to the directors of the Bank of St. George in Genoa, to whom he wrote: "Although my body is here, my heart is still there."[8] A third copy was sent to Hispaniola with his representative, Alonso Sanchez de Carvajal. Columbus left the final copy of the *Book of Privileges* at the monastery of Santa María de las Cuevas with Friar Gorricio to whom he had already entrusted his *majorat*, the will making his son Diego heir to his estate.

Once his worldly affairs were in order, Columbus turned his attention to the spiritual matter that he considered of utmost importance—to make known the apocalyptic significance of his discoveries. Columbus considered this an urgent task, not only for his own soul, but for the sake of the world. For a long time he had been keeping track of passages from both the Old and New Testaments of the Bible, from the Jewish historian Josephus, and from St. Augustine and other church fathers, as well as statements from ancient and medieval philosophers and geographers, including several Muslims, that seemed to prophesy his discoveries and their ultimate meaning. In 1481 Columbus had copied some of the passages into his copy of Pope Pius's *Historia rerum.* Now he wanted to collect additional statements and to gather them all into a book which he intended to present to the sovereigns. No doubt this was a way to encourage them to move more earnestly to take up their parts in the unfolding Christian drama.

Columbus's son Ferdinand called this compilation the *Libro de las profecías* (Book of Prophecies), which is how it is referred to today. That was not the title Columbus gave it, nor was it a book in the conventional sense. Instead of a title, he began as follows:

> Here begins the book, or handbook, of sources, statements, opinions and prophecies on the subject of the recuperation of God's Holy city and Mount Zion, and on the discovery and evangelization of the islands of the Indies and of all other peoples and nations. To Ferdinand and Elizabeth [Isabella], etc., our hispanic rulers.[9]

The *Libro* is the most explicit and extensive expression of Columbus's quest for the liberation of Jerusalem and the way he thought about his discoveries and his role in the fulfillment of Christian prophecy. Written mostly in Latin, it languished unpublished for four hundred years in the library attached to the cathedral in Seville. In 1892 the original Latin version was typeset and printed in an edition of only 560 copies. For almost a hundred more years, it remained untranslated into any modern language: finally, in 1984, it was translated into Spanish. English translations did not appear until the Quincentennial in 1992.[10] Even today, very few people know about the *Libro*, let alone have read it.

Most, but not all, Columbus scholars have dismissed it because it punctured their view of him as the first modern man, and some such as Henry

Harrisse and Henry Vignaud, both French Americans, saw it as evidence of his senility or insanity. Harrisse, for example, calls the *Libro* "a deplorable lucubration" that he hoped would never be published, for in it Columbus claimed not only

> to owe all he knew and all he had accomplished to inspiration from on high,—having been chosen by the Almighty to discover the New World before the whole earth came to an end, which momentous event was certainly to take place within the next fifty years.

Clearly, Harrisse did not read the book very carefully since Columbus had calculated one hundred and fifty-five years. Vignaud commented only to say that the book contained "an order of ideas that permits no critical discussion and one into which we will not enter here." [11]

Yet for Columbus and his contemporaries, the sciences, including the science of navigation, were seen as an aid to revealing the secrets of God's world, not in giving an alternative explanation in competition with it. For Columbus, the primary question was: What is the ultimate meaning of the discovery? That is what he tried to demonstrate in the *Libro de las profecías*.

To give a sense of the size of the undertaking, the first part begins with quotations from sixty-five Psalms that referred either to *Zion* (sometimes spelled *Sion*, both meaning Jerusalem), the dominion of God over all the nations, or the conversion of all peoples. Compiling the source material was a prodigious undertaking for Columbus, emotionally and physically. Emotionally, it was the consummation of his thoughts, reading, and experience. Next to passages that were significant to him, Columbus drew his characteristic finger-pointing hand. Physically, the project was difficult because the painful arthritis in his hands had gotten much worse, which made it impossible for him to write at times. There was no way he could do all the writing himself; he needed help. Analyses of the handwriting in the *Libro* suggest that four people may have been involved in the physical process of writing. While a number of passages were written by Columbus, quite a few are in Gorricio's hand and others, because of the style of writing, have been attributed to an "Italian scribe." A massive part—pages and pages from the biblical books of Isaiah, Jeremiah, Baruch, Ezekiel, Daniel, Hosea, Joel, Amos, Obadiah, Micah, Zephaniah, Zachariah, and Chronicles—was allegedly written out by Columbus's son Ferdinand. This work may have been a happy project that enabled father and son to spend time together discussing the passages and an opportunity for Columbus to give some religious instruction to his son, or it may have been a grueling and tedious task for the young boy. Regardless, whether or not Ferdinand agreed with his father's thinking, he certainly became familiar with it.

From Granada, where Columbus was trying to persuade the sovereigns to sponsor a fourth voyage, he wrote to Friar Gorricio to solicit his help for additional research. The letter shows Columbus in charge, micromanaging the project; he told Gorricio where to look for appropriate biblical passages.

> Reverend and very devoted father: When I came here [i.e., to Spain in 1485], I began to collect in a book excerpts from authoritative sources that seemed to me to refer to Jerusalem; I planned to review them later and to arrange them appropriately. Then I became involved in my other activities and did not have time to proceed with my work; nor do I now. And so I am sending the book to you so that you can look at it. Perhaps your soul will motivate you to continue the project and our Lord will guide you to genuine *auctoritates* [authorities]. The search for texts should be continued in the Bible, and the *Commentary* is often useful and illuminating and should be used for clarification.[12]

The letter shows that Columbus had been thinking about this project for a long time, even before the first voyage, although some scholars dismiss it as a response to his immediate troubles and as a way to ingratiate himself with the sovereigns.[13] More sympathetically, it could be seen as a desperate cry from a despondent soul urging his leaders to make haste to fulfill their ordained role in the world-historical drama in which he, and presumably they, fervently believed. When Gorricio returned the book six months later, his accompanying letter shows that the book had already contained quite a bit of material and was well advanced: he wrote of receiving Columbus's letter and

> the book of prophecies, sayings, and *auctoritates* referring to Mount Zion and Jerusalem and the island peoples and the nations of the universe and . . . in order to comply with your wishes to the best of my meager abilities, I would work on this book as much as I could.

He acknowledged the grandeur of the project and modestly added that since it was quite beyond his own expertise, he would only add some gleanings "after the harvest."[14]

Columbus worked on the project while he was back in Spain, from early 1501 until May of 1502, when he left on his fourth voyage. This extraordinary compilation set out to show that the discovery of islands in the sea was foretold, and that their discovery was an integral part of the great cosmological drama— a sign of the impending end of the world. After he demonstrated that the discovery was such a sign, Columbus went on to take up the conditions necessary to fulfill prophecy, namely the evangelization and conversion of all peoples and the rebuilding of the temple in Jerusalem. Toward the end of the *Libro*, he discussed his own role and that of the sovereigns.

Columbus had to demonstrate that he knew the accepted methods of interpretation that were necessary to extract the often hidden meanings from the biblical texts. He cited St. Thomas Aquinas, who claimed that "the Holy Scripture is expounded by four methods": historical, allegorical, tropological, and anagogical. To illustrate that method, Columbus included a brief paraphrase by Jean Gerson, who had succeeded Pierre d'Ailly as bishop in Paris. Gerson wrote:

> *The literal teaching tells facts;*
> *The allegory tells what you should believe;*
> *The moral interpretation tells how you should act;*
> *The anagogy tells where you are going.*

As a demonstration of the method, Columbus included Gerson's example of Jerusalem; it could not have been closer to his own views.

> In a historical sense, it is the earthly city to which pilgrims travel. Allegorically, it indicates the Church in the world. Tropologically, Jerusalem is the soul of every believer. Anagogically, the word means the Heavenly Jerusalem, the celestial fatherland and kingdom.[15]

The concept of prefigurement was also important for deciphering the meaning of a biblical text. For example, the near sacrifice of Isaac by Abraham in Genesis is, for Christian theologians even today, thought to prefigure the Crucifixion, when God the Father allowed his only son to be sacrificed.[16] Isidore of Seville, a seventh-century theologian, still very influential during Columbus's lifetime, noted that in the Bible the past tense was used even though the event described would happen in the future, "because things that are still future to us, have already happened according to God's viewpoint in eternity."[17] This belief has hardly disappeared among Christians in the twenty-first century.

Regarding the implications of the discovery of the islands, Columbus included the following biblical passage:* "I will set a sign among them . . . to the islands afar off, to them that have not heard of me and have not seen my glory" (Isaiah, 66:19).[18] In the margin next to this passage Columbus wrote "note this," indicating, no doubt, his belief that he was the sign; he was Xpo-ferens, the Christ-bearer sent by God, to the islands "afar off." Surely, he thought that if he could convince the sovereigns that the discovery of the islands was foretold and was an integral part of the religious drama set in motion ages ago, then they would do their part to help fulfill prophecy.

Columbus believed that the islands he discovered were the islands mentioned in the Bible, not the mythical ones such as St. Brendan's, Antilia, or Brasil, and that their discovery was thought to be "one of the events that would precede the end of the world, along with the liberation of the holy sepulchre and the universal conversion of the peoples to the gospel of Christ."[19] He included too many passages to be repeated here, but let the following suffice: "The Lord hath reigned, let the earth rejoice: let many islands be glad" (Psalm 96); "Give ear, ye islands, and hearken, ye people from afar" (Isaiah 49:1); and "For the islands wait for me, and the ships of the sea in the beginning: that I may bring thy sons from afar" (Isaiah 60:9). Columbus could not help but think that he was the one to bring these "sons from afar" to Christ, and that their discovery was a sign prophesying the end. Cultural historian John Gillis has explored the meaning of "islands in the West," and wrote that the

> rising tide of Christian millenarianism in the fifteenth and sixteenth centuries reinvigorated biblical geosophy . . . The Discovery of new islands took on enhanced significance as signs that the Second Coming was at hand. His [Columbus's] voyage was no *fuga mundi*, no escape from the world, but an effort to reconnect *Orbis Terrarum*'s eastern

---

* Biblical quotations are from Christopher Columbus's *Libro de las profecías*. He used an old Vulgate version of the Bible, which sometimes has slightly different numbering for verses.

and western shores, thus bringing closer the end-time as foretold in Revelation.[20]

The discovery of all the islands in the sea revealed millions of people previously unknown to the Europeans—peoples who had to be converted to Christianity before the end. Converting all these newly discovered peoples, let alone the Grand Khan, to the Christian faith, was one of Columbus's primary and most explicitly stated goals.

All the ends of the earth shall remember, and shall be converted to the Lord: And all the kindreds of the Gentiles shall adore in his sight. For the kingdom is the Lord's; and he shall have dominion over the nations (Psalm 21 in the *Libro*, but 22:27–28 in the RSV).

Beyond the natives and the Grand Khan's people, Columbus also had in mind unconverted Gentiles and Jews. He cited the popular commentary by Nicolas of Lyra, *Glossa ordinaria*, to make clear that Jesus did not "die for the Jews only . . . [for] 'other sheep I have, who are not of this sheepfold,' that is, not of the synagogue of the Jews but of the Gentile people."[21] The metaphor of the "sheepfold" and its apocalyptic implications had been significant to Columbus at least since the mid-1480s during the Spanish sovereigns' Reconquista. The metaphor also appeared in passages that Columbus cited from Augustine, St. John Chrysostom, and St. Gregory.

With regard to the conversion of the Jews, Columbus copied out parts of a very long, famous, and widely circulated letter, written in the eleventh century, from Rabbi Samuel of Toledo to his former teacher Rabbi Isaac in Morocco. "Dear Sir," he said, "I fear that the mighty God has quickened and given life to these Gentiles by faith in him, and that he has killed us with unbelief and hardness."[22] The rabbi goes on to say that God's law has not been reserved only for Jews but, citing prophetic statements by Isaiah, Habakkuk, Amos, Jeremiah, Zephaniah, and others, that "many nations shall come from many places." Rabbi Samuel's teacher must have been persuaded for he, too, converted. In the margins, Columbus drew several finger-pointing hands, indicating that the rabbi's letter must have had particular importance to him. The emphasis on conversion may also have been a subtle message to King Ferdinand—an attempt to convert him to embrace the crusader's zeal.

With the discovery of the islands and all the peoples to be evangelized, Columbus had made possible two of the conditions necessary for Christ to return. But that was hardly the end of his mission. The conquest of Jerusalem was still the ultimate goal. To emphasize that point Columbus drew his finger-pointing hand next to a passage from Isaiah 60:1.

Arise, be enlightened, O Jerusalem: for thy light is come, and the glory of the Lord is risen upon thee (*Libro*, p. 179).

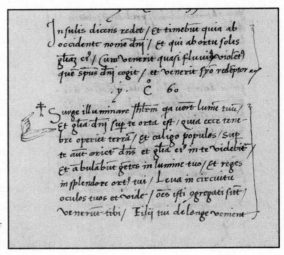

Passage from Isaiah 60 in the
Libro de las profecías. Courtesy of
Biblioteca Colombina.

He must have thought some action would be taken in this regard.

Columbus knew that Pope Alexander VI was a great supporter of crusades, and he might have heard that in March of 1500, the pope had assembled a meeting of ambassadors from several European countries asking that they unite to form a new crusade. And he would have known that only Spain and Italy responded favorably. Sometime later, Alexander issued a papal bull authorizing a crusade against the Turks. A copy of that bull was found in a collection of documents that Columbus had left with Friar Gorricio at the monastery of Santa María de las Cuevas. Perhaps this inspired Columbus to write to the pope with his interpretation of the significance of the discoveries.[23]

Dated February 1502, Columbus wrote a letter to Pope Alexander VI with regrets that he would not be able to visit him as he had planned because the sovereigns were sending him on another voyage. He said he wanted to give His

Holiness some of his writings, most likely the *Libro de las profecías* and a copy of the diary of the first voyage. Although the main point of the letter appears to be his request to send more priests and other religious persons to spread God's word to the universe, out of respect, he put it last.[24] Preceding his request he gave a brief synopsis of what he had discovered to date, namely 1,400 islands and 333 languages in the land of Asia and mines of gold and copper. In addition, he claimed to have found what "so many sacred theologians and saints believed and believe, that there in that region is the Terrestrial Paradise."[25] He reminded the pope that his enterprise was undertaken with the purpose of obtaining gold to restore the Holy Sepulchre to the Holy Church. He claimed that he had already sent 120 *quintals* (about 100 pounds) of gold to the sovereigns and was certain he would find at least that much in the next five years if Satan did not disrupt his plans. With that gold he promised, as he had to the sovereigns, that "in seven years I will be able to pay for 50,000 foot soldiers and 5,000 cavalry and another 50,000 foot soldiers and 5,000 cavalry in the following five years," which amounts to "100,000 foot soldiers and 10,000 cavalry."[26]

Solomon's gold would finance the crusade and restore the Temple. Ten years after his discovery, Columbus was still claiming that Hispaniola was Tharsis and Ophir.[27] He repeated the biblical passage he had used in his arguments with the committee set up to evaluate his first voyage. "The king's ships went to Tharsis with the servants of Hiram, once in three years: and they brought thence gold and silver, and ivory, and apes, and peacocks" (II Chronicles 9:21, in *Libro*, p. 243; also 1 Kings 10:11). Since it had taken Solomon's ships three years to make the round trip from Jerusalem, Columbus had argued, first, that they must have gone to Asia; second, that Asia extended much farther east than thought; and third, that therefore the ocean between Europe and Asia could not be very wide.

In the *Libro*, however, twelve passages about Tharsis were used to emphasize the goods to be found there, namely gold, silver, and exotic birds and animals. Since these were exactly the things Columbus had found, these citations were meant to prove that he had found the fabled Tharsis (aka Ophir), "the name of a province in India, in which there are mountains containing mines of gold."[28] If the discovery of islands in the sea was not enough to convince the sovereigns of the apocalyptic import of the "Enterprise of the Indies," then surely the discovery of Ophir with its gold, silver, and exotic birds and animals would convince them. Perhaps as an admonishment to King Ferdinand, Columbus included a poem—one he may have composed himself:

Remember with careful attention,
O man, whoever you are,
Always to keep your thoughts
upon God and his commandment,
If you wish to rule with him.
Prepare for the future now,
Since death is inevitable
That at the time of your parting
You will see the straight road ahead. (Libro, p. 225)

The words imply that Ferdinand may have strayed in his religious commitment; that if he wished to rule and die properly, he needed to refocus his attention on God and his commandments. In contrast to Ferdinand, Columbus wrote the following to show his own commitment:

Preparing for the last days
Always the saintly men
Separated themselves from the world,
And always served Christ,
Suffering tribulations,
Sacrificing their own desires
Of the flesh, and the pride of life.
Clothed with humility
To restrain their passions. (Libro, p. 225)

Columbus had suffered numerous tribulations in keeping his promises to the sovereigns; indeed, he often compared himself to the biblical Job, who suffered greatly but survived the terrible afflictions God allowed Satan to lay upon him. Columbus had separated himself from worldly affairs, given up a normal life in the comfort of family and friends; he had sacrificed the joys of the flesh; he restrained his passions not only during the long wait before the first voyage was launched but also in his dealings with the rebels on Hispaniola and even his passion for Jerusalem. He had clothed himself in the humble habit of a Franciscan friar and kept his chains until released by the sovereigns. Self-serving or not, this was the portrait of himself he presented to the sovereigns.

Not only did Columbus see his discoveries as an integral part of the Christian story, he also saw them as prophesied by ancient pagan texts. Immediately following the poem quoted above, Columbus wrote out, in his own hand, the prophetic passage from Seneca's *Medea* about how Typhis, the pilot of the Argonauts, would "unfasten the bounds" of the sea and "discover new worlds." After it, however, he reworded the Seneca prophecy so that it would point to himself as the new Typhis, a modern argonaut:

> In the latter years of the world will come certain times in which the Ocean Sea will relax the bonds of things, and a great land will open up, and a new mariner like the one who was the guide of Jason, whose name was Typhis, will discover a new world, and then will the island of Thule no longer be the farthest land (*Libro*, p. 227).

Years later, next to that passage in his own copy of *Medea*, Columbus's son Ferdinand poignantly wrote "This prophecy was fulfilled by my father . . . the Admiral in the year 1492."[29]

The final section of the *Libro*, "Prophecies of the Future. The Last Days," begins with a copy of a 1492 letter from Genoese ambassadors to Queen Isabella and King Ferdinand. Columbus had been at the meeting when that letter was delivered. The ambassadors wrote, "we did read that Joachim the Abbot of Southern Italy has foretold that he is to come from Spain who is to recover again the fortunes of Zion."[30] Immediately following that passage, ten pages of the *Libro de las profecías* were cut out, vandalized by some incensed reader sometime between 1569 and 1576. Ambrose de Morales, a sixteenth-century historian, had seen the manuscript, obviously more than once, for he wrote in the manuscript: "Whoever removed these pages acted badly, for this was the best prophecy in the book." Unfortunately, Morales did not tell us what it was.

As if the book itself were not enough for the Spanish sovereigns to get the point and understand his motives for compiling it, Columbus prefaced it with a letter. It begins: "The reason which I have for the restitution of the Holy Sepulchre to the Holy Church militant is the following," after which he went on to explain how he came to this project and why it was so important. He told them that sailing is a profession that creates a desire to "understand the world's secrets"—a desire he had had for forty years.[31] Columbus felt he had a "calling,"[32] a mission from God whom he credits for giving him the ability to acquire the skills necessary for maritime exploration and for opening his will to undertake the voyages of discovery. He wrote that it was "the Holy Spirit who encouraged me with a *radiance of marvelous illumination* from his Holy Scriptures"; that "was the *fire* that burned within me when I came to visit Your Highnesses."[33] The word *fire* meant more than simple passion; it was then, and still is, a "typical symbol for the Holy Spirit as derived from the fire which came down at Pentacost."[34]

Columbus relayed to the sovereigns his belief that his success in crossing the ocean and discovering the myriad islands was part of God's plan meant to encourage him in the crusade to liberate Jerusalem. The liberation of Jerusalem was so important to Columbus that he said he could cast aside all his experience as a navigator, all the books on science and geography he had read, and would

> hold only to the sacred Holy Scriptures, . . . the forty-four books of the Old Testament, from the four Gospels, from the twenty-three Epistles of the blessed Apostles . . . and to the interpretations of prophecy by certain devout persons who have spoken on this subject by divine illumination.[35]

In an almost heretical statement, he claimed that Revelation can come to anyone, even to "Jews and Moslems, and among all men of every faith," and not just to the educated but also to simple villagers, and by implication sailors.[36] Lesser men were burned at the stake for such beliefs.

By the middle of the letter, Columbus's tone became urgent, warning the sovereigns about the approaching end of the world. The end was not a vague prediction about sometime in the future. History was not open-ended, it had limits both temporally and spatially: the narrative was pre-scripted from beginning to end, from Genesis to Apocalypse. "Saint Augustine says that the end of this world will take place in the seventh millennium after the age of the creation of the world" and Columbus claimed that "theologians of the Church follow this view."[37] Columbus revisited the calculations he had made years earlier and revised the number of years the earth had endured and, thus, how many years were left until the end. He quoted a passage from one of his favorite authors, Cardinal Pierre d'Ailly: "From the creation of the world, or from Adam, until the advent of our Lord Jesus Christ, there were five thousand, three hundred and forty-three years, and three hundred and eighteen days." To which Columbus added: "one thousand, five hundred and one years of waiting [i.e., the year he is writing], this makes a total of six thousand, eight hundred, forty-five years of waiting for the completion of the age." Then, Columbus made it clear: "According to this calculation, only one hundred and fifty-five years are lacking for the completion of the seven thousand years which would be the end of the world." [38]

Only 155 years before the end of the world. No wonder Columbus's writings contain such a sense of urgency. Although Columbus was aware that he would not live to witness Christ's return or be present at the end, the *Libro* was a desperate plea to get the sovereigns to do everything in their power to begin the process of fulfilling the conditions necessary before the end. Columbus warned:

> Our Savior said that before the consummation of this world, first must be fulfilled all the things that were written by the prophets [and emphasized that] much of the prophecies remained to be fulfilled, and I believe that these are great events for the world. I believe that there is evidence that our Lord is hastening these things. This evidence is the fact that the Gospel must now be proclaimed to so many lands in such a short time.[39]

The content of the prophecies was well known. The Gospel had to be preached to all the peoples in the world in order to give them the opportunity to be saved, Jerusalem had to come under Christian control, and the temple had to be rebuilt. These conditions had to be met before Christ could come again. Columbus's letter ended with a repetition of the prophecy of Joachim, who "said that the restorer of the House of Mt. Zion would come out of Spain." Many people believed the prophecy referred to King Ferdinand. After all, he had inherited the title, if not yet the role: King of Jerusalem. If he would only take up the cross and rally the people for a crusade, they were prepared to help him make the kingship a reality.

The *Libro* could be seen as a kind of literary gauntlet thrown down to the sovereigns with the hope they would be persuaded by the logic of the signs that the end of the world was imminent and that, therefore, they would enthusiastically take up their divinely appointed task—the conquest of Jerusalem.

Columbus's passion for the conquest of Jerusalem never ended. While his passion was most explicit in the *Libro de las profecías*, it had been there from the beginning, even if he had not quite understood how it would unfold. But once he had crossed the ocean and understood his discoveries within the wider Christian prophetic tradition, his passion grew stronger and more emphatic. Not only did his passionate quest underpin the patience and perseverance he displayed in pursuit of his vision, it was a vision that would occupy him to the end of his life.

CHAPTER TEN

MAROONED

On March 14, 1502, Columbus received word from the sovereigns to begin preparations for a fourth voyage. They stipulated that this voyage was to be exploratory only; he was "to inquire what gold, silver, pearls, gems, spices, and other products are to be found in the islands and mainland" that he might discover.[1] Any objects he or his men obtained through trade with the natives were to be registered with Francisco de Porras, the comptroller on board, and with the notary who would make a full accounting. If and where it seemed appropriate, Columbus could leave some men to establish an outpost for further trade. However, the sovereigns were adamant that Columbus was not to stop at Hispaniola, the very island he had discovered, and which had made all subsequent voyages, trade, and the colonies possible.

The previous month, the sovereigns had sent Nicolás de Ovando to Hispaniola with thirty-five ships and 2,500 colonists. They had appointed Ovando as governor, which effectively nullified the contract they had made with Columbus. Columbus endured these affronts to his dignity with his characteristic patience, although he did begin legal proceedings for restitution of his titles and privileges. Still, after waiting in Spain for a year and a half, at a time when he was no longer young and was suffering from a variety of ailments, he was thrilled to be going to sea again. What made this voyage especially alluring was the possibility of meeting Vasco da Gama en route. Each of them was sailing to India from different directions and under different sovereigns—da Gama for the Portuguese and Columbus for the Spaniards—neither of them aware that the large landmass Columbus had discovered was not Asia, but another huge continent in the way.[2]

Columbus knew that da Gama had reached India in 1498 when he followed the eastern route blazed by Bartolomeu Dias almost a decade earlier, and he also knew that da Gama was heading there again. Columbus thought that if he could find the strait leading to the Indian Ocean, he would be able to confer the same glory on Spain that da Gama had on Portugal, and even more important, he might be the first to make a complete circumnavigation of the globe. Columbus had formed that idea during the second voyage, but the possibility must have come up again in his discussions with the sovereigns for they gave him a letter of greeting to da Gama should they cross paths—da Gama sailing by way of the East and Columbus from the West. If "by a happy chance . . . you do encounter, you should deal with one another as friends, and as captains and subjects of Kings bound together by love and kinship."[3]

The sovereigns gave permission to Columbus to take his son Ferdinand on this voyage. Over the year while they had worked together on the *Libro de las profecías*, Ferdinand had heard his father's stories about the exotic lands and people he had discovered; the more he heard, the more he must have wanted to go. One can imagine the twelve-year-old boy putting pressure on his father to take him along—after all, the gromets were about the same age. At Columbus's request, the sovereigns agreed that Ferdinand's stipend could be transferred to Diego, who would remain at court. Diego never sailed to Hispaniola with his father, although after Columbus's death he became the second Admiral of the Ocean Sea and Governor of Hispaniola. Instead, Diego was put in charge of his father's legal matters and instructed to consult with Friar Gorricio. Before Columbus left, he entrusted Diego with the care and support of the women in his life for whom he felt responsible. He wrote to Diego: "I commend to you, out of love for me, Beatriz Enriquez, as if she were your own mother"[4] and instructed him to give her ten thousand *maravedis* each year; he also gave the same amount to his sister-in-law. After they said goodbye to Diego and to Friar Gorricio, Columbus and Ferdinand made their way to Sanlúcar de Barrameda, where the ships were being readied.

For this voyage Columbus had 4 ships and 135 men and boys.[5] The contrast with Ovando's huge fleet, despite the different purposes, could not have been more striking. Columbus and Ferdinand sailed on *La Capitana*, but due to Columbus's infirmity, the ship was captained by one of his former and loyal shipmates, Diego Tristan, who had also been his majordomo when they were back in Spain. Columbus's brother Bartholomew came along on this voyage and served as an unpaid captain on the *Santiago de Palos*, also known as the

Bermuda. The comptroller, Francisco de Porras, was given the title and pay, if not the role, of captain, and his brother Diego de Porras was to be the chief auditor of the fleet. Columbus had not wanted to take the Porras brothers but Alonso de Morales,[6] the treasurer of Castile, was having an affair with their sister. Since Morales controlled the funds for the voyage, Columbus was forced to accept them.

This ship also included Diego Méndez,[7] a friend of Columbus's, and six gentlemen volunteers. The third ship, *La Gallega*, was captained by Pedro de Terreros, who had been on every one of Columbus's voyages, and the ship's master was Juan Quintero, who had sailed on the *Pinta* on the first voyage. Finally, the fourth ship, *Vizcaina*, was captained by a fellow Genoese, Bartolomeo Fieschi, whose family had befriended the Columbus family even before Christopher was born.[8] Many of the men who sailed on this voyage had sailed on some of the others, demonstrating their faith and loyalty to Columbus.

Columbus made his way to Cádiz from where the fleet departed on May 9. When they reached the Canaries, Columbus wrote to Gorricio asking him to get in touch with Francisco de Rivarola about the business he had in Rome. This was probably about his request for good friars and the matter of the crusade about which Columbus had written the pope.

Columbus called this voyage *El Alto Viaje* (the High Voyage); perhaps he had an intimation it would be his last. Little did he know that it would also be "a story of adventure which imagination could hardly invent" and the most dangerous.[9] The adventure began even before the Atlantic crossing. Possibly before he sailed, and surely before he reached the Canaries, he heard that Moors were attacking a Portuguese fortress at Arcila on the coast of Morocco. Aware that some of the knights holding the fort were cousins of his deceased wife, Columbus ordered the ships to make a detour in order to scare off the besiegers and aid the Portuguese if necessary. By the time they arrived the Moors had retreated. Learning that the governor of the fort had been wounded, he sent his brother Bartholomew and his son Ferdinand to pay his respects, for as captain of the fleet he could not leave the ship. The governor was so grateful that he sent some of his men, including the cousins of Doña Felipa, to pay a visit to thank Columbus for his courtesy. Ferdinand, who wrote about this incident in his biography, does not say what transpired, but it is clear that the stopover, though friendly, was brief, for they arrived at Grand Canary on May 20.

When the fleet of four finally got under way on May 25, 1502, they made the fastest crossing ever—only sixteen days from the Canaries, making land-fall on Martinique (or possibly Dominica) on June 15.[10] They spent a few days relaxing from the journey, taking time to enjoy fresh water, wash their clothes, and bathe. Columbus was happy. He had his son Ferdinand, his brother Bartholomew, and many old friends and shipmates with him.

The first assault on Columbus's mood and honor came when they arrived at Santo Domingo in Hispaniola. He knew he was not supposed to stop there, but when he saw that a severe hurricane was fast approaching, he had to find shelter quickly, and he decided to go against the sovereigns' orders. Columbus sent Captain Terreros ashore to request entrance to the harbor and to warn Ovando of the impending storm. Ovando had just replaced Bobadilla, who was departing on one of thirty ships Ovando was sending back to Spain. When Columbus learned about their departure, he reiterated his warning about the storm. But Ovando, even more arrogant than Bobadilla, scoffed at the warning and refused Columbus entrance to the harbor of the "land that he had given to Spain for its honor and exaltation."[11] Ovando had already wreaked worse atrocities on the native peoples than had Bobadilla. Las Casas, who had come to Santo Domingo on the ship with Ovando, witnessed a number of his atrocities and wrote about a particularly cruel one that occurred on a seemingly ordinary day: While a cacique and some of his attendants were bringing a supply of bread to a caravel, as they had been doing for some time, one of the fierce dogs kept by the Spaniards broke his leash and attacked the cacique, and "with his powerful jaws tore at the man's stomach, pulling out the intestines as the cacique staggered away." He died soon after. Las Casas noted wryly that "it was a general rule among Spaniards," who were his countrymen, "to be cruel; not just cruel, but extraordinarily cruel so that harsh and bitter treatment would prevent Indians from daring to think of themselves as human beings or even having a minute to think at all."[12]

Ovando, clearly, had reasons for keeping Columbus off the island; he feared that if Columbus found out about his treatment of the Indians, he, too, would be recalled. When the hurricane hit, Ovando must have hoped that Columbus and his ships, without shelter on the open sea, would be destroyed—Nature's way of ridding him of his nemesis. He forgot to consider Columbus's superb navigational skills.

The wind became wild, and beat down with unparalleled ferocity upon all of the ships. Poor little Ferdinand—he had never seen a storm like this before.

Columbus, however, had not only seen such weather, he had survived it, and he used his experience to instruct the other captains how to ride it out. Still, he raved:

> What man has ever lived, not excluding Job, who would not have wished himself dead in my situation: seeking to save my life and that of my son, my brother and my friends. I was at that moment denied access to the very land and ports which, by the will of God and sweating blood, I had conquered for Spain.[13]

The fleet of thirty ships heading for Spain was leaving from the north side of Hispaniola; it had barely departed when the storm hit with full force. The ships were tossed around by the whirling winds, and their captains did not know what to do. Twenty ships went down, along with 200,000 *castellanos* of gold.[14] Other ships were broken to bits, and more than five hundred lives were lost, including Columbus's friend Antonio de Torres, his archenemy Bobadilla, and the rebellious Francisco Roldán. Neither Roldán nor Bobadilla ever had to face an investigation into their behavior. Because there was no opportunity for Columbus to counter the accusations against him made by Bobadilla, the recently found report by Bobadilla, *La caída de Cristóbal Colón*, is highly suspect.

Only one of the ships ever made it to Spain. Through a strange twist of fate, the surviving ship carried Columbus's gold (4,000 gold pesos, or about 1,800,000 *maravedis*) and his other belongings. Upon hearing this, his enemies accused him of witchcraft. Columbus, on the other hand, probably thought the sinking of the other ships was a sign of divine retribution. On July 3, Columbus learned that, miraculously (and because of his instructions), all of his ships and crew had survived. Later, they learned that down with the fleet that Ovando had sent to Spain went the largest nugget of gold "ever found in the West Indies," though there seems to be some confusion about just how large it was; estimates varied from "a monstrous block weighing thirty-five pounds" to the size of a large loaf of bread. Its assessed worth ranged from 36,000 gold pesos down to only 3,600 pesos.[15] This nugget had been found in 1502 by a young native girl who, in Las Casas's imagination,

> was sitting near a brook eating and resting, perhaps meditating upon her sad lot, her captivity and misery, idly poking the ground with a stick . . .

without thinking of what she was doing. She had scratched the ground and the gold nugget began to gleam. Her eyes fell on it, she unearthed it and called her Spanish victimizer.[16]

The miners celebrated with a big feast, perhaps thinking they would all get a share of the gold, but the "governor took it for the monarchs and gave its value in money to the two partners, Francisco de Garay and Miguel Díaz,"[17] for they were the ones who "controlled" that area of the mine and also the people who worked it. We do not know whether the girl who found the nugget received any recompense, but it was a boon to the two men. With the money, Francisco de Garay was able to marry Ana Muniz Perestrello, the sister of Columbus's deceased wife, and the windfall surely made life more comfortable for Miguel Díaz, the man who had fallen in love with a native princess and had moved the settlement from La Isabela to Santo Domingo.

After the storm abated, the ships of Columbus's fleet reconnoitered, during which time they caught a couple of "fish"; one was a sting ray, and the other the natives called a manatee. On earlier voyages, some of the men thought the creature was a mermaid, albeit an ugly one, but this time, young Ferdinand indicated that it might be a mammal and neither a mermaid nor a fish. On July 14, Columbus and the four ships set sail again; none of the ships would ever make it back to Hispaniola, let alone to Spain. The winds and currents took them west along the south coast of Jamaica, up north near Cuba, from where they would set a course south toward the mainland in order to search for the strait that Columbus thought "would open a way to the South Sea and the Lands of Spices."[18]

Reaching Cuba, Columbus passed the Jardín de la Reina (Queen's Garden), which he had discovered on the second voyage. Recalling how the coast veered south, he now set his course to the southwest. Soon they came to another island, called Guanaja (Bonacca), where the people, including women and children, came out in a canoe with an awning "like that which the Venetian gondolas carry," providing protection from sun, wind, and waves. The group seemed to be on a trading mission for they carried many wares for trade—"cotton mantles and sleeveless shirts embroidered and painted in different designs and colors; breechclouts of the same design and cloth as the shawls worn by the women in the canoe, being like the shawls worn by the Moorish women of Granada," some weapons, hatchets of copper, grains, and "wine made of maize that tasted like English beer." Columbus was much impressed by these people for they also displayed modesty—the men covered their genitals and the women their faces—a trait that apparently he and the crew assumed belonged to a more advanced civilization; Columbus could only imagine that he was approaching the edges of the realm of the Grand Khan.

They exchanged some trinkets and one older man accompanied them to the edge of his language area, where Columbus "gave him some presents and sent him home satisfied." [19]

Soon they came to the north coast of what is today Honduras. The people there indicated the existence of a "strait" to the south and east; so the fleet set off in that direction expecting to find the opening to the sea that would lead to Cathay. On the way to find this strait, Columbus wrote that he struggled against wind and current for sixty (later he wrote eighty-eight) days, during which time "there was rain and thunder and lightning continuously, so that it seemed as if it were the end of the world" [20]—hardly just a turn of phrase to Columbus. In a letter he later wrote to the sovereigns, Columbus described this storm as follows:

> My ships were stripped, and anchors, rigging and cables were lost, with the boats and many stores; the crews were weak and all were contrite and many turned to religion; nor was there one who did not make vows and promise pilgrimages. Many times they came to the point of confessing one another. Other storms have been seen, but none has ever endured so long or so terrible.

The terrors of the storm made him think about his sons and his brother for he went on:

> Many who we regarded as men of courage were in a state of great terror and that many times. The distress of my son, whom I had there, racked my soul, and the more since I saw him, at the tender age of thirteen years, so exhausted and for so long a time. Our Lord gave him such courage that he revived the spirit of the others, and he acted as if he had been a sailor for eighty years and he consoled me. I had fallen ill and had many times come to the point of death . . . My brother was in the worst ship and that which was in the greatest danger. My grief was great, and was the greater because I had brought him with me against his will . . .

Another sorrow tore my very heartstrings, and that was for Diego, my son, whom I had left in Spain an orphan and dispossessed of my honour and estate. Yet I was assured that there, as just and grateful princes, you would make restitution to him of all, with increase.[21]

The fleet weathered the storm and proceeded slowly south and slightly east along the coasts of what are, today, Honduras, Nicaragua, and Costa Rica. On September 16, they passed a river that Columbus thought they should explore, and he sent in several of the small boats. One of the boats was overwhelmed by heavy surf and sank; all of its crew drowned. In their honor, Columbus named the river *Río de Desastres*. As they sailed farther south, they came to another group of natives.

The men wore their hair braided about their heads, while the women wore theirs cut as we do. Seeing that we came in peace, they appeared eager to trade their weapons, cotton cloaks and shirts, and the *guanin* pendants which they hang about their necks as we wear an Agnus Dei.[22]

Oddly, instead of exchange, as was his custom, Columbus sent gifts. This gesture confused the people, but they, too, followed his example and sent two young girls as gifts—one girl was about eight years old and the other fourteen. Ferdinand, himself only about thirteen at the time, was clearly impressed by their composure in facing so many strange men; later writing of this incident, he said that the girls

displayed much courage . . . showed no fear or grief but always looked pleasant and modest. On this account they were well treated by the Admiral, who caused them to be clothed and fed and then sent them ashore, where the old man who had brought them and fifty more Indians came out to receive them with much rejoicing.[23]

Early in October 1502, near the site of what would become the Panama Canal, the natives told Columbus about a place called Ciguare situated on the coast, on the other side of a narrow strip of land, about a nine-day journey. At Ciguare, they would find "an infinite amount of gold."[24] This information was enough for Columbus to reason that he was once again near the Golden Chersonese of the Malay peninsula, that the water on the other side was the Indian Ocean, and the gold mines might be those of Solomon. But, alas, the "strait" was an isthmus not a water channel; he had misunderstood what the natives had told him. No doubt he was disappointed for now there was no chance of meeting Vasco de Gama and circumnavigating the world. He was not about to leave the ships behind and go off on a hiking trip, at least not on this voyage. He had just lost some of his men and was also eager to find a suitable spot for the trading post. But in another sense he was pleased, for the geographical information confirmed his view about the size of the earth that he had argued about so long ago. In his letter to the sovereigns, he repeated the passage from Esdras: "The world is small. The dry land is six parts of it; the seventh only is covered with water" and went on to say that "[E]xperience has already shown this, and I have written it in other letters and with illustration from the Holy Scripture concerning the situation of the earthly paradise."[25]

In late November and early December 1502, they encountered a storm so fierce that, not surprisingly, Columbus claimed it "was a second universal deluge."[26] In the biography he wrote of his father, Ferdinand included his own eyewitness account of his experiences and observations on this voyage. Ferdinand wrote that they hardly got any sleep and were very wet; that sailors in "such terrible storms, dread the fire in the lightning flashes, the air for its fury, the water for the waves, and the land for the reefs and rocks." If he, too, was frightened, he didn't admit to it.

> Besides these different terrors, there befell one no less dangerous and wonderful, a waterspout that on Tuesday, December 13th, passed between two ships. Had the sailors not dissolved it by reciting the Gospel according to St. John, it would surely have swamped anything it struck; for it raises the water up to the clouds in a column thicker than a water butt, twisting it about like a whirlwind.[27]

As if the storm and waterspout were not enough to terrify the sailors, there were sharks circling the ships; the men thought that they were waiting, like vultures, in anticipation of a meaty dinner. These signs and omens led the men to think they were in the grip of an impending Apocalypse.

When the storm finally abated, the ships retraced some of their path west, meanwhile discovering new ports and peoples, and spent Christmas near what would be the entrance to the Panama Canal. On January 6, 1503, which on the Christian calendar is Epiphany—the night the wise men brought gifts to the baby Jesus—they found a safe harbor up a river in the area of Veragua, today the part of Panama near the border with Colombia. At the mouth of the river, they maneuvered through a shallow channel and around a sandbar and entered a large basin with plenty of room for the ships; they would be well protected. Columbus called the place Belén, Spanish for Bethlehem.

Their arrival at Belén was greeted in a friendly enough manner. The Quibián, or chief (cacique) of the area, came out to meet Columbus, and the next day went aboard the flagship; they visited back and forth talking in whatever manner they were able with the help of a local interpreter Columbus must have picked up along the way, exchanging pleasantries as well as goods. Later, the Quibián took Bartholomew and a few men to the interior to show them where and how they might find some gold. Apparently, they found grains of it just digging around roots of trees; surely it had been washed down from the mountains where they suspected the mines were located. Because there seemed to be significant amounts of gold in this territory, Columbus decided that this might be a good place to leave some men to make a settlement.

On January 24 they were surprised when the river suddenly flooded. Ferdinand wrote that it was so forceful that the waves knocked out the cables of the flagship, *La Capitana*, and pushed her into the *Gallega*, broke one of her masts, and fouled the lines so that as they drifted, they were "in great peril of going down with all hands."[28] The rains of the past few months and this new storm had silted up the river and made it impossible to get the ships out to the coast. In other words, they were trapped until it rained hard enough: obviously not a good situation. Trying to make the best of it until a channel cleared, Columbus sent his brother Bartholomew and about eighty men ashore to begin the construction of a settlement consisting of some huts with thatched roofs, an arsenal, and storehouse for gold and articles obtained by trade. In the meantime, he packed the *Gallega* with all "the necessities of life, such as wine, biscuit, garlic, vinegar, and cheese, being all the Spanish food they had . . . for greater security aboard," since he planned to leave that ship for the settlers.[29] When the chief saw all this activity, he realized that some of the Europeans were planning to remain on his territory, and he was not pleased. Still, he continued to make a show of friendliness, receiving them in his village and providing information about the location of mines.

During the month of February, Bartholomew and some of his men made several forays into the interior to search for the mines. Every time, they came back with pieces of gold they had found near the roots of trees or acquired through trade, but they had not yet found any mines. Finally, the Quibián supplied him with some guides who led them to the mines; the Quibián was clever, however, for he had the guides take the men to mines in an area that belonged to another Quibián, hoping, no doubt, to get the Europeans to move and leave him alone.

Meanwhile, the men at Belén had built about twelve houses and a separate one for their weapons (some guns, swords, and small cannon) and the gold they would acquire. Columbus must have thought things were proceeding well and was eager to continue his explorations. He and those who were to remain on the ships prayed for rain—ironic given the terrible storms they had so recently weathered—so they could get the ships over the bar of the river and out to the coast.

The natives, sizing up the situation, began visiting the ships. Although arrayed as if for battle, they pretended they were going to attack a neighboring tribe. Those on board grew suspicious; the fragile harmony that had been established between the Europeans and the native people was broken. Diego Méndez offered to investigate. He took one of the small boats and rowed upstream, where he came upon a thousand men in battle gear encamped on the shore. He, too, grew suspicious, returned to inform Columbus, and then volunteered to return and learn more.

Columbus should have insisted on bringing Bartholomew and his men aboard the ships for safety, but he hesitated while Méndez went on his second reconnaissance mission. Brazen and confident, Méndez persuaded some of the native men to take him to see the Quibián with the pretext he had come to obtain a cure for a wound he had sustained in an earlier battle. When Méndez approached the chief's residence he saw that the "stockade was decorated with 300 heads of the men he had killed in battle" during a war against a neighboring group.[30] At Méndez's approach, the women and children made such an uproar that "the son of the cacique came out in great rage, spitting out angry words in his own language . . . and with a big push shoved me far from him." Then came one of the most unusual vignettes of the entire voyage. In his own account, Méndez explained what he did to calm the son and pry his father out of his house.

I whipped out a comb, a pair of scissors, and a mirror, and made Escobar, my companion, comb my hair and cut it. This really astonished him
and the others who were there. I then got him [the cacique's son] to let
Escobar comb his hair and cut it with the scissors; and I presented him
with the scissors, the comb and the brush, and that made him friendly.
I then asked for some food. This they brought immediately, and we ate
and drank in harmony and good fellowship like friends.[31]

Méndez left but he didn't trust the fellowship that had been achieved. When he
reported to Columbus, both agreed they must capture the cacique and his closest associates in order to prevent the planned attack.

At this time, we learned through the interpreter that the Quibián
planned to set fire to the houses and kill all the Christians, the Indians
being greatly offended that we had settled on that river. It was decided to
teach him a lesson and strike fear into his neighbors by taking him and
all his leading men prisoners and sending them to Castile, and to make
his people serve the Christians.[32]

For this purpose, Bartholomew took seventy-four men to visit the Quibián.
Leaving most of them some distance away, he advanced with only five of them
to the house of the chief. The chief was suffering from an arrow wound but went
out to meet Bartholomew, who knelt down to examine the wound but instead
grabbed hold of the Quibián's arm and gave a shout to the others, who quickly
came out from hiding, surrounded the house, captured those inside, including
his children, and seized whatever valuables they saw lying about. Later, when
they reconnoitered with Columbus they were able to present him "with about
300 ducats of booty," mostly gold objects which, after they had "deducted the
royal fifth, they divided the rest among themselves," as was customary.[33] This
skirmish happened so fast that, fortunately, no one was hurt.

After the Quibián, his family, and the others in house had been captured,
they were marched to the small boats waiting to take them to the ships. During
the night, the Quibián complained that the ropes were hurting him, and the
man on guard felt some sympathy and loosened them. The wily chief was able
to quickly slip out of them, jumped overboard, and swam in the dark to shore,
vanishing, wrote Ferdinand, "like a stone fallen in water." The Europeans were

embarrassed and strengthened their hold on their remaining prisoners. When they reached the ships, they put them in the hold of the *Bermuda*. When the Quibián's forces heard about what had happened to him and his family, they were naturally incensed and vowed to retaliate.

Miraculously during that night, the rains came; Columbus could not waste time in futile pursuit and, instead, decided to try to get three of the ships around the sand bar, out to the coast and out of danger. The *Gallega* was left inside the harbor with a few of the men on guard. Bartholomew, Méndez, and about twenty men remained on shore in their tiny settlement. Realizing how vulnerable they were, and assuming that at least three of the ships had sailed away, the natives chose that moment to attack. Nearly four hundred of them, armed with bows and arrows, darts and spears, surrounded the encampment and attacked the men. The Europeans fought bravely; one of the men was killed, seven were wounded including Bartholomew, "who received a dart wound in the chest,"[34] but with their swords and guns, they were able to rebuff the native warriors, who soon retreated.

Meanwhile, Diego Tristan was sent from Columbus's ship in a small boat to get a supply of fresh water for their intended voyage back to Spain. From his boat, Tristan witnessed some of the fighting; he did not join in but proceeded on his orders to get water. At a narrow point in the river, Tristan and the men with him were set upon by a few natives and all but one of them were killed; the lone survivor swam underwater until he was out of sight. When he brought the news of the attack back to Bartholomew, he reported that Tristan had been killed with a spear through the eye; it was not long before the bodies of those who had been killed were floating down the river past the settlement. This terrible sight forced a decision; they had to abandon the settlement and the *Gallega*, which was trapped in the sand.

Columbus, offshore and outside the sandbar, knew nothing of this; days passed without news of what was happening at the settlement. The wait was excruciating; he was distraught and exhausted. While falling asleep on one of these anxious nights of waiting, he had the second of his mystical visions.[35] A voice came to him, saying something like: "O ye of little faith" and reminded him of the "barriers of the Ocean Sea, which were closed with such mighty chains, He hath given thee the keys"—a paraphrase of a passage from Seneca's *Medea* that was so close to Columbus's heart. The voice also reminded him of how God had helped Moses bring his people out of Egypt, how he raised David from a shepherd to become king, and gave Abraham a son in his old age. "His mercy is infinite; thine old age shall not prevent thee from achieving all great things."[36] He awoke from his trance with his faith restored and waited for news of his brother, Méndez, and Tristan.

The prisoners in the hold were becoming restive. One night they succeeded in pushing open the hatch which the man guarding it had thought too high for them to reach and had not secured with chains. The prisoners had cleverly used some of the ballast as stepping-stones and a few of them were able to pull themselves up through the hatch and jump overboard before the crew realized what had happened. Quickly, the guard forced the others back into the hold and fastened the latch. The "next morning it was found that they had hanged themselves." Ferdinand ruefully reflected that "the Quibián would gladly have made peace for the return of his children, but now that we no longer had hostages, there was reason to fear he would wage even crueler war on the town."[37]

The men at the settlement had reached the same conclusion and decided they had to get out to Columbus as quickly as possible. They went to the *Gallega*, where they wrapped up their provisions in sacks that Méndez made from the sails. Lashing together two canoes, the men made several trips between the *Gallega* and the ships where Columbus was waiting, until everyone had been rescued from danger and boarded onto the three remaining ships. Columbus was devastated by the sad news that Diego Tristan was among those killed, but he commended Méndez for his bravery in the rescue and appointed him as captain of *La Capitana*, in place of the dead Tristan. On April 16, 1503, the fleet of three finally "departed in the name of the Holy Trinity on Easter night, with ships rotten, worm-eaten, all full of holes";[38] soon thereafter they had to abandon the leaking *Vizcaina* in Porto Bello, farther down the coast of Panama.[39]

Now only two ships remained and all of the men had to crowd onto them. Columbus was in a quandary; in a letter he would later send to the sovereigns he said that he and the men would have remained at Belén to "maintain the settlement," but since neither the sovereigns nor Ovando knew where he was, they would not know where to send ships with supplies or to rescue them. Columbus wanted to return to Spain, but admitted that "to traverse seven thousand miles of sea and waves, or to die on the way with my son and brother and so many people," was not to be contemplated.[40] So he headed for Hispaniola. Contrary currents and severe winds brought them back to Cuba, which, even at that time, Columbus continued to think was the mainland of China. Columbus wrote that "On 13 May, I reached the province of *Mago* [Mangi] which borders upon the province of Cathay. Thence I sailed for Hispaniola."[41]

They never made it to Hispaniola. The account Columbus wrote—about more terrible storms they encountered, about losing three anchors, about cables bursting—would seem concocted if it were not corroborated by others. They were thrown off course and, instead of Hispaniola, they arrived on the north coast of Jamaica at the place Columbus had visited on the second voyage and had named Santa Gloria (now St. Ann's Bay). The two remaining ships—the *Capitana* and the *Santiago*—were sinking under them, "more riddled with holes than a honeycomb."[42]

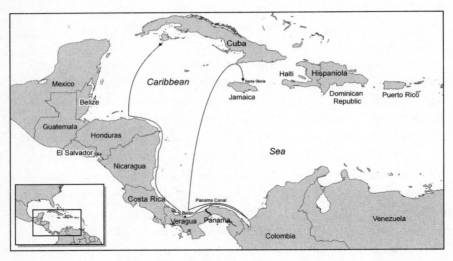

Final explorations of the Fourth Voyage and Marooned ~ July 30, 1502-June 29, 1504.

Prepared by Lynn Carlson, GISP

The date was June 25, 1503. Columbus was shipwrecked for the third time.[43] With him were 116 men and boys but no food. Ferdinand wrote that they ran the ships ashore, close together, and built cabins on top of the decks where they could seem to be taking refuge against possibly hostile natives. More likely, Columbus kept the men on board rather than setting up camp on shore in order to protect the natives from the rapaciousness of the crew.[44] Ferdinand wrote:

Our people being by nature disrespectful, no punishment or order could have stopped them from running about the country and into the Indians' huts to steal what they found and commit outrages on their wives and children, whence would have arisen disputes and quarrels that would have made enemies of them; and if we had taken their food from them by force, we would later have suffered great need and privations. But this did not happen, for the men were confined in the ships and no one could go ashore without getting permission and signing out. The Indians were so grateful for this that they freely brought all we needed in exchange for our things.[45]

Perhaps the natives remembered Columbus's earlier visit which had gone smoothly, for, according to Ferdinand, they were "kind and gentle people" who "presently came in canoes to barter their wares and provisions."[46] Apparently, the Europeans still had some "beads, combs, knives, hawk's bells, fish-hooks and other trading truck" to exchange for food.[47] There were complicated negotiations going on between the natives and the sailors. Columbus sent Méndez ashore with a couple of men to seek out several caciques and to arrange a deal for provisions. They even made a list of agreed upon equivalences, which Ferdinand recorded:

for one or two hutias [large rodent] we gave them a lace point, for a large cake of cassava bread, which is made from grated roots, we gave two or three strings of green or yellow beads; and for a large quantity of anything a hawk's bell, with an occasional gift of a mirror, red cap, or a pair of scissors to the caciques or nobility to keep them happy.[48]

How long this mutually satisfying exchange would last was anyone's guess. In fact, after a few months the natives got fed up and complained that the Spaniards ate more in a day than they did in twenty. By the end of 1503, the situation was getting desperate.

Columbus recognized that he needed to do something extraordinary if he was going to keep his men safe and their relationship with the native people functioning. He must have been reading his copy of the *Ephemerides* and recalled "that in three days' time, at midnight, there would be a total eclipse of the moon."[49] So he sent a messenger to invite the caciques to the ships whereupon he told them that God was angry with them for not continuing to bring them provisions and would punish them with famine if they did not resume. He told them to "attend that night the rising of the moon: She would rise inflamed with wrath, signifying the chastisement God would visit upon them." The eclipse began and as it became more complete,

> the Indians grew so frightened that with great howling and lamentations they came running from all directions to the ships, laden with provisions, and praying the Admiral to intercede with God that He might not vent His wrath upon them, and promising that they would diligently supply all their needs in the future.[50]

Columbus retired to his cabin to "speak with God" and waited through the climax of the eclipse. While there, he actually used the eclipse to figure the longitude (way off) and latitude (almost correct) of his current location. He recorded his observations and the date, February 29, 1504, in the *Libro de las profecías*, an indication that he had taken the book with him on this voyage in order to edit or make additions to it.

After his calculations, he returned on deck and told the cacique he had prayed for him and his people and that God would pardon them as long as they continued to provision the Christians. As the moon began to emerge from the shadow, the natives were much relieved and continued to supply food to the Europeans for the remainder of their stay. Whether or not the devout Columbus had qualms about using God in this fashion, the problem of food was one that he had to resolve.

The more urgent and not so easily resolved problem was how they were going to get off the island. No one on Hispaniola knew where they were, and ships from there would never pass by since there was no gold on Jamaica and, thus, no reason to do so. Columbus and the men knew they could not survive like this forever. They would eventually run out of trading trinkets, and the natives would soon become disaffected. Their small boats had long ago been lost or destroyed; the only possibility of rescue was to send some men to Hispaniola in canoes. It was a desperate move and dangerous because "the passage from the eastern end of Jamaica to the western cape of Hispaniola was 105 miles against wind and current, with another 350 miles to paddle alongshore before reaching Santo Domingo."[51] Because no one wanted to go, the ever-faithful friend, Diego Méndez, volunteered.

On July 7, 1503, just before Méndez's departure, Columbus wrote a rash of letters, hoping that somehow, sometime, Méndez would be able to deliver news to his son Diego and to the queen. He also wrote a short note to Father Gorricio asking for his prayers and telling him that his son Diego would fill him in on the details. The letter Columbus wrote to the queen, known today as *Lettera Raríssima*, was written in haste and while he was exhausted and ill. Nevertheless, it is a long letter in which he recounted the adventures, discoveries, and pitfalls of the fourth voyage. In this letter, he makes an appeal to the sovereigns that would become a persistent refrain once he was back in Spain:

> The people who came with me have suffered incredible toils and dangers. I pray Your Highnesses, since they are poor, that you will command that they be paid immediately and that you will grant rewards to each one of them according to their quality.[52]

In addition, he reiterated his appeal for the quest of Jerusalem and the prophecy that

> Jerusalem and Mount Sion are to be rebuilt by the hand of a Christian; who this is to be, God declares by the mouth of His prophet in the fourteenth psalm. Abbot Joachim said that he was to come from Spain.

He also pledged that, if he returned to Spain, he would take friars to teach the Grand Khan about the Christian faith. Perhaps more surprising given what he experienced on the coast of Veragua is his plea about the extraction of gold from the native people. He was still thinking that a trading post, beneficial to both, should be established.

> Although the gold which the Quibián has in Veragua and which others in that neighborhood have, is, according to accounts, very abundant, it does not appear to me to be well or for the service of Your Highnesses that it should be seized violently.

Carrying these letters, Méndez started out for the other side of the island with one other Christian and six native men, but they had to return when they were attacked by another group of natives. Courageously, Méndez set out again; this time he would have a second canoe that would be "captained" by Bartolomeo Fieschi, a Genoese. Each canoe would have "six Christians and ten Indians, in the hope that at least one dugout could make the passage."[53] Ferdinand, Columbus's son, said that Bartholomew accompanied Méndez and Fieschi across the island with an armed guard, while Las Casas recalled a more benign excursion. He wrote that it was Columbus himself who went with them to the tip of Jamaica and then "returned slowly to his ships, visiting villages along his path and conversing joyfully with their inhabitants and leaving many friends behind."[54]

Méndez and Fieschi set out in these crowded canoes; with the exception of a brief stop on the rocky islet of La Bella Saonese that Columbus had given to Michele de Cuneo on the second voyage, this trip across the channel would take them four days. Due to strenuous paddling under the searing sun, several natives died of thirst or from drinking too much water too quickly.[55] When they finally reached the western tip of Hispaniola, one of the canoes was supposed to return to let Columbus know they had made it. "Bartolomeo Fieschi, standing on his honor as an *hidalgo*, proposed to return as the Admiral had ordered," but the other Christians, feeling they had been "delivered from the whale's belly" like Jonah, refused to go back, and so, too, did the natives.[56] Fieschi could not go alone.

Méndez wrote that he took one canoe and started to paddle along the coast to Santo Domingo; no doubt Fieschi accompanied him part of the way, though Méndez doesn't say. Shortly, they heard that Ovando was in the hinterland trying to quell an uprising. Méndez abandoned his canoe and set off overland to meet him, while Fieschi continued to Santo Domingo. Ovando pretended to be happy to see Méndez, but Méndez reported that Ovando "detained me there seven months until he had burned or hanged 84 caciques, lords of vassals, and with them Anacaona, the chief lady of the island, whom all the natives obeyed and served."[57] Las Casas, who was in Hispaniola by 1504, described this terrible tragedy/travesty visited upon the native people. Las Casas wrote that Anacaona herself had planned a big feast to welcome the new governor and had invited the many chiefs to meet him. Instead of behaving like guests, the Spaniards forced the caciques into a house and set it on fire. "As for the lady chief, they hanged her as a mark of honor." In addition, he described one of the most gratuitous acts of violence: he wrote that if one Spaniard "from pity or greed, snatched a child away to save him from slaughter by lifting him to his horse, someone would come from behind pierce the child with a lance . . . or slash his legs off with a sword." [58] Many months *after* the massacre of these natives, Ovando committed another travesty: he arranged a (mock) trial of the natives he had killed. And he called as witnesses the very men who had killed them. Ovando may have learned this tactic from Bobadilla.

Méndez's persistence to go to Santo Domingo finally paid off. Ovando probably thought that after all that time, with worsening conditions among his men as well as with the natives, Columbus had perished by now, so why not let Méndez go. When Méndez reached Santo Domingo he was able to hire a ship to rescue Columbus and his men. After giving thorough instruction to the crew on how to find the others, Méndez caught a ship returning to Spain to deliver letters and to inform the queen about everything that had happened.

Columbus, of course, didn't know about any of this. Since neither Fieschi nor Méndez nor any of their men had returned, as he had requested, Columbus had no way of knowing whether anyone had made it to Hispaniola; he most likely assumed that all of them had died at sea. Columbus had to prepare mentally and physically for a long wait. Not only did he have to maintain cordial relations with the natives, he also had to keep up the spirits of more than a hundred men and boys. It was an awesome task, especially as they were cooped up on board the two ships for most of the time. In such enforced proximity and under such dire circumstances, father and son must have become close; the famous father worried but proud of his son, and the son full of admiration for his father as is so clear in the biography he later wrote.

But an idyll it was not to be. Some of the men were sick, others began to concoct preposterous theories to explain their plight,

> saying the Admiral had no intention of returning to Spain, whence the Catholic Sovereigns had banished him; and they said he had even less intention of returning to Española, where he had been forbidden to land at the start of that voyage. His true purpose in sending those canoes was not to obtain ships or relief but to enable Méndez and Fieschi to go to Spain to try to fix up the Admiral's business. [59]

The Porras brothers capitalized on the suspicions of the crew. Promising to get them back to Castile, they convinced forty-eight of the remaining men to sign articles of mutiny. Furthermore, they said that Columbus would inflict terrible punishments on them for attempting to leave the island, so if they wanted to save themselves, it would be better to kill him. Yet, Columbus also had at least an equal number of men loyal to him and they, too, had weapons. Even better, they had the protection of the ships. The mutineers commandeered ten canoes that Columbus had diligently secured from the natives and took off for the place from which Méndez and Fieschi had departed. Ferdinand continues:

> Wherever they called, they inflicted outrages on the Indians, robbing their food and other possessions; they told the Indians to collect their pay from the Admiral and authorized them to kill him if he would not pay.[60]

Planning to follow in the wake of Méndez and Fieschi, a few of the mutineers took some Indians and started to cross the channel. But the sea became rough and they were afraid the canoes would sink. In order to lighten their load, they took the nasty expedient of killing some of the Indians and throwing them overboard. In an attempt to avoid that fate, other Indians jumped into the sea but were soon tired from swimming. When they "tried to rest by clinging to the gunwales, their hands were hacked off by the mutineers. They killed eighteen this way." Ferdinand wryly comments, "this was the Indians' reward for listening to their false promises."[61]

While the mutineers were trying to escape, Columbus was surprised and relieved when a small ship from Hispaniola arrived. But his relief turned to dismay when he saw that the captain of the ship was Diego Escobar, who had been one of the rebels under Roldán; no doubt Ovando had sent him as a calculated affront to Columbus. Later, he learned from Méndez that Ovando was afraid that if Columbus returned to Spain "the Catholic Sovereigns would restore the Admiral to his office and deprive him [Ovando] of his government."[62] Ovando had probably hoped that Escobar would find Columbus dead or dying. Escobar told Columbus that Méndez had reached Santo Domingo, but said that Ovando "had no ship large enough to take off all the Admiral's men." Then, like a slap in the face, he tossed them "a barrel of wine and a slab of salt pork . . . [and] immediately returned to the caravel, sailing away the same night without even taking letters from anyone." Columbus did not let his annoyance show but instead consoled the men who had remained loyal to him by telling them "that the caravel was too small to take them all, and he did not want to leave without taking them all." Columbus threw his fate in with theirs.

After Escobar's ship departed, Columbus sent a messenger to inform the Porras mutineers about the visit and the news that Méndez had made it to Santo Domingo. He told them he was assured that another ship, large enough to rescue all of them, would soon arrive. He even offered to pardon them if they would just return to the group. Porras convinced the mutineers that this was a ruse and that the caravel was a "phantasm conjured up by the magic arts of which the Admiral was a master" and so they refused the offer and determined to march on Columbus and take control. "When he learned of their intention, the Admiral sent his brother, the Adelantado, in an effort to bring them to their senses with soft words, but backed him up with a large enough force to repel any attack."⁶³ When Bartholomew and the men loyal to Columbus tried to make peace, the mutineers turned on them and attacked. Bartholomew's men were well armed. Fueled by anger, they rebuffed the mutineers and succeeded in killing several of the worst, wounding others, and capturing Francisco de Porras. The rest of the mutineers escaped as fast as they could. Bartholomew suffered a minor injury and the loyal Pedro de Terreros, the man who had asked Ovando for refuge during the hurricane, and who had captained the *Gallega*, died from wounds he sustained in the battle.

On May 20, 1504, the mutineers who had escaped sent an envoy to Columbus pleading "humbly with the Admiral to be merciful to them, for they were repentant and wished to rejoin his service."⁶⁴ Generously, Columbus granted them full pardon. He kept Francisco de Porras as prisoner and sent the contrite mutineers with one of his trusted associates on a tour of the island to trade with the natives until the rescue ship came. And things turned out just as Columbus had promised. Barely a month later, two ships arrived—one that Méndez had hired and one presumably sent by Ovando. On June 29, all of the men—both the mutineers and the loyal seamen—bid farewell to Jamaica. They had been marooned on Jamaica for a year and five days.

CHAPTER ELEVEN

THE FINAL PASSION:
DISILLUSION AND DEATH

On August 13, 1504, just short of Ferdinand's sixteenth birthday, the weary men from Jamaica arrived in Santo Domingo. In contrast to the relatively quick trip in the canoes by Méndez and Fieschi, it took the rescue ships six weeks to sail from Jamaica to Santo Domingo—longer than most of Columbus's Atlantic crossings. When they arrived, Ovando "received the Admiral very hospitably and lodged him in his own house; but it was a scorpion's kiss" according to Ferdinand.[1] Ovando insulted Columbus by freeing Francisco de Porras, the ringleader of the mutiny, and said he would punish the men who had remained loyal to Columbus, instead of the mutineers.[2]

Columbus suffered in these conditions for a month, while a ship was found for the voyage back to Spain. Out of what little ready cash he had left, Columbus paid the men their wages and chartered and outfitted two ships, names unknown, for this voyage. One of them was the small caravel that had rescued them; a few of the men chose to sail on that ship while Columbus, Bartholomew, Ferdinand, his friend Fieschi, and twenty-two others sailed on the other. Columbus had been ill and bedridden for some time (no doubt his painful arthritis had flared up due to all the stress he had endured), so he hired Diego Rodriguez to captain his ship. They left on September 12, 1504. The rest of the men had had enough of sailing for the time being and decided to remain in Hispaniola.

Since it was still hurricane season it is not surprising that they ran into a serious storm soon after they left. The mainmast of the small caravel broke, and it had to turn back; Columbus continued in the remaining vessel. When its mainmast also broke, they assembled a makeshift one and decided to continue, for the last thing Columbus wanted to do was to return to Santo Domingo and Ovando. Columbus's last voyage would end on November 7, 1504, as the ship pulled into the familiar harbor of Sanlúcar de Barrameda. He was fifty-three, weary and ill and feeling his age; he realized that his career as Admiral of the Ocean Sea was over.

He settled in Seville, informed the sovereigns that he was home, and waited for their invitation to receive him. The court was in Segovia; Columbus was so infirm that he would not be able to ride a horse and did not know how he would get there. A mule would be much better for "only the gentle amble of the sure-footed Andalusian mule could afford ease and safety to one so grievously afflicted with the gout as was the Admiral." Since travel by mule was a high honor, "granted only to nobles and the highest ecclesiastics," Columbus could not take such a privilege for granted.[3] He applied to the King for the permit that was necessary in order to hire a mule.

While waiting for the permit and the royal invitation for an audience, and trying to recoup his strength, he had the company of teenage Ferdinand, but he was also eager to see Diego, who had been promoted from page to bodyguard and confidant of Queen Isabella and could, therefore, inform Columbus about what was going on at court.[4] During this period, Columbus wrote a rash of letters to Diego, ten of which have survived. There was no standardized postal system at this time; instead, Columbus was able to send letters with friends or couriers going to court, which must have been relatively safe since Columbus often enclosed large amounts of gold or money—gold for the Crown and money for Diego, possibly to pay off debts or legal fees.

The first of the letters to Diego from this period is dated November 21, 1504. It begins "very dear son" and is mostly about business matters but includes an account of the Porras brothers' rebellion and his dismay at their release. He ended the letter in his usual way, signing "your father who loves you more than himself," and ending with the pyramid of letters and Xpo-ferens. But then he added a postscript that expressed his concern for the men who had remained loyal to him all along.

I wrote *again* to their Highnesses entreating them to order that these people who went with me should be paid, because they are poor and it is three years since they left their homes. The news which they bring is more than extraordinary. They have endured infinite dangers and hardships.[5]

A week later, Columbus wrote again to his son Diego saying he had received his letters of the 15th and had sent a response by courier eight days prior. His illness troubled him greatly and though he was preparing to go to court, he told Diego that just because of that, "you must not write less often." Then Columbus reiterated his

> wish that their Highnesses would provide for the payment of these poor people who have passed through incredible hardships and have brought them such great news that infinite thanks should be given to God, our Lord, and they should rejoice greatly over it.[6]

The most touching letter is the one written only a few days later, on December 1, 1504. It registers such a familiar parental complaint.

> Very dear son:
> Since I received your letter of November 15 I have heard nothing from you. I wish that you would write me more frequently. I would like to receive a letter from you each hour. Reason must tell you that now I have no other repose. Many couriers come each day, and the news is of such a nature and so abundant that in hearing it, all my hair stands on end . . . Take good care of your brother. He has a good disposition and is no longer a boy. Ten brothers would not be too many for you. I never found better friends to the right or to left than my brothers.[7]

In that same letter, Columbus sent his regards to the queen, saying "May it please the Holy Trinity to give health to the Queen, our Lady, that she may settle what has already been placed under discussion."[8]

Columbus had hoped Isabella would take care of the restitution of his privileges and the various monies owed him. He ended that letter with mounting exasperation about the monies owed to his men:

We must strive to obtain a reply to my letter from their Highnesses, and to have them order that these people be paid. I wrote in regard to this subject four days ago.

Columbus's expression of concern and compassion for his men is also a not so veiled criticism of the sovereigns for their very lack of understanding and their dilatory response in addressing the men's need.

At the end of the letter he added a postscript: "Today is Monday . . . Remember to write me very often and tell Diego Méndez to write at length."[9] In every letter to his son, Columbus mentioned his friend Diego Méndez, who was also at court helping with all the matters related to the fourth voyage. Columbus instructed his son to show Méndez all the letters and said that he would write to Méndez himself, but "[m]y illness permits me to write only at night, because in the daytime my hands are deprived of strength."[10]

Two days later, December 3, Columbus wrote again with even more complaints:

> I wrote you at length day before yesterday . . . I am very much astonished not to receive a letter from you or from any one else, and this astonishment is shared by all who know me. Every one here has letters and I, who have more reason to expect them, have none. Great care should be taken about this matter.[11]

What Columbus had no way of knowing at that point was that Queen Isabella had died on November 26, 1504, after an illness that came and went during the last year of her life. She had suffered from fevers and pains, and doctors at the time believed it was dropsy. Today, some have speculated that it could have been cancer (toward the end, a tumor had become visible, though "just where or what kind is not stated") or endocarditis—an infection of the heart valves.[12] Columbus was devastated when he learned of the queen's death. He had looked forward to seeing her and being able to tell her about the adventures and mishaps of this voyage. Columbus was well aware that King Ferdinand was not as strong a supporter of him as she had been, and he was worried about his status. He also realized that now he would be unable to tell his patron and friend about the mutiny and the perfidiousness of those sent to govern in his place.

Christopher Columbus. Attributed to Ridolfo del
Ghirlandaio. *By permission of the Museo del Mare,
Genoa, Italy.*

Columbus was broken in spirit and in body, his suffering reflected in the
urgent tone of his letters. The queen's illness was probably the reason he had
not been immediately summoned to court, but now, his own illness prevented
him from being present at her funeral and being able to pay his respects. In his
stead, he asked Diego

> to affectionately and with great devotion commend the soul of the
> Queen, our Lady, to God. Her life was always Catholic and Holy and
> ready for all the things of His holy service, and for this reason it must
> be believed that she is in His holy glory and beyond the desires of this
> rough and wearisome world.[13]

The "wearisome world" was clearly weighing heavily on Columbus. He sent
Bartholomew and Ferdinand, "who, although he is a child in days, is not a child
in understanding," in order to give Diego more information about the voyage
and to help him negotiate the family business with the Crown. He told Diego to
"show your uncle due respect and treat your brother as an elder brother should
treat a younger. You have no other brother, and praised be our Lord, he is such
a one as you need very much. He has proved and proves to be very intelligent."[14]

Columbus felt bereft, forsaken, and complained again about not getting any
letters from friends at court. In another letter to Diego, he wrote: "I feel great
sorrow that all the world should have letters from there each day, and I have
nothing, when I have so many people there," including his son. He added a
postscript that his affairs should be "settled according to conscience," and that

he, Diego, as his heir, be "placed in possession." He was referring to the rights (privileges) he had been granted in the Capitulations—especially his titles and his shares of the profits from the Indies—which were heritable. He wrote, however, that although he was owed his "third and eighth and the tenth . . . There will always be opportunity to make reductions from this amount."[15] In other words, it was more important to Columbus to have the contracts about his share in the Indies trade acknowledged than to receive the actual amount of money owed him. All of the contracts were in the *Book of Privileges*, a copy of which he had entrusted to his friend Friar Gaspar Gorricio. Columbus wanted to see them again, and he asked Gorricio "to order a box made of cork and line with wax to hold them," and to send the papers to him by a lay brother.[16] He must have had a special reason to see the contracts, because in his letter he wrote "I do not know yet how to tell you of my desire to see you and communicate something which is not to be written."[17]

Columbus was ill; like any parent, he was concerned about the welfare of his sons in the event of his death and was trying to cement the family ties. With each letter to Diego, Columbus sent gold, but he was getting worried that his supply would dry up if the king did not settle his accounts. In a letter of December 21, for example, he said "I have already told you how necessary it is to be careful in the expenditure of the money, until their Highnesses give us law and justice."[18]

That was not to be. After the queen's death, King Ferdinand reneged on the privileges—the hereditary titles and shares of the profits—made to Columbus in the Capitulations of Santa Fe in April 1492 before he set out on the first voyage and which were reinstated after the third voyage—all except the governorship of Hispaniola. Columbus requested an investigation and a hearing; instead lawyers were assigned to handle his "estate, but not his rights"—that is, they could handle any property he owned, but not his titles and the thirds, eighths, and tenths. While Las Casas had taken that "to mean that the admiral's rights were unquestionably clear," that was not the king's view. Las Casas comments:

> As for the Catholic King Ferdinand, I do not know why he was not only ungrateful in words and deeds but actually harmed Columbus whenever possible, although his words belied his actions. It was believed that if, in good conscience and without losing face, he could have violated all the articles of the privileges that he and the Queen had justly granted him

for his services, he would indeed have done so. I have never been able to ascertain the reason for this dislike and unkingly conduct toward one whose unparalleled services no other monarch ever received. Perhaps he was unduly impressed by the arguments and false testimonies of the admiral's enemies and rivals.[19]

The king did not share the zeal of both Columbus and Isabella over the issue of the conquest of Jerusalem. Instead of mounting a crusade to liberate Jerusalem, Ferdinand sent Peter Martyr to the sultan to persuade him to protect the holy places for Christian pilgrims. Columbus, with good reason, was despondent; not only did he *feel* cheated out of the honors and rewards that he was promised, he *was* cheated. Las Casas agreed; in his *Historia de las Indias*, written many years after these events, and even after belatedly becoming an advocate for the Indians, he viewed Columbus kindly. While recognizing Columbus's shortcomings in the administration of the colonies, Las Casas still claimed that Columbus was far better and fairer than either Bobadilla or Ovando or any of those who came later. Unfairly, their names are forgotten and so too their misdeeds, while Columbus has become the symbol for all that went wrong in the Indies.

Columbus was concerned not only about the monies owed to him, but also those owed to his men. He could not understand why the king was so remiss. In frustration, he wrote again to Diego on December 29, 1504, saying:

The payment of the people who went with me has been delayed. I have provided for them here what I have been able. They are poor and are obliged to go in order to earn a living. They decided to go yonder[,][20]

that is, to court, no doubt hoping that if they presented their case in person, they would be paid. Columbus empathized with them, for he, too, was a victim of the king's injustice. "[O]n the one hand, the faithful members of his exploring expedition—the loyal companions of his last voyage—are unpaid and unrewarded; while, on the other, he beholds the mutinous and rebellious going unpunished and protected."[21]

He especially wanted Gonzalo Camacho to be punished. He had been one of the most troublesome of the mutineers, and he was now trying to steal the inheritance of Pedro de Terreros by forging a will that made himself heir at the exclusion of de Terreros's natural heirs. De Terreros was one of Columbus's most loyal sailors; he had been on all four of Columbus's voyages, and on the last one he was captain of the *Gallega*. In addition, when the men arrived at Hispaniola and saw signs of the impending hurricane, he was the one who went into Santo Domingo "to beg that the little fleet might take refuge in the harbour during the coming storm." [22] On the third voyage, after Columbus realized that he had found *tierra infinita*—the huge landmass we recognize as South America—he sent de Terreros in to take possession of it because he was too ill to move. And on the final voyage, de Terreros had defended Columbus against the rebels and died on May 29, 1504, from the wounds they had inflicted. It was outrageous that Camacho should try to steal his inheritance, which included de Terreros's substantial wages as ship captain. Columbus was as loyal to the dead de Terreros as the latter had been to him. Columbus wrote again to Diego and assured him that the relatives of de Terreros had another recent will and said that he was prepared to help them obtain their rightful inheritance. Columbus was able to have warrants sworn for Camacho's arrest, but when Camacho heard of this, he spent eight days hiding out in a church during the Christmas holidays. And he was not punished.

The king was unmoved by all of Columbus's pleas. He tried to buy him off with the offer of an estate in Castile and a guaranteed income, but Columbus refused. His honor was at stake; he wanted only what was due him, and not really even for himself but for his sons and family—his legacy. He spent the remaining months of his life trying to get his privileges acknowledged. Diego, as legal heir, would inherit most of the estate, although Columbus had made provisions for Ferdinand and his brothers among others. Ferdinand would continue to help his brother through long, drawn-out legal battles to reinstate their father's rights—battles that would continue long after Columbus's death.

Columbus also hoped to have some say over what would become of Hispaniola before he died. Since he was aware he would never be able to sail again or return there as governor, he asked King Ferdinand to bestow the governorship on his son Diego. Columbus also wanted to be able to suggest the names of men who should be appointed as bishops on the island—men who would take seriously the need to instruct the natives in the Christian faith.

Columbus had planned to visit the pope (Julius II) in Rome to discuss his concern about this issue, but he was far too ill for such a trip. In a letter to Diego of December 29, 1504, Columbus wrote that he enclosed "a copy of a letter which I wrote to the Holy Father in regard to the affairs of the Indies that he might not complain of me any more,"[23] meaning that Columbus had not yet responded to a letter he had received from the pope. He asked Diego to show his reply to the king and the archbishop in order to inform them of its contents and to make sure it was properly worded.

During the month of January, 1505, Méndez, who had been at court trying to help settle the accounts of the fourth voyage, went to stay with Columbus in Seville. During that time, he had the opportunity to ask a favor of Columbus. He requested to be named *alguacil mayor* (a kind of sheriff) of Hispaniola as a reward for his extraordinary service. Méndez recorded that Columbus "replied that he would do so very willingly and that that was but slight return for the great services I had performed."[24] Being very ill, Columbus told Méndez to communicate to Diego his wishes about the post he wanted Méndez to have. In a letter of January 18, 1505, Columbus informed Diego that Méndez would be leaving Seville shortly to return to the court and would be carrying "a full pouch" of letters. One of the letters must have included the business about Méndez's appointment, for Méndez wrote that Diego responded "that if his father conferred it upon me with one hand, he, on his part, conferred it upon me with both."[25]

Méndez stayed with Columbus for about a month and left on February 3. Two days later, Columbus wrote to Diego saying,

> I talked with Americus Vespucius, the bearer of this letter, who is going yonder where he is called in regard to matters of navigation. He was always desirous of pleasing me. He is a very honourable man. Fortune has been adverse to him as it has been to many others. His labours have not profited him as much as reason demands. He goes for me and is very desirous of doing something to benefit me if it is in his power.[26]

Columbus and Vespucci knew each other and were friends, perhaps since 1493, for Vespucci worked with the firm of Bernardi that helped to outfit the ships for the second voyage. Still, today, there is poignancy in reading the letter, for we know what happened. It seemed that the world conspired to deprive Columbus of his legacy. John Boyd Thacher, a nineteenth-century American who made a voluminous study of Columbus, wrote that "Columbus was deprived of the honour of having his name given to the New World. It was an injustice. But this injustice lies not at the door of Vespucius."[27] Las Casas agreed but thought

Vespucci was a fraud and had wangled the situation in his favor. In his *Historia de las Indias*, he wrote "that Vespucci was in bad faith and deliberately sought to steal the admiral's glory . . . to have the world acknowledge him as the discoverer of the largest part of the Indies."[28] In a pamphlet, *Mundus Novus* (New World), published in 1503, Vespucci claimed to have found a new part of the world—the fourth. Because this was such a shocking idea disrupting the centuries-long, biblically based belief that there were only three parts, it was widely published in numerous languages—more so than Columbus's letter about his 1492 discovery. Yet Columbus *had* discovered the South American continent on the third voyage, but he never claimed it was a new one, a fourth one; instead he assumed it was an unknown part of Asia.

Then in 1504, in what is referred to as the Letter to Soderini, Vespucci claimed to have discovered the continent in 1497, a year *before* Columbus had come to the conclusion that what he had first thought was an island, Gracia, was actually *tierra firma*, a continent. Although Vespucci claimed to have accompanied Alonso de Hojeda to Paria, on the South American coast, we know that Hojeda's first voyage there was not until 1499. Recall that after reaching Paria, Hojeda sailed to Santo Domingo while Columbus was in the midst of negotiating with Roldán and the rebels. When Hojeda told Columbus he had just come from Paria, where he had found gold, pearls, and other things of value, Columbus was angry because, according to the Capitulations, he alone had the right to authorize voyages in those parts and, thus, he realized that the sovereigns had violated their contract with him. When Columbus wrote about Hojeda's visit in 1499, he did not mention Vespucci. If he had actually accompanied Hojeda, Columbus would surely have noted it.

The debate about the naming of America was still raging in the nineteenth century. Washington Irving took up the cause as did Ralph Waldo Emerson, who decried how "broad America must wear the name of a thief . . . [who] managed in this lying world to supplant Columbus and baptize half the Earth with his own dishonest name."[29] Scholars today believe that Vespucci did not write the letters, that they had been forged, perhaps by Florentines trying to take the credit away from the Genoese. Nevertheless, at the time the letters were so popular that, not surprisingly, a copy came to the attention of a German cartographer. While Vespucci may have wanted his name attached to the continent discovered by Columbus, it was actually bestowed by a man he was unlikely to know—Martin Waldseemüller—whose map of 1507 is the first one to name the continent America.[30] Regardless, fate is cruel. It was an injustice that the continent would be named after Amerigo rather than its discoverer. Fortunately, Columbus would never know.

Columbus's last extant letter to his son Diego is dated February 25, 1505. It is brief and merely informed Diego that he had sent a letter via Vespucci with information that would help the case of two men who were being prosecuted by King Ferdinand. He asked that his petition be given to Méndez, who should, in turn, give it "to his Highness during Holy Week, for pardon."[31] He does not give the names of the men he is trying to help, though presumably both Diego and Méndez knew who they were. Around this time the king granted Columbus permission to ride a mule so that he might, finally, come to the court. According to Morison it was "the only favor that King Ferdinand ever granted to the Discoverer of America."[32]

In May, when the soft weather of spring arrived, Columbus set off on a mule for the journey from Seville to Segovia with the purpose of petitioning the king to reinstate his hereditary titles. At Segovia, the king procrastinated and said there were some issues that still had to be investigated and sent the various claims to an arbitration committee. In the summer of 1505, while Columbus waited for the results of the king's investigations, he amended the *majorat*—the will he had first drawn up in February 1498—that had specified monies for his heirs, for the people of Genoa, and also for the instruction in the Christian faith for the native people in Hispaniola. The will included a directive about what to do if a schism should again occur in the church, and specified a fund to be used for the crusade for the conquest of Jerusalem. Columbus now made several new stipulations. He made a *majorat* for Ferdinand to ensure he would have a proper income; he reiterated the need to help any of their kin who were poor; and at the end he added a list of people, most of them Genoese—old friends and employers, including the heirs of Spinola, de Negro, and Centurione—whom he wished to honor with a gift of money "given in a manner that they may not know who orders it to be given to them."[33]

Columbus also brought closure to an important part of his life. He directed Diego, his son and heir,

to make provision for Beatriz Enriquez, mother of Don Fernando, my son, so that she may be able to live honestly, being a person to whom I am under very great obligation. And this shall be done for the satisfaction of my conscience, because this matter weighs heavily upon my soul. The reason for which, it is not fitting to write here.[34]

Perhaps his neglect of Beatriz had been nagging at the back of Columbus's mind for some time; given his condition, it had forced its way to the forefront. Whatever it was that bothered him, he declined to put it in writing; clearly he felt some responsibility toward her. He had been sending her money but felt compelled to ensure that the practice would be continued after his death. Columbus's provision for her was unusual in an age when that was hardly mandated even for those who had been married.[35]

Columbus followed the court when it moved to Valladolid, where he rented a building that is, today, a small museum called Casa de Colón. His condition was getting worse; the sand in his hourglass was running out. At age fifty-six he was dying with his most cherished goal unfulfilled, his legal cases inconclusive, and his deeds unrecognized and unrewarded. Friends and relatives, aware that his end was near, began to arrive at his bedside. His two sons were there, so too were Méndez and Fieschi, the two men who risked their lives to save him. His brother Diego was there, but Bartholomew was away on their business. On May 19, his will and its codicil were authorized. A priest was called and administered the last rites. Then, according to several witnesses' statements, on May 20, 1506, the Feast of the Ascension, Columbus, with his dying breath, said:

> *In manus tuas, Domine, commendo spiritum meum.*
> (Into thy hands, Lord, I commend my spirit.)

In the millennial year, 2000, a bronze plaque engraved with an image that had been designed by Columbus's son Ferdinand was placed in the floor of the Seville Cathedral.[36] Surrounding the family's coat of arms, words simply and clearly acknowledge Columbus's extraordinary accomplishment: "To Castile and Leon, Columbus gave a New World."

COLUMBUS, APOCALYPTIC, AND JERUSALEM

Columbus has been dead for more than five hundred years, but he does not rest in peace. Heated debates about his legacy that began to coalesce around the Quincentennial commemorating his landfall continue to the present, and every year protests against him mar a holiday weekend in October. Like a fallen angel who was proposed for canonization in the nineteenth century, he has crashed to earth in the late twentieth and early twenty-first centuries. Where once he was celebrated for the discovery of a new world, now he is blamed for all the calamities that befell that world. The "presentist" perspective that dominates the contemporary view, even among some academics, holds him responsible for consequences he did not intend, expect, or endorse. Judging Columbus from a contemporary perspective rather than from the values and practices of his own time misjudges his motivations and his accomplishment.

Because Columbus has been such an important figure in the collective imagination of Americans, what we make of him affects both how we view our history and imagine our future. In what follows, I wish, first, to disentangle Columbus's motivations from the accusations that have been brought against him and then to trace briefly the transformations of the apocalyptic scenario and the place of Jerusalem that figured so centrally in his quest. To distance ourselves from his religious views obscures how deeply influential they have been, and continue to be, in our national and political consciousness.

Can we even say that Columbus "discovered" a new world when there were already millions of people living here? Can we say he discovered "America" when he reached only islands in the Bahamas and the Caribbean and did not know he had found a different continent—a fourth part of the world—when he landed on the north coast of South America? Columbus did not know it was a new world he had found; he died believing he had reached the periphery of Asia. What he did discover was a new way to get there—not "by land, by which way it is customary to go, but by the route to the West, by which route we do not know for certain that anyone previously has passed" (*Diario*, p. 19).

Columbus set forth on his voyage with the intention to deliver letters to the Grand Khan from Queen Isabella and King Ferdinand and to set up a trading post to trade for the gold and spices he had read about in Marco Polo's book. The stated purpose of that trade was to obtain enough gold to finance a crusade to retake Jerusalem from the Muslims as a prerequisite to rebuilding the temple for Christ's return before the end of the world. Because events of the "fourteenth and fifteenth centuries had heightened expectations of an imminent, decisive confrontation between good and evil, thus encouraging apocalyptic beliefs . . . [about] the approaching end of the world,"[1] his project was seen as eminently worthwhile by his contemporaries.

Columbus did not intend to supplant the native peoples with Europeans or steal their land; later, faced with rebellion, he capitulated to the settlers' demands, and Isabella eventually approved land grants to them. He surely did not intend to commit genocide, of which he has been accused. He wanted to enlist the khan and his people on his side, not to destroy them. Nor was his intention to obtain slaves; there was no possibility of enslaving the people in the civilized, luxurious world of the Grand Khan. When he met the native people, he thought that they were attractive and intelligent and because they had no false *sectas*, that they could easily become Christian: indeed, he thought they were already natural Christians. "I believe that in the world there are no better people or a better land. They love their neighbors as themselves, and they have the sweetest speech in the world; and [they are] gentle and are always laughing" (*Diario*, p. 281).

Later when he proposed sending some of the natives back to Spain as slaves, he distinguished between the friendly ones he knew and the warlike people called *canibales* or *Caribes* who were "idolators" said to eat human flesh. People who waged war against Christians or contravened the law of nature by such primitive, inhuman practices as cannibalism could be enslaved according to papal policy at the time. Thus Columbus thought it "could not be anything but well" to take them to Spain, where they would lose that habit and thereby save their souls, and he specifically requested that they be better treated than other slaves.

This is not to deny that the distinction between the different groups of natives may have been blurred in some instances and some non-Caribs were sent to Spain as slaves.[2] Slavery under any circumstances is deplorable. But Columbus was doing nothing new or different from what was common and legitimate practice in Europe, and people in the "new world" were enslaving their own neighbors before he arrived. Nor should we forget that long after Columbus's death, Las Casas, who belatedly came to the defense of the Indians, proposed that blacks be imported from Africa in their stead.

There is also no question about the terrible devastation and depopulation that was visited upon the native people due to disease and slaughter. Yet atrocities often occurred when Columbus was not even there—for example, at Navidad— or was on board ship when his men disobeyed his explicit orders and went on rampages of which he continually complained. Today, however, he is held responsible while the names of those who committed the terrible deeds have been forgotten. In addition to the ravages of disease and the carnage of conquest on the bodies of the native people, which occurred to a much greater extent with the conquistadors, was the conquest of native souls and the imperious and often forceful conversion to Christianity. Recall, however, that Columbus repeatedly asked for friars who would learn the native language and instruct the natives about the religion rather than assume they had become Christian simply by the act of baptism. For that very purpose, he also left money in his will.

Columbus was neither an angel nor a monster; he was a man of his time, and his ideas and goals were formed in that context. An extraordinarily talented navigator and seaman, he was ill prepared to manage an unruly colony and was often disgusted by the behavior of his men. Deeply devout, he fervently believed in the Christian mission and felt he had an important role to play.

Situating Columbus within a Christian apocalyptic scenario helps to broaden the debate about him and relocate some of the responsibility for the consequences of the momentous encounter between Europeans and the native peoples of America. But it also forces us to take a closer look at the very beliefs that motivated and sustained him, precisely because the millennial, apocalyptic scenario that stirred Columbus and his contemporaries did not die with him. It persists today, not only in America and among Christians, but is held in slightly different versions by some Jews and Muslims. The imperialistic pretensions of Christianity and Islam, the exclusivity of Judaism, and the beliefs of all three monotheistic, Abrahamic religions—that one cannot be among the chosen, the saved, or the elect unless one believes in God, the particular tenets of faith, and performs the appropriate practices—wreak a terrible vengeance on those who do not. Thus, they remain a major source of conflict in the world today. An investigation of the implications and permutations of the myth of the Apocalypse may help us gain a new perspective on the possible conse-quences we could expect from such views. Columbus's story can be read as a parable for our times.

The crusading impulse withered after Columbus's death despite a few subse-quent attempts. The world was changing dramatically and the Church was under siege. Not only had the Ottomans continued their successful advance into Eu-rope, but by 1517 they had taken Jerusalem from the Mamluks (another Muslim group) and would hold it for the next four hundred years. In the same year Mar-tin Luther posted his "theses" at Wittenberg, a move that would challenge the papacy's hegemony over faith. Luther also translated the Bible from Latin into German so that those who could read their own language might see how far the pope and his minions had strayed from Jesus' teaching. To accompany the text, he commissioned paintings and a series of double woodcuts from Lucas Cran-ach that juxtaposed the pope's actions with those of Jesus. One of the woodcuts showed Jesus kneeling as he washed the feet of a leper while the other showed the resplendent pope sitting on his throne while supplicants kneeled and kissed his feet. Clearly, something was wrong with that picture. In his 1520 treatise, *The Babylonian Captivity of the Church*, Luther wrote: "The papacy is indeed nothing but the kingdom of Babylon and of the true Antichrist."[3] Although he also as-sociated the threat of the "Turk" with the Antichrist, that idea lost ground as he focused more and more on the papacy. When Luther finally turned his attention to the last book of the Christian Bible, the Apocalypse (or Revelation), he began to see parallels between the tribulations elaborated in the text and papacy's devil-ish actions and concluded that the end was fast approaching.

Luther was not the first to refer to the pope as the Antichrist; others such as John Hus and John Wycliff had come to the same conclusion and others quickly followed, including Philipp Melanchthon, Ulrich Zwingli, John Calvin, and John Knox. Recently, one scholar has claimed that "the Reformation wouldn't have happened without the conviction that the pope was Antichrist," for, if he is not, "what right do you have to be split" from the Catholic church?[4]

Luther's translation of the Bible into the vernacular meant that the people themselves could interpret its meaning and no longer had to depend on their priests. This led ultimately to the fragmentation of the church into numerous denominations. The apocalyptic scenario, which has always been an integral theme in Christianity, receded into the background in the Catholic church as it became more prominent, but transformed, in a number of the Protestant churches. With the Puritans it made its second transatlantic crossing and became firmly planted in the American landscape. Leaving what they saw as a corrupt world, the Puritans had crossed the ocean to establish a godly city, a "new Jerusalem" in New England. For the Puritans, Jerusalem became a metaphor, a symbol—a crusade to capture the ancient holy city was no longer necessary; they would build a new and better one for Christ's return.

Columbus's vision was transformed as his mantel was transferred to American shoulders. America was to be the place of redemption, and the "city on a hill" would be a light unto the nations. This idea persisted even as it underwent secularization when Enlightenment ideas began to take hold of some of the influential thinkers in the new republic. The Enlightenment fostered the idea that human reason, rather than religion, was the source of authority. Yet, even as adherents to its philosophy began to criticize traditional beliefs and institutions, many of the religious ideas persisted in nonsectarian but still Christian forms or thinly veiled secular guise. For example, the very secular notion of progress, brought about not by faith in God but by faith in science, was portrayed as leading to a more perfect and peaceful world, that is, the millennium. Today, the issue of global warming is interpreted by some as the coming Apocalypse, others dismiss it, while still others, including a number of members of the U.S. Congress, believe that God will provide. For example, one congressman "dismissed the dangers of climate change by quoting Genesis 8:22: As long as the earth endures, seedtime and harvest, cold and heat, summer and winter, day and night will never cease." He added, "I believe that's the infallible word of God, and that's the way it's going to be for His Creation."[5]

The belief that this nation has a divinely supported manifest destiny, sometimes referred to as "American exceptionalism," not only legitimated its expansion west and the suppression of the native people, but also ordained its global *mission* to spread the American way of life and its values around the world, sometimes at the point of a sword.

Despite the separation of church and state, many Americans believe the United States is a God-supported, if not explicitly a Christian, nation. Since 1954, our Pledge of Allegiance has reminded us that we are "one nation under

God"; presidents take their oaths on the Bible, and until recently, witnesses had to swear they were telling the whole truth and nothing but the truth "so help me God." Even our money proclaims "In God We Trust." The United States is supposed to be a secular country, but these examples show that is hardly the case.

Secularization that was part of the Enlightenment did, however, change ideas about religion: religion was no longer supposed to have a public, political role, but was relegated to the private, personal realm. Not only that, there was a recognition that there are many religions and each was to be tolerated and respected. Because religion was a personal matter, a person could "shop" and choose his or her religion or even choose not to have one at all. These views, however, are not accepted by many Americans who continue to insist that there is only one, true faith and want this to be a Christian nation.

But what version of Christian? As the Protestant denominations splintered, so too did notions of what constitutes Christianity and with it different interpretations of the millennium, the return of Christ, and the Apocalypse. The most prominent differences—premillennialism, postmillennialism, and dispensationalism—concern the sequence of events, whether the tribulation occurs before or after the millennium, or at what point the "Rapture" occurs. These ideas are far too complicated to enter into here except to note that they tend to be held most strongly by denominations referred to as evangelical, "born again," or fundamentalist. Some groups have separated themselves from the "corrupt" world while they await Christ's return, the Rapture, or the Apocalypse itself. As the second Christian millennium approached, Americans witnessed a couple of separatist millenarian groups—the Branch Davidians and Heaven's Gate—come to tragic ends.

Most people saw these groups as fringe phenomena with very little connection or relevance to the general population or to politics and so dismissed them. The same cannot be said of the wildly popular Left Behind series by Tim LaHaye and Jerry Jenkins. The sixteen books, so far, have sold more than 65 million copies, have been made into movies and video games, and translated into several languages. The books have promoted the idea of the "Rapture" based on 1 Thessalonians 4:16–17:

> For the Lord himself will descend from heaven . . . with the sound of the
> trumpet of God. And the dead in Christ will rise first; then we who are

alive, who are left, shall be caught up together with them in the clouds to meet the Lord in the air; and so we shall always be with the Lord.

The faithful will be saved, "raptured" up to heaven, while all others will be "left behind" to suffer terrible tribulations. The books' popularity is a clear indication that apocalyptic thinking is alive and thriving in the United States.

The Left Behind series are not the only books prophesying the end of the world as we know it. At the time of the first Gulf War there was an efflorescence of apocalyptic books. For example, *The Rise of Babylon: Sign of the End Times*[6] asked on the front cover whether "ours could be the last generation?" In this instance, Saddam Hussein was portrayed as the Antichrist and his rebuilding of Babylon was taken as a sign that Armageddon was nigh. During the more recent invasion of Iraq, Saddam was labeled the "Evil One," Babylon was bombed, and the Antichrist was killed.[7] But the outcome has not been peace, only more war. In the volatile Middle East, however, Israel is the thorn in the side of peace. While there has always been an apocalyptic aura surrounding nuclear weapons, many believe that a nuclear holocaust is a real possibility and could likely begin over claims to Jerusalem.

This is hardly the place to try to explicate the extremely complicated and contentious history of Jerusalem, but certainly an outline is warranted.[8] Soon after the Ottomans took Constantinople, they quickly took over Syria, Palestine, and Egypt. In Jerusalem, the Ottoman sultan known as Suleiman the Magnificent made plans for the area known to Muslims as Al-Haram al-Sharif and to Jews as the Temple Mount. Suleiman requisitioned the building of the beautiful mosaic-tiled golden Dome of the Rock and the Al-Aqsa mosque; he also allocated an area at the Western Wall where Jews were allowed to pray. After Mecca and Medina, Jerusalem is the third holiest place in Islam; the Haram area is sacred to Muslims because it is where Muhammad is said to have made his ascent to heaven. To Jews it is the site of the original Temple; some also believe it is Mt. Moriah, where Abraham's faith was demonstrated as he made preparations to sacrifice his son.

Each of the Abrahamic religions—Judaism, Christianity, and Islam—has claims to Jerusalem. Jerusalem is for Jews their most sacred city, but it is the Temple Mount that is the holiest place; until the Temple is rebuilt, the Messiah cannot return. Some Christians argue that Jerusalem is theirs because the message of Jesus, as the son of God, superseded that of the Old Testament, and it is the place where Christ will return. Muslims believe that although Muhammad was the last prophet, he was recalling people back to the original religion given to Abraham, so they can imagine they have the prior claim. To this anthropologist, it seems these sibling faiths are like three brothers fighting over the patrimony—who has the true interpretation of God's will and who, therefore, will inherit His promises.

From the mid-nineteenth century on, spurred by anti-Semitic sentiments in Europe as well as Zionist rhetoric, many European Jews migrated to Palestine and to the city of Jerusalem. In 1917, their desire for a homeland was incorporated into the Balfour Declaration. In that year, despite the Arab rebellion helped by T. E. Lawrence (Lawrence of Arabia), the British army marched in and took over the city. Once again, Jerusalem was under Christian control; however, the situation was tense and tenuous. During the British mandate, Arabs felt they were being overrun as many thousands of Jews migrated to the city, and there were bloody encounters. During World War II the British turned the problem over to the United Nations, which tried to work out a division of the land and the city. However, on May 14, 1948, just eight hours before the British mandate was to end, David Ben-Gurion announced the establishment of the state of Israel.[9] During the 1967 war between Israel and the United Arab Republic, Israel captured more territory: the Sinai peninsula and the West Bank up to the Jordan River. Although the UN called for them to relinquish these territories, the Israelis continue to build settlements in some of these occupied spaces, which inflames the passions of Palestinian Arabs. The tension continues, and attempts to peacefully coexist have yet to succeed. One hopes the conflict will not end at Armageddon, today's Megiddo, which sits close to the West Bank.

Meanwhile, 1948 and the "in-gathering" of the Jews to their ancient homeland was for fundamentalist Christians the beginning of the countdown to the Apocalypse. Many moved to Jerusalem to try to convert the Jews; others have joined with radical Jewish groups plotting to blow up the Dome of the Rock and the Al-Aqsa mosque because they believe that these Muslim holy sites occupy and desecrate the very spot on which the ancient Temple stood. One goal of ultranationalist Orthodox Jews, such as the Gush Emunim, is to clear the ground so they can rebuild the Temple; this dovetails with the desire of certain Christian groups who, like Columbus, believe that rebuilding the Temple is necessary for Christ's return.

Today, the quest for Jerusalem has come full circle; no longer is it a meta-phor or symbol for the eternal city. Instead, as it was for Columbus, the quest is for the physical place. According to Gershom Gorenberg, long an observer of apocalyptic activities and an associate at the Center for Millennial Studies at Boston University, the Temple Mount is easily the "the most contested piece of real estate on earth."[10] There, an act of destruction could ignite a passion that might quickly spread into a worldwide conflagration. Of course, some true believers want to "bring it on," for it would fulfill the signs they read from the book of Revelation. They fervently believe that world events are fulfilling bibli-cal prophecy instead of the reverse—that the Bible itself with its apocalyptic scenario is a force propelling these events. If Columbus's story can be read as a parable, with a tale to tell and a warning about the unintended consequences of religious intentions believed to be good, it is well to keep in mind that today's world is very different from his. With biological, chemical, and nuclear weap-ons at our disposal, *we* could easily bring about the Apocalypse. Concerned about this possibility, Gorenberg asks: "[W]hich commitment is deeper, to-wards human beings or the grand millennial story?"—to which I would simply add: How can we diffuse the power of the apocalyptic myth before its destruc-tive, self-fulfilling prophecy becomes a reality? On that the fate of our world may depend.

~ Acknowledgments ~

"Are you prepared to sleep with Columbus for five years?" That was one of the first questions my wonderful agent, Wendy Strothman, asked me when I proposed my book to her. I was a bit taken aback, but she was right; it aptly captures the process of writing a book such as this. Not only have my days been filled with reading material by and about Columbus, but my sleep has been disturbed with dreams of the fifteenth century, the rolling of the tall ship, and composing the perfect sentences that I forget by morning.

First, however, I wish to acknowledge Norman Fiering, the former director of the John Carter Brown Library at Brown University, for taking a chance on an anthropologist with no "track record" in medieval history or Columbian studies and for recommending me for one of its fellowships. And to Ted Widmer, the current director, for letting me stay on as an Invited Research Scholar. Members of the staff were extremely helpful: Susan Newberry and Rick Ring commented judiciously on an early draft and Richard Hurley and Leslie Tobias Olson performed technical wizardry, computerizing some of the images. Susan Danforth's expertise with maps gave me a sense of fifteenth-century geography, while Lynn Carlson, a geographic information system professional at Brown, conveyed modern equivalents through numerous discussions and the elegant charts and maps she provided. Ken Ward's expertise in Latin American history was invaluable for locating important material. James Muldoon, professor emeritus, Rutgers University, and longtime Invited Research Scholar at the library, graciously answered my many questions about medieval history and the papacy and steered me to pertinent sources.

The generosity of Gianni Carosio at the Galata Museo del Mare in Genoa for quickly giving me permission to use photographs of some of their valuable

Columbus documents was unprecedented. *Gracias* also to D. José Manuel Calderón and D. Jorge González García at the Casa de Alba, and Nuria Casquete de Prado at the Biblioteca Colombina for some of the other illustrations.

I am indebted to a number of scholars who have shared generously their time, thoughts, and knowledge—Stan Aronson, Ralph Bauer, Tim Buckley, Jorge Canizares, Anunciada Colón, Robert Dankoff, Evelyn Lincoln, Mary Malloy, William Monroe, Carla Rahn Phillips, William Phillips, Amy Remensyder, Richard Unger, Pauline Moffitt Watts, and Nicolas Wey-Gomez. To all of you, thank you, and to those I may have forgotten, please forgive me.

Lauren Sarat and Linda Rosenberg, freelance editors, helped me transform my academic writing style to appeal more to general readers whom I wished to engage; it has been one of the most interesting and difficult intellectual experiences I have ever had. After many drafts when I thought I was losing the thread, Deborah Kaspin, a former classmate at the University of Chicago, helped me pick it up again.

It is a much better book due to the careful reading, reorganizations, comments, and suggestions of Emily Loose and Leah Miller, my editors at Simon & Schuster; for any residual confusion, mistakes, or misrepresentations, I take full responsibility.

Many thanks for the warm tolerance of family and friends who look forward to actually reading the book they have been hearing about so long.

Christopher Columbus traveled almost as much dead as when he was alive, and there is considerable debate about where his body actually lies. He was first buried at the Church of San Francisco in Valladolid, but in 1509 his body was moved to the monastery of Las Cuevas in Seville. His son Diego specified in his will that both he and his father should be buried in Santo Domingo. When Diego died in 1526, presumably, his body was buried in Santo Domingo, and in 1541, Columbus's remains were taken there as well. In 1795, when Santo Domingo came under French rule, their bodies were exhumed and removed to Cuba, though some speculate that only Diego's body was moved. When Cuba became independent, Columbus's remains were, supposedly, taken back to Seville and placed in a huge monument within the cathedral. However, that is not the end of the story. In 1877 when builders were expanding the church in Santo Domingo, they came upon a lead box inscribed with the name Don Cristóbal Colón. This box remains at the El Faro a Colón—a lighthouse museum in Santo Domingo. However, Anunciada Colón, a descendant of Columbus, is quite sure that the remains of Columbus are encased in the monument in the Seville Cathedral. DNA samples have been taken from remains in Santo Domingo and Seville, but the results are inconclusive; some of Columbus's remains may be in both places as well as in a small vial in Genoa.

King Ferdinand (1452–1516) "was no longer king in Castile" after Queen Isabella's death, but from 1508 he ruled as regent for his mentally unstable daughter, Juana. He waged several wars, conquered Tripoli, and led a campaign against

France. A year after Isabella's death, Ferdinand married Germaine de Foix, who was the niece of Louis XII of France. Although a son was born to them, the baby lived only a day. When Ferdinand was nearing the end of his reign, he apparently submitted several projects for the conquest of Jerusalem to the Cortes (Spanish parliament), but nothing came of them. At his death, Ferdinand was buried next to Isabella in Granada as he had desired.[1]

Don Bartholomew (ca. 1461–ca. 1515), Columbus's brother, who became his second-in-command as *adelantado*, died in 1514 or 1515, probably in Santo Domingo, where he had served under the new viceroy, his nephew, Columbus's son Diego. He was buried, however, at the monastery of Las Cuevas, where Columbus's body had been moved in 1509. Some researchers think Bartholomew's body was taken to Santo Domingo instead of Christopher's; if so, the remains at the lighthouse are his.

Don Diego (ca. 1468–ca. 1515), known as Giacomo in Italian, was a younger brother of Columbus. Upon return from Hispaniola, he became a Spanish subject, devoted himself to religious matters, and died in the home of Francisco Gorricio (thought to be a brother of Gaspar). He never received the bishopric that Columbus had hoped to obtain for him.

Don Diego (ca. 1480–1526), Columbus's son, became the Second Admiral of the Ocean Sea and Viceroy, and in 1509 he went to Hispaniola as Governor. He sued the Crown for the privileges that should have been his according to the Capitulations of Santa Fe, which the sovereigns had negotiated with his father. The documents of the court case, known as the *Pleitos Colombinos*, contain much information about Columbus and the voyages. Diego is alleged to have had two children out of wedlock before he married a noblewoman, a cousin of King Ferdinand—Doña María de Toledo—with whom he had seven children including Luis (see below). He was recalled to Spain in 1514 for discussions about his administration and remained there until 1520. Diego was recalled again in 1523 and remained in Spain until his death in 1526. His bones, along with those of his father, were later taken to Santo Domingo and buried in the cathedral; some scholars believe that it was his remains subsequently dug up there that were transferred first to Cuba and then to Seville. After Diego's death, Doña María ruled in his stead until rebuked by the king.

Ferdinand Columbus (1488–1539), son of Columbus and Beatriz de Harana, had an eager mind and liked books; while some scholars attribute this to his education at court, Columbus must also have inspired this passion in his son. Surely something of Columbus's bookish interests and his curiosity about the world and its peoples rubbed off on the boy both before and during their voyage together. Ferdinand became a bibliophile and amassed one of the largest libraries in all of Europe, more than 15,000 volumes that included many of Columbus's manuscripts and annotated books as well as music of the era.[2] Ferdinand also "devised a plan for indexing and classifying the contents of his library that one scholar called "worthy of a modern school of the science of bibliography."[3] Upon his death on July 12, 1539, he was buried in the cathedral in Seville. In accordance with his will, his library became the property of his nephew Luis, who was supposed to oversee it and attempt to have it stored in some place where it would be open to scholars. Luis was in Santo Domingo at the time and neglected to do anything about the library for years. During that time many volumes were lost or damaged. Eventually, what remained of it went to the cathedral in Seville. There it languished for years and much of it "suffered shameful neglect and losses from vandalism. By the early eighteenth century it seems to have been absolutely abandoned; it is said that children were permitted to play in its galleries and amuse themselves with the miniatures adorning the precious manuscripts."[4] There are rumors that when Napoleon's troops were in Seville, they used some of the papers for toilet tissue. The remains of the collection, fewer than two thousand of his books, are now stored at the Biblioteca Colombina attached to the cathedral. Ferdinand's biography of his father, known as the *Historie* (it has a very long title),[5] and other family papers passed to the widow of his brother Diego and ultimately to Luis, her oldest child.

Don Luis Colón (1521–1572), son of Diego Columbus and Doña María de Toledo, became the third Admiral and Viceroy of the Indies until his mother was finally able to get him to exchange the post of viceroy and other titles inherited from Columbus for the duchy of Veragua. He was a profligate son, a gambler, and a polygamist. He was able to have his first "marriage" annulled, but he was arrested when his second wife accused him of marrying yet another while he was still married to her. Luis was arrested and confined for five years in various places in Spain, during which he contracted another "marriage." This resulted in a stiffer sentence—he was exiled to Oran, North Africa, where he died.

Though entrusted with Ferdinand's library, Don Luis sold off many pieces to pay for his debts and other debaucheries. Ferdinand's biography of his father, the *Historie*, was sold to a Genoese physician who took it to Venice, where it was translated into Italian and finally published in 1571. The original is lost. Of the family papers that had been in Luis's possession, some were distributed, but many have disappeared.

Beatriz de Harana (ca. 1465–1522) was the mistress of Columbus and mother of their son Ferdinand. Despite Columbus's stipulation in his will that Beatriz be provided an annual pension, Diego cut her off after he took charge of the estate. In 1521, she brought a court case to attempt to collect on monies owed her. She died the next year. Her own estate, which consisted "of a house with a workshop and a wine press, two orchards, and three vineyard plots, went to her son Fernando. The latter, on August 17, 1525, gave this property as a gift to his cousin Pedro de Arana, one of the sons of Beatriz's only brother."[6] Perhaps to make up for his negligence, Diego, in his own will dated September 8, 1532, stipulated that all the monies owed to Beatriz should be paid to her heirs; some of it probably went to Ferdinand.

Diego Méndez (ca. 1472–ca. 1536) had an adventurous life, but like his friend and mentor, he had trouble securing the honors and rewards promised to him for his valiant service. He was knighted by the king in 1511 and awarded a coat of arms that displayed a canoe and two Indians in recognition of his brave trip from Jamaica to Hispaniola to requisition a ship to rescue Columbus and the men marooned there. After Columbus's death, Méndez helped Diego with his business and legal issues and, in 1520, accompanied him when he went to Santo Domingo as governor. Méndez served Doña María de Toledo until his death; he was "devoted to her and her children and aided them in the defense of their privileges, but had to be let go."[7]

Diego Columbus did not appoint Méndez *alguacil mayor* as he had promised; instead when the time came, he gave the post to his uncle, the *adelantado*, Columbus's brother Bartholomew, who in turn gave it to Francisco de Garay. It was a terrible way to repay Méndez for all he had done for the family. After many years, he eventually did get the post, but it was not exactly what he imagined or hoped for. Again like his mentor, he was involved in a number of lawsuits and "[b]ecause he was strong willed, he never yielded—no matter how many years, how much money, how many *probanzas*, appeals, reversals, counter-appeals, and reviews these litigations might provoke." Méndez is said to have been present at Columbus's bedside at his death, though others dispute this. Like Columbus, he asked to be buried in a friar's habit at a Franciscan monastery.[8]

Bartolomeo Fieschi (ca. 1470–ca. 1530), a Genoese gentleman, sailed with Columbus on the fourth voyage as captain of the *Vizcaína*. He, along with Diego Méndez, risked his life when he went by canoe from Jamaica to Hispaniola in order to obtain ships to rescue Columbus and the rest of the men. Apparently, he too was at Columbus's bedside at his death. Soon thereafter, Fieschi is believed to have returned to Genoa, where one chronicler identified him as the same person as Bartolomeo Flisco, who was "an instigator of a popular uprising in Genoa in July 1506." If Fieschi was that person, he was exiled to France but returned again to Genoa in 1525, and "was elected captain of a fleet of fifteen Genoese ships that sailed to fight France. In 1527, he was declared *padre del comune* (city father)." After that the record is silent.[9]

Nicolás de Ovando (ca. 1460–1518) became governor of Hispaniola after Columbus was relieved of that post. While Ovando may have achieved some peace on the island, it was achieved at great human cost. When Diego Columbus was leaving Spain to replace Ovando and become the second Admiral and governor of Hispaniola, King Ferdinand wrote him "several letters" in which "he praised Ovando, hoping his successor would follow his example."[10] Ferdinand's interests diverged considerably from those of Columbus and Isabella; he was interested in gold for secular purposes and believed it was important that the colony be disciplined, even if cruelly.

Bartolomé de Las Casas (1484–1566) is one of the most important sources for information about Columbus's first voyage because he had a copy of Columbus's diary. He also had a copy of Ferdinand Columbus's *Historie* and frequently cited it in his own *Historia de las Indias*.[11] Las Casas was eight years old when he witnessed the return of Columbus from the first voyage. Later, he knew members of the Columbus family and admired Christopher, who he thought had been chosen "'among all the sons of Adam' for the providential task of opening 'the doors of the Ocean Sea.' He saw a divine design in the pattern of his life until his arrival in Castile, endows him with great virtues, and bitterly criticizes the injustice and ingratitude with which the Spanish monarchs treated him and his family." [12]

Today, Las Casas is widely known as the great defender of the Indians, but during the time he knew Columbus, he supported the practice of slavery and owned slaves. Even after Las Casas was ordained in 1510, he helped suppress a native rebellion. Las Casas never heard the fiery sermon by Montesinos in Hispaniola in 1511 that condemned the treatment of the Indians; not until more than a decade after Columbus's death did his thinking slowly begin to change, and he began to protest the treatment of the Indians. Even as late as 1544 he wrote to Charles V asking permission to import some African blacks to help at his bishopric in what is now Venezuela. In other words, at the time, he seems not to have been against slavery per se, but only against the enslavement of the native Americans. After the mid-sixteenth century he regretted his suggestion. Between 1551 and 1552 he engaged in a publicized debate with Juan Gimés Sepulveda about the inhumane treatment of the Indians. His work on this subject, for which he has become justly famous, occupied him for the rest of his life. I write this because Las Casas is remembered only for his defense of the Indians; what is forgotten is that he owned slaves and endorsed and operated *encomiendas,* while Columbus, who never owned slaves, is reviled and blamed for everything that went wrong in the Indies.

~~ NOTES ~~

INTRODUCTION: THE PASSIONS OF COLUMBUS

1. See Phelan, *Millennial Kingdom*; Hamdani, "Columbus and the Recovery of Jerusalem"; Milhou, *Colón y su mentalidad;* Watts, "Prophecy and Discovery," "Apocalypse Then," and "The New World and the End of the World"; Sweet, "Christopher Columbus and the Millennial Vision of the New World"; West, "Wallowing in a Theological Stupor"; and West and Kling, *The* Libro de las profecías *of Christopher Columbus.*

2. Sweet, "Christopher Columbus and the Millennial Vision, p. 370."

3. McNeill, *Mythistory,* p. 3.

4. I acknowledge the insights of historians Lynn White ("Christian Myth and Christian History"), William McNeill (*Mythistory*), Wilfred Cantwell Smith (*The Meaning and End of Religion*), a theologian and one of my professors at Harvard Divinity School who also wrote extensively about Islam; and, for their views about culture, two anthropologists: Clifford Geertz ("Religion as a Cultural System"), and David Schneider ("Kinship, Nationality, and Religion" and "Notes Toward a Theory of Culture").

5. Geertz, "Religion as a Cultural System," p. 89.

6. Some places refuse to acknowledge Columbus Day; some states do not grant a holiday. A 2009 vote by Brown University faculty decided to change the name of the Columbus Day holiday weekend to Fall Weekend.

7. From Francisco López de Gómara's *Historia General de las Indias* ca. 1552. See Jane, *Four Voyages*, or Keen's translation of Ferdinand Columbus's biography of his father, (Ferdinand Columbus, *Life*, p. xxiii). In contrast, a modern extreme view brands "him as cruel and greedy," and links him to the process whereby "the West has ravaged the world for five hundred years, under the flag of a master-slave theory which

in our finest hour of hypocrisy was called the 'white man's burden'" (König, *Colum-bus: His Enterprise*).

8. The best explanation of this can be found in the first two chapters of Wilfred Cantwell Smith's *The Meaning and End of Religion*.

9. Scarfi, *Mapping Paradise*, p. 45.

10. The word *Apocalypse*, from the Greek, means "the disclosure of the hidden divine purpose in history, to which common usage has added the dimension of imminent crisis." Reeves, "The Development of Apocalyptic Thought," p. 40.

11. The much-debated issue of Columbus's birthplace will be discussed in chapter 2.

CHAPTER ONE: OMENS OF THE APOCALYPSE

1. Fleet, *European and Islamic Trade*, p. 122. Ironically, it was the lack of foresight and strategy on the part of the Roman church regarding the enormity of the Ottoman threat that contributed to the outcome.

2. After the conquest of Constantinople, the term *kizil elma* was tranferred to Rome or Vienna—cities yet to be conquered—always the prize just out of grasp.

3. Crowley, *1453: The Holy War for Constantinople*, p. 115. This is an excellent and very readable account, blow by blow, of the Ottoman siege against Constantinople.

4. Leonard's letter was written on August 16, 1453; see Melville-Jones, *The Siege of Constantinople*, p. 13.

5. The Venetians did not send any ships until the end of April, and then only one, not sixteen as originally promised; another left Venice on May 11, but its departure was too late. Neither made it to Constantinople.

6. Barbaro, *Diary of the Siege of Constantinople*, pp. 48–49.

7. The word *Antichrist* occurs only in the epistles of John (1 John 2:18 and 2:22; and 2 John 1:7). Some believe that the same John wrote the book of Revelation, the last book in the Christian Bible, which discusses in more vivid detail all that will transpire during the last days.

8. The Janissaries were men who, as young boys, were collected in a process known as the devşirme, mostly from Christian families living in Ottoman territories. They were taken to the sultan's palace, where they were educated and converted with the intention that they would serve in the elite military corps. They never saw their families again.

9. This incident was reported by two eyewitnesses, Leonard of Chios in his letter to Pope Nicholas V (see Melville-Jones *The Siege of Constantinople*, pp. 36–37, and Barbaro, *Diary*, p. 65). Apparently, Giustiniani had lied because the Turks had not yet entered the city.

10. Tursun Beğ, secretary to the sultan's council, quoted by Lewis, *Istanbul*, p .7.

11. Today, Aya Sofya is a museum—and declared a world heritage site. The images have been uncovered and restored as much as was possible. Renovations have been going on for years.

12. Cardinal Bessarion, July 13, 1453, to Francesco Foscari, Doge of Venice. In Ross and McLaughlin (eds.), *Renaissance Reader*, p. 71. Despite his reflections and in addition to the three-day rampage, Mehmet allowed himself the pleasures of a number of young Christian boys who had been taken as captives; those who resisted were slain.

13. Barbaro, *Diary*, p. 67.

14. Melville-Jones, *Constantinople*, p. 13.

15. Although the Holy Sepulchre was destroyed in 1009, it took time for the news to reach Europe and more time before the Europeans considered a crusade. In mid-century they were also embroiled over the schism between the Eastern and Western parts of the Christian church.

16. Schein, *Gateway to the Heavenly City*, p. 38.

17. Mintz, *Hurban*; Spiegel, *The Last Trial*; Delaney, *Abraham on Trial*.

18. Said by "Peter of Cluny in his sermon of 1146 on the theme of the Holy Sepulchre," in Schein, *Gateway*, p. 39.

19. Schein, *Gateway*, pp. 162ff.

20. Pazzelli, *St. Francis and the Third Order*, p. 73.

21. Ibid., p. 178, note 21.

22. Komroff, *The Travels of Marco Polo*, p. 123.

23. Herrin, *Byzantium*, p. 266.

24. The crusading impulse continues. As one historian has noted, "invaders of strange continents assumed an innate and absolute superiority over all other peoples because of divine endowment; their descendants would eventually secularize the endowment to claim it from nature instead of God, but would leave its absolute and innate qualities unchanged." Jennings, *The Invasion of America*, p. 5. See also Muldoon, "John Marshall and the Rights of Indians." It should not be surprising that some Muslims interpret American invasions of their countries as "crusades."

25. Quoted in Ziegler, *Black Death*, p. 50.

26. Information about the Black Death is from Aberth, *Black Death*; Herlihy, *Black Death*; Ziegler, *Black Death*.

27. For instance, there was an outbreak near Genoa around the time Columbus was born; there was also one in Seville in 1481–82, just before Columbus arrived there.

At that time, more than a third of the population of Seville succumbed. See Reston, *Dogs of God*, p. 82. Yet, when the plague is mentioned in relation to that city, only the Great Plague of the mid-sixteenth century is noted. There have even been outbreaks of plague in the United States in the twentieth century, but today we have antibiotics to deal with it.

28. See Schwartz, *All Can Be Saved*, who claims, on page 3, that the voyages of expansion and missionary efforts were carried out in the shadow of God's plan of redemption and individual salvation; however, despite the title, he asserts that by the fifteenth century the prevailing view was that salvation could only happen through the church.

29. Liss, *Isabel the Queen*, pp 35–37.

CHAPTER TWO: LEARNING THE "SECRETS OF THE WORLD"

1. As with everything else related to Columbus, his birthplace and ethnicity are contested. Claims have been made that he was Catalan, Portuguese, the illegitimate son of a French nobleman, or Jewish. The most persistent claim, that he was Jewish, was made by Madriaga in *Christopher Columbus*. Columbus did focus a fair amount of attention on the Old Testament but so do many Christians who search the Old Testament for prophecies that are expected to be fulfilled in the New Testament. Columbus may have had a Jewish ancestor but, if so, he seems to have been unaware of it, and was most avowedly a Christian. Among claims that Columbus was Portuguese is that of Manuel da Silva Rosa; he asserts that Columbus was "a Portuguese double-agent working for King John II." See *O Mistério Colombo Revelado* and *Colombo Português*. Yet given Columbus's interactions with John/João, it seems highly unlikely. Friends such as Michele de Cuneo, Bartolomé de Las Casas, and Bartolomeo Fieschi all said he was Genoese, and so did his son Ferdinand in his biography of his father,* though his account of the family genealogy is inaccurate. Columbus himself said he was Genoese, and he left money in his will for his relatives in Genoa.

2. Simon Boccanegra was made Genoa's first perpetual doge in 1339 after a successful uprising of the people. His son became the second doge but was murdered. Thereafter began the assent of the Adorno and Fregoso factions. Simon's grandfather built the Palazzo San Giorgio. For a good source on Genoese history, see Epstein, *Genoa*.

---

* See Ferdinand Columbus, *Life*, in the bibliography.
READERS NOTE: Whenever Ferdinand is cited as author, I am referring to Columbus's son Ferdinand, not King Ferdinand. I use Ferdinand instead of Columbus to avoid confusing him with his father.

3. Document in the Genoese archives. See Dotson and Agosto, *Christopher Columbus and His Family*, #9, p. 34..

4. Originally there were only three gates, built into the walls in the twelfth century; but as the city expanded, new walls and two new gates were built.

5. Dotson and Agosto, *Columbus and His Family*, commenting on document #9, p. 383.

6. The quote, from Voragine's *Chronicon januense*, a history of Genoa, is cited in a pamphlet about the Cathedral of Saint Laurence (San Lorenzo), published by the Archdiocese of Genoa, 2004:47. Voragine also wrote the *Golden Legend* about lives of the saints which became one of the most famous books of the medieval period.

7. Mormando, *The Preacher's Demons*.

8. A copy of that letter does not survive, but he mentioned that he had written to her and her husband in a letter he wrote to Nicoló Oderigo in Genoa, March 21, 1502, before setting out on his third voyage.

9. See Hughes, *Catherine of Genoa*. During an outbreak of the plague that hit Genoa in 1493, Caterina became ill attending to the sick, but although four-fifths of the population succumbed, she survived and lived until 1510.

10. A prize white female slave between the ages of twenty-six and thirty would cost 100 lira at a time when a sailor's annual pay was only about 58 lira or about as much as the modest house of a weaver or twice as much as his loom. Spufford, *Power and Profit*, p. 339. See also Fleet, *European and Islamic Trade*.

11. Columbus's book, in Latin, had the title *De consuetudanibus et conditionibus orientalium regionum* (Concerning the customs and conditions of peoples in the East). Along with *Imago Mundi* (The Image of the World), a work of cosmography by Pierre d'Ailly; and *Historia rerum ubique gestarum* (History of Deeds Done Everywhere) by Aeneas Sylvius Piccolomini (Pope Pius II), it is one of his most heavily annotated books—with 366 postilles. The other surviving books from his library are Pliny's *Historia naturalis*; Plutarch's *Las vidas de los ilustres Varones*; *Concordantiae Bibliae Cardinalis*; St. Antoninus of Florence, *Sumula confessionis*; Seneca's *Tragedies*; and Azcuto's *Almanach perpetuum, cuius radix est annun*. For the list and discussion of the rest of his library see West and Kling, *Libro*, p. 24. For works on Marco Polo see: Komroff, *Travels of Marco Polo*; Larner, *Marco Polo and the Discovery*; and Bergreen, *Marco Polo*.

12. Marco Polo in Komroff, *Travels of Marco Polo*, p. 264.

13. Ibid.

14. Ibid., p. 254.

15. Delumeau, *History of Paradise*, p. 71. Although the legend sometimes places Prester John in Ethiopia or India, Columbus followed Marco Polo who placed him in Central Asia where he fought with Genghis Khan. The story is that Genghis had outraged Prester John by asking for his daughter in marriage. They fought and Genghis killed John and married his daughter. Mandeville also noted that there were many islands in the vicinity and in some of them the people go naked.

16. Quotations are from Mandeville, *Travels*, pp. 44, 101, 76, 85, 87, and 95.

17. See Nunn, "The *Imago Mundi*," and Nunn, *Geographical Concessions*. Samuel Eliot Morison, who joined the Harvard Expedition in 1939 that followed the route and directions from Columbus's diary, agrees with Nunn. See *Morison*, Journals, Vol. I, chapter 7, note 30.

18. Nader, *Book of Privileges*, p. 164, believes Latin was taught by memorizing biblical passages, yet that appears to conflict with her belief that these passages were "functional tools for a business career . . . [for] businessmen needed to be able to read contracts and political documents in Latin because it was the language of church and government records throughout Italy."

19. Michele's father might have welcomed the inquisitive Christopher as an inspiration to his more high-spirited son for it is always easier to learn with a friend. With Michele, he may have improved his grasp of Latin, and from him he may also have acquired his aristocratic tastes and manners.

20. In the Gulf of Genoa, the young Columbus probably learned how to steer a small boat through those turbulent waters and to keep it from capsizing; he may even have done so with Giovanni Caboto (John Cabot), for there is speculation that Cabot was born or lived in Genoa or Savona before becoming a citizen of Venice and going on to become a discoverer for England. David Boyle claims that Cabot and Columbus may have become acquainted with each other as youths or in their business dealings, and that Cabot may have helped to finance one of Columbus's voyages. See Boyle, *Toward the Setting Sun*.

21. Emphasis mine. Ferdinand Columbus, *Life*, p. 10. This is quoted from a letter Columbus sent to the Spanish sovereigns in 1501 which serves as a preface to his book, *Libro de las profecías*.

22. Document # 74 in Dotson and Agosto, *Columbus*, witnessed on October 30, 1470, attests that Christopher at the age of "more than 19" owed money for a consignment of wine (his father stood surety). Document #86, March 20, probably 1482, was drawn up in Savona, with Columbus himself as a witness, and he is specified as a wool merchant of Genoa.

23. Pérez-Mallaína, *Spain's Men of the Sea*, p. 77. Originally published in Spanish in time for the Quincentenary of Columbus's first voyage, this wonderful book is full of information about the training and hierarchy of sailors. Although the book is constructed from sixteenth-century documents, much of it is applicable to the late fifteenth century. See also Morison, *Journals*, Vol. 1, pp. 220–236.

24. Unali, *Marinai*. The danger was ever-present, and whoever seized a ship was considered a pirate by the other. For example (p. 133), a document from Barcelona in 1457 cited fourteen events of seizure—mostly for oil, fish, and wine.

25. This is taken from a letter Columbus sent to the Spanish sovereigns from Hispaniola, January 1495, years after the event. Quoted in Ferdinand, *Life*, p. 11. Version in Spanish and Italian in Taviani, Rusconi, and Varela, *Cristoforo Colombo*, p. 15. The letter does not say to whom the galleass belonged nor whether they were able to capture it.

26. This episode is noted in both Taviani, *Christopher Columbus*, pp. 60–62, and Ferdinand, *Life*, p. 13, though their versions differ. Ferdinand got the date (1485 rather than 1476) and the identity of the attackers (Venetians rather than the French) wrong, confusing a 1485 battle, which Columbus could not have engaged in, with the 1476 one. However, he described that battle correctly—the ships did grapple and they did catch on fire which is why I have kept his description.

27. Hamdami, "Ottoman Response," p. 324, citing the 1453 account by Gomez Eanes de Azurara.

28. Columbus cited in Ferdinand, *Life*, p. 11. Also, in Taviani, Rusconi, and Varela, *Cristoforo Colombo*. See note 25 above.

29. Quinn, "Columbus and the North," p. 284.

30. One note in Italian appears in Pliny's *Historia naturalis*, and the other in *The Libro de las profecías*, West and Kling, p. 224.

31. Dotson and Agosto, *Columbus*, document #113, page 139.

32. Some scholars believe they may have married as early as 1477 and that Doña Felipa may have gone to Porto Santo to be with relatives while Columbus was off on the sugar voyage (Morison, *Journals*, Vol. 1, p. 59, note 19), but most seem to accept 1479 and that they stayed with her mother in Lisbon before leaving for Porto Santo.

33. Ferdinand, *Life*, p. 14.

34. Ibid., p. 10.

35. Ibid., p. 14.

36. Las Casas, ca. 1527, cited in Morison, *Journals*, Vol. 1, p. 63. Most people know Las Casas primarily for his defense of the Indians. They do not know that at the time he knew Columbus, he was not yet a priest; he went to Hispaniola as a colonist, owned slaves, and had two *encomiendas*. He was not ordained until years after Columbus's death, was not converted to the Indian cause by the fiery sermon of Friar Antonio Montesinos in 1511 denouncing their treatment by the Spanish. Only much later did Las Casas come to that conclusion, but even then it seems he was not so much against slavery as he was against the enslavement of the Indians for he suggested that the Spanish import blacks from Africa instead.

37. According to New Testament scholar Ernst Kasemann, quoted in McGinn, *Visions of the End*, p. 1.

38. Daniel, *Franciscan Concept*, p. 28.

39. Ozment, *Age of Reform*, p. 107.

40. Dawson, *Mission to Asia*, p. xxx. In addition to Rubruck's *Journey*, and John de Plano Carpini's *History of the Mongols*—both of which are more engagingly written than Marco Polo's *Travels*—Dawson included copies of correspondence between Pope Innocent IV (1245) and Guyuk Khan (1246). These are extraordinary for the arrogance each expressed about the superiority of his own religious views and the request each made that the other submit.

41. According to Ralph Bauer, the phrase can also refer to *the Book of Secrets*, about the alchemical system in which the mystery of the elements would also be revealed. His book, *A New World of Secrets: The Esoteric Hermeneutics of Discovery in the Early Americas*, is in progress.

42. Columbus cited in West and Kling, *Libro*, pp. 89–90. Columbus's inscription also shows that he probably acquired his copy of Pope Pius's book during his time on Porto Santo.

43. Perhaps he imagined he would meet the descendants of Domenico Ilioni, a Genoese merchant family that had been living in China in the mid-fourteenth century, who might help him make contact with the Grand Khan and be sympathetic and useful associates. See Spence, *Chan's Great Continent*, p. 10.

CHAPTER THREE: THE PLAN BEGINS TO TAKE SHAPE

1. Later, the fort would become a conduit for the slave trade, but that was years after Columbus's visit. Some scholars have asserted that Columbus's mission across the ocean was motivated by the lure of trade in slaves.

2. See Richard W. Unger's "Portuguese Shipbuilding and the Early Voyages," pp. 43–63.

3. Although Isabella proclaimed herself queen in 1474 after the death of Henry who had specified her as his heir, wars of succession ensued and she did not officially become queen until 1479.

4. Taviani, *Christopher Columbus*, p. 368. Also noted in Ferdinand, *Life*, p. 11.

5. While initiated by King Alfonso, the correspondence was conducted through Fernão Martins, a Florentine canon serving in Lisbon.

6. Morison, *Journals*, p. 14, translation of the Toscanelli letter. See also Ferdinand, *Life*, p. 21. There are some slight differences between the versions of the letter cited by Ferdinand and that included by Morison. I have used portions of each depending on felicity of phrase.

7. This is from Ferdinand's copy of the letter, pp. 20–21. There has been some misunderstanding about the distances Toscanelli described because while he wrote of leagues, both Morison and the translator of Ferdinand's biography convert them into miles, making the distance about 6,500 miles—much greater than he meant or what Columbus would have considered. We do not know what kind of league Toscanelli was using.

8. Ferdinand, *Life*, p. 20.

9. Ibid., p. 22. There has been considerable debate over the authenticity of the Toscanelli correspondence but today most scholars believe it was genuine. Regarding the "Christians," he was probably referring to the Nestorian community in the East, Prester John, or the descendants of a Genoese family who allegedly had traded with the Grand Khan (see note 43, p. 262).

10. Ferdinand, *Life*, p. 35.

11. He did not go immediately and when he did, according to Columbus's son Ferdinand, he was set upon by pirates and robbed of all his maps and other belongings so that it took him some time before he was in a position to approach the king. Bartholomew was very skillful in making maps and on one of those that Ferdinand found among his papers, he had written, in Latin, a poem and a note saying that he, Bartholomew Columbus, a native of Genoa, had published the work in London on February 13, 1498—surely another indication of Columbus's Genoese origins.

12. Pérez, *Spanish Inquisition*, p. 11.

13. Ibid., p. 20.

14. Ibid., pp. 147–148. See also Reston, *Dogs of God*. For the second kind of torture, the prisoner would be hung by a rope tied around his wrists, with weights attached to his feet, and for the third the rack would pull apart the muscles and break bones.

15. Accounts of how many people were actually tortured or burned at the stake vary considerably. One account suggests that 90 percent of the accused were not tortured, but another claims that during Torquemada's fifteen years as grand inquisitor (1483–1498), 8,800 people were burned at the stake and more than 9,000 had other punishments. Pérez, *Spanish Inquisition*, pp. 148, 170. Reston, *Dogs of God*, claims that those burned numbered no more than 3,000 during the same period.

16. Liss, *Isabel the Queen*, p. 12.

17. Morison, *Admiral*, Vol. 1, p. 108, from the *Pleitos*, the court cases brought to the Spanish crown in 1513, after Columbus's death.

18. There is some debate about whether Juan Pérez was the presiding friar at La Rábida at the time of Columbus's arrival in 1485. He was there at the time of Columbus's departure in 1492. In any case, Marchena was the one influential in obtaining Columbus's audience with Queen Isabella.

19. A fragment of a letter Columbus wrote to the Spanish sovereigns sometime between 1498 and 1500. See Varela, *Cristóbal Colón*, document XXXII, p. 407; see also the citation and translation by West and Kling of Columbus's *Libro de las profecías*, p. 57.

20. Thacher, *Christopher Columbus*, Vol. 1, p. 412. The letter was written only a few days after Columbus's return from the first voyage.

21. Anderson, *Hispanic Costume*, p. 12. "The yearly income of a high nobleman ran between three and forty million maravedis, 8,000–106,666 ducats" (note 4, page 251). Citing Gonzalo de Baeza who was treasurer for Queen Isabella, Anderson claims the following equivalencies: "Three hundred seventy-five maravedis equaled one ducat. A *sueldo* or *escudo* was worth 18 maravedis, a *real* 31, a *florin* 265, a *dobla* 365, a *castellano* 485. He goes on to say that the worth of a gold *marco* was equal to 50 *castellanos* or 24,250 maravedis."

22. Greenfield, *A Perfect Red*, pp. 3, 24–28.

23. See Carla Phillips, "The Portraits of Columbus," pp. 1–28. However, a ceramic bas relief at La Rábida is thought to be an authentic likeness, and some believe that the image of Reprobus carrying Christ across the water on the map by Juan de la Cosa is actually a likeness of Columbus.

24. Angelo Trevisan, 1501, cited in Morison, *Journals*, Vol. 1, p. 161.

25. Ferdinand, *Life*, p. 9. According to contemporaries, Columbus's hair was still reddish when he first met Isabella. Nor did it all turn white at age thirty; perhaps Ferdinand used age thirty loosely since he wasn't even born until Columbus was thirty-seven. The Spanish text says his hair was *rubio*, which in Columbus's time meant *el color*

roxo claro, u de color oro, that is, light red or the color of gold, which can tend to reddish or to yellow. Also, the translation "bright red" probably meant easily sunburned.

26. Columbus's letter to the sovereigns that prefaces the diary of the first voyage. I have substituted the word *secta* in place of "religion" which is how Dunn and Kelley translated it (*Diario*, p. 19). Yet the word *secta* did not mean "religion" as we know it, but would have meant the false beliefs and ways of life of non-Christians.

27. Morison, *Admiral*, Vol. 1, p. 87.

28. Though this statement was written to the sovereigns during the Third Voyage, it was part of his original argument. In Taviani, *Nuova*, Vol. 6, letter 6, p. 391, emphasis in the original. See also Major, *Select Letters*, p. 140; Quinn, *New American World*, Vol. 1, p. 23; and *Opus Majus* by Roger Bacon (1214–1292) whom Columbus cites via d'Ailly. The reference to Seneca comes from his *Quaestiones naturales*, where he wrote: "For what after all is the space that lies from India to the farthest shores of Spain? A few days journey if a prosperous wind waft the vessel." Quinn, *New American World*, Vol. 1, p. 8.

29. Stone, *Marriage and Friendship*, p. 33.

30. Taviani, *Christopher Columbus*, p. 471.

31. Brundage, *Law, Sex, and Christian Society*, pp. 119, 125.

32. Columbus in Morison, *Admiral*, Vol. 1, p. 99—original is postil #24 in d'Ailly's *Imago Mundi*.

33. Also known as *Paseábase el Rey Moro* (The Moorish King Was Riding). Because it provoked rage against the Christians, the Moors were forbidden to sing it. A sixteenth century version, by Luys de Narváez, can be heard on a CD along with many other songs and music from the time of Isabella: *Isabel I Reina de Castilla*, put out by Hesperion with Jordi Savall, director (Alia Vox #9838 recording).

34. The information in this paragraph and the quotation are taken from Liss, *Isabel the Queen*, p. 223.

35. Morison, *Admiral*, Vol. 1, p. 131.

36. Ibid., pp. 131–132; also Ferdinand, *Life*, chapter 12. Nicolas Wey-Gomez's *Tropics of Empire* is a scholarly treatise that discusses the scientific theories about zones and the antipodes.

37. Zamora, *Reading Columbus*, p. 124.

38. Morison, *Admiral*, Vol. 1, pp. 115–116.

39. Liss, *Isabel the Queen*, p. 250.

40. Ibid., p. 222.

41. Columbus, *Diario*, trans. Dunn and Kelley, p. 17 (see Readers Note below).

42. Reston, *Dogs of God*, p. 143.

43. Even if they could sell their houses, they were not allowed to take any gold or silver out of the country. Somewhere between 50,000 and 100,000 Jews left Spain by August 2, 1492, to destinations in North Africa, Greece, or Constantinople where the Ottoman Muslims accepted them graciously.

CHAPTER FOUR: VISION BECOMES REALITY

READERS NOTE: No original version of Columbus's *Diario* exists. Bartolomé de Las Casas made a transcription of it, which is the version used and translated by Dunn and Kelley. When I quote directly from the diary, I will put page numbers from their edition. Because Las Casas paraphrased parts of it, he will often use third person "he" or "the Admiral"; when he quotes verbatim, he uses "I."

1. Thacher, *Columbus*, Vol. 1, p. 443.

2. Morison, *Journals*, p. 31. Both letters are in Morison, *Journals*, pp. 30–31.

3. Columbus cites this letter in his *Libro de las profecías* (see West and Kling, *Libro*, p. 239). Specifying Spain as the place from which the Last World Emperor would arise probably derives from Arnold of Villanova, one of Joachim's followers, with whose work Columbus, and maybe Isabella, was familiar.

4. Morison, *Admiral*, Vol. 1, p. 151.

5. The saying is attributed to Anacharis, a sixth-century B.C. Scythian-Greek, who excelled in pithy statements that often overturned received wisdom.

6. Morison, *Admiral*, Vol. 1, pp. 151–152, and Martinez-Hidalgo, *Columbus's Ships*, pp. 40–41 where he cites Ferdinand who claimed that the *Santa María* drew three Genoese fathoms or about 5.71 feet.

7. Pérez-Mallaína, *Spain's Men of the Sea*, p. 84. This book is one of the very few to describe what life was like on board sixteenth-century Spanish ships. At that time, ships were frequently plying the *Carrera de Indias* (the route to the Indies); still, much of what he describes is applicable to the fifteenth century.

8. For the list of the crew on Columbus's first voyage, see Gould, *Nueva lista documentadad de los tripulantes de Colón en 1492*. For a list in English see Morison, *Admiral*, Vol. 1, pp. 190–192, or Martinez-Hidalgo, *Columbus's Ships*, pp. 72–73 and 90–93.

9. Morison, *Admiral*, Vol. 1, p. 187; Hamdani ("Columbus and the Recovery," 1979, p. 47, note 39) believes that Columbus also hoped to speak with Arab merchants he might encounter in the Orient though there is no record of this.

10. Most of the information about the crew is taken from Morison (*Admiral*, Vol. 1) and Pérez-Mallaína, *Spain's Men of the Sea*.

11. Parry, *The Age of Reconnaissance*, p. 73. This also agrees with the amount of the daily ration of sherry calculated from an order the queen sent with Juan de Aguado when he sailed in 1495 to the colony that had been established after the second voyage. Rations were low—she specified that they should receive half an arroba every two weeks and a pint a day. An arroba was four gallons, so they received two gallons every two weeks plus a pint a day. She added that they could receive more once they received the new shipment (Parry and Keith, *The Caribbean*, p. 206). On the first voyage they must have been allotted more than a quart.

12. Pérez-Mallaína, *Spain's Men of the Sea*, 2005, pp. 128 and 170–175.

13. For a sense of the contents of sailors' chests see: Bedini, *Columbus*, p. 172, and Martinez-Hidalgo, *Columbus's Ships*, pp. 79–80.

14. For a full list see Friedman, *Monstrous Races*, pp. 5–15.

15. Such theories have hardly passed away. Contemporary anthropological theory has had to deal with the same issue in somewhat different form. Either all peoples descended from one group in Africa—the monogenist explanation and the theory most widely believed, or there were different centers of origination—the polygenist explanation, in which case they might not all be equally human. In either case, racist elements creep in; in the first instance, cultural differences easily can be, and have been, attributed to "degeneration." In the polygenist theory, people are "naturally" different. In both, different peoples have been ranged on a graduated scale from savage to civilized.

16. The belief in the curse of Cain might also be related to the fact that his name, spelled Cham in the Middle Ages, was easy to confuse with Cain in medieval orthography. Most of the information about monsters in this paragraph is taken from Friedman, *Monstrous Races*, pp.100–102.

17. Ibid.

18. Gillis, *Islands of the Mind*, p. 52.

19. Newton, *Travel and Travellers*, p. 162.

20. It is believed that somewhere between 50,000 and 100,000 left Spain by August 2, 1492, that is, at the very same time Columbus would leave on his voyage. Unlike Columbus, who sailed west, many of the Jews sailed east to ports in North Africa, Greece, and Constantinople where the Ottoman Muslims received them graciously. Descendants of the Jewish community that began its new life in Constantinople continue to live in the city renamed Istanbul. See Brink-Danan, *Jewish Life*.

21. The letter, or what some scholars call a "prologue," has been the subject of much debate. For example, Zamora thinks it is not a "preface" because it was written after the departure and addressed to the Crown as a way to legitimize the voyage (*Reading Columbus*, pp. 21–38). To me, the timing seems irrelevant since many authors write a "preface" after a work is completed. Whatever term one wishes to affix to this letter, it seems to confirm, in writing, what had previously been discussed.

22. Young, *Columbus Memorial*, no page number.

23. Nader in Bedini, *Columbus and the Age of Exploration*, pp. 750–753.

24. See Morison, *Admiral*, Vol. 1, p. 221 and note 3, p. 236, where he gives indications of watches in Columbus's *Diario*; and Pérez-Mallaína, *Spain's Men*, 1998, p. 70.

25. The origin of clocks is not well documented. According to the *Encyclopaedia Britannica*, there were some public "clocks" in the fourteenth century but they didn't strike the hours or have hands on a dial! Apparently, they were used to alert monks to ring the bells at canonical hours which, due to the changing length of daylight over the seasons, change accordingly. Henlein used the invention of the mainspring to replace the weights that had been used to drive clocks. Galileo in 1582 noticed that pendulums could be used for timekeeping but this insight was not applied to clocks until 1656.

26. Morison, *Admiral*, Vol. 1, pp. 224 and 233.

27. Morison, ibid., p. 233, includes music for this Benedictine chant, "Salve Regina," but his notation may not accurately capture the sound of the chant at that time. Nevertheless, one might get a fleeting sense of that "ancient hymn of praise to the Queen of Heaven that floated over uncharted waters every evening, as the caravels slipped along."

28. Morison, *Admiral*, Vol. 1, p. 244. The following discussion about Columbus's methods is taken from ibid., pp. 240–256, and 270.

29. Ibid., p. 252.

30. Ibid., pp. 252–253.

31. Parry, *Age of Reconnaissance*, pp. 87–88. Part I of this book is an excellent resource about the technicalities of navigation. Parry claims that the use of a calibrated knotted rope to check speed was not invented until the sixteenth century; it is from that we get the term "knots" to describe speed at sea.

32. Ibid., pp. 88ff. and Morison, *Admiral*, Vol. 1, pp. xxi–xlv, 247 for more information about ships and sailing.

33. Dunn and Kelley in transl. *Diario*, p. 117, claim a *braças* is 2.5 feet; Fuson, in *Log of*

Columbus, p. 48, says 5.5 feet, and Morison, *Journals*, p. 83, says that twelve Castilian *brazas* equal about eleven of our six-foot fathoms.

34. Morison, *Admiral*, Vol. 1, p. 242.

35. He was able to do so in 1494 and in 1504.

36. The explanation given in the diary is that "the cause was that the North Star appears to move and not the compasses" (*Diario*, pp. 33–35). As we know, the original diary is lost, and the version we have is what Las Casas excerpted and edited; and there are instances when it is clear that he inserted his own opinions, sometimes in retrospect. What Columbus noticed was not the movement of Polaris, as Las Casas and the modern editors Dunn and Kelley assert, but was—according to experienced navigators Thomas Buckley, Mary Malloy, and Richard Unger, whom I consulted—magnetic variation.

37. The quotation is from Ferdinand, *Life*, p. 56. The sovereign's promise is not mentioned in the *Diario* until October 11; see p. 63.

38. According to the *Pleitos de Colón* (Vols. 1 and 2), court cases brought up after Columbus's death. At the time there was debate over just who promised to turn back if they did not find land in three days. And some wanted to claim Pinzón as the discoverer.

39. Columbus, rather than Rodrigo, claimed the reward of 10,000 *maravedis* perhaps, as his son believed, because he "had first seen the light amid the darkness, signifying the spiritual light with which he was to illuminate those parts" (Ferdinand, *Life*, pp. 58–59). Scholars have felt Columbus's claim was a very cruel gesture, and so it may have been. However it may also have been a way to stave off arguments among the crew on board the *Pinta*, or even on the *Niña*, about who had first sighted land.

CHAPTER FIVE: DAYS OF WONDER

1. Ferdinand, *Life*, p. 59.

2. Ibid.

3. Ibid.

4. See Muldoon, *Popes, Lawyers, and Infidels*, Hanke, *Spanish Struggle*, and Seed, *Ceremonies of Possession*, about notions of "possession." The date recorded, as everyone knows, was October 12, 1492, except that Columbus was using the Julian calendar. Our current calendar, the Gregorian, was not instituted until 1582, and between the two is a difference of ten days.

5. Columbus refers to the Indians simply as *gente* (people). Although an October 11 entry in the diary says: "they had reached an islet of the Lucayas which was called Guanahani in the language of the Indians," this has to be a retrospective addition by

Las Casas, since on October 11 Columbus had not yet seen any natives, could not have known the name of the island nor the group of islands called the Lucayas.

6. Whatever symbolic significance the body paint may have had, Columbus later learned that they also painted themselves to prevent sunburn (*Diario*, p. 275).

7. There is debate over whether he came ashore on Samana Cay or on Watling Island (San Salvador).

8. It is important to note that Columbus used the word for servant, not slave, because several recent scholars argue that his mission was motivated to obtain slaves. Yet, that was hardly the case since he expected to meet the Grand Khan and his sophisticated subjects.

9. Leonard Sweet, "Christopher Columbus and the Millennial Vision," p. 383.

10. *Lettera Rarissima*, July 7, 1503, sent from Jamaica, in Thacher, *Columbus*, Vol. 2, p. 695; also in Jane, *Four Voyages*, Vol. 2, p. 104, and Morison, *Journals*, p. 383.

11. Some scholars believe that Columbus kidnapped the natives who would act as guides but it is also possible that some of them wanted to go, because that became a common request.

12. Ferdinand, *Life*, pp. 66–67.

13. Today, doctors think he may have suffered from a severe form of rheumatoid arthritis called Reiter's syndrome. See Taviani, "Columbus's Health," in *Nuova*, Vol. 6, Part II.

14. Morison, *Admiral*, Vol. 1, p. 165.

15. That Columbus recognized the importance of learning their language if he was ever to understand the natives and their culture is in sharp contrast to the famous French anthropologist Claude Levi-Strauss who assumed he could decipher the culture of Amazonian peoples without learning the language.

16. The groups he first encountered and who befriended him remained unnamed. *Arawak* was never a term used by the natives themselves. It first appears in 1540 as *Aruaca* in writings of Fray Gregorio Betela, Bishop of Cartagena. The name *Taino* was bestowed by Cornelius Rafinesque in 1836 (see Hulme, *Colonial Encounters*, p. 59).

17. Las Casas in Thacher, *Columbus*, Vol. 1, p. 561.

18. This is the first appearance in the diary of the word *canibales* from which we get *cannibal*. For a long time, cannibalism has been the trope through which Europeans have made distinctions between savage and civilized. It is the subject of long debate that is beyond the scope of this book. Whether it was ever practiced in the Caribbean or elsewhere, the reasons for the intense interest among Europeans is, at least,

as interesting. Some scholars suggest that this interest is not so much because the practice is alien, but because it is too close—an unconscious projection of the central sacred ritual among Christians—the ritual eating of the body and blood of Christ that is the Eucharist. For debates about cannibalism in the Caribbean see Pagden, *The Fall of Natural Man*, Hulme, *Colonial Encounters*, and Stover, "The Other Side of the Story."

19. Although I have used Dunn and Kelley's translation of the *Diario* throughout, which has the Spanish on the facing page, the word *Indio* does not appear in Columbus's entry for that day, November 23, 1492.

20. To Columbus, the notion of family, from the Latin *famulus*, meant all those who were considered dependents of the male head of the family, not just wife and children, but also slaves, so he naturally assumed patrilineal kinship as depicted in the Bible, whereas the indigenous people were probably organized matrilineally. At that time, however, Europeans were unaware of matrilineally organized societies. See also Pagden, *The Fall*, p. 53.

21. Hodgen, *Early Anthropology*, p. 20. While Hodgen uses "Carib" as a cover term for all the natives, Columbus was more specific and used it only for a particular, hostile group who were said to be enemies of those with whom he had become acquainted. In retrospect, they were most likely all of the same ethnic stock with somewhat related languages and customs.

22. Delumeau, *History of Paradise*, p. 112.

23. Fuson, *Log of Columbus*, p. 32.

24. On January 2, Columbus wrote that he left thirty-nine men "and, over them, as his lieutenants, Diego de Arana, a native of Cordova, and Pedro Gutiérrez steward of the king's dias and a servant of the chief steward, and Rodrigo Descobedo, a native of Segovia" (*Diario*, p. 303). But on January 13 he wrote of the thirty-nine men he left at Navidad (ibid., p. 335).

25. I have borrowed this notion from Fleming, "Christopher Columbus as a Scriptural Exegete," p. 196, except that he used the phrase "from the *bowels* of the ship called Mary," to describe the birth of the first Christian settlement in the new world. But it is an odd word choice—body or belly is far more appropriate!

26. Thacher, *Columbus*, Vol. 1, p. 632, citing Las Casas who is quoting Columbus.

27. He took either six or ten, though in another place he said he planned to take seven.

28. The display of evidence was an integral part of exploration and conquest; Columbus was following the custom of the Spanish in the Canaries and the Portuguese in Africa (Phillips, *Medieval Expansion*, p. 162). Four hundred years later, the practice was

repeated at the Columbian Exposition (World's Fair 1892) when a number of Native Americans of different tribes were brought from their lands to be displayed along the Midway in Chicago.

29. For interpretations see: Thacher, *Columbus*, Vol. 3, pp. 454–459, West and Kling, *Libro*, pp. 71–73, and Milhou, *Colón*, pp. 53–90.

30. I offer this interpretation as my contribution to the issue. Seven was, of course, a special number, and not only because of the supposed seven millenia of the world's duration. Mandeville wrote that "the height of the earth is divided into seven parts, which are called seven climates after the seven planets." See Mandeville, *Travels*, p. 130.

31. Columbus originally used the term *gente* (people) to refer to the natives; in the *Diario* the term *Indio* is occasionally used but whether Columbus began to use it or whether this is Las Casas's retrospective insertion is unclear. Regardless, the term *Indio* can hardly be seen as a derogatory term at the time; instead it makes perfect sense since Columbus assumed he was in the Indies.

32. Ferdinand, *Life*, p. 88.

33. Fuson, *Log of Christopher Columbus*, pp. 29 and 31.

34. Ferdinand, *Life*, p. 89.

35. Ibid., p. 91.

36. Ibid., p. 92.

37. Ibid., p. 96.

38. Ibid., p. 97.

39. Ibid., p. 92.

40. When the ship did not sink, Columbus may have retrieved the letter and sent it overland from Lisbon to the Spanish sovereigns. This letter, along with copies of several other documents written by Columbus, emerged in 1985 when a Catalan bookseller presented them to the Centro Nacional del Tesoro Documental y Bibliographico Español. The bookseller claimed the documents were bought from an estate on Majorca. Bound together, these documents have come to be known as *Libro Copiador*. The book contains nine letters—five thought to be in Columbus's hand (1, 3, 5, 6, and 8); a copy by Las Casas (4); a legal copy (2); a draft of a letter (7); and a copy of a letter by Columbus from a later period, July 7, 1503. They were first published in 1989 by Antonio Rumeu de Armas. The first English translation of the March 4 letter appeared in Zamora, *Reading Columbus*, but a new edition of the *Libro Copiador* was published, along with an English translation of all the documents, in the *Nuova Raccolta Colombina*, edited by Taviani, Varela, Gil, and Conti, in 1994.

41. Zamora, *Reading Columbus*, p. 196. Villacorta and several others were also mentioned in a memo Columbus sent back to the sovereigns in February 1494.

42. Columbus, *Libro Copiador*, Letter #1, in Taviani et al., *Nuova*, Vol. 6, Part 2, p. 193.

CHAPTER SIX: TRIUMPH AND DISASTER

1. Most commentaries declare that Pinzón arrived later the same day, stole off quietly to his house and a few days later died of grief, but I have yet to find the source of that information. Instead, I am following Ferdinand, Columbus's son, who said that Columbus had already left for Seville *before* Pinzón arrived which makes more sense.

2. Ferdinand, *Life*, p. 101.

3. Columbus used the word for Christendom (*Christiandad*), not Christianity (*Christianismo*), which is a later concept. Then, in Las Casas's excerpt of the diary, he added: "These are the final words of the Admiral Don Christobal Colón concerning his first voyage to the Indies and their discovery. Thanks be to God."

4. Las Casas, *History of the Indies*, p. 37.

5. The story is told in Matt. 21; Mark 11; Luke 19; and John12, of the New Testament.

6. See also Morison, *Admiral*, Vol. 2, p. 7.

7. This quotation, from Francisco López de Gomara's *Historia General de las Indias* (1552), is frequently cited. See Jane, *Four Voyages*, p. xv, or Ferdinand, *Life*, p. xxiii.

8. See Fernández-Armesto, *Ferdinand and Isabella*, pp. 115–118, for an account of this event.

9. Although most accounts claim that Columbus arrived in Barcelona sometime between April 15th and 20th, that seems impossible. While a royal courier, or a series of couriers, on horseback might have been able to deliver a letter from Barcelona to Seville in seven or eight days, an entourage like that of Columbus could never have traversed the distance so quickly. Most people could cover between twenty and thirty miles a day and even that could not be sustained day after day. Noble entourages were even slower. So, either Columbus's reply arrived in mid-April informing the sovereigns that he was on his way, or historians have the dates wrong. The description of their meeting was taken from Morison, *Admiral*.

10. Las Casas quoted in Thacher, *Columbus*, p. 669.

11. Godparenthood (*compadrazgo*) has been an important relationship in Spanish culture for a long time. Normally, it is a bond between *compadres*—the natural parents and the godparents who, together, commit to sharing responsibilities toward a par-

ticular child. They are to see to the child's education in the faith, his moral training, and to provide financial help when needed.

12. If the wording of Martyr's letter is correct, it would imply that Columbus arrived in Barcelona sometime early in May, not mid-April, which would make much more sense given the distance he had to travel.

13. English translations can be found in many places; I have quoted from Morison, *Journals*, pp. 185–187. Since there is no original of the diary, and later Las Casas paraphrased much of it, it is difficult to know whether the word *Indio* was given by Columbus or was added later by Las Casas, as were a number of other names in the diary. The verbatim quotes tend to use the word *gente* (people) for the natives except for the *canibales*, the Caribs.

14. See note 40, chapter 5. In this letter, Columbus also reminds them of his service to them, not only the years of waiting but also of having left wife and children behind and of coming from his homeland to serve them. Some scholars have taken this to mean that Dõna Felipa de Moniz was still alive and that they had had another child. In contrast, I think it implies he thought of Beatriz as his wife, in spirit if not in law, that the children were Diego and Ferdinand, and that the homeland he referred to was Genoa, hardly Porto Santo or even Lisbon.

15. For those interested in this issue, see Cecil Jane's "The Letter of Columbus," pp. 33–50.

16. Five hundred years later, we are still singing of these events. Every schoolchild knows "In 1492, Columbus sailed the ocean blue . . ."

17. Phillips and Phillips, *Worlds of Columbus*, p. 189. The menage in Seville, which eventually included Columbus's brothers, two nephews, and three other siblings of his late wife, would have made it difficult for him to bring Beatriz and little Ferdinand there.

18. Las Casas claims that Columbus's memo to the sovereigns was written on April 8, 9, or 10, 1493, and begun, if not finished, in Seville. If so, that is even more evidence that he could not have arrived in Barcelona in mid-April.

19. Columbus's "Memorial Policy to the Sovereigns on Colonial Policy, April 1493," in Morison, *Journals*, p. 201.

20. Instructions of the sovereigns to Columbus for his Second Voyage to the Indies were "the first set of laws promulaged by a European sovereign for an American colony." Morison, *Journals*, p. 203.

21. Ibid., p. 204.

22. Thacher, *Columbus*, Vol. 2, p. 284.

23. Royal letter to Fonseca, August 18, 1493, in Parry and Keith, *The Caribbean*, pp. 75–76.

24. Bartolomé de Las Casas in Morison, *Admiral*, Vol. 2, p. 57.

25. Columbus's account and this assessment of Pane's work are recounted verbatim in Ferdinand, *Life*, pp. 151–153. Ferdinand includes the full account by Pane.

26. Morison, *Admiral*, Vol. 2, p. 50.

27. Ferdinand, *Life*, p. 110.

28. De Cuneo, October 15–28, 1495, translation in Morison, *Journals*, p. 227.

29. Dr. Chanca's letter in Jane, *Four Voyages*, Vol 1, p. 26.

30. De Cuneo's letter in Morison, *Journals*, p. 212.

31. Dr. Chanca in Jane, *Four Voyages*, Vol. 1, p. 30.

32. Columbus, letter to the sovereigns, ca. January or February, 1494, in Taviani et al., *Nuova*, Vol. 6, Part I, p. 207; letter 2 from the *Libro Copiador*.

33. Morison, *Admiral*, Vol. 2, pp. 96–97.

34. Ibid., p. 82.

35. De Cuneo's letter in Morison, *Journals*, p. 212.

36. Columbus letter to the sovereigns, ca. January or February, 1494. In Taviani et al., *Nuova*, Vol. 6, Part I, p. 219.

37. Morison *Admiral*, Vol. 2, p. 95.

38. Columbus, Letter #2, from *Libro Copiador*, in Taviani et al., *Nuova*, Vol. 6, part II, p. 227.

39. Deagan and Cruxent, *Columbus's Outpost among the Taínos*, p. 50.

40. Ibid., p. 51.

41. Ibid., pp. 51–52.

42. Jane, *Four Voyages*, Vol. 1, p. 104.

43. Fifteenth-century music was often religious in nature, but some beautiful exultant marches, tender laments, and love songs exist. Although some of the instruments no longer exist, one can get a sense of the music, and thus the emotional tone of the times, from several recordings: *El Cancionero de la Colombina* (music from Ferdinand Columbus's collection) and *Isabel I Reina De Castilla*, both recorded on CD by Hespèrion XX with Jordi Savall, are excellent. Hear also Johannes Cornago's *Missa de la mapa mundi*, along with secular music of the fifteenth century, CD by Harmonia mundi with the Newberry Consort; and somewhat later, *La Barca d'Amore*, cornett music of the sixteenth century, with Le Concert Brisé, CD by Accent Plus.

44. Las Casas, *History of the Indies*, p. 47.

45. Morison, *Journals*, p. 213.

46. Deagan and Cruxent, *Columbus's Outpost*, p. 147.

47. The remains of the kiln and thousands of tiles have been found at the site. In the judgment of the archaeologists, this was an excellent site, just as Columbus thought, and much more extensive than anyone previously had believed. See Deagan and Cruxent, *Columbus's Outpost*.

48. Columbus, February 26, 1495. Taviani et al., *Nuova*, Vol. 6, Part 1, p. 269.

49. Dr. Chanca, translated in Jane, *The Four Voyages*, Vol. 1, p. 64.

50. Deagan and Cruxent, *Columbus's Outpost*, p. 136.

51. From the letter Coma sent to Syllacio, who translated it into Latin and sent it on to the Duke of Milan, December 13, 1494, in Morison, *Journals*, p. 244.

52. Columbus, "The de Torres Memorandum," January 30, 1494, in *Christopher Columbus: Accounts and Letters of the Second, Third, and Fourth Voyages*, Vol. 6, Part I, p. 15, of Taviani et al., *Nuova*. For an account of Hojeda's trip to Cibao, see also Nicolò Syllacio's letter of December 14, 1494, in Morison, *Journals*.

53. Columbus, letter #2, *Libro Copiador*, p. 237, in Taviani et al., *Nuova*.

54. This is the opinion of Dr. Francis Guerra, see Taviani, "Columbus's Health," in Taviani et al., *Nuova*, Vol. 6, Part II, pp. 127–138.

55. This quotation comes from letter 2, that Columbus sent to the sovereigns along with his memo (*Nuova*, Vol. 6, part I, p. 235).

56. Whether or not Columbus was so specific in his requests as the list the Crown sent to Fonesca of the supplies to be sent to him is not known. For lists of items requested see Parry and Keith, *The Caribbean*, pp. 185–188, or Deagan and Cruxent, *Columbus's Outpost*, pp. 137 and 154.

57. Apparently the quicksilver mines in Almaden are some of the richest in the world and have been mined for centuries. Jane, *Four Voyages*, Vol. 1, p. 111, note 1. Columbus elaborated his request in Letter #3 in *Libro Copiador*.

58. Morison, *Admiral*, Vol. 2, p. 108. Columbus wrote another letter to the sovereigns in April, 1494, even though de Torres had already left. He said he had taken Bernal de Pisa as prisoner but, given his rank, he was reluctant to punish him. Thus, he hoped to send him back to Spain on the next ship.

59. Some historians claim they also carried 30,000 ducats of gold, but it seems more likely this is confused with a later shipment, for the men had had very little time to collect so much gold and had gathered only a few samples on their expedition to the hinterlands.

60. Because the Canarians were seen as living a very primitive kind of life, like animals, they could be enslaved; Christianization was thought to be a civilizing influence. The

quotation is from page 91 in an excellent article by Muldoon, "Spiritual Freedom—Physical Slavery."

61. Columbus's memo sent with de Torres, Jane, *Four Voyages*, Vol. 1, p. 88, or Parry and Keith, *The Caribbean*, p. 182.

62. Ibid. Note that Columbus was distinguishing between the cannibal/Caribs and the other natives. Despicable as slavery is, it was nothing new. Although Columbus is blamed for introducing it to the Caribbean, it was already being practiced by the indigenous peoples. Beyond that, Columbus was merely following long-standing practice legitimized by the papacy. Catholic policy followed the Bull of Alfonso V (1455) which had given Portugal the right to conquer and enslave Africans, and the Spanish used the same rationale when they conquered and enslaved the Guanches of the Canary Islands. Now, Pope Alexander VI gave such rights to Spain vis-à-vis the lands and peoples of the Caribbean. If the conquered people resisted Christianization, they were presumed enemies and could be enslaved. The papacy and Columbus could refer to biblical passages as inspiration for their policies:

> Ask of me and I shall give thee the heathen for thine inheritance, and the uttermost parts of the earth for thy possession (Psalm 2:8).
>
> Let every soul be subject unto the higher powers. For there is no power but of God: the powers that be are ordained of God. Whosoever therefore resisteth the power, resisteth the ordinance of God: and they that resist shall receive to themselves damnation (Romans 13:2).

63. Columbus memo, in Jane, *Four Voyages*, Vol. 1, p. 90.

64. Columbus's letter to the Spanish sovereigns, #2, *Libro Copiador*, in *Nuova*, Vol. 6, Part I, pp. 211–212. There is no date but was probably sent along with the De Torres Memorandum in February 1494 or with another letter in April. Hitherto unknown letter summarizing the second voyage.

65. It is not clear when the animosity between Friar Buil and Columbus began, but it was surely exacerbated when Buil wanted revenge against Guacanagarí. Despite his lack of success with the natives, he was appointed as the Vatican's chief legate to the New World and sailed with John Cabot on his second voyage in 1498. The ship he was aboard survived; the other four did not.

66. Columbus letter #4, *Libro Copiador*, in Taviani et al., *Nuova*, Vol. 6, Part I, p. 323.

67. Columbus, "de Torres Memorandum," in Taviani et al., *Nuova*, Vol. 6, Part I, p. 27.

68. Ibid., p. 31

CHAPTER SEVEN: UNRULY PASSIONS: THE COLONIES

1. Quote from Morison, *Journals*, p. 215. The following information is from Anderson, *Hispanic Costume*, 1979, note 4. Two thousand *castellanos* would equal approximately 870,000 *maravedis* while a nugget weighing 24 *castellanos* would equal 11,640 *maravedis*—more than a seaman's annual salary. According to Thacher (*Columbus*, Vol. 2, p. 351), one *castellano* weighed 1/50 of a German mark and a mark weighed eight ounces. He went on to say that Diego Colón, Columbus's Indian interpreter-godson, wore a necklace that weighed 600 *castellanos*, 12 marks or 96 ounces.

2. Swine flu was later referred to as Spanish flu.

3. Columbus's Instructions to Mosen Pedro Margarit, April 9, 1494, in Taviani et al., *Nuova*, Vol. 6, Part I, p. 45. See also Parry and Keith, *The Caribbean*, pp. 203–206.

4. De Cuneo's letter, Morison, *Journals*, pp. 215 and 227. This letter is one of the best records we have of the second voyage.

5. Columbus's written instructions to Margarit, April 9, 1494. In Parry and Keith, *The Caribbean*, p. 205.

6. Columbus, *Libro Copiador*, letter #3, April 1494, to the sovereigns. In Taviani et al., *Nuova*, Vol. 6, Part I, p. 255.

7. Las Casas in Morison, *Admiral*, Vol. 2, p. 114.

8. Columbus, *Libro Copiador*, letter #4, February 26, 1495, to the sovereigns. In Taviani et al., *Nuova*, Vol. 6, Part I, p. 275.

9. Columbus, ibid., p. 277.

10. Columbus, ibid., p. 287; and Morison, *Admiral*, Vol. 2, pp. 117ff.

11. Andrés Bernáldez, from the diary of Columbus's second voyage that he included in his *Historia de los Reyes Católicos*, cited in Jane, *Four Voyages*, Vol. 1, p. 152.

12. Fernand Pérez de Luna in Thacher, *Columbus*, Vol. 2, pp. 322ff. This gave rise to a scholarly discussion that Columbus required the men to swear an oath that Cuba was the mainland and enforced a penalty if they would not. Thacher claims that Columbus did no such thing, that de Luna, on his own authority, imposed the penalty by threatening he would cut off the tongues of men who contradicted their statements. De Cuneo's letter (Morison, *Journals*, p. 227) discussed this business.

13. Morison, *Admiral*, Vol. 2, pp. 140–141.

14. Bernáldez in Jane, *Four Voyages*, Vol. 1, p. 118.

15. Mandeville, *Travels*, p. 128.

16. Columbus, *Libro Copiador*, letter #4, p. 279, in Taviani et al., *Nuova*.

17. In his *Historia de los Reyes Católicos*, Andrés Bernáldez also commented on Columbus's idea to circumnavigate the world.

18. Ferdinand, *Life*, p. 142.

19. Columbus, *Libro Copiador*, letter #4, p. 315, in Taviani et al., *Nuova*.

20. Columbus, ibid., p. 317.

21. De Cuneo, October 28, 1495, in Morison, *Journals*, 224.

22. See Ted Widmer, *New York Times*, June 30, 2007.

23. Five and a half hours seems not too far off to me; however, according to Morison, Columbus's calculations were "completely wild" (Morison, *Admiral*, Vol. 1, p. 255). The data is confusing. Morison is calculating between Saona and Cape St. Vincent in Portugal, Ferdinand between Saona and Cádiz, and perhaps Columbus had calculated first from Hispaniola to Nuremberg and subtracted the difference. In addition, on page 255 Morison says "solar" eclipse where in Vol. 2, p. 158, he says it was a lunar eclipse.

24. Columbus, *Libro Copiador*, letter #4, p. 321, in Taviani et al., *Nuova*.

25. Cited in "Columbus's Health," in Taviani et al., *Nuova*, Vol. 6, Part II, p. 130.

26. Ferdinand, *Life*, p. 145.

27. West and Kling, *Libro*, p. 79, cites Gerald Weissmann, director of rheumatology at New York University School of Medicine, for making this diagnosis. This was also the opinion of Dr. Francisco Guerra; see Taviani et al., "Columbus's Health," in *Nuova*, Vol. 6, Part 2, where he writes that the contributing factors to "reactive arthritis" are "strong emotions; excessive physical exertion; prolonged fatigue, both mental and physical; and, above all, exposure to humidity, rain, and cold" (p. 135)—all of which Columbus had experienced beginning with the first shipwreck when he swam to shore in Portugal in 1476. Curiously, however, Columbus did not seem to be plagued by the illnesses that affected many of the men who came with him.

28. Las Casas in Morison, *Admiral*, Vol. 2, p. 164.

29. Columbus, *Libro Copiador*, letter #3, p. 251, in Taviani et al., *Nuova*.

30. From Las Casas's *Historia de las Indias*, in Parry and Keith, *The Caribbean*, Vol. 2, p. 227.

31. Columbus, *Libro Copiador*, Letter #3, pp. 253 and 265, in Taviani et al., *Nuova*.

32. Peter Martyr in Parry and Keith, *The Caribbean*, Vol. 2, p. 210.

33. For these royal instructions, see Parry and Keith, ibid., p. 206.

34. Thacher, *Columbus*, Vol. 3, p. 340.

35. Jane, *Four Voyages*, p. cxlix.

36. Quinn, "John Day and Columbus." Later, Columbus probably learned that Friar Buil, his nemesis, accompanied Cabot on his second, ill-fated voyage. Buil's ship survived but the other four, including Cabot's, went down. See letter from Pedro de Ayala to Ferdinand and Isabella, July 25, 1498, in Quinn, *America from Concept to Discovery*, p. 101.

37. Thacher, *Columbus*, Vol. 3, p. 643.

38. Ibid., p. 652. This bequest ought to silence those who doubt Columbus's origins in Genoa. A translation of Columbus's *majorat*, his will, and its addenda, can be found in ibid., pp. 643–660.

39. Columbus in ibid., pp. 653–654.

40. The reason it took almost a year before the will was signed was that the sovereigns were engulfed in mourning; their son Don Juan died five months after his wedding, and they had to console the young widow. Columbus's sons, who had been Don Juan's pages, were now assigned to the queen.

41. Eleven letters to Diego, Columbus's elder son, survive. In 1498 Diego was about eighteen years old and Ferdinand about ten. Others letters will be discussed in chapter 8.

42. Thacher, *Columbus*, Vol. 3, p. 123, lacuna in original.

43. This quotation and the following five are in the orders of Ferdinand and Isabella, June 15, 1497, trans. Parry and Keith, *The Caribbean*, pp. 217–220.

44. Morison, *Admiral*, Vol. 2, p. 226.

45. Parry and Keith, *The Caribbean*, p. 218.

46. Information for this paragraph is from Morison, *Admiral*, Vol. 2, pp. 226ff.

47. Columbus in Morison, *Journals*, p. 263.

48. Morison, *Admiral*, Vol. 2, p. 229.

49. Las Casas in Parry and Keith, *The Caribbean*, p. 223.

50. Some histories claim that Columbus's younger brother, Diego, was still in Hispaniola and was standing watch over the storehouse. But that conflicts with reports that he returned with de Torres at the same time as did Michele de Cuneo.

51. More than 160 of the Spanish men became ill with the disease. Ferdinand Columbus referred to what we know as syphilis as the "French sickness." The name for the disease changed depending on the nationality of the diseased; that is, the Spanish called it the French sickness, the French called it the Spanish or Italian disease, the Turks called it the Christian disease. Apparently, the first outbreak in Europe was reported in 1494 among French troops in Naples. But it may have been transmitted, somehow, from Spanish troops who had been serving under King Charles of France.

CHAPTER EIGHT: PARADISE FOUND AND LOST

1. Cited in Morison, *Admiral*, Vol. 2, p. 234.

2. All quotations from Ferrer's letter in Thacher, *Columbus*, Vol. 2, pp. 368–369.

3. Columbus in Jane, *Four Voyages*, Vol. 2, p. 10.

4. Las Casas's abstract of Columbus's journal of the third voyage in Morison, *Journals*, p. 261.

5. Ibid., p. 264.

6. Ibid., p. 265.

7. Columbus's letter to the sovereigns, in Jane, *Four Voyages*, Vol. 2, p. 14; Las Casas's abstract in Morison, *Journals*, p. 268.

8. Often erroneously translated as "tambourine."

9. Las Casas's abstract of Columbus's journal, in Morison, *Journals*, p. 269, also Jane *Four Voyages*, Vol. 2, pp. 16–18.

10. Columbus in Morison, *Journals*, p. 270.

11. This was Marco Polo's name for monkeys; as pet cats were commonly named "Tom," it is thought that pet monkeys were named "Paul." See Morison, Admiral, Vol. 2, p. 272, note 20.

12. In his writing, Columbus used the normal Spanish word for "take" (*tomar*); while he may have taken them against their will, it is also possible, as has been seen before, that some of them wanted to sail with him.

13. Las Casas's abstract of Columbus's journal, in Morison, *Journals*, p. 281.

14. Ibid., p. 278; see also Parry and Keith, *The Caribbean*, p. 99.

15. Morison, *Journals*, p. 279. The use of the word continent in the translation conveys a false sense of what Columbus imagined. He knew it was a huge landmass, but it could only be an unknown part of one of the three "parts" of the world, not a totally new part.

16. The calculations, and the deductions Columbus made from them, are rather complicated. Those interested should consult the discussion in Jane, *Four Voyages*, Vol. 2, p. 28, and Morison, *Admiral*, Vol. 2, pp. 282 ff.

17. Columbus's letter to Ferdinand and Isabella, written August 31, 1498. He was not able to send it until October 18, 1498, from Santo Domingo. See Jane, *Four Voyages*, Vol. 2, p. 30; also in Morison, *Journals*, p. 286.

18. Jane, *Four Voyages*, Vol. 2, p. 32. The Hebrew word we translate as "east"is more ambiguous and has both a spatial and temporal meaning—"away to the east" or "from the beginning" (Scarfi, *Mapping Paradise*, p. 35), yet Europeans have generally adhered to the spatial meaning. Although Jerome, an early church father, chose

the temporal, "the translators of the Septuagint, the *Vetus Latina*, and the English Authorized Version all chose to give the expression a spatial meaning" (ibid.), that is, Eden, the earthly paradise, has always been imagined to lie in "the east."

19. See Delumeau, *History of Paradise*, p. 55, regarding Pedro de Rates Hanequim of Brazil. Beyond that, some archaeologists believe the Garden of Eden described in the Bible was located in Bahrain, though they have not found it. Eden, *The New York Times* reported on May 1, 2009, might be located on the southwest coast of Africa, for that is where anthropological geneticists believe humans originated.

20. Delumeau, *History of Paradise*, p. 34.

21. Mandeville, *Travels*, pp. 184–185. Although now known to be fictitious, it was thought to be a true description of the world. "Martin Frobisher took it with him when he sailed in 1576 to discover the Northwest Passage," and some of the "best geographers of the Renaissance" such as Richard Hakluyt also consulted the book (Delumeau, *History of Paradise*, p. 52). See Columbus's letter to the sovereigns, dated August 31, 1498, but not sent until October 18. Jane, *Four Voyages*, Vol. 2, pp. 2–47. (Columbus also wrote a note in the margin next to a similar description in his copy of *Imago Mundi*.)

22. Scarfi, *Mapping Paradise*, pp. 47–48.

23. Ibid., p. 55. This analogy is well known among students of the Bible, but Scarfi has made a study of these extra-biblical stories and beliefs.

24. Ibid., p. 56.

25. Ibid.

26. Columbus in Jane, *Four Voyages*, Vol. 2, p. 4.

27. Las Casas's abstract of Columbus's journal of the third voyage, in Morison, *Journals*, p. 276.

28. Columbus's letter to the sovereigns, in Jane, *Four Voyages*, Vol. 2, p. 4. It should be noted that although Morison also includes this letter in his 1963 book, he begins it several pages from the beginning, that is, leaving out all the religious references.

29. Columbus's letter to the sovereigns, p. 288, and in his own journal, p.276, both in Morison, *Journals*.

30. Both quotoations in this paragraph from Morison, *Admiral*, Vol. 2, pp. 285 and 286.

31. Ferdinand, *Life*, p. 201.

32. Columbus cited by Las Casas in Parry and Keith, *The Caribbean*, p. 232.

33. Ferdinand, *Life*, p. 201.

34. For both quotes, ibid., pp. 209–210.

35. Ballester cited by Las Casas in Parry and Keith, *The Caribbean*, p. 231.

36. Ferdinand, *Life*, p. 206.

37. Columbus quoted by Las Casas in Parry and Keith, *The Caribbean*, p. 232.

38. Ferdinand, *Life*, p. 224.

39. Ibid., quoting Roldán, pp. 209 and 214.

40. Provost, *Columbus Dictionary*, p. 47.

41. Liss, *Isabel the Queen*, p. 305.

42. Columbus, letter 8, from *Libro Copiador*, in Taviani et al., *Nuova*, Vol. 6, Part 2, pp. 401 and 403. The translation was awkward so I have paraphrased somewhat.

43. At the time, both Hojeda and Columbus continued to assume the continent was part of Asia, part of the Indies. After Columbus's death, in a court dispute with Columbus's brother Diego, Hojeda claimed he had been the first to discover the continent. Columbus's own writings, and testimony of a number of men who had been on Columbus's third voyage verified that it was Columbus who had been the first to discover and set foot on the continent.

44. Ferdinand, *Life*, p. 218.

45. Isabella quoted by Las Casas in Parry and Keith, *The Caribbean*, p. 235.

46. Nader, *The Book of Privileges*, p. 212, note 14.

47. Ferdinand, *Life*, p. 223.

48. Las Casas, in Parry and Keith, *The Caribbean*, p. 241.

49. Las Casas, *History of the Indies*, p. 79.

50. Ibid., p. 80.

51. "The Fall of Christopher Columbus: The Judgment of Bobadilla," Consuelo Varela (ed.), from a transcription by Isabel Aguirre, Marcial Pons Historia, 2006. A copy of this testimony was recently found in the archives at Simancas by Isabel Aguirre. The editors take it at face value without any discussion of the way it was possibly contrived. The investigation was begun by Bobadilla in late September; Columbus was in chains and imprisoned, and at no time was he given the opportunity to counter the accusations.

52. Las Casas in Parry and Keith, *The Caribbean*, p. 239.

53. Columbus's letter to Doña Juana, in ibid., p. 247–248.

54. Ferdinand, *Life*, p. 223.

55. Written in 1500, Jane, *Four Voyages*, Vol. 2, p. 48; Morison, *Journals*, p. 290, and Parry and Keith, *The Caribbean*, pp. 242–248

56. Columbus in Jane, *Four Voyages*, Vol. 2, p. 50.

57. Jane, ibid., also has "new earth," but Columbus does not . . . so I just left it out—Morison has merely New Heaven and Earth but capitalized them.

Chapter Nine: Privileges and Prophecies:
Columbus's Stake in the Future

1. I have found three different dates for Columbus's arrival in Cádiz: end of October (Morison); November 20 (Ferdinand says that Columbus wrote on that date to the sovereigns to inform them he had landed); and November 25 (Martinez-Hidalgo).

2. Las Casas in Parry, *Age of Reconnaissance*, p. 42. This report is probably not the recently found document published as *La Caída de Cristóbal Colón*, since the investigation was not begun until late September and Columbus left in early October, 1500. Perhaps it was a partial letter describing what Bobadilla found upon arrival.

3. The recently found document of Bobadilla's "testimony" claims that Columbus had executed Violante's husband, Miguel Moliart. Yet, since Moliart was a relative of Columbus, it seems far more likely that the rebels had killed him. If so, they may have done it after Columbus left, in which case, Columbus would not yet have known of his death. If he did know, the task of conveying the news would have been difficult.

4. Ferdinand, *Life*, p. 223.

5. Ibid., p. 224.

6. Ibid., pp. 220–221.

7. The letter, dated March 21, 1502, was sent via Columbus's long-time business associate, Francesco di Rivarola, who had lived in Seville for many years (Nader, p. 188).

8. Columbus, April 2, 1502, in Nader, p. 189. These copies and the letters that accompanied them further bolster the case for Columbus's Genoese origins. Various theories that he was Jewish, Catalan, Portuguese, and Spanish have been proposed despite the considerable evidence that he was from Genoa or its environs. Several letters including the one to Oderigo and the *Book of Privileges* remain in Genoa where they are on permanent display at the Museo de Mare located at the harbor.

9. West and Kling, *Libro*, p. 101.

10. The same year that the Spanish version was printed, 1984, Delno West found a copy of the printed Latin version of 1892 in the Princeton Library. Its pages were still uncut, untouched, unread. He, along with August Kling, would prepare the first definitive study and translation into English, published in 1991 just in time for the Quincentennial. Rusconi made another scholarly edition in 1997. I use quotations from both. In 1991, Kay Brigham published excerpts and personal reflections, but it was published in Spain and did not receive as much attention as West and Kling's edition. Today, with the increase of religiousness and especially its fundamentalist, apocalyptic forms, we are in a better position to reassess the *Libro*. But first, we must

take it seriously as a desperate cry from a despondent soul urging his government to make haste to fulfill the conditions necessary before Christ's return.

11. Henry Harrisse, *Notes on Columbus*, p. 156. Vignaud's opinion was cited by Watts, "Prophecy and Discovery," p. 83, note 20.

12. Columbus, September 13, 1501, translation in Rusconi, *The Book of Prophecies*, p. 55.

13. For a long time, many academics have not taken religion very seriously as a primary motivating factor in people's lives but have tended to reduce it to a reflection of political or economic contexts. With the rise of fundamentalism in the late twentieth and early twenty-first centuries, they are paying more attention. The few scholars who have dealt with Columbus's religious views have not reached a general readership. Noteworthy is the work of J. L. Phelan, Alain Milhou, and Pauline Moffitt Watts.

14. Gorricio, March 23, 1502, in Rusconi, *Book of Prophecies*, p. 57. See also West and Kling, *Libro*, p. 84.

15. West and Kling, *Libro*, p. 101.

16. See my book, *Abraham on Trial*.

17. West and Kling, *Libro*, p. 103.

18. I have taken the biblical passages from West and Kling's edition of the *Libro*. As noted the numbering, however, does not always coincide with the standard English versions of the Bible because Columbus used the Latin Vulgate version.

19. Rusconi, *Book of Prophecies*, p. 33.

20. Gillis, *Islands of the Mind*, p. 43.

21. West and Kling, *Libro*, p. 229.

22. Ibid., p. 139.

23. Gorricio, as guardian of Columbus's papers, made an inventory of them after Columbus's death. Columbus's son Diego consulted the documents during his testimonies in court, but since then, many of the documents have disappeared. Scholars debate whether the letter to Pope Alexander VI was ever sent. However, it hardly matters because it shows clearly Columbus's thinking about Ophir, Jerusalem, and the crusade.

24. He asked the pope to contact the superiors of religious orders—Carthusians, Jeronomites, Franciscans—to give him the power to select six priests or religious persons and to guarantee that if they should return to their orders they should be well treated, even better than others, because of what they will have accomplished. (See Varela, *Cristóbal Colón*, pp. 479–481.)

25. West and Kling, *Libro*, p. 18; also Varela, *Cristóbal Colón*, p. 479.

26. Columbus's letter to Pope Alexander VI, in Varela, *Cristóbal Colón*, p. 481.

27. He also said it was Cethia and Cipango—an indication either of his confusion or the desire to make the reality fit his vision. See also Romm, "Biblical History," for a fuller discussion of the significance of Ophir in Columbus's thinking.

28. Columbus included a commentary from Nicholas of Lyra's *Glossa ordinaria* (West and Kling, *Libro*, p. 241).

29. Morison, *Admiral*, Vol. 1, p. 69. A copy of the 1510 *Medea* can be seen at Harvard's rare book library, but it does not have Ferdinand's poignant annotation. His book remains at the Biblioteca Colombina in Seville. With time, his writing has become blurred and the page could not be easily reproduced.

30. West and Kling, *Libro*, p. 239.

31. Columbus in ibid., p. 105.

32. Although he did not use the word *calling*, which would become so famous with Martin Luther, it seems clear that Columbus felt he was called by God for a particular mission.

33. West and Kling, *Libro*, p. 105, emphasis mine. West and Kling note that "Columbus's affirmation of his direct spiritual illumination from the Bible and the Holy Spirit is the most striking aspect of the *Libro de las profecías*. It is repeated many times here and in letters" (Ibid., p. 261, note 9).

34. West, "Wallowing in a Theological Stupor," p. 54, note 6.

35. Columbus in West and Kling, *Libro*, pp. 105 and 107.

36. Columbus in ibid., p. 107.

37. Ibid., p. 109.

38. Ibid. The editors made a mistake in translation and wrote one hundred and fifty years, not one hundred and fifty-five which is correct.

39. Columbus in West and Kling, *Libro*, pp. 109 and 111.

CHAPTER TEN: MAROONED

1. Ferdinand and Isabella, in Parry, *Age of Reconnaissance*, p. 106.

2. In 1500, Pedro Álvares Cabral tried to follow de Gama's route to India, but went off course and came upon Brazil. The Portuguese showed little interest in the place until after 1530, instead continuing with their route around Africa.

3. The daughter of the Spanish sovereigns, Doña María, married Don Manuel of Portugal.

4. Columbus in Taviani, *Christopher Colombus*, p. 471; Varela, *Cristóbal Colón*, p. 477.

5. Ferdinand and Isabella, March 14, 1502, in Parry and Keith, *The Caribbean*, p. 106.

The list and names of the men, compiled by Diego de Porras, survives. Apparently, three men deserted at Cádiz, before the voyage began. For the list see ibid., pp. 108–111, or Morison, *Journals*, pp. 314–320.

6. This is not Ambrose de Morales, who pointed out pages missing from the *Libro de las profecías*.

7. Méndez left a will in which he recorded a great deal of information about the fourth voyage. Due to Columbus's arthritis, he may also have kept his logbook. Other major sources for the fourth voyage are the royal instructions, the roster and payroll, and an account by Oviedo, a younger contemporary of Columbus who had access to some of these materials and was able to speak with some of the participants; and of course, Ferdinand Columbus's account in the biography of his father.

8. Further evidence, if any is needed, that Columbus was Genoese. (Information about the ships is taken from Morison, *Admiral*, Vol. 2, pp. 320–321.)

9. Ibid., p. 319.

10. It would appear the actual number of days of the crossing was twenty-one; however, as one nineteenth-century biographer noted, the fact that "he *landed* at Martinique on the 15th does not militate against his having sighted Barbados or the neighboring islands two or three days earlier" (MacKie, *Last Voyages*, p. 428). Also, almost alone of any English commentators until the 1990s, MacKie had read the newly published Latin edition of the *Libro de las profecías* and took it as a serious project of Columbus.

11. Ferdinand, *Life*, p. 229.

12. Las Casas, *History of the Indies*, pp. 91 and 94.

13. Letter #9, pages 405 and 407 in *Libro Copiador*. In Taviani et al., ed, *Nuova*, Vol. 6, Part 2, with Italian and English translations. A similar statement is found in the letter known as *Lettera Rarissima*. See Jane, *Four Voyages*, Vol. 2, p. 74, and also Morison, *Journals*, pp. 371–385.

14. There were 485 *maravedis* to one *castellano*; thus 97 million *maravedis* were lost. To give some perspective, the salary for a ship captain was about 35,000 *maravedis* per year and about 7,920 for a gromet or ship's boy.

15. Thacher, *Christopher Columbus*, Vol. 3, p. 341; Las Casas, *History of the Indies*, p. 85; Morison, *Journals*, Vol. 2, p. 325.

16. Las Casas, *History of the Indies*, p. 85.

17. Ibid., p. 86.

18. Ferdinand, *Life*, p. 233.

19. All of the quotations about Guanaja are from Ferdinand's biography of his father, *Life*, p. 232.

20. Columbus in Jane, *Four Voyages*, Vol. 2, p. 76 says the storm lasted sixty days, but on the next page, 78, he claims the storm had lasted eighty-eight days.

21. The letter is known as *Lettera Rarissima*, and Columbus did not write it until July 7, 1503. However, it described events that had occurred earlier. Apparently no original Spanish text survives. Instead, the earliest printed text is an Italian translation published in 1505. The versions we have were translated from Italian back into Spanish (Morison, *Journals*, pp. 371–374). It is the same letter that Cecil Jane calls *Quarta Viage de Colon*, where he has both Spanish and English versions. I have quoted from his version (*Four Voyages*, Vol. 2, pp. 78–79). Varela and Gil have a somewhat different Spanish version which they call *Relación del Cuarto Viaje*.

22. Ferdinand, *Life*, p. 236.

23. Ibid., p. 237.

24. Columbus in Jane, *Four Voyages*, Vol. 2, p. 82.

25. Ibid., p. 84.

26. Ibid., p. 86.

27. Ferdinand, *Life*, pp. 246 and 247.

28. Ferdinand, *Life*, p. 251.

29. Ibid., p. 253.

30. Méndez in Morison, *Journals*, p. 389. Méndéz left a will which includes a very long account of the fourth voyage. It is now in the Archives of the Indies in Seville but many good translations exist. See ibid., pp. 386–398.

31. Ibid.

32. Ferdinand, *Life*, p. 256.

33. Ibid., p. 257–258.

34. Ibid., p. 259.

35. The first vision had occurred when he was much younger. A voice had told him he would accomplish great things.

36. Columbus in Jane, *Four Voyages*, Vol. 2, p. 92.

37. This and the previous quotation from Ferdinand, *Life*, p. 262.

38. Columbus in Jane, *Four Voyages*, Vol. 2, p. 94.

39. Underwater archaeologists have recently claimed that a shipwreck near Nombre de Dios, not far from Porto Bello, is that of the *Vizcaina*. See Brinkbäumer and Höges, *Voyage of the Vizcaina*. It makes an interesting read but there are quite a number of factual errors. In addition, although one chapter is entitled "The Secret

Behind the Great Enterprise," they never once mention Jerusalem or the plan for a Crusade.

40. Columbus in Jane, *Four Voyages*, Vol. 2, p. 94.

41. Columbus in Morison, *Journals*, p. 379.

42. Ibid., pp. 379–380.

43. The first time that he was shipwrecked led to his sojourn in Portugal after the Genoese ships on which he was sailing were attacked by pirates. The second shipwreck was when the *Santa María* went aground on Christmas eve, 1492, at the place Columbus called Navidad.

44. Hans König, a severe critic of Columbus, has wondered why the men didn't use the wood from the ships to make huts, why they didn't plant gardens, and why they didn't fish. This lack of industriousness was not from laziness or arrogance but from Columbus's experience of the outrages that the crew perpetrated on the Indians. (See König, *Columbus: His Enterprise.*)

45. Ferdinand, *Life*, pp. 265–266.

46. Ibid., p. 265.

47. Méndez's will, in Morison, *Journals*, p. 392.

48. Ferdinand, *Life*, p. 266.

49. Ibid., p. 272.

50. Ibid., p. 273.

51. Morison, *Admiral*, Vol. 2, p. 391.

52. Columbus in Jane, *Four Voyages*, Vol. 2, pp. 104–106 and next two quotations.

53. Morison, *Admiral*, Vol. 2, p. 394.

54. Las Casas, *History of the Indies*, p. 135. The two differing reports may have been about the two different attempts to sail to Hispaniola.

55. Today we are all aware of the perils experienced by those who attempt this crossing to Haiti. Theoretically they have better boats, charts, and technical experience, but despite these modern aids, many of them also die. Méndez and Fieschi had none of these things.

56. Ferdinand, *Life*, p. 277.

57. Méndez in Morison, *Journals*, p. 395.

58. Las Casas, *History of the Indies*, p. 99.

59. Ferdinand, *Life*, p. 268.

60. Ibid., p. 270.

61. Ibid., p. 271.

62. Quotations in this paragraph taken from Ferdinand, *Life*, pp. 274 and 275.

63. Quotations in this paragraph from Ferdinand, *Life*, pp. 279 and 280.
64. Ferdinand, *Life*, p. 281.

CHAPTER ELEVEN: THE FINAL PASSION: DISILLUSION AND DEATH

Passion: from Medieval Latin *passio, passion-*, sufferings of Jesus or a martyr, from Late Latin, physical suffering, martyrdom, sinful desire, from Latin, an undergoing, from *passus*, past participle of *pati*, to suffer (*American Heritage Dictionary*).

1. Ferdinand, *Life*, p. 282.
2. Later, Porras was given a government post on Jamaica when it was settled (Morison, *Admiral*, Vol. 2, p. 409); fortunately Columbus did not live to learn of this.
3. Thacher, *Columbus*, Vol. 3, p. 353.
4. Morison, *Admiral*, Vol. 2, p. 411.
5. Columbus in Thacher, *Columbus*, Vol. 3, p. 299, emphasis mine.
6. Ibid., p. 306.
7. Ibid., pp. 318, 322.
8. Ibid., p. 318.
9. Ibid., p. 323.
10. Ibid.
11. Ibid., p. 329.
12. Liss, *Isabel the Queen*, pp. 340–351.
13. Columbus in Thacher, *Columbus*, Vol. 3, p. 332.
14. Ibid., p. 348.
15. Ibid., p. 377. The "third" was not part of the Capitulations, but Columbus had learned that a former Admiral had been granted a third of all profits found "at sea" and felt he was entitled to the same percentage. However, unlike the former Admiral, he was not authorized to capture ships and their booty; his voyage was for discovery and exploration, therefore the Crown did not grant him a third of the profits from his enterprise. (See Thacher, *Columbus,* Vol. 1, pp. 438–441.)
16. Ibid., p. 387.
17. Ibid. My sense is that what he did not wish to put in writing had to do with Beatriz, for when he ratified his will, he made provisions for her.
18. Ibid., p. 356.
19. Las Casas, *History of the Indies*, pp. 138, 140.
20. Columbus in Thacher, *Columbus*, Vol. 3, p. 374.
21. Ibid., p. 369. Thacher commentary on Columbus letter of December 24, 1504.
22. Ibid., p. 370.

23. Ibid., p. 374.

24. Méndez's will, Morison, *Journals*, p. 396; also in Jane, *Four Voyages*, Vol. 2, p. 136.

25. Morison, ibid., see appendix for what happened to Méndez.

26. Columbus in Thacher, *Columbus*, Vol. 3, p. 398.

27. Ibid., p. 395. See also Felipe Fernández-Armesto, *Amerigo*.

28. Las Casas, *History of the Indies*, p. 62.

29. Emerson in Lester, *The Fourth Part of the World*, p. 5.

30. For the history of the Waldseemüller map, see the engaging account by Toby Lester, *Fourth Part of the World*. The only copy of this map is now in the United States. It was bought by the Library of Congress in 2003 for $10 million. Lester also tells how strange it is that this map, made in 1507, showed the American continent surrounded by water, yet Europeans did not know of the Pacific until 1513. Although Columbus knew that there was a huge body of water across the isthmus of Panama, he thought it was the Indian Ocean.

31. Columbus in Thacher, *Columbus*, Vol. 3, p. 403.

32. Morison, *Admiral*, Vol. 2, p. 415.

33. Thacher, *Columbus*, Vol. 3, p. 660.

34. Ibid., p. 659.

35. This gesture raised my opinion of Columbus. Today, in the United States, the situation of alimony and/or child support is abysmal at all levels of society. Furthermore, regarding public support for families (welfare), the United States is almost at the bottom of the list of industrial nations with regard to public family support; only Ireland and Israel are worse.

36. Ferdinand had drawn the image on his own will; it includes the Columbus family coat of arms and the inscription. While there were, apparently, earlier plaques in marble installed in the sixteenth century and replaced in the nineteenth, they may not have carried the same image because a description of one of the earlier ones mentioned a globe and two compasses, and this image does not appear on the current plaque.

AFTERWARDS: COLUMBUS, APOCALYPTIC, AND JERUSALEM

1. Ozment, *Age of Reform*, p. 111.

2. Today, it is believed that all the natives were of one stock, but Columbus and others noticed significant differences in behavior, language, technology, and adornment.

3. Cited in McGinn, *Antichrist*, p. 203.

4. Philip Cary, *Luther, Gospel, Law and Reformation*, Vol. I, p. 155, cited by Pettibone, "Martin Luther's views on the Antichrist," pp. 81–82.

5. The congressman was John Shimkus, a contender for the chairmanship of the House Committee on Energy and Commence. Cited in Kolbert, "Uncomfortable Climate." She also noted that others, such as John Boehner, new majority leader in the House, don't believe carbon dioxide has anything to do with global warming or that there is anything humans can do to alter its course.

6. Dyer, *The Rise of Babylon*.

7. Biblical language, especially apocalyptic references, were part of the Bush presidency and his 2004 reelection. Vice President Dick Cheney conjured fears of Armageddon if Senator Kerry should be elected. More recently, the Project for the New American Century, founded by William Kristol, that created President Bush's rationale for the Iraq war, centered on the idea that the United States should project its power in the world in order to be a force for good.

8. A more detailed history of Jerusalem may be found in Armstrong's *Jerusalem*.

9. Pfeiffer, *Jerusalem Through the Ages*, p. 85.

10. This and the next quotation are from Gorenberg's *The End of Days*, pp. 11 and 227. Gorenberg is an American-born journalist living in Israel.

APPENDIX: WHAT HAPPENED TO OTHER KEY PLAYERS

1. Liss in Bedini, *Columbus and Age of Exploration*, p. 385; Sweet, "Christopher Columbus and the Millennial Vision," p. 379; see also Fernández-Armesto, *Ferdinand and Isabella*, p. 133.

2. Keen (1992, viii) says Ferdinand's library contained 15,370 items, while Provost (1991) claims only 4,231—perhaps that was the number of Columbus's books and other material, most of which has been lost. As mentioned, some of the music in his collection is available—*El Cancionero de la Colombina* (1451–1506) with Jordi Savall, put out by Astrée. Music of the fifteenth century can also be found on *Isabel I: Reina de Castilla*, also with Jordi Savall, on an AliaVox CD; and *Missa de la mapa mundi: secular music of 15th century Spain*, with the Newberry Consort, on Harmonia mundi label.

3. Keen in Ferdinand, *Life*, p. ix, quoting Thacher.

4. Thacher, *Columbus*, Vol. 3, p. 451.

5. Ferdinand's biography was published in Venice in 1571. The long title is: *Historie del S. D. Fernando Colombo; Nelle quali s'ha particolare, & vera relatione della vita, & de' fatta dell'Ammiraglio D. Cristofor Colombo, suo padre: Et dello scoprimento, ch'egli fece dell' Indie Occidentali, dette Mondo Nuovo, hor possedute dal Sereniss. Re Catolico: Nuovamente de lingua Spagnuola tradotte nell'Italiana dal S. Alfonso Ulloa.* (See Ferdinand, *Life*, p. 287.)

6. Taviani in Bedini, *Columbus and Age of Exploration*, p. 25.

7. "In 1534 she (Doña María) appointed Méndez and Diego de Arana"(Vigneras, Diego Méndez, p. 693) to help with her cause. If this Diego de Arana was related to Beatriz, he was also a relative of Columbus's son Ferdinand. If so, this is clear indication that the Columbus family kept in close contact with Beatriz's family.

8. See Vigneras, "Diego Méndez," pp. 676–696, and Méndez's will for account of some of these events, in Morison, *Journals*.

9. Taviani in Bedini, *Columbus and Age of Exploration*, p. 273.

10. Vigneras, "Diego Méndez," p. 682.

11. See Ferdinand, *Life*, pp. xv–xvi, for a more detailed account.

12. Keen in Bedini, *Columbus and Age of Exploration*, p. 412.

~ BIBLIOGRAPHY ~

Aberth, John. *The Black Death: The Great Mortality of 1348–1350: A Brief History with Documents.* Boston and New York: St. Martin's, 2005.

Anderson, Ruth Matilda. *Hispanic Costume, 1480–1530.* New York: Printed by order of the Trustees of The Hispanic Society, 1979.

Armstrong, Karen. *Jerusalem: One City, Three Faiths.* New York: Ballantine Books, 1997.

Ávalos, Héctor Ignacio. "Columbus as Biblical Exegete: A Study of the *Libro de las profecías*," in *Religion in the Age of Exploration: The Case of Spain and New Spain,* edited by Bryan F. Le Beau and Menachem Mor. Omaha: Creighton University Press, 1996.

———. "The Biblical Sources of Columbus's *Libro de las profecías*," in *Traditio: Studies in Ancient and Medieval History, Thought and Religion.* 49 (1994): 331–35.

Barbaro, Nicolò. *Diary of the Siege of Constantinople,* trans. J. R. Jones. New York: Exposition Press, 1969 [1453].

Bedini, Silvio A., ed. *Christopher Columbus and the Age of Exploration: An Encyclopedia.* New York: Da Capo Press, 1998.

Bergreen, Laurence. *Marco Polo: From Venice to Xanadu.* New York: Alfred A. Knopf, 2007.

Bernáldez, Andrés. *Historia de los reyes católicos D. Fernando y Da. Isabel.* 2 Vols., Granada: Zamora. 1856.

Boyle, David. *Toward the Setting Sun: Columbus, Cabot, and Vespucci: The Race for America.* New York: Walker, 2008.

Brigham, Kay. *Christopher Columbus: His Life and Discovery in the Light of his Prophecies.* Barcelona: Libros CLIE, 1990.

Brink-Danan, Marcy. *Jewish Life in 21st Century Turkey: The Other Side of Tolerance.* Bloomington, IN: Indiana University Press, forthcoming.

Brinkbäumer. Klaus, and Clemens Höges. *The Voyage of the* Vizcaína: *The Mystery of Christopher Columbus's Last Ship.* New York: Harcourt, Inc., 2006.

Brundage, James A. *Law, Sex, and Christian Society in Medieval Europe.* Chicago: University of Chicago Press, 1987.

Bullough, Vern L., and James A. Brundage. *Sexual Practices and the Medieval Church.* Buffalo, NY: Prometheus Books, 1982.

Campbell, Mary. B. *The Witness and the Other World: Exotic European Travel Writing, 400–1600.* Ithaca, NY: Cornell University Press, 1988.

Columbus, Christopher. *The* Diario *of Christopher Columbus's First Voyage to America, 1492–1493.* Abstracted by Fray Bartolomé de Las Casas, transcribed and translated into English by Oliver Dunn and James E. Kelley, Jr. Norman, OK: University of Oklahoma Press, 1988.

———. *The* Libro de las profecías *of Christopher Columbus.* Translation and commentary by Delno C. West and August Kling. Gainesville: University of Florida Press, 1991.

Columbus, Ferdinand. *The Life of the Admiral Christopher Columbus by His Son Ferdinand.* Translated and annotated by Benjamin Keen. New Brunswick, NJ: Rutgers University Press, 1992 [1959].

Crowley, Roger. *1453: The Holy War for Constantinople and the Clash of Islam and the West.* New York: Hyperion, 2005.

Daniel, E. Randolph. *The Franciscan Concept of Mission in the High Middle Ages.* Lexington: University of Kentucky Press, 1975.

Davidson, Miles H. *Columbus Then and Now: A Life Reexamined.* Norman: University of Oklahoma Press, 1997.

Dawson, Christopher. *Mission to Asia.* Toronto: University of Toronto Press for the Medieval Academy of America, 1980 [1966].

Deagan, Kathleen, and José Maria Cruxent. *Columbus's Outpost among the Taínos: Spain and La Isabela, 1493–1498.* New Haven, CT: Yale University Press, 2002.

Delaney, Carol. "Columbus's Ultimate Goal: Jerusalem." *Comparative Studies in Society and History*, 48, No. 2 (2006): 260–92.

———. *Abraham on Trial: The Social Legacy of Biblical Myth.* Princeton, NJ: Princeton University Press, 1998.

Delumeau, Jean. *History of Paradise: The Garden of Eden in Myth and Tradition.* New York: Continuum, 1995.

Dor-Ner, Zvi. *Columbus and the Age of Discovery.* New York: William Morrow, 1991.

Dotson, John, and Aldo Agosto., ed. and trans. *Christopher Columbus and His Family: The Genoese and Ligurian Documents.* Vol. 4, *Repertorium Columbianum*, Turnhout, Belgium: Brepols,1998.

Dugard, Martin. *The Last Voyage of Columbus: Being the Epic Tale of the Great Captain's*

Fourth Expedition, Including Acounts of Swordfight, Mutiny, Shipwreck, Gold, War, Hurricane, and Discovery. New York: Little, Brown, 2005.

Dunn, Oliver, and James E. Kelley, Jr. See Columbus, Christopher: *Diario*.

Dyer, Charles H. (with Angela Elwell Hung). *The Rise of Babylon: Sign of the End Times*. Wheaton, IL: Tyndale House Publishers, 1991.

Edwards, John. *Religion and Society in Spain c. 1492*. Aldershott, UK: Variorum, 1996.

Emmerson, Richard K., and Ronald B. Herzman. *The Apocalyptic Imagination in Medieval Literature*. Philadelphia: University of Pennsylvania Press, 1992.

Emmerson, Richard K., and Bernard McGinn. *The Apocalypse in the Middle Ages*. Ithaca, NY: Cornell University Press, 1992.

Epstein, Steven. *Genoa and the Genoese, 958–1528*. Chapel Hill: The University of North Carolina Press, 1996.

Ferdinand. See Columbus, Ferdinand.

Fernández-Armesto, Felipe. *Amerigo: The Man Who Gave His Name to America*. New York: Random House, 2007.

———. *Columbus*. Oxford: Oxford University Press, 1991.

———. *Ferdinand and Isabella*. New York: Taplinger, 1975.

———. *Columbus and the Conquest of the Impossible*. London: Phoenix Press, 1974.

Fiske, John. *The Discovery of America with Some Account of Ancient America and the Spanish Conquest*. Boston: Houghton, Mifflin, 1982.

Fleet, Kate. *European and Islamic Trade in the Early Ottoman State: The Merchants of Genoa and Turkey*. Cambridge: Cambridge University Press, 1999.

Fleming, John V. "Christopher Columbus as a Scriptural Exegete." *Lutheran Quarterly* 5, No. 2 (1991): 187–98.

Flint, Valerie I. *The Imaginative Landscape of Christopher Columbus*. Princeton, NJ: Princeton University Press, 1992.

France, John. *The Crusades and the Expansion of Catholic Christendom, 1000–1714*. London and New York: Routledge, 2005.

Friedman, John Block. *The Monstrous Races in Medieval Art and Thought*. Cambridge, MA: Harvard University Press, 1981.

———. "Cultural Conflicts in Medieval World Maps," in *Implicit Understandings*, edited by Stuart Schwartz. Cambridge: Cambridge University Press, 1994.

Fuson, Robert H., trans. *The Log of Christopher Columbus*. Camden, ME: International Marine Publishing, 1992.

Gardiner, Robert, ed., and Richard W. Unger, consultant ed., *Cogs, Caravels, and Galleons: The Sailing Ship, 1000–1650*. Annapolis, MD: Naval Institute Press, 1994.

Geertz, Clifford. "Religion as a Cultural System," in Clifford Geertz, *Interpretation of Culture*. New York, Basic Books, 1973.

Gillis, John R. *Islands of the Mind: How the Human Imagination Created the Atlantic World*. New York: Palgrave Macmillan, 2004.

Gorenberg, Gershom. *The End of Days: Fundamentalism and the Struggle for the Temple Mount*. Oxford: Oxford University Press, 2002 [2000].

Gould, Alice Bache. *Nueva lista documentadad de los tripulantes de Colón en 1492*. Madrid: Real Academia de la Historia, 1984.

Grafton, Anthony. *New Worlds, Ancient Texts: The Power of Tradition and the Shock of Discovery*. Cambridge, MA: Harvard University Press, 1992.

Granzotto, Gianni. *Christopher Columbus*. New York: Doubleday, 1995.

Greenblatt, Stephen. *Marvelous Possessions: The Wonder of the New World*. Chicago: University of Chicago Press, 1991.

Greenfield, Amy Butler. *A Perfect Red: Empire, Espionage, and the Quest for the Color of Desire*. New York: Harper Perennial, 2005.

Gurevich, A. J. *Categories of Medieval Culture*, translated by G. L. Campbell. London: Routledge & Kegan Paul, 1985.

Gužauskytė, Evelina. "Stars of the Sky, Gems of the Earth: Place Names Related to 'Planets' and Metals in Columbus's *Diario*." *Colonial Latin American Reviews*, 18, No. 2 (2009): 261–82.

Hamdami, Abbas. "Ottoman Response to the Discovery of America and the New Route to India," *Journal of the American Oriental Society*, 101, No. 3 (1981): 323–30.

———. "Columbus and the Recovery of Jerusalem," in *Journal of the American Oriental Society*, 99, No.1 (1979): 39-48.

Hanke, Lewis. *The Spanish Struggle for Justice in the Conquest of America*. Boston: Little, Brown, 1965 [1949].

Harley, J. B., and David Woodward, eds. *The History of Cartography*, Vol. 1. Chicago: University of Chicago Press, 1987.

Harrisse, Henry. *Notes on Columbus*. New York: Privately printed, 1866.

Hearder, Harry. *Italy: A Short History*. Cambridge: Cambridge University Press, 1990.

Henige, David. *In Search of Columbus: The Sources for the First Voyage*. Tucson: University of Arizona Press, 1991.

Herlihy, David. *The Black Death and the Transformation of the West*. Cambridge, MA: Harvard University Press, 1997.

Herrin, Judith. *Byzantium: The Surprising Life of a Medieval Empire*, Princeton: Princeton University Press, 2007.

Highfield, Roger. *Spain in the Fifteenth Century: 1369–1516*. London: Macmillan, 1972.

Hodgen, Margaret. *Early Anthropology in the Sixteenth and Seventeenth Centuries*. Philadelphia: University of Pennsylvania Press, 1964.

Hughes, Serge, trans. *Catherine of Genoa: Purgation and Purgatory, the Spiritual Dialogue*. New York: Paulist Press, 1979.

Hulme, Peter. *Colonial Encounters: Europe and the Native Caribbean, 1492–1797*. London: Methuen, 1986.

———. "Tales of Distinction: European Ethnography and the Caribbean," in *Implicit Understandings*, edited by Stuart Schwartz. Cambridge: Cambridge University Press, 1994.

Irving, Washington. *The Life and Voyages of Christopher Columbus*. New York: John B. Alden, Publisher, 1884.

Jane, Cecil. *The Four Voyages of Columbus*, New York: Dover Publications, Inc., 1988.

———. "The Letter of Columbus." *Hispanic American Historical Review* 10 (1930): 33–50.

Jennings, Francis. *The Invasion of America: Indians, Colonialism, and the Cant of Conquest*. Chapel Hill: University of North Carolina Press, 1992.

Kadir, Djelal. *Columbus and the Ends of the Earth: Europe's Prophetic Rhetoric as Conquering Ideology*. Berkeley: University of California Press, 1992.

Kamen, Henry. *Spain, 1469–1714: A Society in Conflict*. Harlow, UK: Pearson Educational Limited, 2005 [1983].

Katz, David. S., and Richard H. Popkin. *Messianic Revolution: Radical Religious Politics to the End of the Second Millennium*. New York: Hill and Wang, 1999.

Keen, Benjamin, See Columbus, Ferdinand.

Kinross, Lord. *The Ottoman Centuries: The Rise and Fall of the Turkish Empire*. New York: Morrow Quill Paperbacks, 1977.

Kolbert, Elizabeth. "Uncomfortable Climate." *New Yorker*, November 22, 2010.

Komroff, Manual. *The Travels of Marco Polo*. New York: Garden City Publishing, 1926.

König, Hans. *Columbus: His Enterprise: Exploding the Myth*. New York: Monthly Review Press, 1976.

Kupperman, Karen Ordahl. *America in European Consciousness: 1493–1750*. Chapel Hill: University of North Carolina Press, 1995.

Ladner, Gerhart B. *God, Cosmos, and Humankind: The World of Early Christian Symbolism*, translated by Thomas Dunlap. Berkeley: University of California Press, 1995.

Larner, John. *Marco Polo and the Discovery of the World*. New Haven: Yale University Press, 1999.

Las Casas, Bartolomé de. *An Account, Much Abbreviated, of the Destruction of the Indies*, edited by Franklin W. Knight, and translated by Andrew Hurley. Indianapolis: Hackett Publishing, 2003.

———. *Las Casas on Columbus: The Third Voyage*, edited by Geoffrey Symcox and Jesús Carrillo; translated by Michael Hammer and Blair Sullivan. Turnhout, Belgium: Brepols, 2001.

———. *History of the Indies*, translated by Andrée Collard. New York: Harper and Row, 1971.

LeBeau, Bryan F., and Menachem Mor, eds. *Religion in the Age of Exploration: The Case of Spain and New Spain*. Omaha: Creighton University Press, 1996.

Leppäkari, Maria. *Apocalyptic Representations of Jerusalem*. Leiden: Brill, 2006.

Lester, Toby. *The Fourth Part of the World: The Race to the Ends of the Earth, and the Epic Story of the Map That Gave America its Name*. New York: Free Press, 2009.

Lewis, Bernard. *Istanbul and the Civilization of the Ottoman Empire*. Norman: University of Oklahoma Press, 1963.

Liss, Peggy. *Isabel the Queen: Life and Times*. New York and Oxford: Oxford University Press, 1992.

López de Gómara, Francisco. *La historia general de las Indias*. En Anuers: Martin Nucio, ca. 1554.

MacKie, Charles Paul. *The Last Voyages of the Admiral of the Ocean Sea*. Chicago: A. C. McClurg, 1892.

Madriaga, Salvador. *Christopher Columbus: Being the Life of the Very Magnificent Lord Don Cristobal Colón*. Westport, CT: Greenwood, 1979.

Major, R. H. *Select Letters of Christopher Columbus*. London: Printed for the Hakluyt Society, 1847.

Mallett, Michael E. *The Florentine Galleys in the Fifteenth Century*. Oxford, UK: Clarendon Press, 1967.

Mandeville, Sir John. *The Travels of Sir John Mandeville*, translated and edited by C. W. R. D. Moseley. New York: Penguin Books, 2005 [1983].

Mariéjol, Jean Hippolyte. *The Spain of Ferdinand and Isabella*. Benjamin Keen, trans. and ed. New Brunswick, NJ: Rutgers University Press, 1961.

Martínez-Hidalgo, Jose María. *Columbus's Ships*, edited by Howard I. Chapelle. Barre, MA: Barre Publishers, 1966.

McGinn, Bernard, ed. *The Encyclopedia of Apocalypticism*. 2 vols. New York: Continuum, 1998.

———. *Antichrist: Two Thousand Years of the Human Fascination with Evil*. San Francisco: HarperSanFrancisco, 1994.

———. *Visions of the End: Apocalyptic Traditions in the Middle Ages*. New York: Columbia University Press, 1979.

McGovern, James. R., ed. *The World of Columbus*. Macon, GA: Mercer University Press, 1992.

McNeill, William H. *Mythistory and Other Essays*. Chicago: University of Chicago Press, 1986.

———. *Venice: The Hinge of Europe: 1081–1797*. Chicago: University of Chicago Press, 1974.

Melville-Jones, J. R. *The Siege of Constantinople 1453: Seven Contemporary Accounts*. Amsterdam: Adolf M. Hakkert, Publisher, 1972.

Milani, Virgil I. *The Written Language of Christopher Columbus*. Forum Italicum: University of South Florida, 1973.

Milhou, Alain. *Colón y su mentalidad mesianica en el ambiente franciscanista español*. Valladolid, Spain: Seminario Americanista de la Universidad, 1983.

Mintz, Allan. *Hurban*. New York: Columbia University Press, 1984.

Morison, Samuel Eliot, trans. and ed. *Journals and Other Documents on the Life and Voyages of Christopher Columbus*. New York: Heritage Press, 1963.

———. *Admiral of the Ocean Sea: A Life of Christopher Columbus*, 2 vols. Boston: Little, Brown, 1942.

Mormando, Franco. *The Preacher's Demons: Bernardino of Sienna and the Social Underworld of Early Renaissance Italy*. Chicago: University of Chicago Press, 1999.

———. "Signs of the the Apocalypse in Late Medieval Italy: The Popular Preaching of Bernardino of Sienna," *Medievalia et Humanistica*, No. 24 (1997).

Muldoon, James. "Spiritual Freedom—Physical Slavery: The Medieval Church and Slavery," in *Ave Maria Law Review* 3, No. 1 (2005): 69–93.

———. "John Marshall and the Rights of Indians." In *Latin America and the Atlantic World*, edited by Renate Pieper and Peer Schmidt. Köln, Weimar, Wein: Böhlau Verlag, 2005.

———. *Popes, Lawyers, and Infidels: The Church and the non-Christian world*. Philadelphia: University of Pennsylvania Press, 1979.

Nader, Helen, ed. and trans. *The Book of Privileges Issued to Christopher Columbus by King Fernando and Queen Isabel, 1492–1502*. Vol. 2 of *Repertorium Columbianum*. Berkeley: University of California Press, 1996.

———. Entry on Columbus's Adolescence and Youth. In *Christopher Columbus and the Age of Exploration: An Encyclopedia*, edited by Silvio A. Bedini. New York: Da Capo Press, 1992.

Nebenzahl, Kenneth. *Atlas of Columbus and The Great Discoveries*. New York: Rand McNally, 1990.

Newton, Arthur Percival, ed. *Travel and Travellers of the Middle Ages*. London: Routledge & Kegan Paul, 1949.

Nicolle, D., J. Haldon, and S. Turnbull. *The Fall of Constantinople: The Ottoman Conquest of Byzantium*. Oxford: Osprey Publishing, 2007.

Nunn, G. E. "The *Imago Mundi* and Columbus." In *American Historical Review*, 40, No. 4 (1935): 646–61.

———. *Geographical Conceptions of Columbus*. New York: Douglas C. McMurtie, 1924.

Oviedo on Columbus. Carrillo, Jesús, ed. Vol. 9 of *Repertorium Columbianum*. Turnhout, Belgium: Brepols, 2000.

Ozment, Steven. *The Age of Reform, 1250–1550: An Intellectual and Religious History of Late Medieval and Reformation Europe*. New Haven, CT: Yale University Press, 1980.

Pagden, Anthony. *The Fall of Natural Man: The American Indian and the Origins of Comparative Ethnology*. Cambridge: Cambridge University Press, 1986.

Paolucci, Anne, and Henry Paolucci, eds. *Columbus, America, and the World*. Published for the Council on National Literatures by Griffon House Publications, 1992.

———. *Columbus: Selected Papers on Columbus and His Time*. Published for the Council on National Literatures. Whitestone, NY: Griffon House Publications, 1989.

Parry, J. H. *The Age of Reconnaissance: Discovery, Exploration, and Settlement 1450–1650*. Berkeley: University of California Press, 1981 [1963].

Parry, John H., and Robert G. Keith. *The Caribbean*, Vol. 2 of *New Iberian World: A Documentary History of the Discovery and Settlement of Latin America to the Early 17th Century*. New York: Times Books, 1994.

Pazzelli, Raffaele, T.O.R. *St. Francis and the Third Order: The Franciscan and Pre-Franciscan Penitential Movement*. Chicago: Franciscan Herald Press, 1989.

Pérez, Joseph. *The Spanish Inquisition*. New Haven, CT: Yale University Press, 2005.

Pérez-Mallaína, Pablo E. *Spain's Men of the Sea*, translated by Carla Rahn Phillips. Baltimore: Johns Hopkins University Press, 1998.

Pettibone, Dennis. "Martin Luther's Views on the Antichrist." *Journal of the Adventist Theological Society* 18, No. 1 (2007): 81–82.

Pfeiffer, Charles F. *Jerusalem Through the Ages*. Baker Studies in Biblical Archaeology. Grand Rapids, MI: Baker Book House, 1967.

Phelan, J. L. *The Millennial Kingdom of the Franciscans in the New World*. Berkeley and Los Angeles: University of California Press, 1970.

Phillips, Carla Rahn. "The Portraits of Columbus: Heavy Traffic at the Intersection of Art and Life." *Terrae Incognitae: The Journal for the History of Discoveries*, No. 24 (1992): 1–28.

Phillips, J. R. S. *The Medieval Expansion of Europe*. Oxford, UK: Clarendon Press, 1998 [1988].

Phillips, William D., Jr., and Carla Rahn Phillips. *The Worlds of Christopher Columbus*. Cambridge: Cambridge University Press, 1992.

Pike, Ruth. *Enterprise and Adventure: The Genoese in Seville and the Opening of the New World*. Ithaca, NY: Cornell University Press, 1966.

Provost, Foster. *Columbus Dictionary*. Detroit: Omnigraphics, 1991.

———. *Columbus: An Annotated Guide to the Scholarship on His Life and Writings, 1750–1988*. Detroit: Omnigraphics, 1991.

———. "Columbus's Seven Years in Spain Prior to 1492." *Columbus and His World*. Proceedings of the First San Salvador Conference, edited by T. Gerace. San Salvador, Bahamas, 1986.

Pryor, John H. *Commerce, Shipping and Naval Warfare in the Medieval Mediterranean*. London: Variorum, 1987.

Quinn, David B. "Columbus and the North: England, Iceland, and Ireland," in *William and Mary Quarterly* 49, No. 2 (1992): 278–97.

———, ed. *America from Concept to Discovery. Early Exploration of North America*, Vol. I of *New American World: A Documentary History of North America to 1612*. New York: Arno Press, 1979.

———. "John Day and Columbus," *Geographical Journal* 133, Issue 2 (1967): 205–9.

Rawlings, Helen. *Church, Religion and Society in Early Modern Spain*. Basingstoke, UK, and New York: Palgrave, 2002.

Reeves, Margorie. *Joachim of Fiore and the Prophetic Future: A Medieval Study in Historical Thinking*. Stroud: Sutton, 1999.

———. "The Development of Apocalyptic Thought: Medieval Attitudes." In *The Apocalypse in English and Renaissance Thought and Literature*, edited by C. Patrides and J. Wittreich. Ithaca, NY: Cornell University Press, 1984.

———. *The Influence of Prophecy in the Later Middle Ages: A Study of Joachimism*. Oxford: Oxford University Press, 1969.

Reston, James, Jr. *Dogs of God: Columbus, the Inquisition, and the Defeat of the Moors*. New York: Anchor Books, 2005.

Robinson, James Harvey. *An Introduction to the History of Western Europe*. Boston: Ginn and Company, 1934.

Romm, James. "Biblical History and the Americas: The Legend of Solomon's Ophir, 1492–1591." In Paolo Bernardini and Norman Fiering, eds., *The Jews and the Expansion of Europe to the West, 1450–1880*. New York: Berghahn Books (2001): 27–46.

Rosa, Manuel da Silva. *Colombo Portugués*. Lisboa: Esquilo Ediciones y Multimedia, 2009.

———. *O Mistério Columbo Revelado*. Lisboa: Esquilo Ediciones y Multimedia, 2006.

Ross, James Bruce, and Mary Martin McLaughlin, eds. *Portable Renaissance Reader*, New York: Viking Press, 1953.

Ruiz, Jean-Pierre. "The Exegesis of Empire: Toward a Postcolonial Reading of Christopher Columbus's *Libro de las profecías*." Personal copy of paper presented at the annual meeting of the Catholic Biblical Association of America, San Francisco, 2003.

Rumeu de Armas, Antonio. *Libro Copiador de Cristóbal Colón*. Madrid: Testimonio Compañia Editorial, 1989.

Runciman, Steven. *The Fall of Constantinople*. Cambridge: Cambridge University Press, 1965.

———. *A History of the Crusades*. Vol. 1 of *The First Crusade and the Foundation of the Kingdom of Jerusalem*. Cambridge: Cambridge University Press, 1951.

Rusconi, R., ed., and B. Sullivan, trans. *The Book of Prophecies Edited by Christopher Columbus*. Berkeley: University of California Press, 1997.

Russell, Jeffrey Burton. *Inventing the Flat Earth: Columbus and Modern Historians*. New York: Praeger, 1991.

Sanders, Ronald. *Lost Tribes and Promised Lands: The Origins of American Racism*. Boston: Little, Brown, 1978.

Sauer, Carl Orwin. *The Early Spanish Main*. Berkeley: University of California Press, 1966.

Scarfi, Alessandro. *Mapping Paradise: A History of Heaven on Earth*. Chicago: University of Chicago Press, 2006.

Schein, Sylvia. *Gateway to the Heavenly City: Crusader Jerusalem and the Catholic West (1099–1187)*. Hants, UK: Ashgate, 2005.

Schnaubelt, Joseph, OSA, and Frederick Van Fleteren, eds. *Columbus and the New World*. New York: Peter Lang, 1998.

Schneider, David. "Kinship, Nationality and Religion: Toward a Definition of Kinship," in *Symbolic Anthropology*, edited by J. Dolgin, D. Kemnitzer, and D. Schneider. New York: Columbia University Press, 1977.

———. "Notes Toward a Theory of Culture," in *Meaning in Anthropology*, edited by Keith Basso and Henry A. Selby. Albuquerque: University of New Mexico Press, 1976.

Schwartz, Stuart. *All Can Be Saved: Religious Tolerance in the Iberian Atlantic World.* New Haven, CT: Yale University Press, 2008.

———. *Implicit Understandings: Observing, Reporting and Reflection on the Encounters between Europeans and Other Peoples in the Early Modern Era.* Cambridge: Cambridge University Press, 1994.

Seed, Patricia. *Ceremonies of Possession in Europe's Conquest of the New World, 1492–1620.* New York: Cambridge University Press, 1995.

Smith, Wilfred Cantwell. *The Meaning and End of Religion.* New York: A Mentor Book, 1964.

Spence, Jonathan D. *The Chan's Great Continent: China in Western Minds.* New York: W. W. Norton, 1998.

Spiegel, Shalom. *The Last Trial: On the Legends and Lore of the Command to Abraham to Offer Isaac as a Sacrifice: The Akedah.* New York: Schocken Press, 1969 [1950].

Spufford, Peter. *Power and Profit: The Merchant in Medieval Europe.* New York: Thames and Hudson, 2002.

Stein, Stephen, ed. *The Encyclopedia of Apocalypticism*, Vol. 3. New York: Continuum, 1998.

Stevens-Arroyo, Anthony M. "The Inter-Atlantic Paradigm: The Failure of Spanish Medieval Colonization of the Canary and Caribbean Islands," *Comparative Studies in Society and History* 35, No. 3 (1993): 515–43.

Stone, Marilyn. *Marriage and Friendship in Medieval Spain: Social Relations; According to the Fourth Partida of Alfonso X.* New York: Peter Lang, 1990.

Stover, Dale. "The Other Side of the Story: Indigenous Interpretations of Contact with Europeans." In *Religion in the Age of Exploration: The Case of Spain and New Spain.* Omaha: Creighton University Press, 1996.

Sweet, Leonard. "Christopher Columbus and the Millennial Vision of the New World," *Catholic Historical Review*, Vol. 72, No. 3 (1986): 369–82, 715–16.

Symcox, Geoffrey, Giovanna Rabitti, and Peter D. Diehl, eds. and trans. *Italian Reports on America, 1493–1522: Letters, Dispatches, and Papal Bulls.* Vol. 10 of *Repertorium Columbianum.* Turnhout, Belgium: Brepols, 2001.

Symcox, Geoffrey, Luciano Formisano, and Theodore J. Cachey, Jr., eds. and trans. *Italian Reports on America 1493–1522: Accounts by Contemporary Observers.* Vol. 12 of *Repertorium Columbianum.* Turnhout, Belgium: Brepols, 2002.

Taviani, Paolo Emilio. *Christopher Columbus: The Grand Design.* London: Orbis Publishing, 1985.

———. "Columbus's Health." In *Nuova Raccolta*, edited by Taviani et al., Vol. 6, Part 2, 127–38.

———, Roberto Rusconi, and Consuelo Varela, eds. *Cristoforo Colombo: Lettere e Scritti, 1495–1506*. Rome: Istituto Poligrafico e Zecca dello Stato, 1993.

Taviani, Pablo, Consuelo Varela, Juan Gil, and Marina Conti, eds. *Nuova Raccolta Colombina*. Roma: Istituto Poligrafico e Zecca dello Stato, for the Ministry of Cultural and Environmental Assets. Many volumes; see especially Vol. 6, *Christopher Columbus: Accounts and Letters of the Second, Third, and Fourth Voyages* (1994). English translation by Luciano F. Farina and Marc A. Beckwith.

Thacher, John Boyd. *Christopher Columbus: His Life, His Work, His Remains*, 3 vols. New York: G. P. Putnam's Sons, 1903–1904.

Thomas, Hugh. *Rivers of Gold: The Rise of the Spanish Empire from Columbus to Magellan*. New York: Random House, 2003.

Traboulay, David. *Columbus and Las Casas: The Conquest and Christianization of America, 1492–1566*. Lanham, MD: University Press of America. 1994.

Unali, Anna. *Marinai, pirati e corsari catalani nel basso Medioevo*. Bologna: Cappelli editore, 1983.

Unger, Richard W. "Portuguese Shipbuilding and the Early Voyages to the Guinea Coast," in *The European Opportunity*, edited by Felipe Fernández-Armesto. Cambridge: Cambridge University Press, for Variorum, 2 (1987): 43–63. Reprinted from *Vice-Almirante A. Teixeira Da Mota in Memoriam*, Vol. 1. Lisbon: Academia de Marinha & Instituto de Investigaçao Cientifica Tropical, (1987): 229–49.

———. *The Ship in the Medieval Economy 600–1600*. London: Croom Helm, 1980.

Varela, Consuelo. *La Caída de Cristóbal Colón: El juicio de Bobadilla*. After the transcription by Isabel Aguirre. Madrid: Marcial Pons Historia, 2006.

———, ed., and Juan Gil. *Cristóbal Colón: Textos y documentos completos*. Madrid: Alianza Universidad, 2003.

Vigneras, Louis André. "Diego Méndez, Secretary of Christopher Columbus and *Alguacil Mayor* of Santo Domingo: A Biographical Sketch," in *Hispanic American Historical Review* 58, No. 4 (1978): 676–696.

Von Martels, Zweder. *Travel Fact and Travel Fiction*. Leiden: E. J. Brill, 1994.

Voragine, Jacobus de. *The Golden Legend* (13th century), translated by Granger Ryan and Helmut Ripperger. New York: Longmans, Green, 1941.

Watts, Pauline Moffitt. "Apocalypse Then: Christopher Columbus's Conception of History and Prophecy," *Medievalia et Humanistica*, New Series, No. 19 (1993): 1–10.

———. "The New World and the End of the World: Evangelizing Sixteenth-Century Mexico," in *Imagining the New World: Columbian Iconography*. Exhibit sponsored by the New York Historical Society and the Istituto della Enciclopedia Italiana, 1991, 29–39.

————. "Prophecy and Discovery: On the Spiritual Origins of Christopher Columbus's 'Enterprise of the Indies.'" *American Historical Review* 90, No. 1 (1985): 73–102.

West, Delno C. "Wallowing in a Theological Stupor or a Steadfast and Consuming Faith: Scholarly Encounters with Columbus's *Libro de las profecías.*" In Donald T. Gerace, ed., *Columbus and His World*. Proceedings of the First San Salvador Conference. Fort Lauderdale, FL: College Center of the Finger Lakes, 1987, 45–57.

West, Delno C., and August Kling, eds. *The* Libro de las profecías *of Christopher Columbus*. Gainesville, FL: University of Florida Press, 1991.

Wey-Gomez, Nicolas. *Tropics of Empire*. Cambridge, MA: MIT Press, 2008.

White, Lynn. "Christian Myth and Christian History." *Journal of the History of Ideas* 3 (1942): 145–58.

Widmer, Ted. "Little America," *New York Times*, June 30, 2007.

Wilford, John Noble. *The Mysterious History of Columbus*. New York: Alfred A. Knopf, 1991.

Woodward, David. "Reality, Symbolism, Time and Space in Medieval World Maps." *Annals of the Association of American Geographers* 75, No. 4 (1985): 510–21.

Young, George, ed. *The Columbus Memorial*. Philadelphia: Jordan Bros., 1863.

Zamora, Margarita. *Reading Columbus*. Berkeley: University of California Press, 1993.

Ziegler, Philip. *The Black Death*. London: Collins, 1969.

INDEX

Page numbers in *italics* refer to illustrations and maps. Those followed by *n* are in the notes section.

ABOUT THE AUTHOR

Carol Delaney received a BA from Boston University, an MTS from Harvard Divinity School, and a PhD in Cultural Anthropology from the University of Chicago. She was the assistant director of the Center for the Study of World Religions at Harvard and a visiting professor in the Department of Religious Studies at Brown University. She is an emerita professor, Stanford University, where she taught for eighteen years, and is an Invited Research Scholar, John Carter Brown Library at Brown University. Delaney is the author of several books, including *The Seed and the Soil: Gender and Cosmology in Turkish Village Society; Abraham on Trial: The Social Legacy of Biblical Myth; Naturalizing Power: Essays in Feminist Cultural Criticism* (coeditor/contributor); and *Investigating Culture: An Experiential Introduction to Anthropology.*